Praise for

THE ODYSSEY

"In her powerful new translation, Emily Wilson . . . has chosen immediacy and naturalism over majestic formality. She preserves the musicality of Homer's poetry, opting for an iambic pentameter whose approachable storytelling tone invites us in, only to startle us with eruptions of beauty. . . . Wilson's transformation of such a familiar and foundational work is . . . astonishing."
—Rebecca Newberger Goldstein, *Atlantic*

"When I first read these lines . . . , I was floored. I'd never read an *Odyssey* that sounded like this. It had such directness, the lines feeling not as if they were being fed into iambic pentameter because of some strategic decision but because the meter was a natural mode for its speaker."
—Wyatt Mason, *New York Times Magazine*

"Wilson's translation is a superb achievement and a striking departure from the tradition of Homeric translation into English. . . . There is no elaborate or antiquated diction, just a crispness and clear-headedness that will seem quite alien to anyone familiar with earlier versions. . . . Wilson has produced a wonderfully distinctive—and modern—version of the poem."
—Henry Power, *Evening Standard*

"This translation is a marvel! Bold and timely and ever so exciting. . . . As majestic as literature gets."
—Max Porter, author of *Grief Is the Thing With Feathers*

"Dispenses gracefully with unnecessary archaisms and flourishes. . . . Wilson's project is basically a progressive one: to scrape away all the centuries of verbal and ideological buildup . . . to reveal something fresh and clean. . . . In all its morphing and slippery layers, its winks and double meanings, Wilson's *Odyssey* contains a laughing, democratic undercurrent."
—Annalisa Quinn, NPR Books

"Wilson . . . does a magnificent job of bringing this archaic poem to a new audience. Fresh, crisp, and thoughtful, the translation reflects smart choices across the board. . . . The resulting poetry is both moving and readable."
—Natalie Haynes, *The i Paper*

"There are many *other* stunning things about Wilson's translation, from the five-beat lines to the straightforward speech free from the elegant clunkiness that we usually see when scholars try to carry words over from one language to another. But one of them is certainly an awareness of her own daring."
—Yung In Chae, *Eidolon*

"It is immensely satisfying to see *The Odyssey* in the hands of such a careful and creative scholar. . . . [P]erhaps Wilson's greatest achievement is to disprove the increasingly held view that versions of ancient texts require an established poet to be parachuted in, like a literary James Bond, to rescue their English lines from the prosaic. For a translation of *The Odyssey* that knows what it is talking about and sings as it speaks, this is the one to read."
—Josephine Balmer, *New Statesman*

"One of the great narratives of all time. You think you know it? Not until you read this one. A stunning translation."
—Susan Hill

"An energetic verse rendition. . . . Wilson offers a fluent, straightforward, and accessible version of the Homeric epic; a solid reading edition."
—*Library Journal*

"The words are short, mostly monosyllables. Almost none have French or Latin roots. None is independently striking; their force comes from their juxtaposition with one another—*pat pat pat*, like raindrops on a metal roof. If Wilson's version has an English model, it is the moving plainness of Matthew Arnold's 'Sohrab and Rustum.' . . . Though he never produced a translation himself, I think [Arnold] would have recognized his Homer—a poet 'eminently rapid . . . , eminently plain and direct'—in Wilson's."
—Gregory Hays, *New York Times Book Review*

"Wilson's version is an exciting one, all the better I guess for forcing us to think how approachable, how weird, how everyday Homeric language ever was."
—Mary Beard, *Times Literary Supplement*

"A perceptive reading of *The Odyssey*. . . . Readers who want to get a feeling for the poem will find Wilson's translation full of insights."
—Colin Burrow, *London Review of Books*

"One of the very best verse translations ever completed in English—of any book. . . . For any lover of traditional English verse, Wilson is the most pleasant news we have had since Robert Frost. Gone is the amorphous 'six-beat line,' gone is the verse which ends when the writer decides to hit return. Frost said that poetry without meter was playing tennis without a net: Wilson reads like a Wimbledon champion."

—John Byron Kuhner, *University Bookman*

"Wilson's *Odyssey* feels like a restoration of an old, familiar building that had over the years been encrusted with too much gilt. . . . She scrapes away at old encrusted layers, until she exposes what lies beneath."

—Nilanjana Roy, *Financial Times*

"This translation reminds us of the plot's cinematic urgency, its cliff-hangers. . . . Wilson's *Odyssey*, for all its plainness, breaks into moments of lyrical beauty. . . . [It] is not only well suited to dramatic interpretation, but is ideal for students." —A.E. Stallings, *Spectator*

"Poetry that reads like a thriller."

—R.L. Stine, author of the *Goosebumps* series

"The new Emily Wilson translation of the *Odyssey* is brilliant and sharp and swift and funny and will repay the reader a thousand times over."

—Katherine Rundell, author of *The Explorer*

"This translation is SO GOOD."

—Celeste Ng, author of *Little Fires Everywhere*

OTHER BOOKS BY EMILY WILSON

Mocked with Death: Tragic Overliving from Sophocles to Milton

The Death of Socrates: Hero, Villain, Chatterbox, Saint

The Greatest Empire: A Life of Seneca

TRANSLATIONS

Seneca: Six Tragedies

Four Tragedies of Euripides

HOMER

THE ODYSSEY

TRANSLATED BY EMILY WILSON

W. W. NORTON & COMPANY, INC.
Independent Publishers Since 1923
New York • London

First published as a Norton paperback 2018

Manufacturing by Lightning Source
Book design by Chris Welch Design
Production manager: Julia Druskin

Library of Congress Cataloging-in-Publication Data

Names: Homer, author. | Wilson, Emily R., 1971– editor, translator.
Title: The Odyssey / Homer ; translated by Emily Wilson.
Other titles: Odyssey. English
Description: New York : London : W. W. Norton & Company, 2018.
Identifiers: LCCN 2017027185 | ISBN 9780393089059 (hardcover)
Classification: LCC PA4025.A5 W56 2018 | DDC 883/.01—dc23
LC record available at https://lccn.loc.gov/2017027185

ISBN 978-0-393-35625-0 pbk.

W. W. Norton & Company, Inc. 500 Fifth Avenue, New York, N.Y. 10110
www.wwnorton.com

W. W. Norton & Company Ltd. 15 Carlisle Street, London W1D 3BS

Authorized EU representative: EAS, Mustamäe tee 50, 10621 Tallinn, Estonia

24 25 26 27 28 29 30

To my daughters,
Imogen, Psyche, and Freya

CONTENTS

INTRODUCTION

The Odyssey, composed almost three thousand years ago, is an epic poem: "epic" both in the sense that it is long, and in the sense that it presents itself as telling an important story, in the traditional, formulaic language used by archaic poets for singing the tales of gods, wars, journeys, and the collective memories and experience of the Greek-speaking world.

Modern connotations of the word "epic" are in some ways misleading when we turn to the Homeric poems, the texts that began the Western epic tradition. The Greek word *epos* means simply "word" or "story" or "song." It is related to a verb meaning "to say" or "to tell," which is used (in a form with a prefix) in the first line of the poem. The narrator commands the Muse, "Tell me": *enn-epe.* An epic poem is, at its root, simply a tale that is told.

The Odyssey is grand or (in modern terms) "epic" in scope: it is over twelve thousand lines long. The poem is elevated in style, composed entirely in a regular poetic rhythm, a six-beat line (dactylic hexameter), and its vocabulary was not that used by ordinary Greeks in everyday speech, in any time or place. The language contains a strange mixture of words from different periods of time, and from Greek dialects associated with different regions. A handful of words in Homer were incomprehensible to Greeks of the classical period (in the fifth and fourth centuries BCE). The syntax is relatively simple, but the words and phrases, in these combinations, are unlike the way that anybody ever actually spoke. The style is, from a modern perspective, strange: it is full of repetitions, redundancies, and formulaic expressions. These mark the poem's debt to a long tradition of storytelling and suggest that we are in a world that is at least partly continuous with a distant, half-forgotten past.

But in some ways, the story told in this long piece of verse is small and ordinary. It is a story, as the first word of the original Greek tells us, about "a man" (*andra*). He is not "the" man, but one of many men—albeit a man of extraordinary cognitive, psychological, and military power, one who can win any competition, outwit any opponent, and manage, against all odds, to survive. The poem tells us how he makes his circuitous way back home across stormy seas after many years at war. We may expect the hero of an "epic" narrative to confront evil forces, perform a superhuman task, and rescue vast numbers of people from an extraordinary kind of threat. Failing that, we might hope at least for a great quest unexpectedly achieved, despite perils all around; an action that saves the world, or at least changes it in some momentous way—like Jason claiming the Golden Fleece, Launcelot glimpsing the Holy Grail, or Aeneas beginning the foundation of Rome. In *The Odyssey,* we find instead the story of a man whose grand adventure is simply to go back to his own home, where he tries to turn everything back to the way it was before he went away. For this hero, mere survival is the most amazing feat of all.

Only a portion of the twenty-four books of *The Odyssey* describes the magical wanderings of Odysseus on his journey back to Ithaca. These adventures are presented as a backstory partly told by the hero himself (in Books 5 through 12). The poem cuts between far-distant and diverse locations, from Olympus to earth, from Calypso's island to the palace at Ithaca, from the underworld to the cottage of the swineherd. Sometimes the setting feels entirely realistic, even mundane—a world where a mother packs a wholesome lunch of bread and cheese for her daughter, where there is a particular joy in taking a hot bath, where men listen to music and play checkers, and lively, pretty girls have fun playing ball games together. At other moments, we are in the realm of pure fantasy, inhabited by cannibals, witches, and goddesses with six barking heads, where it is possible to cross the streams of Ocean (the mythical river that encircles the known world), and come to the land of asphodel, where the spirits of dead heroes live forever. Different characters tell their own inset stories—some true, some false, of past lives, adventures, dreams, memories, and troubles. The poem weaves and unweaves a multilayered narrative that is both simple and artful in its patterning and composition.

The story begins in an unexpected place, *in medias res* ("in the middle of things"—the proper starting point for an epic, according to Horace). It is not the start of the Trojan War, which began with the Judgment of Paris and the Abduction of Helen and was fought for ten years. Nor does the poem start at the beginning of Odysseus' journey home, which has been in progress for almost as many years as the war. Instead, it begins when nothing much seems to be happening at all; Odysseus, his son, and his wife are all stuck in a state of frustration and paralysis that has been continuing for years and is becoming unbearable.

Odysseus, at the start of the poem, is trapped by the goddess Calypso, who wants to have him stay there as her husband for eternity. He could choose to evade death and old age and stay always with her; but movingly, he prefers "to see even just the smoke that rises / from his own homeland, and he wants to die." Odysseus longs to recover his own identity, not as a victim of shipwreck or a coddled plaything of a powerful goddess, but as a master of his home and household, as a father and as a husband. He sits sobbing by the shore of the island every day, desperately staring at the "fruitless sea" for a boat that might take him back home.

Meanwhile, in Ithaca, Odysseus' wife, Penelope, is surrounded by young men who have forced their way into her home and are making merry with daily feasts, wasting the provisions of the household, waiting for her to agree to give up on Odysseus and marry one of them. Penelope has a deep loyalty both to her lost husband, for whom she weeps every night and whom she misses "all the time," and also to the "beautiful rich house" in which she lives, which she risks losing forever if she remarries.

She has devised clever ways to put off the suitors, but it is clear that she cannot do so forever; eventually, she will have to choose one of them as her husband and perhaps leave the household of Odysseus for a new home. When that happens, either the suitors will divide the wealth of Odysseus between them—as they sometimes threaten—or the dominant suitor may gain the throne of Ithaca for himself. The ambiguity about what the suitors are seeking matches an even more central ambiguity, about what Penelope herself wants. Indefinitely, tearfully, Penelope waits, keeping everyone guessing about her innermost feelings and intentions. As the chief suitor complains, "She offers hope to all, sends signs to each, / but all the while her mind moves somewhere else." This premise allows for artful resonances with earlier moments in the myth of Troy. Much-courted Penelope resembles Helen, the woman to whom all the Greek heroes came as suitors (Menelaus, her husband, eventually won her hand by lot), and whom Paris, Prince of Troy, later stole away. Like Paris, Penelope's suitors threaten to steal away a married woman as if she were a bride. Penelope's house also echoes the besieged town of Troy, when the Greeks were fighting to take Helen back home—but there is here no strong Hector to defend the inhabitants.

Telemachus, Odysseus' almost-adult son, is in a particularly precarious situation. Left as a "little newborn baby" when Odysseus sailed for Troy, he must be twenty or twenty-one years old at the time of the poem's action, but he seems in many ways younger. To fight off the suitors and take control of the household himself, he would need great physical and emotional strength, a strong group of supporters, and the capacity to plan a difficult military and political operation—none of which he possesses. Telemachus must complete several difficult quests in the course of the poem: to survive the mortal danger posed by the suitors; to mature and grow up to manhood; to find his lost father, and help him regain control of the house. The journey with which the story begins is not that of Odysseus himself but of Telemachus, who sets out to find news of his absent father. The son's journey away from home parallels the father's quest in the opposite direction. The poem intertwines the story of these three central characters—the father, the mother, the son—and shows us how something different is at stake for each of them, in the gradual and difficult struggle to rebuild their lost nuclear family.

The Odyssey puts us into a world that is a peculiar mixture of the strange and the familiar. The tension between strangeness and familiarity is in fact the poem's central subject. Its setting, in the islands of the Mediterranean and Aegean Seas, would have been vaguely familiar to any Greek-speaking reader; but this version of the region includes sea-monsters and giants who eat humans, as well as gods who walk the earth and talk with select favorites among the mortals. We encounter a surprisingly varied range of different characters and types of incident: giants and beggars, arrogant young men and vulnerable old slaves, a princess who does laundry and a dead warrior who misses the sunshine, gods, goddesses, and ghosts, brave deeds, love affairs, spells, dreams, songs, and stories. Odysseus himself seems to contain multitudes: he is a migrant, a pirate, a carpenter, a king, an athlete, a beggar, a husband, a lover, a father, a son, a fighter, a liar, a leader, and a thief. He is a man who cries, takes naps, and feels homesick, but he is also a man who has a special relationship with the goddess who transforms his appearance at will and ensures that his schemes succeed. The poem promotes but also questions its own fantasies and ideals, such as the idea that time and change can be undone, and the notion that there is such a thing as home, where people and relationships can stay forever the same.

Who Was Homer?

The authorship of the Homeric poems is a complex and difficult topic, because these written texts emerge from a long oral tradition. Marks of this distinctive legacy are visible in *The Odyssey* on the level of style. Dawn appears some twenty times in *The Odyssey*, and the poem repeats the same line, word for word, each time: *emos d'erigeneia phane rhododaktulos eos*: "But when early-born rosy-fingered Dawn appeared . . ." There is a vast array of such formulaic expressions in Homeric verse, which suggest that things have an eternal, infinitely repeatable presence. Different things will happen every day, but Dawn always appears, always with rosy fingers, always early. Characters and objects all have their own descriptive terms in Homer; these are known as epithets, rather than adjectives, because they express an essential quality or characteristic, rather than a trait that the object or person possesses only in a particular moment. Ships are "black," "hollow," "swift," or "curved," never "brown," "slow," or "wobbly." Chairs are "well-carved" or "polished," never "uncomfortable" or "expensive." Penelope is "prudent Penelope," never "swift-footed Penelope" even if she is moving quickly. Telemachus is "thoughtful," even when he seems particularly immature. Moreover, many types of scene follow a certain predictable pattern. There is a fixed sequence of events described, with variations, whenever someone gets dressed or puts on armor, whenever a meal is prepared, or whenever a person is killed. Through its formulaic mode, *The Odyssey* assures us that, once we know the patterns, the world will follow a predictable rhythm. This feature of the Homeric poems is a mark of their debt to a Greek oral tradition of poetic song that extends back hundreds of years before the poems in their current forms came into existence.

In *The Odyssey* itself we meet two singers who play the lyre while they give their performances of traditional tales at the banquets of the rich. The first is Demodocus at the court of King Alcinous of Phaeacia, who tells stories about Odysseus himself and the Trojan Horse, as well as about the affair between the god Ares and the goddess Aphrodite. The second is Phemius, who performs under compulsion for the suitors of Penelope. These characters give us some important insights into the composition of the poem, and the person (or people) who composed it. In an obviously self-interested spirit, *The Odyssey* suggests that poets have a particularly honorable place in society. But the singer is also presented as a servant, perhaps a slave, who earns food and a place to rest by giving performances that are enjoyed by wealthy banqueters. Demodocus does not read out his poetry from a script; his inability to do so is underlined by the fact that he is blind (not incidentally, no one in the entire *Odyssey* reads or writes anything). Moreover, Demodocus does not invent an original story of his own composition. Instead, Demodocus is inspired by the Muse to sing the "deeds of heroes"—which are, at least in outline, already well-known to his audience. The skill and inspiration of these illiterate singers is shown not in the invention of entirely new stories, but in their ability to retell ancient stories, and to transport their audience to the scenes they describe.

But Homer himself—if there was such a person—was not exactly a Demodocus. A blind, illiterate bard could not, by himself, have written the monumental *Iliad* and *Odyssey*. Homer is usually described in Greek sources not as a singer (*aoidos*) or rhapsode ("song-stitcher"), but as a poet, *poietes*—a word that means "maker." Indeed, a normal way to refer to Homer in Greek is as "the Poet"—the name Homer can be omitted, since there is only one primary poet in the canon.

The Odyssey as we know it is based, like almost all the Graeco-Roman literature we have, on medieval manuscripts. But there is an important difference with this text. The medieval manuscripts of an author like Virgil or Horace are based on earlier manuscripts, based in turn on earlier manuscripts, and so on, each scribe copying the work of a predecessor, and moving back from the medieval codex (a leaved book written on animal skin parchment) to the Byzantine and then ancient papyrus (a scroll written on a kind of thick paper made from papyrus leaves).

The Odyssey and *The Iliad* are different, not only because they are older than other ancient texts, but because of the specific difficulties of understanding how these poems were created—not, or not simply, from the mind of an individual creator, but also from a long oral tradition, which has been transformed into two monumental written texts. How exactly did this process happen? Did a single, particularly talented folk-poet learn to write? Or did an illiterate singer collaborate with scribes? Was there one creator, or many? At what time in the process of composition did writing enter the picture?

This takes us to what is known as the Homeric Question, which is really a whole cluster of questions about the composition of *The Iliad* and *The Odyssey*. The Question is given a capital Q, because scholars still disagree on some crucial issues even after a couple of centuries of discussion. How exactly did the Homeric poems as we have them emerge from the oral tradition that preceded them? Who was Homer? Was there a single author of *The Odyssey*, or several? Did the same person produce *The Iliad* and *The Odyssey*? When exactly did the poems get written down, and how? Can we trace earlier and later parts of the poems, or tie particular passages to different geographical locations? And to what extent do the poems reflect real historical events, cultures, and peoples—a real Trojan War, or the real Mycenean civilization of late Bronze Age Greece (which existed from the sixteenth to the twelfth centuries BCE)? Most generally, how exactly did multiple people over hundreds of years across the Greek-speaking world work together to create this magnificent, challenging, and coherent work of poetic storytelling? Design "by committee" has a very bad name, and yet *The Odyssey* seems like an unexpected success. How was it done?

During the Renaissance, when the Homeric poems were rediscovered in Europe, Homer was assumed to have been a writer, in the same way that Virgil or Dante were writers—albeit a writer from an ancient time. But in the seventeenth and eighteenth centuries, dissenting voices began to emerge. In 1664, the Abbé d'Aubignac attacked Homer, arguing that *The Iliad* and *Odyssey* were incoherent, immoral, and tasteless poems, cobbled together out of an oral folk tradition. A generation later, the British scholar Richard Bentley studied Homer's language, and proved that it was much earlier than classical (fifth- and fourth-century) Greek, because it still showed traces of a letter of the alphabet that dropped out of the language: the digamma. Bentley argued that "Homer" was a prehistoric oral poet of about 1,000 BCE, whose disparate and rambling songs were not gathered into the epics we have until the late sixth century. Scholars began to apply new methods of historical and linguistic analysis, and to ask new questions about how and when these texts were produced. In his *Prolegomena to Homer* of 1795, a pioneering work in this "new philology," Friedrich August Wolf argued that the Homeric poems were transmitted orally, and that they had undergone a long period of change and adaptation, through multiple oral reperformances and multiple reformulations by literate editors to suit changing contemporary tastes. He suggested that the poems, which he saw as the product of "the whole Greek people," were forged into their state of apparent unity only at the stage of transcription. Wolf's new vision initiated a fresh discussion of how the original Homer, or the original building blocks of the poem, might be uncovered out of the text as we have it.

During the nineteenth century, Homeric scholarship was divided between the Analytic and Unitarian schools. The Unitarians opposed Wolf's ideas, largely on literary grounds, and argued that the poems as we have them are not an aggregate of earlier, shorter compositions, but were composed by a lone author with a single overarching structure in mind. The Analysts, by contrast, argued that the epics were produced by many different hands. There were multiple theories about how exactly the compilation took place, and what the original kernel might have been. Some argued that there was an original core narrative, an *ur-Odyssey*, which had been encrusted with many later and clumsier accretions; their scholarly task was to strip away the layers of later sub-Homeric narrative and restore the original purity of the poems. Others believed that the poems as we have them are a compilation of originally separate folk stories welded together. The Analysts shared the view that the earlier, more original layers of the poems were superior to the later additions and edits, although they disagreed about where exactly the original Homer could be located in the poems as we have them. Even in more recent times, Homerists have been slow to shake off the notion that earlier means better, as well as to rid themselves of the hope that one might chisel a more perfect poem out of the rough marble of the text we have.

Up until the start of the twentieth century, scholars took the oral roots of Homeric poetry more or less for granted, not fully understanding the degree to which they can help us explain important features of Homeric style and narrative technique. The emergence of Homeric poetry from folk traditions explained its "primitive" style, but the generic and stylistic structures of oral poetry and folk traditions were not examined in a systematic way. The state of Homeric scholarship changed radically and permanently in the early 1930s, when a young American classicist named Milman Parry traveled to the then-Yugoslavia with recording equipment and began to study the living oral tradition of illiterate and semiliterate Serbo-Croat bards, who told poetic folk tales about the mythical and semihistorical events of the Serbian past. Parry died at the age of thirty-three from an accidental gunshot, and research was further interrupted by the Second World War. But Parry's student Albert Lord continued his work on Homer, and published his findings in 1960, under the title *The Singer of Tales*. Lord and Parry proved definitively that the Homeric poems show the mark of oral composition.

The "Parry-Lord hypothesis" was that oral poetry, from every culture where it exists, has certain distinctive features, and that we can see these features in the Homeric poems—specifically, in the use of formulae, which enable the oral poet to compose at the speed of speech. A writer can pause for as long as she or he wants, to ponder the most fitting adjective for a particular scene; she can also go back and change it afterwards, on further reflection—as in the famous anecdote about Oscar Wilde, who labored all morning to add a comma, and worked all afternoon taking it out. Oral performers do not use commas, and do not have the luxury of time to ponder their choice of words. They need to be able to maintain fluency, and formulaic features make this possible.

Subsequent studies, building on the work of Parry and Lord, have shown that there are marked differences in the ways that oral and literate cultures think about memory, originality, and repetition. In highly literate cultures, there is a tendency to dismiss repetitive or formulaic discourse as cliché; we think of it as boring or lazy writing. In primarily oral cultures, repetition tends to be much more highly valued. Repeated phrases, stories, or tropes can be preserved to some extent over many generations without the use of writing, allowing people in an oral culture to remember their own past. In Greek mythology, Memory (*Mnemosyne*) is said to be the mother of the Muses, because poetry, music, and storytelling are all imagined as modes by which people remember the times before they were born.

It is now generally agreed that, in broad terms, Parry and Lord were right. Many features of the Homeric poems are indeed formulaic (such as those standard "epithets" and those formulaic "type-scenes" of arming or eating), and must have originated from an oral tradition. But there is still a very wide range of opinion about how, exactly, the words of many generations of illiterate and semiliterate bards turned into the written texts of Homer that we have. Several essential factors need to be accounted for by any viable theory. Most obviously, the Homeric poems are written texts, not oral performances. Writing must have played a central part in the process of composition, so it is very misleading to describe *The Odyssey* simply as an "oral" poem, as is far too often done. It is a written text based on an oral tradition, which is not at all the same as being an actual oral composition. Moreover, these texts are far too long for any singer to perform them on a single occasion, and far too long for any individual to hold in memory without the use of writing. Songs that had an influence on the Homeric poems were sung for hundreds of years in preliterate Greece; but none of them was *The Odyssey.*

These are written texts that display the legacy of a long oral tradition. In important ways the poems are a patchwork. The language is a mishmash of several different dialects, which marks the fact that the Greek singers and storytellers lived and developed their legends in multiple different locations across the Greek-speaking world. Moreover, there are small inconsistencies in the narrative itself, which usually pass unnoticed by the casual reader (such as a slight confusion about how many cloaks Eumaeus possesses, and an apparent switch in who sets up the axes for the contest in which the suitors and Odysseus compete for Penelope's hand). The inconsistencies could mark the text's emergence from multiple different earlier versions of the story of Odysseus, or they might suggest multiple stages of composition and revision, by one poet or by many. Yet despite their mixed language, and despite the few inconsistencies, both *The Iliad* and *The Odyssey* display striking structural coherence. There is a grand architecture to the storytelling, which might seem to imply the careful planning of a single architect, or architects.

It is possible, as Albert Lord argued, that an oral poet worked closely with a literate scribe or scribes over the course of many days, weeks, or months. On this model, the composition of *The Odyssey* may have been not so different from that of *Paradise Lost*, composed by a blind poet who dictated his work over a long period to a number of amanuenses. Lord and Parry thought that the composer of the poem could not have been literate, because in the Yugoslavian context, singers who acquired literacy tended to lose their ability to compose oral poetry. But it has now been shown that oral traditions, or "orature," can interact with literacy in a number of different ways, and they are not necessarily driven out as soon as literacy arrives; in Somalia, for example, oral poets have been able to continue their oral compositions even after acquiring literacy. Oral literature is more diverse than Parry, with a single point of cultural comparison, could discern.

Some scholars argue that *The Odyssey* was composed by a single person who was well acquainted with the oral tradition but had become literate. This is certainly possible, but there is really no evidence one way or the other. Alternatively, perhaps the poem was composed when one particularly talented illiterate or semiliterate poet (or several) teamed up with a scribe or a group of scribes. Perhaps the scribe or scribes were entirely passive in the process of writing down what the poet composed; or perhaps there was an ongoing collaboration between two or more members of a group. Again, it is difficult to adjudicate between these various possibilities, in the absence of any solid evidence, or a time machine.

The same person could, in theory, have composed *The Iliad* and *The Odyssey*, though many scholars believe that different individuals wrote the two poems, because they are notably different in terms of language as well as narrative content. It certainly seems likely that the person or people who composed *The Odyssey* were aware of *The Iliad*, since *The Odyssey* supplements but does not repeat any incidents from *The Iliad*—which is unlikely to have happened by chance.

Scholars who claim that *The Odyssey* was composed by a single person acknowledge that this poet drew on a long and complex set of earlier poetic and folkloric traditions, and that the initial composition underwent considerable alteration in subsequent years, decades, and centuries. Homer—whoever he, she, or they may have been—composed this definitive version of the homecoming of Odysseus with a deep awareness of multiple different versions of the story, as well as a deep knowledge of multiple other parallel folk traditions and myths. For instance, there were probably versions of the story in which Penelope was aware of Odysseus' plans to slaughter the suitors at a much earlier stage, and thus proposed the Contest of the Bow in full knowledge that it would help further her husband's plot. *The Odyssey* is also influenced by other related archaic legends, originating both around the Mediterranean and the Near East; for instance, the ancient myth of Jason and the Argonauts seems to hover behind the story of Odysseus and his wanderings.

Maybe an individual genius, a "Homer," had a particularly important role in the creation of *The Odyssey*. But we should question the notion that a unified structure and coherent creative product must necessarily be seen as the result of an individual's work. Scholars have tended to assume so, because many long-form narrative genres that we are familiar with, like novels, are produced that way. However, we are also familiar with long narratives that do not have single authors. Many movies, for example, are the product of a team. Most contemporary long-form television drama series are put together by multiple people, even if there is a single creator who came up with the show's initial premise. It may be helpful to think in these terms when considering the authorship of *The Odyssey*. Perhaps we are more prepared than readers of the past to approach *The Odyssey* as a poem that exists as a mostly unified whole, but which was created by multiple different people, over a long period of time.

When Was *The Odyssey* Composed?

The date of the poem, no less than its authorship, is a matter of serious disagreement. In the middle of the eighth century BCE, the inhabitants of Greece began to adopt a modified version of the Phoenician alphabet to write down their language. The Homeric poems may have been one of the earliest products of this new literacy. If so, they would have been composed some time in the late eighth century. But some scholars have suggested a significantly later date, in the early, middle, or late seventh century BCE; others, less plausibly, have suggested even later dates of composition. The near consensus is that, at some point between the late eighth and late seventh century, a hundred-year-long window, *The Odyssey* was composed.

It is frustratingly difficult to be any more precise. Arguments about dating the Homeric poems usually involve an appeal to material evidence. Objects can often be dated with some precision, especially since the advent of carbon dating and other technological advances in archaeology. People use different artifacts as time goes by, or behave differently in ways that leave a material record: for instance, we know that people in the Mediterranean world switched from using bronze weapons to using, primarily, iron, once new metallurgical techniques developed. Ceramics survive well over thousands of years and are useful for tracking cultural change, since pottery fashions often change fairly rapidly. But it is extremely difficult to use any such evidence to date *The Odyssey*. For example, inscribed on a clay drinking cup that was found on the Italian island of Ischia there is the fragment "Nestor's cup, good to drink from." Some scholars, citing an extensive description of King Nestor's magnificent golden cup in *The Iliad*, have claimed that this inscription must be an allusion to the poem. It is nice to imagine that the words are a kind of joke: this simple, ordinary piece of crockery is identifying itself as a magnificent, heroic item. The cup can be dated to 750–700 BCE, so if this really is an allusion, *The Iliad* cannot be later than that date. But it is also quite possible that there were other poems and traditions about Nestor; the cup does not actually quote *The Iliad*, so it is not conclusive evidence that its maker knew the Homeric poem as such, rather than a set of associated Trojan legends—which we know also circulated in non-Homeric versions throughout the archaic period.

The Homeric poems reflect a mixture of artifacts and practices that existed at different historical times (such as divergent funeral practices, by burial or cremation, and different dowry practices). Indeed, the poems seem to have no interest in conveying an accurate, realistic account of the culture in which they were produced. Rather, they combine elements of a fictionalized, heroicized past with details of the more recent or contemporary world. Consider, as one example, the diets of characters in Homer. *The Odyssey*'s noble classes subsist on bread and, especially, wine and meat—usually large, impressive domesticated animals like pigs, sheep, and cattle (not chickens or geese, although Penelope dreams of geese and geese are kept in the palace). Nobody ever drinks water, and the men eat fish only when the alternative is starvation—as when Odysseus and his men are stranded on the island of Thrinacia. In real life, as the archaeological record shows and as common sense would predict, the people who lived around the Mediterranean ate fish, vegetables, cheese, and fruit. It has been suggested that the diet of these heroes might reflect a vague memory of even more ancient Indo-European civilizations; the nomadic people of the steppes by the Black Sea ate far more meat than the Greeks ever did. But it seems most likely that Homeric elites do not eat meat as a reflection of reality, but because it is a way for the poem to demonstrate their distinguished and extraordinary status. Meat makes them strong, and it shows how strong and important they already are—the stuff of legends.

Questions of dating are further complicated by the fact that the Homeric poems, or sections of them, were performed regularly by rhapsodes for several hundred years. These "song-stitchers"—professional poetry performers—competed in public competitions, and imagined themselves as stitching together a quilt of poetic narrative out of an already existing cloth, one often presented as the poetry of "Homer." It seems likely that rhapsodes made use of written texts to learn their lines of Homer, although they may also have ad-libbed and riffed off the script. Rhapsodes presumably introduced variations on the texts in performance, until the first Homeric scholars, men associated with the library of ancient Alexandria in the second century BCE, tried to "correct" the texts. By this time there must have been many slight textual variants in the Homeric poems, and the Alexandrians tried to come up with the "best" reading at each moment when their manuscripts did not agree. We have evidence of the type of variant that existed in the texts of Homer in circulation in the classical period, because quotations of Homer by authors such as Plato are sometimes a little different from the text as we have it.

But *The Odyssey* as read by Sophocles or Plato in fifth- or fourth-century Athens was presumably not significantly different from our own. Minor variations aside, the Homeric poems existed by the late seventh century BCE, and they quickly claimed a canonical place all over the Greek world. By the sixth century, they had acquired a central place in the cultural institutions of ancient Athens. In 566 BCE, Pisistratus, the tyrant of the city (which was not yet a democracy), instituted a civic and religious festival, the Panathenaia, which included a poetic competition, featuring performances of the Homeric poems. The institution is particularly significant because we are told that the Homeric poems had to be performed "correctly," which implies the canonization of a particular written text of *The Iliad* and *The Odyssey* at this date. From that time onward, if not before, *The Iliad* and *Odyssey* acquired a central place in the cultural and educational life of ancient Greece and Rome. There was no holy scripture in the classical world, but everyone knew the stories of Achilles and Odysseus as told in the Homeric poems.

Homer's World

The geographical setting of *The Odyssey* is almost as hard to pin down as its temporal location. Some of the places visited by Odysseus are obviously fictional or mythical—the Land of the Dead, the island of the Sirens, the home of the monster Scylla and the whirlpool Charybdis, or the city of the giant, cannibalistic Laestrygonians. But even the places that seem less clearly unrealistic are often difficult to plot onto an accurate map. Ethiopia is the most distant place imaginable, located "between the sunset and the dawn." Libya is a mythically wealthy place where sheep produce lambs three times a year. Egypt is a little less hazy, but still not described with any precision: it is the fertile land of the Nile, where traders or visitors (like Menelaus) can acquire fabulous amounts of wealth. Even the island of Ithaca itself is described in a muddled way. This may be a sign that the traditions that informed the poem developed primarily in the eastern part of the Greek world, so that the composer(s) had only a vague notion of the actual geography of the western islands like Ithaca. It is also a sign that the poem has little interest in the realistic depiction of geography.

Nevertheless, readers since antiquity have tried to locate the wanderings of Odysseus in the real Mediterranean and Aegean world. By the third century BCE, certain traditional identifications of Homeric geography with real geography had developed. Scylla and Charybdis were identified with the Straits of Messina (where there are often rough currents, though never six-headed sea-monsters). Sicily was identified as the Island of the Cyclops—a rich, fertile land inhabited by non-Greek people, whose customs and agricultural practices are different from those of Greece.

These identifications reflect an awareness that there is some correspondence between the world of Homer and the real world, although the relationship is partial and inexact; see Map 1, which depicts the fictional wanderings of the hero, in contrast to Maps 2, 3, and 4, which depict the geographical realities on which the fantasy is loosely based. *The Odyssey* explores the relationship of its central character, a man from the western Greek world, with people, gods, and monsters from many different regions, each of which has its own separate identity, and which correspond in wildly different degrees to real life.

"Greece," as a unified entity, is an invention of the classical age; in the sixth and especially the fifth centuries BCE, Greek-speaking people began to define themselves as Hellenes, in contrast to the "barbarian" (meaning "non-Greek-speaking") peoples of other civilizations, such as the Persians and the Egyptians. But in Homer, as Thucydides points out, there is no single term for all Greek people. Those who sail to attack Troy from places that would later be defined as "Greek" are categorized by names for smaller ethnic tribes, or as the followers of individual leaders: the Danaeans, the Achaeans, the Myrmidons, and so on.

The Odyssey reflects an awareness of the many diverse peoples who inhabited the territories around mainland Greece. During the Bronze Age, in the fourth to second millennia BCE, the Minoans, who may have been proto-Greek speakers, inhabited Crete, while other proto-Greek speakers lived on the Cycladic islands of the Aegean, and others again on the mainland. These people left tantalizing glimpses of their cultures, through material remains, including wall paintings and pottery and ruined palaces and homes. In the sixteenth to twelfth centuries BCE, the so-called Mycenean Greeks established a powerful civilization on the

Greek mainland, with grand palaces in locations such as Mycenae itself, but also in many other cities, including Pylos (home, in *The Odyssey*, of old King Nestor). The Myceneans had a system of writing known as Linear B, a syllabic script that was used by scribes to make administrative records on clay tablets. But when Mycenean civilization fell—perhaps due to invasion by non-Greek people or, more likely, because of civil warfare and possibly climate change—the great palaces were destroyed and, with them, the Linear B writing system was lost.

In the Greek "dark ages," from the twelfth to the eighth centuries BCE, Greece was illiterate, and it was in this period that the oral poetic tradition that led into *The Odyssey* developed. The stories and myths that circulated in this period reflected memories and fantasies about the lost cultures of the Minoans and the Myceneans—although they were also drawn from neighboring cultures, such as the civilizations of the ancient Near East (including Egypt, Iran, the Levant, Mesopotamia, and Asia Minor). The oral tradition provided Greek-speaking people with a way to remember and memorialize the cultures that had been lost, including the wealthy and hierarchical civilization of the Myceneans.

The legends of the Trojan War—tales of a great conflict, the fall of a mighty people, and the attempts of scattered survivors to regain or build new homes—are informed by folk memory of this fallen culture. *The Iliad* tells the story of a conflict between two elite warrior kings, Agamemnon of Mycenae and Achilles of Thessaly—perhaps echoing a real collapse of Mycenean civilization through civil war. In *The Odyssey*, the rich palaces of Nestor on Pylos and Menelaus in Sparta may reflect folk memories of Mycenean grandeur. Crete is another important point of reference in *The Odyssey*. When Odysseus in Ithaca tells false tales about himself, he often says that he comes from Crete—which may echo archaic Minoan or Mycenean myths, and reflect a cultural memory of the days when Crete was at the center of Greek-speaking civilization.

It is hard to say how much the Homeric poems depict the realities of actual historical events, such as "the" Trojan War. In the late nineteenth century, an amateur archaeologist named Heinrich Schliemann excavated a site in Turkey, Hissarlik, that he theorized was the original Troy.

He made some extraordinary discoveries, including a cache of gold that he labeled "Priam's treasure"; later, on a different excavation in Mycenae, he claimed to have uncovered the real tomb of Agamemnon. Modern archaeologists tend to be more skeptical, and to lament the way in which Schliemann—like other archaeologists of his time—rashly shoveled his way into the earth, destroying a vast amount of evidence in the process. Hissarlik is still identified as the site of Troy, but it is now generally believed that there were at least nine towns built in the area over the course of some three millennia, from early Bronze Age settlements to a Roman imperial city. Some of these cities were destroyed by natural means, such as earthquakes, and others were destroyed by fire and war; but we cannot identify any one of these multiple destructions with the single sacking of Troy described in Homer.

It was from the Phoenicians that, in the middle of the eighth century, the Greeks adapted their alphabetic system of writing. The Phoenicians, a trading, seafaring people who originated from the western part of the Fertile Crescent (in the area which now includes Lebanon, Syria, Israel, and Jordan), are portrayed in the poem as rich traders who are liable to trick, rob, and enslave the unwary. Odysseus tells his swineherd, Eumaeus, an elaborate false story that he came from Crete, stayed in Egypt for seven years getting rich, and then was tricked by a "cunning man" from Phoenicia into sailing with him; the Phoenician hoped to trade him as a slave, for a profit. Eumaeus replies with his own, presumably more truthful story, which again involves being tricked and trafficked into slavery—which explains how he has ended up in Odysseus' own household.

These sinister, deceitful, profit-mongering Phoenicians are ostensibly contrasted with Odysseus himself. Similarly, the seafaring people of Taphos are described as "pirates," who live by looting, robbing, and enslaving their neighbors—in contrast to the maritime wanderings of Odysseus, whose only goal is to reach his home. But the line is uncomfortably difficult to draw. Odysseus is depicted as a master of deceit, a compulsive liar; he is also, like a Phoenician or Taphian trader or pirate, hoping to return home with as large a pile of loot as he can. He enriches himself from the sacked city of Troy, and from various other places along the way, where the inhabitants either willingly equip him with presents (as in the case of Calypso, Circe, Aeolus, and the Phaeacians) or are robbed by Odysseus and his men. When telling the story of his various adventures to the Phaeacians, Odysseus begins with an episode in which he and his men stop by the city of the Cicones. He explains,

I sacked
the town and killed the men. We took their wives
and shared their riches equally among us. (9.41–43)

No justification is given for this act of plunder; it is presented simply as the kind of thing that Odysseus does, or perhaps the kind of thing that any Greek man would do, given the chance. A little later, Polyphemus the Cyclops asks Odysseus suspiciously if he is a "pirate," like people who "risk their lives at sea to bring disaster / to other people." Odysseus' answer is notably equivocal. He declares that he and his men are part of the great expedition to Troy, and claims

We are proud to be the men of Agamemnon,
the son of Atreus, whose fame is greatest
under the sky, for sacking that vast city
and killing many people. (9.263–66)

Being a "hero," *heros*—which in archaic Greek suggests a warrior, and does not imply virtue—is different from being a "pirate" in that it is a much more positive term, which a man can proudly apply to himself; nobody in Homer admits to being a pirate. Like pirates, warriors sack towns and kill the inhabitants; the main difference is scale. Odysseus goes on to infiltrate the enemy's dwelling, maim him, and poach his beloved sheep, the wealth of his household—an act that is clearly analogous to the hero's previous triumph over the Trojans.

The late eighth century was a period of increasing trade across the Mediterranean world—including trade of objects, stories, skills (like writing), ideas, and people. It was also a period in which Greek speakers had begun to create colonies. Colonization was a way to improve trading opportunities and increase the wealth of the originating city or settlement, as well as to house a growing population. Greek colonies developed in Libya, in southern France, along the Black Sea, and on the southern coast of Italy and Sicily—later known as Magna Graecia, "Big Greece." *The Odyssey* shows an acute awareness of the processes of colonization, and Odysseus himself seems sometimes to think as much like a colonizer as a pirate. When scoping out the uninhabited island adjacent to that of the Cyclopes, he gives a description that sounds like an advertisement for prospective colonial inhabitants, as well as a critique, from the colonizer's point of view, of the natives who have failed to exploit their country's natural resources:

Cyclopic people have no red-cheeked ships
and no shipwright among them who could build
boats, to enable them to row across
to other cities, as most people do,
crossing the sea to visit one another.
With boats they could have turned this island into
a fertile colony, with proper harvests.
By the gray shore there lie well-watered meadows,
where vines would never fail. There is flat land
for plowing, and abundant crops would grow
in the autumn; there is richness underground. (9.125–35)

It is not surprising that the island was identified in antiquity with Sicily, given both the lush natural resources of this location in the poem, and the ways that the Polyphemus episode seems to meditate uneasily on the processes of colonization. In real life, we know frustratingly little about the process by which the Greeks established their control. The Greek invaders quickly imported their own agricultural products—olives for oil, and grapes for wine—and later used slaves, perhaps including native Sicilians, to construct monumental architecture, vast temples to the Greek gods to represent Hellenic dominance in the region. The various tribes who inhabited Sicily before the Greeks took over do not seem to have managed to fight back against the invaders, and there is no way to reconstruct what they felt about it all.

We can see in *The Odyssey* a complex response by the Greeks to their own growing dominance as traders, travelers, colonizers, pirates, leaders, and warriors. The Polyphemus episode, for example, can be read as an attempt to justify Greek exploitation of non-Greek peoples. Odysseus enters the Cyclops' cave without the host's permission, and then tricks, blinds, robs, and abuses the native inhabitant. As narrator, he makes his actions seem acceptable or even admirable, by emphasizing morally irrelevant considerations—such as the fact that the Cyclops lives by herding animals rather than growing crops (as presumably was also true of the native Sicilians), and by presenting his victim as loud, ugly, and oversized. Of course, Polyphemus also has the nasty habit of eating his human visitors. By this means, the text invites us to imagine that all non-Greek and pastoralist societies should be seen as barbaric and cannibalistic.

The narrative is told only through the mouth of Odysseus himself, and we may well see him as an unreliable narrator. Odysseus implies that the Cyclopic people (also known as the "Cyclopes," plural of Cyclops) are "lawless," or lacking in customs; but Polyphemus does his chores in an entirely regular and predictable fashion. Odysseus implies that these people are loners who care nothing for one another; but Polyphemus' neighbors arrive promptly when they hear him calling for help, and the Cyclops treats his animals with attentive care and affection—his blind petting of his favorite "sweet ram" is particularly touching. Odysseus first tells us that the Cyclopes "put their trust in gods," who provide them with crops (implying that these people can be blamed for their lazy lack of Greek-style agricultural practices), but then suggests that a failure to welcome strangers should be construed as an insult to "the gods," or at least to Zeus, the god of strangers—suggesting that the gods are all on the Greek side. In fact, Polyphemus, the son of Poseidon, has some powerful divine backing of his own.

The Odyssey looks back to a lost heroic age, the time before the Greek dark ages, when elite Mycenean families, living in great palaces, dominated the surrounded regions, clashed with one another, and maintained power through wealth, military prowess, and a traditional way of life. But the poem also meditates on the social and geographical changes undergone by Greek society in the late eighth century, as the new literacy enabled new forms of communication with outsiders, and as colonizers, traders, and pirates pushed outward across the Mediterranean, encountering alien cultures and alien peoples.

Friends, Strangers, Guests

Before approaching the island of the Cyclopes, Odysseus tells his men that he has to find out some important information: whether the inhabitants are "lawless aggressors," or people who welcome strangers. Odysseus presents these categories as if they are mutually exclusive: the willingness to welcome strangers is figured as enough, in itself, to guarantee that a person or culture can be counted as law-abiding and "civilized." The Cyclopes would have good reason to be suspicious of these visitors, who have looted and slaughtered the inhabitants of the previous island that they visited. But the dichotomy hints at the importance in *The Odyssey* of *xenia*, a word that means both "hospitality" and "friendship." The cognate word *xenos* can mean both "stranger" and "friend"; it is the root from which we get the English word "xenophobia," the fear of strangers or foreigners, as well as the sadly less common "xenophilia," the love of strangers or of unknown objects.

Hospitality is important in all human cultures, ancient and modern; in this respect, there is nothing special about archaic Greece. What is distinctive about the customs surrounding hospitality in this culture is that elite men who have entered one another's homes and have been entertained appropriately are understood to have created a bond of "guest-friendship" (*xenia*) between their households that will continue into future generations. Guest-friendship is different from *philia*, the friendship, affection, love, and loyalty that connects a person to his or her family members and neighborhood friends. It is created not by proximity and kinship, but by a set of behaviors that create bonds between people who are geographically distant from each other. *Xenia* is thus a networking tool that allows for the expansion of Greek power, from the unit of the family to the city-state and then across the Mediterranean world. It is the means by which unrelated elite families can connect to one another as equals, without having to fight for dominance. It is no coincidence that the origin of the Trojan War, the abduction of Menelaus' wife by his guest, Paris, is presented in Greek literature as an abuse of *xenia,* since the laws of hospitality are what stave off a world where men kill those who are different from themselves. When *xenia* is absent or is abused, violence follows.

Xenia acquired an extra importance in the era when Greek men were expanding their world. Travelers, in an era before money, hotels, or public transportation, had to rely on the munificence of strangers to find food and lodging and aid with their onward journey. *The Odyssey* suggests that it was the responsibility of male householders to offer hospitality of this kind to any visitor, even uninvited guests, strangers, and homeless beggars. Those who traveled to an unfamiliar land used the norms and expectations of *xenia* to form bonds with people who might otherwise have treated them as too ragged and dirty to deserve a welcome, or as too dangerous to accept into their home. Conversely, the promotion of Greek *xenia* as a quasi-universal and quasi-ethical concept can be used as imaginative justification for robbing, killing, enslaving, or colonizing those who are reluctant to welcome a group of possible bandits or pirates into their home. *The Odyssey* shows us both sides of this complex concept, which hovers in an uneasy space between ethics and etiquette.

The poem's episodes can be seen as a sequence of case studies in the concept of *xenia*. In the first four books—known as the Telemachy, the story of Telemachus—Odysseus' young son grapples with the suitors, who are presented as bad guests: they have taken over Odysseus' household without his permission and are abusing its resources and inhabitants. By contrast, Telemachus shows that he himself is capable of being a good, polite guest who is more or less able to overcome his crippling shyness with the magical help of Athena. He thanks his hosts appropriately, and does not overstay his welcome. He manages to be a good host also, when he welcomes a stranger in need, Theoclymenus, on board his ship. He even manages to circumvent a tricky dilemma of etiquette—how to avoid having to make a second visit with touchy, long-winded Nestor, without being rude to the old man—although only at the cost of putting his friend, Nestor's son, in a difficult position.

Telemachus' visits to the homes of Nestor and Menelaus provide contrasting examples of elite hospitality. The first is old-fashioned, pious, rich in horses and sons, presided over by moralizing old Nestor. The second is piled high with newly acquired treasure, brought by blustering, self-pitying Menelaus, and the dominant figure is beautiful, magical Helen, who has frightening drugs that can take away all pain and grief. But in both Pylos and Sparta, the visit follows a set pattern. The guest is welcomed, washed by slave women, given an honorable and comfortable place to sit, and offered food and wine. Only after he has eaten and had some wine is he asked to tell his story. The visitor is then given lodging for the night, and when it is time to leave, the host provides gifts and some practical help with the onward journey. As Menelaus pompously declares, "To force a visitor to stay / is just as bad as pushing him to go." Providing help with the next leg of the trip—*pompe* in Greek, "sending," a common word and essential concept in the *Odyssey*—is thus an important component in hospitality. Nestor, for example, gives Telemachus a horse-drawn chariot to get to Sparta, and sends along his youngest son, Pisistratus, as a companion.

Odysseus is not so lucky in some of his hosts. We first see him suffering the burdens of a hospitality even more insistently lavish than that of Nestor. Calypso gives her human guest more than enough of everything a visitor could ask for, except the final crucial ingredient: *pompe*—the ability to get away. When, thanks to divine intervention, Calypso finally lets Odysseus build a raft and be on his way—an unorthodox "sending" in which the guest has to construct his own means of transportation—his next hosts are challenging in different ways. The shipwrecked, naked stranger finds himself rescued by a young princess of marriageable age, among a nation of sailors, and has to muster all his powers of flattery and politeness. Nausicaa, the Phaeacian princess, warns Odysseus that her people are not welcoming to strangers; yet the court of Arete and Alcinous seems in many ways ideally hospitable. Odysseus is bathed, wined and dined, entertained with poetic song, and given the chance to tell his own story at great length. He watches and then is put to the test in the Phaeacian contests, performing far better than expected—an episode that anticipates the later challenges and contests back home in Ithaca. The Phaeacians then give him the most lavish possible *pompe*—a magical boat that sails itself—at a high personal cost to themselves; Poseidon punishes them by crushing their boat with a mountain hurled into the sea, thus blocking their island from the outside world forever after and curtailing any future Phaeacian generosity.

The limits and antonyms of *xenia* are explored in Odysseus' account to the Phaeacian king of his wanderings to other fantastical, monstrous places he has visited. Each of these hosts seems to offer a perversion or a frightening exaggeration of the ordinary modes of hospitality. Aeolus, the god of the winds, provides Odysseus with a means of transportation or "sending" that is more powerful than he or his men can handle: the bag of winds, once opened, blasts the ship back in entirely the wrong direction. A normal host may provide his guests with poetic and musical entertainment before he goes to sleep; the Sirens entice their visitors with a song so fascinating that they want to stay forever, and never go home again. Many of these hosts pervert the ordinary way that guests are given food and drink. The Lotus-Eaters share a plant that makes those who eat it forget all thoughts of going home. In order to meet the dead, Odysseus himself has to act like a peculiar kind of host, welcoming them into the world of the living—by allowing them to drink blood from a ditch. The witchlike goddess Circe provides her guests with a magical drink that turns them into pigs.

Several of those whom Odysseus visits—the giant Polyphemus, the gigantic Laestrygonians, the thirsty whirlpool Charybdis, and the six-headed Scylla—are defined as monstrous because they do not feed their guests: instead, they eat them (or, in the case of Charybdis, gulp them down like drink). The majority of Odysseus' men are devoured alive. Some are eaten by the Cyclops; many more are skewered in the water by the Laestrygonians and devoured, like fish. Later, Odysseus watches Scylla eating six of his men and hears them "still screaming, / still reaching out to me in their death throes."

After this climactic moment, the ship—the last left from Odysseus' fleet—sails directly on to Thrinacia, the island of the Sun God (Helius), and is becalmed there. Supplies dwindle and the men grow hungry. While Odysseus is absent, taking a nap in a cave, the men kill and eat the Cattle of the Sun, although they know that it is forbidden. This momentous choice is made for understandable reasons: the men are hungry and desperate, and they choose to risk the anger of the gods rather than endure the pain and slow humiliation of death by starvation. The ringleader of the insurrection, Eurylochus, speaks bravely, urging the others not to worry about the Sun God's response:

"If he is so angry
about these cows that he decides to wreck
our ship, and if the other gods agree—
I would prefer to drink the sea and die
at once, than perish slowly, shriveled up
here on this desert island." (12.347–52)

The language is inspiring, as if from a rousing battle speech. We may well wonder what exactly is wrong with Eurylochus' suggestion. The episode hints at an important idea in the poem: that the willingness to die for honor, which is valued so highly on the battlefield, is not always useful in these strange new worlds. Military valor, in the world of *The Odyssey,* risks looking too much like impatience. The poem shows us the rewards that come to the "much-enduring" or "long-suffering" protagonist through his willingness to wait for the right moment to act, without ever giving up the goal. Moreover, the determination of this crew member to eat even forbidden foods, and to drink even "the sea," represents a kind of self-assertion that is out of keeping with his place both in society and in the narrative. He is usurping the leadership role of Odysseus.

This act of forbidden consumption is a terrible mistake, which condemns the men to death and deprives them of their chance of getting home. Helius, the Sun God, responds to the eating of his cattle as if the men had taken a bite out of the god himself, and Zeus backs him up by drowning them all. Eating is important in *The Odyssey,* and eating the wrong things or eating in the wrong way results in violence or death.

Like the Cyclops or the Laestrygonians, the suitors who have taken over Odysseus' palace in Ithaca are defined as abnormal and monstrous eaters. We are repeatedly told that they are "devouring" and "wasting" the household wealth of Odysseus, by consuming his fattest animals and drinking his wine in their constant feasts, and failing to repay the absent owner or take care of the estate. It is, of course, a violation of hospitality to enter a person's home uninvited and remain there day after day, using up his food stores, wine, and wealth. The poem emphasizes that it is also unjust: the norms of behavior require a person to pay back what he or she owes, and a guest is supposed to give presents to a generous host, rather than simply enjoy the benefits of hospitality without giving anything in return.

Greed, ingratitude, and rudeness are annoying but, one might think, rather trivial faults. These boorish, selfish, immature young men are certainly unpleasant to be around, but not necessarily the epitome of evil, and it may be difficult to understand how anybody could think they really deserve death. The poem itself invites us to feel a degree of horror at Odysseus' violence, and sympathy for the murdered boys. On the other hand, the language in which *The Odyssey* presents the suitors' eating and drinking magnifies the enormity of their crime. The standard epithets applied to the suitors often emphasize their excessive desire to be "above" or "beyond" others (*hyper*: above and beyond): they are *hyper-phialos* or *hyper-thymos* ("self-indulgent," "heedless," "overbearing"). These words can be neutral or even positive (suggesting "noble" or "high-minded"—above the norms in a good way), but they acquire a sinister connotation here, since they are also applied to the man-eating Laestrygonians and Cyclops. We are repeatedly told that the suitors are devouring not only the literal "property" of Odysseus, but also, metonymically, his "house" and hence his "livelihood" or "life"—the words *bios* and *biotos* can mean both "way of making a living" and "life" itself. It is as if in eating Odysseus' animals, the suitors are metaphorically eating the man himself, and his son. Telemachus complains that the suitors are "consuming my whole house, and soon they may / destroy me too." The rage Odysseus musters against his uninvited guests seems to stem from a desperate need to preserve not only his wealth but even his identity from the mouths of those who are eating him alive.

But people who feel oppressed can become more dangerous than the people they fear. Once he reaches Ithaca, Odysseus is in the position of a guest in his own home, disguised as an old beggar. He is given a modest but warm welcome by the slave pig-keeper, Eumaeus, while the suitors act as unfriendly, hostile hosts, mocking and throwing stools at their ragged guest. However, when Odysseus is restored to his own persona, taking charge again of his household, the roles of guest and host make a sudden switch. The poor old visitor is now the householder himself. Odysseus becomes one of the most terrifying hosts of all, defending his property against unwanted visitors as thoroughly and violently as the Laestrygonians or the Sun God himself.

Gods

Xenia is particularly important to the gods in general, and especially to Zeus, the father and king of all the gods. One of the standard titles of Zeus was Xenios ("God of Strangers"). He is the god who presides over visitors, foreigners, and beggars, and who is invoked to defend the rights of guests or of hosts, when people fail to adhere to the norms of *xenia*. Zeus is also the god associated most closely with justice—*dike* in Greek, a notion linked to the idea of balance, and hence to the idea of retribution. Some readers have assumed that the gods in this poem—or at least Zeus—are defenders not only of *xenia* (which is, as we have seen, only partly an ethical concept), but also of morality in general. Some leap to the further notion that the triumph of Odysseus over the suitors represents an ethical victory, sanctioned by the gods. This certainly goes too far. Odysseus is presented as a morally complex character, as ancient readers recognized. The gods in *The Odyssey*, like those of *The Iliad*, are self-interested beings, whose interventions in human lives are motivated primarily by their own desires, whims, and preferences rather than by a consistent commitment to uphold moral law.

The main difference between gods and humans is that gods are far more powerful and, unlike mortals, immune from old age and death. Humans in the poem, especially Telemachus and Odysseus himself, invoke the gods as guardians of what is "right," but it is less clear that the gods see themselves in quite this way.

At the start of *The Odyssey*, Zeus is contemplating a problem in the human world. Agamemnon, king of Mycenae, had raised troops to help his brother Menelaus reclaim his wife, Helen, who had been taken to Troy by Paris, son of Priam, king of Troy. But in Agamemnon's absence, Aegisthus, who had an alternative claim to the throne of Mycenae, seduced Agamemnon's wife, Clytemnestra, seized control of his kingdom, and murdered Agamemnon when he came back home from Troy. Later, Agamemnon's young son Orestes—who had been sent away for his own protection—returned to Mycenae and killed both Aegisthus and his own mother, Clytemnestra, in revenge for the killing of his father.

Zeus presents the story of Aegisthus as an object lesson in human folly. People are already destined to suffer a certain amount, and yet sometimes they increase their quota of suffering by making bad choices—as Aegisthus did in killing Agamemnon and partnering with Clytemnestra, despite the warnings of the gods. Athena replies by reminding her father that Odysseus is stuck on Calypso's island, thanks to "bad luck," the hostility of Poseidon, and the negligence of Zeus himself—although perhaps also, we may speculate, thanks to his own decisions.

This first exchange between divine father and divine daughter has sometimes been read to imply that the gods of *The Odyssey* ensure that good people, like Odysseus, are rewarded for their virtue, while bad people, like the suitors, are punished. Aristotle, the philosopher of the fourth century BCE, may hint at this interpretation in a very brief allusion to the poem: he says that *The Odyssey* has a double structure, and ends in opposite ways for the "better" and "worse" characters (*Poetics* 1453a). But "better" is not the same as "good," and the word Aristotle uses can mean simply "more noble" or "higher class." In fact, neither Zeus' words nor the narrative of the poem suggests that morally good behavior guarantees a happy life. Zeus says nothing about virtue as such in this speech. Although one may speculate that the gods warned Aegisthus because they are on the side of ethical behavior (against adultery, murder, and usurpation), this is not what Zeus himself says. Rather, he insists that Aegisthus was imprudent and foolish in pursuing a course of action that he should have known would result in his doom. When Athena urges Zeus to help Odysseus, she does not claim that her favorite human is morally superior to all others—a case that would be hard to make about this lying, self-interested sacker of cities. Instead Athena reminds Zeus that Odysseus "is more sensible than other humans." His intelligence sets him apart from other adulterers and murderers. Gods usually favor people who are exceptionally talented in some way, and the poem makes it clear that it is Odysseus' special form of cleverness that has earned him the attention of Athena.

Moreover, Odysseus has made the prudent habit of regular sacrifice to the gods. The gods in this poem, like the human characters, prefer people who show them respect and provide plenty of lavish gifts. Gods in Homer, like humans, care about eating and drinking, and associate the proper forms of consumption with honor and identity. The consumption of meat and wine demonstrates the heroes' close relationship to the gods, since these, unlike other foodstuffs, are always offered to the gods: a splash of wine from any drinking occasion is always poured for the gods (as a libation), and animals that are killed are always "sacrificed," never merely butchered. The gods are the most important guests who are always present at human feasts.

Gods have their own particular interests. As father and king of the gods, Zeus takes a special interest in masculine political power. Chieftains in Homer, whether or not they descend from Zeus in terms of lineage, are often given the epithet *diotrephes,* "sprung from Zeus"; in *The*

Odyssey, this epithet is applied exclusively to Odysseus himself, whose role as king of Ithaca is apparently important to Zeus. Zeus is associated with the eagle, the king of the birds, and at more than one key moment in the poem (including the omen in Book 3, and the dream in Book 18), eagles represent Odysseus himself as the king whose power as king, and capacity to exact retribution on his enemies, seem to be favored by Zeus. In Book 1, Telemachus' attempt to speak out against the suitors is valorized by Zeus, who sends two eagles to swoop into the assembled crowd:

they wheeled and whirred and flapped their mighty wings,
swooping at each man's head with eyes like death. (2.152–53)

The birds anticipate the moment, twenty-two books later, when Telemachus and Odysseus together will slaughter the suitors. The day before the massacre, in a memorably creepy episode, the prophet Theoclymenus is able to foresee the suitors' deaths, when they lose control of their own faces, and their cooked meat begins to drip with blood; the prophet declares,

"Your faces, heads and bodies are wrapped up
in night; your screams are blazing out like fire.
The ornate palace ceilings and the walls
are spattered with your blood. The porch is full
of ghosts, as is the courtyard—ghosts descending
into the dark of Erebus. The sun
has vanished from the sky, and gloomy mist
is all around." (20.353–60)

Even before their deaths at the human hands of Odysseus and his helpers, the suitors are doomed by a divinely ordained fate.

But there is more than one god in this poem, and more than one point of view from which to look at Odysseus. The god most hostile to the hero is Zeus' brother Poseidon, the god of the sea, storms, and earthquakes. Indeed, the narrative of the poem can be seen as an extended balancing act between Athena's desire to restore Odysseus to a place of honor and stability in his household, and Poseidon's to curse him with eternal wandering. Poseidon is understandably angry that Odysseus tricks and blinds his son, Polyphemus the Cyclops, who in Book 9 calls on his father to curse the homeward journey of the man who maimed him. Poseidon is less prominent as a character in the poem than his rival, Athena; he gets far fewer speeches and far fewer appearances interacting with the human characters. But we can see his work behind every storm and shipwreck, and behind every disaster that befalls Odysseus' unlucky fellow travelers.

Homer presents us with a world where gods mingle with humans, and may touch their lives in ways that are not always visible to the mortals involved. Great charm and magic comes from the notion that the divine and human worlds are less separate than we might otherwise imagine. Telemachus, for example, is guided by Athena on his journey, and the presence of the goddess imparts a special comfort and joy even to the most mundane moments of the trip.

Wind blew the middle sail; the purple wave
was splashing loudly round the moving keel.
The goddess surfed the waves and smoothed the way.
The quick black ship held steady, so they fastened
the tackle down, and filled their cups with wine.
They poured libations to the deathless gods,
especially to the bright-eyed child of Zeus.
All through the night till dawn the ship sailed on. (2.427–34)

Mortal characters, and their accessories, are very frequently referred to by the standard approbatory epithet, "godlike" (or variations thereof), and one of the most common epithets of all, *dios*—often translated as "noble" or "shining"—literally suggests "associated with Zeus" (the word has the same root as the Latin *deus*, "god"). The sixth-century BCE philosopher Thales said, "The world is full of gods." This is certainly true of the world of Odysseus. On his travels, he meets a number of minor deities, including the "nymph" Calypso. "Nymph" is the normal Greek word for a human young bride, but it is also applied to goddesses who are particularly closely associated with the natural landscape in particular places; there are nymphs of the sea (Nereids), nymphs of the woods (Dryads), and nymphs of caves (like Calypso herself, whose name suggests "hidden," and like the unnamed nymphs whom Odysseus greets as soon as he arrives back in Ithaca). Every place has its own special deity—some welcoming or helpful, like the White Goddess who rescues Odysseus from shipwreck, and some hostile, like Scylla and Charybdis—goddesses who emerge from the dangerous natural world.

A particularly important god in this poem about journeys and interactions between people from different cultures and different households is Hermes, the messenger god, the god of travelers. Hermes is a son of Zeus who has the ability to fly at supernatural speed, bringing news or passengers from one realm to another, wearing the magical sandals "of everlasting gold with which he flies / on breath of air across the sea and land." Hermes can dive from sky to earth and down to the underworld, and can flash through water to travel across the sea:

He touched Pieria, then from the sky
he plunged into the sea and swooped between
the waves, just like a seagull catching fish,
wetting its whirring wings in tireless brine. (5.50–53)

Hermes has a certain elusive quality, appearing and disappearing at will; he is, like Odysseus himself, a trickster. In the (post-Odyssean) "Homeric Hymn to Hermes," this clever, deceitful thief acquires an epithet often used of Odysseus himself—*polytropos*, "much-turning." Hermes plays a key role at three important junctures. He is the one who is sent down unwillingly from Olympus, to the distant island of Calypso, to persuade the goddess to release Odysseus; he saves Odysseus and his men from Circe; and in the final book, he is the one who leads the spirits of the suitors to the underworld.

The most important deity in the poem, however, is Athena, the goddess of technical expertise and strategic thinking. She is a military deity, often represented as dressed in battle armor, and she reminds Odysseus that she is the one who helped him sack the city of Troy, inspiring the construction of the Wooden Horse. Athena also presides over activities associated more with peacetime; Penelope's weaving, no less than Odysseus' fighting, is done under the aegis of Athena. Whereas Poseidon favors the untamed world of the stormy sea, Athena loves fixed settlements and the olive tree—a crop whose oil was used in archaic Greece for cooking and skin care. Poseidon makes the earth shake; Athena makes even the most rugged, barren landscape available for cultivation.

Athena's most common epithet, *glaucopis,* suggests bright or shimmering eyes. The poem constantly reminds us that Athena is alert to whatever is happening to Odysseus and Telemachus; nothing escapes her intelligent, careful notice. We can detect her presence in the narrative, her sharp eyes, even at moments when she is not visible to the human characters. For instance, when Odysseus and his men put out the eye of the Cyclops, they do so with a staff made of olive wood. When Odysseus meets Athena in person on Ithaca, she tells him that she has always been watching over him and helping him, even during the terrible storms at sea when Odysseus thought that she was giving him no protection: "I am Athena, child of Zeus. I always / stand near you and take care of you, in all / your hardships," she declares.

Athena's ultimate motives are mixed and not always benevolent, as befits a divine being in the Greek imagination. She presents herself as consistently the defender of Odysseus and his male line. However, we are also reminded (in Book 5) that the storms which scattered the Greek fleet after the sack of Troy were caused by Athena herself, working alongside Poseidon, since she was enraged at how the Greeks defiled the Trojan temples—and she wanted to increase the glory of her favorite when, after long delays, he finally returns to slaughter the suitors. When Odysseus is in disguise in Ithaca, Athena goads him to greater and greater rage, and prompts the suitors to mistreat him. Athena loves violence, and knows how to manipulate events so as to maximize her own pleasure in battle. Her skill in weaving clothing for domestic use sits uneasily with her ability to weave deception and military strategy for the tapestry of war.

The major Olympian gods do not usually appear in their own true form to mortals. Athena appears in multiple different guises to Telemachus and Odysseus. She can be a bird of prey, not an eagle (the bird of her father Zeus) or a hawk (bird of Apollo), but a European vulture (an ossifrage) or an owl. The cult of Athena in Greece may have originated from that of a Minoan owl goddess. When disguised as a human, Athena appears as Odysseus' old guest-friend, Mentor. But she also assumes other guises. In Phaeacia, she is a little girl, carrying water from the well. When she has her most extensive conversation with Odysseus, in Book 13, she appears first as a well-dressed young man; then, as if to make herself recognizable to him, she transforms herself again, this time into a beautiful woman. Athena transforms Odysseus as well as herself. She can change him into a ragged old man, and then into a tall, handsome, strong man in the prime of life. Athena can mask places, too: she casts a magical mist to make Ithaca unrecognizable, even to Odysseus himself.

Athena's powers of transformation and disguise are part of her cunning, the quality she shares with Odysseus. In myth, Athena's mother is Metis, a goddess who is the personification of Odysseus' central quality: *metis*, which means "cunning," "skill," "scheming," or "purpose." It is the kind of cleverness that enables one to prepare for any new challenge and to come out as a winner. Metis was supposedly swallowed up by Zeus, and Athena emerged whole from the head of her father—a myth that hints at how the archaic Greeks imagined this potentially dangerous and unattractive quality as one that could become acceptable, even admirable, in the right contexts. Unlike the English word "wisdom," which tends to suggest a staid, peaceful, possibly moral kind of intelligence acquired by long years of experience, *metis* suggests cunning plots and deception employed in the service of self-interest. It is not necessarily seen as a bad thing; *metis* is a very useful quality for a person who hopes to survive in a dangerous environment.

Odysseus is often described as *polymetis*, a term that suggests an abundance of *metis*. When the man and the goddess meet face-to-face in Book 13, they agree that they share a capacity for scheming, for deceit, for transformation, and for telling elaborate lies, as well as an ability to wait a surprisingly long time to achieve their ends. Athena tells him,

> *"No man can plan and talk like you,*
> *and I am known among the gods for insight*
> *and craftiness."* (13.298–300)

These shared characteristics explain why the man and the goddess get along so well together. The relationship between Athena and Odysseus has a flirtatious quality that is made all the more interesting by the fact that they come from different worlds—she a goddess, he a mortal—and by the fact that she is a mostly female character who has the absolute upper hand, as well as the power of life, death, and identity, over this dominant Greek male. The relationships of Odysseus with Calypso, Circe, and especially Athena give us glimpses of an alternative to the "normal" mortal world, in which female characters are always less powerful than their male partners.

Goddesses, Wives, Princesses, and Slave Girls

We know frustratingly little about the lives of women in archaic Greece. The Homeric poems themselves are rich sources of information about Mediterranean society in the eighth century BCE, although both are highly artificial literary texts, and both were presumably created primarily by and for men. We see in *The Iliad* a world in which women were often treated by elite warrior men as if they were objects, prizes traded in war for men's honor, along with other possessions, like bronze tripods and piles of treasure. But women also had their own distinctive work (as mothers, wives, weavers, and caretakers), and their own perspective on the male-dominated world of war. They fed, washed, and clothed the men who left them to fight among themselves for honor, and they washed, wrapped, and wept for the dead bodies that returned. They gave birth and cared for their children, and cried when men hurled them from the city walls. Fathers traded their daughters to other men as wives, and they were passed on to yet more men as trafficked slaves.

But perhaps life for women in archaic Greece was not always as bleak as this. *The Odyssey* allows us to imagine a far more varied array of possible female lives. Its various settings—in multiple different islands, homes, and palaces, in peacetime rather than war—are mostly places where women or goddesses have a defined position and a voice. Some scholars have tried to find buried memories in *The Odyssey* of an ancient, pre-Greek matriarchal society—for example, in the peculiarly high status of Queen Arete in Phaeacia, who sometimes, confusingly, seems more important than her husband, or in Penelope's power in Ithaca over even the male members of her household, most prominently Telemachus. But these elements in the poem probably tell us more about male fears and fantasies, both ancient and modern, than about the historical realities of archaic or pre-archaic women's lives.

Samuel Butler famously suggested in the nineteenth century that the *Odyssey* must have been written by a woman, because it has so many interesting and sympathetically portrayed female characters: "People always write by preference of what they know best, and they know best what they most are, and have most to do with." Few modern scholars would agree: we have, sadly, no evidence for women participating in the archaic Greek epic tradition as composers or rhapsodes. Moreover, Butler's claim relied on the dubious assumptions that only a woman would want to write about female characters in any depth, and that all the elements he regarded as ham-fisted could be explained by positing a young, unmarried girl as the "authoress"—in contrast to *The Iliad,* which was clearly the work of an adult man, a person capable of writing convincing battle scenes.

It is more plausible to view *The Odyssey* as the product of archaic male imaginations, questioning and defending the inequalities of male dominance within the status quo. The poem meditates on what women might be capable of, and the degree to which their potential can or should be suppressed. We are shown differences in how men and women behave—for instance, women in Homer do not fight, attack, or kill one another, or travel to foreign countries for trade or war. There are also similarities: both men and women speak, sing, cry, steal, think, plan, deceive, celebrate, organize, give orders, and feel a whole range of emotions—grief, surprise, frustration, rage, embarrassment, shame, loneliness, and joy.

The Odyssey is a poem in which certain females have far more power than real women ever did in the society of archaic Greece. Most obviously, the goddess Athena, born from the head of her father, guides Odysseus through all his wanderings and all his plots, schemes, disguises, and battles back in Ithaca. Only through female divine power can his patriarchal dominance over his household be regained. On a human level, it is essential for the plot that Penelope has the power to choose in her husband's absence to marry one of her suitors, and that if she does so, the suitors will either divide the wealth of the house, or the new bridegroom will take control of the whole palace. It never seems to have been a normal Greek custom for power over the household to transfer through the woman to a new husband. But the notion is vitally important in *The Odyssey*: if Penelope remarries, Odysseus will lose not only a person he loves, but also, perhaps more important, all his economic wealth and social status. It is at least hinted as a possibility that the wife in this poem, unlike most wives in real archaic society, has the power to choose the man who will have control over her household.

In many respects, the text reflects social roles that presumably existed in real life. Girls and women in *The Odyssey* occupy different social spheres from those of men and boys, and their particular types of expertise are different. Female slaves (like Eurycleia) take care of children inside the house and perform domestic labor, like making the beds and lighting the torches, while some male slaves (like the old swineherd Eumaeus) take care of animals and others (like Dolius and his sons) do farmwork and gardening. The task of feeding and clothing the elite is also divided along gender lines. Women slaves grind the grain, bake the bread, and set and clear the tables, while male slaves prepare and serve the meat and pour the wine. Women slaves (like Eurycleia and Eurynome) are the ones who wash, scrub, and anoint the bodies of male guests, and female slaves help elite women make the household clothes and linens, by spinning and weaving cloth, and help them take care of the clothes by doing laundry. Girls make the daily trip to fetch water for the household. Carpenters, shipbuilders, construction workers, ironmongers, priests, fishermen, hunters, pirates, tradesmen, and poets are male.

Among the elite, too, there are clear distinctions between male and female kinds of activity. Powerful men participate in male-only council meetings, and they are the ones who lead troops to war or (what is presented as much the same thing) on raids to kill and rob from neighboring settlements. Elite men are the primary participants in athletic competitions, although we glimpse girls playing ball in their spare time. Men predominate at feasts and banquets, although exceptional noblewomen (such as Helen, and Arete, queen of Phaeacia) are present. Elite women have a separate suite in the house, a set of "upper" or "inmost" rooms, such that Penelope is able to withdraw from the rowdy bustle of the suitors to her own tearstained bed.

The poem circles around the question of whether an elite woman's worth depends entirely on sexual fidelity. Odysseus has affairs with Calypso and Circe in the course of his wanderings, as well as a carefully calibrated flirtation with young Nausicaa. These episodes are not presented as a sign of disloyalty to his wife or a blot on his character—although it is notable that he is rather selective in his final account of these adventures when he tells Penelope about his journey. By contrast, the poem presents it as a matter of the utmost importance that Penelope must keep her suitors at bay and wait indefinitely for her absent husband. Female fidelity is important for maintaining a husband's sense of honor and control; it is associated with the preservation of a particular wealthy household and the perpetuation of a particular elite family line. The double standard creates a particular kind of vulnerability for both men and women within the system.

But the story of the affair between the god Ares and the goddess Aphrodite, told by the poet Demodocus in Book 8, reminds us that female fidelity may be important only in specific human social environments. Hephaestus, Aphrodite's husband, is furious about the affair, traps the lovers in bed, and wants to punish Ares; but the other male gods (with the important exception of Poseidon) treat the whole thing as an amusing joke. The divine lovers, male and female, skip away unharmed, with apparently no damage done to their reputation or status. Odysseus, whose greatest fear is that Penelope will act like Aphrodite, reacts oddly to this narrative: he is delighted. Perhaps there is a kind of relief in imagining a situation so different from his own—a world in which an adulterous affair does not result in loss of status, loss of wealth, and loss of life.

The most insistent declarations that women's value depends entirely on their loyalty to their husbands comes in the mouth of the murdered Agamemnon, who has good reason to be upset about adulterous wives; his wife's sexual infidelity represents the takeover of his household by Aegisthus. Odysseus meets the ghost of Agamemnon in Book 11 and is given a stern warning to keep a close watch on Penelope—lest she act as Agamemnon's wife, Clytemnestra, did, murdering him when he comes home and allowing the suitors to take control of Ithaca. Later, in Book 24, the spirit of Agamemnon meets the spirits of the murdered suitors, learns their story, and responds by exclaiming how lucky Odysseus was to have such a faithful, intelligent wife, whose fame should be made the subject of a divine poem—perhaps a poem like *The Odyssey* itself, but one that would allow a more prominent role for "intelligent Penelope."

The story of Aegisthus, Agamemnon, Clytemnestra, and Orestes recurs repeatedly in *The Odyssey* as the shadowy parallel to the story of the suitors, Odysseus, Penelope, and Telemachus. This parallel homecoming serves as a dark warning of what could have happened to Odysseus if he had arrived home openly, as Agamemnon did, rather than in disguise. The story of Agamemnon's death invites us to read Odysseus' slaughter of the suitors in terms of preemptive self-defense, as if he had to kill them in order to avoid being killed in turn. It is also presented as an important lesson for Telemachus. Without a son mature and determined enough to kill Aegisthus, Agamemnon's murder would have been left unavenged. Telemachus' growth to maturity seems in some ways to threaten Odysseus' position in the household: there would be less need for the father to return and regain control, if the son were already adult enough to manage everything and keep his mother's suitors at bay. Conversely, the example of Orestes presents a case where the son's maturity unambiguously benefits his father, albeit only after the father's death.

In some versions of the Agamemnon story, Clytemnestra actually kills her husband, with Aegisthus merely the accessory to the crime. This is the version used by Aeschylus in his later tragedy, the *Agamemnon*; but it was likely that this version of the myth was already known at the time of the composition of *The Odyssey*. Why, then, is Clytemnestra's role sometimes minimized in the references to the story here? A possible reason is that presenting Clytemnestra as eager to sleep with her suitor and murder her husband would cast a disturbing light on Odysseus' own wife, Penelope. The Agamemnon story is thus not simply contrasted with the Odysseus story, but also made parallel to it: in both cases, the wife is a decent person whose loyalty is tested when her husband is away at war. But the shadowy presence of the Agamemnon story may also underline our awareness that Penelope may not be able to wait forever for her absent husband. Moreover, in other early versions of the myth (as in Aeschylus), Orestes kills not only Aegisthus but also his own mother, Clytemnestra. In *The Odyssey*, we are told only that Orestes killed Aegisthus; the matricide is carefully erased from the story. But the uneasy relationship between Penelope and Telemachus clearly shows us that the interests of mothers and sons need not coincide. This parallel story acts as a reminder of the importance of Penelope's loyalty, and also reminds us that a sensible wife whose husband is long gone might have to move on.

The idea that male power depends on female sexual fidelity is also central to the myth of Clytemnestra's sister, Helen, whose abduction by Paris led to the Trojan War. In *The Odyssey*, we meet the beautiful and frighteningly intelligent Helen back home in Sparta, with her wealthy, blustering, and rather less intelligent husband, Menelaus. The affair between Helen and Paris, like the affair of Aegisthus and Clytemnestra, can be seen as another alternative but parallel narrative, showing what might happen if Penelope decided to go off with one of the suitors. But this counternarrative complicates the idea that it would be a disaster if Penelope had an affair, since Helen and Menelaus seem to have suffered no obvious ill effects from her escapade—beyond the fact that so many people decided to engage in the war and died as a result. The marriage seems, if anything, cemented by a shared sense of regret and a shared interest in the wonderful consumer goods they have acquired through their foreign conquests. At the moment when Penelope and Odysseus are reunited, Penelope speaks of Helen, and draws a complex, confusing comparison between her own situation—vulnerable to any deceitful stranger who may show up—and that of Helen, who left her husband for Paris. Penelope seems to suggest that Helen was forced into adultery (because Aphrodite compelled her and Paris tricked her), and also that, insofar as she made a choice, it was informed, as perhaps most choices are, by limited knowledge of the outcome. She could not know that "the Greeks would march to war / and bring her home again."

Should war, defined in *The Iliad* as "the work of men," be seen as ultimately the fault of a woman—because Helen inspired Paris to abduct her? The question is left largely unanswered in Homer. In *The Iliad,* Helen tells Priam she wishes she had "chosen death" rather than leave her husband for Paris—suggesting that she did have some kind of choice, but also that her only alternative was suicide. The affair is not presented as something that she actually desired. In *The Odyssey,* a much more self-possessed and cheerful Helen declares that the Greeks made war "for the sake of" her face—a formulation that suggests that the woman's appearance is the men's supposed motive, but does not imply that it, let alone its owner, can be blamed for their actions.

Helen describes her face, the face that, in Christopher Marlowe's famous words, "launched a thousand ships," not as beautiful but as "doglike"; it is a face that (in this translation) "hounded" the Greeks to war. The idea that women or goddesses, especially desirable ones who sleep with men outside marriage, are like dogs, or have doglike faces, recurs at several moments in the poem: Hephaestus uses the same term of his unfaithful, divinely beautiful wife, Aphrodite; the dead Agamemnon calls his murderous wife a "she-dog"; and the pretty slave girl Melantho is called a "dog" by both Penelope and Odysseus. As a term of insult, "dog" is applied not only to women. Odysseus also calls the suitors "dogs" when he inveighs against their greedy, shameless consumption of his food supplies, and he suggests that the human belly is also always like a whining dog: it begs for food, even in circumstances where it is not appropriate or possible to eat. The night before the slaughter of the suitors, Odysseus feels his heart "bark" inside him, like a "mother dog" defending her puppies. Odysseus has to restrain his doglike heart, because it is nudging him to act too soon, rather than follow through carefully on his plan. In our culture, "bitch" is used as an insult term only for women, and it implies a kind of malice that is imagined as specifically feminine. In *The Odyssey*, to be "doglike" does not usually connote this kind of malice or cruelty (which is why "bitch" would be a misleading translation). Instead, it suggests an insistent drive, to be fed or satisfied or noticed, which is impatient and oblivious to social cues and constraints. Dogs are kept not as pets, but as guards of the house and for hunting; they are low on the household hierarchy, but valued for their persistence and quick powers of observation—shown most touchingly by Odysseus' old dog, Argos, who recognizes his old master even after twenty years' absence. Women, more than men, are like dogs, because they are put low on the social hierarchy, and because they might be scarily capable of seeing through social conventions, and might refuse to stay in their place. But the idea that it is not the woman or goddess herself, but her face, that is like a dog suggests that it might be male perceptions of women, rather than female desires themselves, that threaten the social fabric.

Characteristics that are ostensibly presented as particularly "feminine" often turn out to be rather more complicated in their metaphorical gendering. For example, female characters tend to achieve their ends by seduction, deceit, or witchcraft, rather than by open aggression. Helen, who has a particular power to control perceptions and see through appearances, puts a special drug in her guests' cup which can enable them to forget all that they have suffered and even be numb to the greatest possible grief or loss:

Whoever drinks this mixture from the bowl
will shed no tears that day, not even if
her mother or her father die, nor even

if soldiers kill her brother or her darling
son with bronze spears before her very eyes. (4.223–27)

Helen's drug is a frightening exaggeration of the normal cheering power of wine, and it hints at her witchlike powers of fascination: in Helen's house, all eyes are always on Helen. The goddess Circe and the Sirens also have the power to trap their victims through enchantment. But it remains unclear whether deceit is being presented as a naturally feminine mode of operation, since Odysseus himself is the most prominent liar and trickster in the poem; nor is deceit necessarily seen as a bad thing in the world of *The Odyssey*.

Prudent, clever Penelope shows her capacity for clever deceit and false storytelling, as well as her technical expertise (as a weaver), which in many ways parallels the sharp wits and practical abilities of her husband. The suitors are attracted to her not only for her wealth and her beauty, but also for her mind; even the brashest of them, Antinous, can wax eloquent in describing Penelope's abilities.

Athena blessed her with intelligence,
great artistry and skill, a finer mind
than anyone has ever had before,
even the braided girls of ancient Greece. (2.116–19)

She weaves a great piece of cloth that is supposedly the shroud in which Laertes will be buried and convinces the suitors that she cannot marry any of them until the task is completed. This delaying tactic shows her capacity for deceptive storytelling—a quality shared by her husband—as well as her technical skill in weaving, which is analogous to her husband's competence as a construction worker. But we should also notice differences. The things Odysseus constructs (such as the Wooden Horse, his raft to get away from Calypso, and his bed) are finished, and are supposed to remain finished. Penelope's weaving is designed to be undone. Moreover, whereas the deceptive plots of Odysseus are geared towards a particular end (to invade a city, to reach his home, or to destroy the suitors), the deceptive plot of Penelope serves in the opposite direction: to hold off an end point, to avoid the end of the story. It is meant to be forever in a state of becoming, not completion.

We get only glimpses of Penelope's state of mind, which is repeatedly described as ambiguous or opaque. What comes across most clearly is her emotional pain. She is in a state of constant apprehension for her young, vulnerable son, constant grief for her lost husband, and constant doubt about how long she can put off the suitors. Penelope knows that marriage to one of them will mean an enormous, wrenching loss; for one thing, remarriage may uproot her from the house to which she feels a deep attachment, the house in which she has lived for her whole adult life: "this beautiful rich house, so full of life / my lovely bridal home. I think I will / remember it forever, even in / my dreams." But she also knows that she may ultimately have little choice; she cannot hold the suitors off forever. In an evocative passage from Book 19, she tells Odysseus—whom she has still not recognized—about her nightly tears:

As when the daughter of Pandareus,
the pale gray nightingale, sings beautifully
when spring has come, and sits among the leaves
that crowd the trees, and warbles up and down
a symphony of sound, in mourning for
her son by Zethus, darling Itylus,
whom she herself had killed in ignorance. (19.520–26)

The simile suggests that Penelope feels a desperate and ambiguous kind of guilt about the husband and son whom she may be forced to "betray," through no fault of her own. Later in the same passage, Penelope tells the story of a dream she had in which there were geese in her house, eating her grain, which were destroyed by an eagle. Odysseus, in his guise as a beggar, immediately interprets the dream to his own advantage: the dream shows, he says, that her husband will return and rout the suitors from the hall. It is, he assumes, unambiguously positive. But Odysseus' interpretation entirely ignores the most striking feature: Penelope says that in the dream, she "wept and wailed" at the death of the geese. This dream response suggests that on some level, Penelope might not want her husband to come home. This would be a perfectly reasonable feeling, since her position in the household is not markedly improved by his return. But when she learns that her suitors really are dead, Penelope is "overjoyed"—although she still refuses to accept that the old beggar might be her husband in disguise. Penelope's feelings are mixed and confusing.

Some readers have argued that this clever woman may well have recognized her husband much earlier than she lets on, or at least half-recognized him. Perhaps she has; the text seems to allow for this possibility, although it gives us little evidence for it. But it is important to see what is at stake in the decision to interpret Penelope as either cognizant or ignorant of her husband's identity. Some critics have been understandably motivated by a desire not to see female characters as victims—and therefore want to see her as more in control than she may appear. Alternatively, one can emphasize the ways that female characters can be disempowered in a male-dominated environment, through no fault of their own; one can then argue that Athena and Odysseus work together to keep Penelope in the dark about her husband's return. In this view, she is presented as an intelligent woman whose capacity for planning and forethought is comparable to her husband's—but who lacks the apparatus of divine and human help that enable Odysseus to achieve his ends with confidence. Penelope's cognitive disadvantage parallels the sexual double standards by which Odysseus' infidelities are treated as normal, and Penelope's twenty-year sexual loyalty is seen by certain characters within the poem (such as the dead Agamemnon) as the centerpiece of her moral worth.

These radically different interpretations are possible because the text keeps the reader or listener of the poem to a large extent in the dark about Penelope's state of mind. This might be a mark of discomfort with the gender inequalities implicit in the plot or a mark of the text's particular kinds of blindness. There are certain particularly ambiguous moments in the depiction of Penelope that underline this narrative tension. For instance, in Book 18, Penelope suddenly decides to show herself before the suitors, although she has previously shunned them. We are told that the reason is to increase their desire for her and promote her own honor. One can assume that it is Athena, not the mortal woman, who is controlling events at this point and who has decided to make Penelope show herself. Or one can argue that Penelope herself has recognized her husband, and has decided to do this to continue her plot to deceive the suitors about her true intentions. Or one may argue that Penelope has not recognized Odysseus, but simply feels the impulse to gain greater attention from the suitors for herself—a possibility that has been neglected by most critics only because it is assumed, with obvious sexism, that a "good" woman would not behave in such a way. The most important point to notice here is how ambiguous the text itself is about these various possibilities, a fact reinforced by Penelope's "mysterious" laugh as she makes the proposal. Penelope's desires and motivations are defined as unknown.

Becoming a Man

The Odyssey tells the story not only of Odysseus and Penelope, but also of their son, Telemachus, whose slow and incomplete journey to adulthood is charted in the course of the poem. Telemachus is the most vulnerable member of the family: the suitors plot to murder him, and we see him break down in tears after a failed attempt to speak up and assert himself in the men's assembly. The boy must be at least twenty years old at the time of the poem's action, and he is physically an adult, full grown and handsome. But he struggles to grow to psychological maturity, to become man enough to help his father defeat the suitors. Telemachus' standard epithet, *pepnumenos*, suggests "of sound understanding" or "thoughtful"; the poem traces the boy's developing cognitive maturity, as he begins to learn what adult masculinity might mean.

In the course of Telemachus' journey in search of news about his father, he meets two alternative father-figures: the controlling, long-winded Nestor, and the rich, narcissistic, uxorious Menelaus. Each of these men seem to echo character traits in Telemachus' own father—as does the old

Sea God Proteus described by Menelaus, a slippery character who can change his shape at will. Back in Ithaca, the swineherd Eumaeus is an even more devoted alternative father: he greets Telemachus on his return like a long-lost son,

Just as a father, when he sees
his own dear son, his only son, his dear
most precious boy, returned from foreign lands
after ten years of grieving for his loss,
welcomes him; so the swineherd wrapped his arms
around godlike Telemachus and kissed him,
as if he were returning from the dead. (16.17–23)

Eumaeus, Nestor, and Menelaus all show their deep, fatherlike love for Telemachus, and each models for the boy, in significantly different ways, the skill of hospitality, which is an essential aspect of elite masculine adulthood.

But only his real father, Odysseus himself, can help Telemachus achieve what he most wants: a position of greater power in his own household. When father and son are reunited, they weep together, as if for Telemachus' lost, fatherless childhood:

They both felt deep desire for lamentation,
and wailed with cries as shrill as birds, like eagles
or vultures, when the hunters have deprived them
of fledglings who have not yet learned to fly. (16.216–19)

After these tears, Telemachus seems more sure of himself, and he can begin the process of joining the adult, male world, by plotting with his father how to kill the suitors.

Telemachus is an only child; his lack of brothers is emphasized in the poem and was presumably unusual in the context of archaic Greek society. He seems markedly more confident after he has formed a close friendship with Pisistratus, Nestor's son, who becomes like a brother to him. The suitors—boys roughly his own age, who act like bullying older brothers—threaten his life and his position in his own home. Unable to stand up to the suitors by himself, Telemachus instead practices masculine self-assertion by putting down his mother.

The relationship between Penelope and Telemachus is painful, full of conflict and secrecy. She sees his vulnerability too clearly and worries for him, which makes him all the more eager to distance himself from her. Penelope cannot do for her son what a father could do, which is introduce him to the world of male power. Under the instructions of Athena, Telemachus pointedly keeps his journey from Ithaca a secret from his mother. Underlining his emotional distance from his mother by insisting that her feelings matter only insofar as they might affect her looks, he tells Eurycleia, who is in on the secret,

> *"Promise me you will not tell*
> *Mother, until she notices me gone.*
> *Say nothing for twelve days, so she will not*
> *start crying; it would spoil her pretty skin."* (2.373–76)

Eurycleia is an alternative mother-figure for Telemachus, and a preferable one, in that—being a slave—she always does exactly what he tells her to do. Athena is a second and even better mother-figure: she enables him to succeed on his trip away from Ithaca, proving his ability to act independently of his human parents, albeit always under her watchful eyes.

Telemachus makes several attempts to put his real mother in (what he regards as) her place. In Book 1, Penelope tries to stop the singer Phemius from telling of the disastrous homecoming of the Greeks from Troy, because it makes her cry too much; Telemachus roughly intervenes, telling his mother,

> *"Go in and do your work.*
> *Stick to the loom and distaff. Tell your slaves*
> *to do their chores as well. It is for men*
> *to talk, especially me. I am the master."* (1.356–59)

The passage is echoed in Book 21, when Odysseus, disguised as an old homeless beggar, asks to be given a turn at the ongoing contest to string the great bow. The suitors try to prevent it, but Penelope insists that the stranger ought to be treated with dignity and kindness, and should be allowed to try the bow, if he so desires. At that, young Telemachus intervenes, scolding his mother for speaking as if she had the authority to decide who should and who should not have access to the weapons of his father. He sends her back upstairs to the women's quarters, declaring,

> *"Go up and work*
> *with loom and distaff; tell your girls the same.*
> *The bow is work for men, especially me.*
> *I am the one with power in this house."* (21.350–53)

These outbursts are startling, since most of the time Telemachus carefully avoids direct confrontations with his mother—as if nervous that he might not be able to hold his own against her. The lines in Book 21 seem to allude to a moment in *The Iliad* when Hector tells his wife, Andromache, that she should not attempt to prevent him from going back to the battlefront, although he may be killed. It is, he declares, his task, as an elite male warrior, to fight on the front lines and risk his life to gain honor—just as it is the task of women to do the household chores and weaving. "War," says Hector, "is work for men, especially me." Telemachus is trying to assert his masculinity and adult status by assuming the role of the heroic fighter who risks his life for his honor and the defense of his city. But the reference does not entirely suit the situation: Telemachus is not planning to fight with the bow himself, only to have control over who else gets access to it. Moreover, the person who is about to assume "power in the house" is not Telemachus but Odysseus, to whom the boy will give the bow. Telemachus is overjoyed at being taken under his father's wing, but he is also overshadowed by his father's position as the eternal head of the household. It would be a problem for the poem's narrative if Telemachus grew up all the way, since there must be only one man running the house in Ithaca forever, and that man needs to be Odysseus.

Telemachus is consistent in his notion that masculine maturity means the suppression and exclusion of women and the suppression of female voices. When Odysseus slaughters the suitors, he leaves a final task to his son, Telemachus: the killing of the "doglike" slave women who have been sleeping with the suitors. Odysseus instructs his son to hack at the girls with swords, to eradicate all life from their bodies and all memory of what they did with the murdered men:

"They will forget the things
the suitors made them do with them in secret." (22.444–45)

The episode is one of the most horrible and haunting of the whole poem, the culmination of a pattern in which the homecoming of Odysseus prevents other people—elite boys and slave girls alike—from reaching their homes and their comfortable beds:

As doves or thrushes spread their wings to fly
home to their nests, but someone sets a trap—
they crash into a net, a bitter bedtime. (22.468–70)

These terrible murders are not quite presented as punishments for a nonexistent crime; these women are slaves, who presumably had little choice about their treatment by the suitors. Rather, Odysseus wants the girls dead because their memories threaten his total ownership of his household. As long as they are still alive, the trace of the suitors is still present in their bodies and their minds, and hence in his home. By slashing them with "long swords," Odysseus suggests that his own male line can regain complete control.

But Telemachus takes initiative, to an almost unprecedented degree, and decides that the women should instead be hanged, saying,

"I refuse to grant these girls
a clean death, since they poured down shame on me
and Mother, when they lay beside the suitors." (22.462–64)

This puzzling, disturbing intervention is a defining moment for Telemachus. Why exactly does he want them hanged, rather than hacked to death with swords? One possible answer has to do with cleanliness and pollution. Despite Odysseus' various attempts to present his killings as revenge for moral outrages committed against him, it is clear that at least some of the murders are primarily motivated by a desire to restore a sense of purity to a house that has been subject to imaginary dirt. The choice of hanging over hacking is beneficial in that it keeps the girls' dirty blood off the clean floors, and maintains the "tainted" bodies in their self-contained state. Hanging also allows young Telemachus to avoid being too close to these girls' abused, sexualized bodies. The boy here demonstrates a newfound maturity in two highly problematic ways: he asserts himself by defying his father's instructions, and he belittles the women he slaughters. But Telemachus is still resisting the adult male role of the warrior, which involves a quasi-sexual act of penetration—using a sharp weapon to pierce and kill human bodies at close quarters.

In the final book of the poem, Telemachus has one more chance to prove himself a man, by fighting, yet again, beside his father. With their little band of supporters, Odysseus, Laertes, and Telemachus prepare together to fight against the family members of those whom they have killed. Odysseus calls on Telemachus not to "shame your father's family," which is "known across the world for courage / and manliness." Telemachus responds eagerly, "Just watch me, Father," and Laertes beams with pride: "A happy day for me! My son and grandson / are arguing about how tough they are!" The fight is curtailed by Athena's intervention, so Telemachus never gets to prove his full worth as a fighter, although he has demonstrated his eagerness to participate in the military aggression of his male family members. Readers may disagree about the extent to which Telemachus ever fully grows up in *The Odyssey*—as well as about whether growing up to manhood, as this boy imagines it, would really be a good thing.

Slaves

Many of the most prominent characters in *The Odyssey*—such as the father, mother, son, and the suitors—are elite people who live in what is figured as a large, palatial house (although it is clearly modest from the perspective of later forms of kingship). Odysseus is a leader in war, not a mere foot soldier, and in Ithaca, the house of Odysseus is the richest and most powerful of the neighborhood. But the poem also includes a number of characters who are not rich or powerful. In *The Iliad*, the only named non-elite character, Thersites, is presented as ugly and annoying; when he speaks out of turn, Odysseus beats him up. *The Odyssey* includes a far richer array of characters who are not lords or ladies, kings or princesses. Slaves and homeless beggars are presented in this text as human beings who deserve respect and even empathy—at least as long as they remain in their limited social place.

The possibility that people of any rank might be enslaved—through trafficking or war—is assumed as a fact about the world; *The Odyssey* is not an abolitionist text. But we are given glimpses of the hard lives of those who serve and feed the privileged people who are the main focus of the narrative. In Book 20, the prayer of an unnamed, frail slave, grinding the grain, reminds us that the labor of food production is exhausting: it hurts her knees. Odysseus, who has his own agenda, treats the prayer simply as a good omen for his own plans. But the reader or listener can momentarily see the cost of running the elite household in terms of human labor and human suffering—a cost that may be reduced but will not end, even when the banquets of the suitors cease.

Slave owners favor slaves who ally themselves most closely with their master's interests, rather than taking the risky step of switching to a new set of masters. Only one of the slaves who slept with the suitors is named: Melantho, who is characterized as having a mind of her own and a will to talk back to her mistress. The orifices of female slaves, including their mouths, are a source of particular concern; the rope deprives Melantho of her attempt to have an autonomous voice. Male slaves are imagined not as mouths but limbs of their masters; a "bad" male slave uses his capacity to work or fight or procreate to serve an alternative master. Melantho's brother, Melanthius, who serves as a herdsman for the suitors, is trussed up like an animal, and then, in a particularly brutal scene, his nose, ears, genitals, hands, and feet are slashed off. This "limb" of the wrong masters is robbed of his own bodily appendages. Melantho and Melanthius—whose names both suggest "black flower"—are the children of Dolius, the herdsman who is treated as a trusted favorite, loyal to Odysseus. We are not told how he feels about the slaughter of his children, but it is clear that, in Odysseus' remade household, there will be no possibility of expressing such grief. The name Dolius suggests "crafty" or "deceitful"; the poem shows us why dishonesty is the most essential survival tool for the "good" slave.

The pair of young "bad" slaves are mirrored by a pair of old "good" slaves, who are loyal to Odysseus and his family. Eurycleia, the old slave woman who took care of Telemachus as a baby and now protects the master's domestic stores, provides a counterpart to the threats posed by Melantho. She is old enough to pose no sexual threat, and she controls her voice for the sake of her masters—by keeping the secrets of Telemachus' journey and Odysseus' identity, and by restraining her impulse to shout in triumph over the slaughter of the suitors. Melantho's physical intimacy with the wrong set of owners is presented as a threat to the household. Eurycleia, by contrast, maintains the household by taking care of the bodies of Odysseus and his family—by helping Telemachus get dressed, and by washing Odysseus' feet.

The most prominent slave character in the poem is the swineherd Eumaeus, the "good" counterpart to the "bad" goatherd, Melanthius. Eumaeus welcomes Odysseus, in his guise as beggar, into his simple cottage. Eumaeus' humble but affectionate offering of *xenia* contrasts with the rudeness of the suitors, and we are clearly supposed to admire this "noble slave" for identifying his own interests with those of his owner; he is the one who "cared most about preserving / the master's property." No other character is addressed directly by the narrator, but Eumaeus is often addressed in the second person ("You, swineherd"), a stylistic detail that creates a particular intimacy between the reader or listener and this odd character. Eumaeus is also described repeatedly in the terms of military heroism, as the "commander" of his pigs—a trope that serves both to elevate this quasi-heroic character and to mock him. Eumaeus is a "noble slave" for two incompatible reasons. On the one hand, paradoxically, he is noble because he is so slavish: he refuses to disentangle his own interests and perspective from that of his master. But he is also genuinely noble, both in birth and in behavior: he performs the aristocratic customs of *xenia* even in his poor, dung-piled shack, and he tells the memorable, grim story of how he was born into an elite foreign household, before he was trafficked and sold as a slave. The "good" slave is one who responds to the trauma of enslavement by identifying with his or her owners, and imagining those in power as loving parents rather than overlords. *The Odyssey* seems to have it both ways in the depiction of slave characters. We are reminded that a good slave can be more loyal and more hospitable than a rude, overprivileged young man, but we are also invited to imagine that slaves are good only insofar as they subdue their own identities to those of their owners.

The poem suggests a similar contrast between the "good" and the "bad" way to occupy another lowly social position: that of the penniless, homeless migrant. When Odysseus is in disguise as a poor beggar, the ways that people respond to him are presented as the test of their moral worth. It is a black mark against the suitors that they fail to behave politely or warmly to the wrinkled, ragged, hungry old stranger who shows up in the palace where they are living it up on somebody else's meat and wine. But the "real" beggar, Irus—who is not an elite warrior in disguise, but a genuinely poor, dirty homeless person—is depicted in entirely negative terms. Odysseus wrestles with him, wins, and humiliates him, and the text seems to invite us to celebrate his victory. There is thus a certain uneasiness about the proper way to respond to social and economic hierarchies. Elite people are supposed to treat slaves and homeless beggars well; but slaves and homeless beggars are themselves to be despised, unless they are royalty in disguise. Odysseus can become old, poor, weak and homeless; but his "real" identity is (apparently, but perhaps debatably) as the king and warrior who fights to gain massive wealth and assert his own masculine prowess, using deceit and violence to slaughter his enemies—both on the battlefield of Troy and even in his own lovely home.

Odysseus presents himself as someone who has endured exceptional trials and tribulations and has managed, alone, to survive the perils and dangers of his journey back from Troy. After listening to the swineherd Eumaeus tell the story of how he was captured and trafficked as a child, entering a lifelong position as a lowly slave, Odysseus comments that Eumaeus' sufferings can hardly match his own: "Your life is good. / But as for me, I am still lost." Odysseus suggests that his own inability to reach his homeland, even after twenty years' absence, is the ultimate form of suffering, which trumps all other pain. But it is notable that Odysseus travels in elite fashion, without ever touching the oars himself. That lowly hard labor is performed for him by others, men who are uncompensated for their labor, and who all, eventually, die before reaching their homes.

The Choice of Odysseus

At the start of the poem, we see Odysseus making a momentous and defining choice: to return to Penelope, his mortal wife, rather than stay forever with the goddess Calypso. This goddess is divinely beautiful, and her island is marked by luxuriant, dense complexity; it is a place of secrets and tangled mixtures.

The scent of citrus and of brittle pine
suffused the island. Inside, she was singing
and weaving with a shuttle made of gold.
Her voice was beautiful. Around the cave
a luscious forest flourished: alder, poplar,
and scented cypress. It was full of wings.
Birds nested there but hunted out at sea:
the owls, the hawks, the gulls with gaping beaks.
A ripe and luscious vine, hung thick with grapes,
was stretched to coil around her cave. Four springs

spurted with sparkling water as they laced
with crisscross currents intertwined together.
The meadow softly bloomed with celery
and violets. (5.60–73)

The god Hermes, visiting Calypso's home, is understandably "full of wonder." But Odysseus, in this magical, mysterious place where he shares the bed of a majestic goddess, is miserable.

His eyes were always
tearful; he wept sweet life away, in longing
to go back home, since she no longer pleased him.
He had no choice. He spent his nights with her
inside her hollow cave, not wanting her
though she still wanted him. By day he sat
out on the rocky beach, in tears and grief,
staring in heartbreak at the fruitless sea. (5.151–58)

The text implies that for some (carefully unspecified) amount of time, Odysseus willingly enjoyed the company of the goddess. Calypso rescued him when he crawled, ragged and half drowned, onto the shore of her island, and he spends a good seven years—the majority of time spent returning from the war—sharing her bed. She has given him shelter from the storm and has provided him with a home that seems in certain very obvious ways superior to his original home on Ithaca. As she herself reminds him with touching defensiveness, the goddess is much more attractive than Penelope. Moreover, Calypso's island is lush and fertile, in contrast to barren Ithaca—and, what ought to be a clinching argument in the case, she has the power to make Odysseus immortal and free from aging forever. She offers him everything, except a way back to his original, human home. Outraged at his rejection of her love, she asks him,

"Do you really want
to go back to that home you love so much?

Well then, good-bye! But if you understood
how glutted you will be with suffering
before you reach your home, you would stay here
with me and be immortal—though you might
still wish to see that wife you always pine for.
And anyway, I know my body is
better than hers is. I am taller too.
Mortals can never rival the immortals
in beauty." (5.204–14)

The depiction of Calypso, a powerful but emotionally open female character, frustrated in her desire for the human she has rescued, is one of the most memorable sequences in the poem. She perhaps does herself a disservice in emphasizing only her superior good looks. She also has a superior mind, and she is particularly well matched with Odysseus, who shares her fondness for secrets. Like Circe and Athena, Calypso appreciates and understands Odysseus' capacity for deceit and scheming, because she has similar qualities herself—albeit at a divine, more than mortal level. She praises him for mistrusting her, saying, "You scalawag! What you have said / shows that you understand how these things work." Penelope, for obvious reasons, shows far less appreciation for Odysseus the liar, Odysseus the trickster, Odysseus the "scalawag." Her looks are ordinary compared with those of the goddess; her love for Odysseus is more careful, more suspicious, and her understanding of him is less complete; and in choosing Penelope, Odysseus is also choosing to become old and, eventually, to die. In reply to the goddess, Odysseus acknowledges the truth of everything she says. But then he adds simply, "But even so, I want to go back home, / and every day I hope that day will come."

Why exactly does Odysseus make this surprising choice? The poem never gives us an explicit answer—an omission that makes the hero's yearning for home all the more resonant and moving. Calypso, an obviously prejudiced observer, suggests that Odysseus' choice to go home is masochistic: a deliberate embrace of suffering, and a perverse preference for something worse over something better. The tactful hero does not correct her.

Presumably, Odysseus is inspired by a deep loyalty to his wife, son, father, and the place of his birth, and moved by a deep and constant love for those he left behind. But we must avoid projecting the anachronistic ideas of chivalric romantic love onto Odysseus, who is not a medieval knight performing valiant deeds for the sake of a beautiful lady. To explain the meaning of Odysseus' choice in Homeric terms, it is useful to look back to *The Iliad*. In that poem, the central character, Achilles, makes the momentous choice to stay and fight at Troy, to gain honor among his fellow Greek warriors, rather than return home to his young son and dying father, where he might have lived a long life in obscurity. The choice of Odysseus is parallel to the choice of Achilles, in that it is a decision to be mortal in order to gain a particular kind of masculine honor. If Odysseus had stayed with Calypso, he would have been alive forever, and never grown old; but he would have been forever subservient to a being more powerful than himself. He would have lost forever the possibility of being king of Ithaca, owner of the richest and most dominant household on his island—an estate wealthy in pigs, sheep, goats, fruit, grain, wine, and slaves, with an old father, a young son, and a desirable, much-courted, and valuable wife all devoted to him, and all increasing his value in the eyes of his neighbors.

But strangely, Odysseus' choice to be in the mortal world does not seem to imply any willingness to submit to the exigencies of change. The hero wants to maintain his dominant position in his household, not for a moment but for all time. His choice to be subject to age and mortality is presented as if it were itself a permanent fact, a choice that he might be able to go on making forever. *The Odyssey* thus makes a paradoxical set of claims about the possibility of permanence, either in relationships or in the lives of any individual person. Odysseus' choice to be with Penelope is associated not only with an admission of human mortality, but also with its opposite: an insistence that a man (it has to be a man) might be able to claim or reclaim a permanent position at the head of his particular social ladder. Odysseus seems to be magically able to evade the pressure of time on mortals and rise above all challenges of circumstance.

Athena changes Odysseus into a weak, bent old man, as a disguise. But when needed, she changes him back into the physical appearance that is figured as his "true" self, a man of the utmost vigor, in the prime of youth. In real life, a man who had left home in his twenties, spent ten years fighting a war, and then another ten lost at sea, would be more likely to look wrinkled, bent, and old—especially in an archaic society without modern medicine, when life expectancy was far shorter than in most contemporary Western cultures. But *The Odyssey* insists that Odysseus is fundamentally unchanged by his adventures. Through his determination and smart mind, and with divine help, he can restore his marriage and his household permanently to the state that they were in when he first went away. Leaving Calypso is thus not only a choice to accept mortality and impermanence, but also, incompatibly, a choice to insist on the fantasy of permanent patriarchal dominance over a carefully regulated human household.

Odysseus is an odd figure to represent permanence, since he seems to be constantly changing—in appearance, behavior, and social role. He is able to be, at different times, young or old, strong or weak, a beggar or a home owner, a victim or an aggressor. What makes Odysseus special is that he is, to a far larger extent than most human beings, in control of his various different changes and manifestations. Gods can disguise themselves and walk unseen through the midst of mortals; Odysseus is able to do the same. He switches roles not only through the magical power of Athena, which transforms his appearance, but also through the magical power of his own words, through which he creates multiple different identities for himself.

Most of the epithets applied to Odysseus begin with the prefix *poly-*, meaning "much" or "many": he is a figure who possesses many attributes, and possesses them intensely. Far more than other mortals, Odysseus is able to change himself to adapt to changing circumstances. A wonderful simile in Book 5, after Odysseus is shipwrecked and clings, just barely, to the rocks of the Phaeacian shore, compares his skinned fingers to the suckers of an octopus:

As when an octopus dragged from its den,
has many pebbles sticking to its suckers,
so his strong hands were skinned against the rocks. (5.432–34)

In archaic Greek lore, the octopus was known as the "boneless one," the creature that (supposedly) survives hunger by eating its own tentacles (or "feet," of which, luckily, it has eight). In the Homeric image, it is a creature defined by its tenacity. It is resistant to change (it has to be dragged from its den), but also changed by its altered environment (the sticking pebbles). Odysseus' fingers are like the pebbles of the den, ripped by the octopus; but he is also himself octopuslike in his stubbornness, his power of survival, his capacity to adapt to new environments, his multiplicity, and his slippery, boneless, self-devouring ability to change. It is this power of self-transformation that gives him the ability to reinvent himself into the most marvelous persona of all: the self he was twenty years ago, before he went to war. The ideal of total autonomy and permanent essence depends on the process of constant self-reinvention.

An essential aspect of Odysseus' multiplicity is his rhetorical ability and capacity for deceit. He is able to spin tall tales, to take over from the poet Demodocus and tell the fantastic story of his own adventures as an entertainment for the Phaeacians. In Ithaca, he constructs multiple different autobiographies, usually claiming to have come from Crete—the traditional home of liars. Odysseus' grandfather Autolycus prides himself on "telling lies and stealing"; Odysseus has inherited these traits. He is the hero who always has an answer, a solution, a fix, a good line, a quick reply to any challenge. He is the master of finding the right words in any situation.

Odysseus is in disguise in Ithaca and has to be recognized by a series of different characters in turn. The poem is virtuosic in its variations on the otherwise formulaic "recognition scene"—each character recognizes Odysseus by a different means, and each character recognizes a different Odysseus. Athena, who has no trouble recognizing Odysseus, begins the sequence in Book 13 by allowing him to recognize her and, in so doing, to recognize himself, as the man defined by cleverness and an infinite capacity for scheming and deceit. Argos, the old dog, recognizes Odysseus by his smell and remembers him as the vigorous man who took him on hunting trips. Eumaeus knows Odysseus as a benevolent owner, a quasi-family-member, who may perhaps reward his lifelong loyalty with a short period of freedom before he dies. Telemachus knows Odysseus as his role-model father, the man on whom his own honor and status in the world of adult men depends. Eurycleia, the old slave nurse, remembers Odysseus as a boy wonder, who killed a boar single-handedly even in his earliest youth. Old Laertes knows Odysseus as his son and heir; he is the boy who was taught to name all the trees in the orchard, and he is the man on whom the future of the whole estate depends. Antinous and the other suitors recognize, with horror, that the weak old beggar in their midst is actually a muscular, murderous fighter, the man who will slaughter them all.

The most complex and extensive recognition is that of Penelope. The process by which she comes to acknowledge the old stranger as her difficult, secretive, aggressive husband is extraordinarily long-drawn-out, and the exact moment at which she truly recognizes him remains a mystery—like so much else about Penelope. After the murder of the suitors, she is told by both Eurycleia and Telemachus that the strange old beggar is really Odysseus. To Telemachus' irritation, however, she refuses to acknowledge him as her husband. "Cautious Penelope" displays her central quality by resisting any quick resolution. Perhaps she suspects or half-knows who he is much earlier than she admits; or perhaps she genuinely remains unsure about who the mysterious stranger is.

But if she does recognize him, or half-recognize him, she also manages to gain an upper hand in the relationship, provoking Odysseus into "proving" his identity. She tells the slave to make up the bed for him outside the bedroom, which devastates and enrages him: "Woman!" he asks, "Who moved my bed?" The bed, it turns out, is not supposed to be movable; Odysseus claims to have built it himself, using an olive tree that grew inside the palace as a bedpost. The bed that can be moved only by cutting down the trunk and destroying the structure is a metonymic symbol for the interdependence of the marriage and the house;

the destruction of either means ruin for the other. Odysseus asks, in disbelief as well as horror, what "man" has moved his bed: the quasi-immovable bed represents a fantasy that it would be almost impossible for Penelope ever to sleep with another man. No other marriage would involve such deep roots.

The tree-bed is the ultimate answer to the question raised at the start of the poem: What does Odysseus choose when he rejects Calypso's offer? It is something deeply characteristic of Odysseus himself: like his most famous invention, the Wooden Horse, the bed is a wood structure that contains humans and a secret, and allows close friends to inhabit a hidden place of safety, even surrounded by enemies. Odysseus, the master storyteller, is also the master builder—of horses, ships, beds, plans of attack, and means of escape. As soon as Calypso allows her lover to leave her island, he begins work constructing a raft; his detailed, obsessive account of how he built his marriage bed echoes that earlier moment of construction. In leaving Calypso, Odysseus chooses something that he built with his own mind and hands, rather than something given to him. Whereas Calypso longs to hide, clothe, feed, and possess him, Athena enables Odysseus to construct his own schemes out of the materials she provides.

But the bed is a product of nature, as well as of human labor; it is growing, alive, and divinely blessed. Trees are not, in fact, permanent or immovable objects; Odysseus cuts down trees to make his raft. This bed is thus a rather different kind of symbol from the nailed-down bed to which the frustrated narrator of Charlotte Perkins Gilman's "The Yellow Wallpaper" is confined (a symbol of the restrictions imposed on women in nineteenth-century New England). Odysseus' bed is difficult to move, but not immovable. Its permanence and its mutability stem from the same cause—the life of the olive tree. In returning to Ithaca and to this bed, Odysseus has chosen a world in which his own work is part of something larger than himself, and where he is woven into relationships that are both rooted and changing.

When Penelope and Odysseus are finally reunited, Odysseus puts his arms around his wife, and a simile invokes the experience of shipwrecked swimmers, suddenly catching sight of land, and crawling to shore, "their skin all caked with brine." We must initially think that this image applies primarily to Odysseus himself—who is the one embracing Penelope when the image begins and who has, in real life, experienced shipwreck. But the narrator then suggests that it is Penelope, not Odysseus, who is like these survivors: "So glad she was to see her own dear husband, / and her white arms would not let go his neck." A surprising slippage happens through the imagery, from the man's to the woman's point of view. With Calypso, Odysseus would have been frozen into the role of the weak, dependent survivor of shipwreck. The mortal Penelope may not know all of Odysseus' many identities and may not have plumbed his capacity for lies. But she understands his suffering, because she too has lived through twenty years of pain—caused by his own absence, in war and with Calypso.

Hated Odysseus

Odysseus is defined by his mutual loving relationships—with his wife, Penelope; his patron goddess, Athena; his father, Laertes; his dead mother, Anticleia; his son, Telemachus—and by his less-mutual loving relationships with Calypso, Nausicaa, Eurycleia, and Circe. He is also defined, even more explicitly, by his enemies, those who hate him and dislike him. In Book 19, we learn about Odysseus' grandfather Autolycus, whose own name suggests "Real Wolf," and "who was the best / of all mankind at telling lies and stealing." Autolycus gave the baby Odysseus his name, based on the fact that he himself has managed to make so many enemies:

> *"I am*
> *disliked by many, all across the world,*
> *and I dislike them back."* (19.406–8)

The verb *odussomai,* meaning "to be angry at," "to dislike," or "to hate," sounds similar to Odysseus. Athena connects Odysseus with the same verb in Book 1, asking Zeus why he bears a grudge against her favorite: "Why do you dismiss Odysseus?" she asks. The etymology suggests that Odysseus is himself much disliked, by both gods and other human beings, and also that he takes after his grandfather by acting in hostile fashion to other people: he tricks, steals from, and hates. Poseidon is, of course, his most powerful enemy, but Odysseus arouses dislike, hatred, and anger in many others during the course of the narrative, and displays his own capacity for rage.

Odysseus is the hero of his own story, and the poem to some extent glorifies its protagonist and valorizes his claims to dominance. But it also articulates some important questions about the moral qualities of this liar, pirate, colonizer, deceiver, and thief, who is so often in disguise, absent, or napping, while other people—those he owns, those he leads—suffer and die, and who directly kills so many people.

Odysseus' use of aggression and violence is presented as problematic in certain ways. The poem raises questions about whether Odysseus, as a fighter who has spent ten years at war, sacking and pillaging a foreign city, can adapt himself enough to succeed in an entirely different context—or whether he will bring the battlefield home with him. In some cases, we see Odysseus managing to modify the conventions of the Homeric battlefield to fit a new challenge. For instance, when he first meets the young Phaeacian princess Nausicaa, he supplicates her—an action familiar from warriors on the Trojan battlefield, when one man kneels in abjection and touches the knees and beard of another, to beg for his life. But in this new version of the formulaic supplication scene, Odysseus is kneeling before somebody who has no beard and who poses no kind of military threat. The supplicator, in this version, is rather more physically threatening than the person to whom he prays. Odysseus studiously avoids the traditional touching of the knees, which would only alarm the girl, and shows his own ability to adapt techniques practiced at Troy for entirely different situations.

But the poem also seems to question how fully this epic hero can adapt to a new, nonmilitary world. When Odysseus is about to go through the straits between Scylla and Charybdis, Circe warns him not to put on his armor and try to fight against Scylla, which will be futile and will only make the situation worse. But Odysseus insists on doing so—increasing the danger to his men. Similarly, in leaving the island of Polyphemus the Cyclops, Odysseus is unable to resist shouting back,

> *"Cyclops! If any mortal asks you how*
> *your eye was mutilated and made blind,*
> *say that Odysseus, the city-sacker,*
> *Laertes' son, who lives in Ithaca,*
> *destroyed your sight."* (9.502–6)

Odysseus cannot resist the urge to gain *kleos*—the honor that comes from being the named subject of heroic legend. He is able to become nameless ("No man") only for a little while.

One of the epithets most commonly used of Odysseus is *polytlas*, which means "much-enduring." It may suggest how much Odysseus has endured and suffered, and it may also suggest how much he is capable of enduring: his stubbornness, his tenacity, his courage, his relentless drive to achieve his own ends. In modern terms, we can see Odysseus as a veteran soldier with his own version of PTSD: he is moody, prone to weeping, often withdrawn, and liable to sudden fits of aggression. We can also, rather differently, see Odysseus as a man who keeps on repeating the same behavior patterns that he has displayed in Troy. He succeeded in taking the foreign city by a mixture of aggression with deceitful infiltration, in the Wooden Horse, which the Trojans themselves took into their town; he succeeds in taking back his own household through much the same means, sneaking inside the house in hidden form (not inside a horse, but inside the body of a beggar), and emerging to slaughter the inhabitants.

Odysseus seems to have complicated feelings about his own past history. The temptation offered by the Sirens is to listen forever, and know everything that the Greeks and Trojans suffered in the war. One might think that Odysseus would want this, above all, as an ego boost: the Sirens address him as the "glory of the Greeks," and their songs promise an endless retelling of Odysseus' own finest hours; they call to him to listen,

"since we know everything the Greeks and Trojans
suffered in Troy, by gods' will; and we know
whatever happens anywhere on earth." (12.189–91)

The temptation is as much knowledge as glory. The Sirens offer Odysseus what no single individual engaged in the conflict can have: a full and complete understanding of what happened in the war and what it meant. In resisting the Sirens, Odysseus acknowledges that he will have to go on acting out the consequences of the war, without ever being able fully to know what it was all about.

Odysseus puts in a special request to Demodocus, the Phaeacian bard, to sing the story of the Wooden Horse—the trick that Odysseus himself devised in order to infiltrate and sack the city. Demodocus complies, and tells how the Greek warriors, including Odysseus, hid inside the manufactured horse; how the Trojans pulled the horse inside, and left it at the summit of their city, as an offering to the gods; and how, during the night, the gang of fighters jumped out of the hollow cavity, scattered across the city, and began slaughtering the people of Troy. One might expect that Odysseus would be happy to hear the story of his own greatest military triumph—a story that, after all, he had just asked to hear. But his response is surprising. Rather than being glad (as he was glad to hear the story of Aphrodite committing adultery), he bursts into tears, and a striking simile seems to conflate his emotional response with that of his own victims.

Odysseus was melting into tears;
his cheeks were wet with weeping, as a woman
weeps, as she falls to wrap her arms around
her husband, fallen fighting for his home
and children. (8.521–25)

The simile compares the desperate weeping of Odysseus, a military conqueror, to the grief of a woman who is a victim of war, a woman whose husband is dying and who knows that she herself, and her children, will soon be led off into slavery by the victors. Perhaps the comparison suggests that Odysseus himself feels some kind of deep guilt over the suffering that he himself has caused, in his instrumental role in sacking not only Troy but many other towns and settlements. Or perhaps the simile works to downplay Odysseus' responsibility for the suffering he has caused, by inviting us to see him as a suffering victim, even in his role as the sacker of cities.

In the final book of the *Odyssey*, after Odysseus has slaughtered the suitors, Eupeithes, the father of one of the dead men, urges the people of Ithaca to rise up together and kill Odysseus in revenge. He offers a searing indictment of Odysseus.

"This scheming man,
my friends, has done us all most monstrous wrongs.
First, he took many good men off to sail
with him, and lost the ships, and killed the men!
Now he has come and murdered all the best
of Cephallenia. Come on, before
he sneaks away to Pylos or to Elis,
we have to act! We will be shamed forever
unless we take revenge on him for killing
our sons and brothers. I would have no wish
to live; I would prefer to die and join
the boys already dead. We have to stop them
escaping overseas! Come on, right now!" (24.425–37)

The words come from the mouth of a grieving parent whose young son has been shot by Odysseus the day before. It represents a limited, highly personal point of view. Moreover, Eupeithes presumably does not know how unpleasantly his son behaved, when he had the chance to lord it up in the household of the absent Odysseus.

But Eupeithes, whose name means "Persuasive," is making a point that readers of the poem may find surprisingly persuasive—as do the people of Ithaca. Antinous is depicted as an arrogant, supercilious young man, who drinks too much, exploits the resources of an absent home owner, treats Penelope and Telemachus with disrespect, and is cruel and unwelcoming to Odysseus in his guise as a poor migrant. Yet the grief of his father reminds us that the murdered Antinous was very young, probably not much older than Telemachus. Young men often behave oafishly, but they may mature in time—unless they get an arrow through the neck first. Eupeithes' speech reminds us also that the killing of the suitors is not an isolated incident; Odysseus has made an unfortunate habit of leading young men to their deaths. When Odysseus addresses the men who row his ship, he repeatedly calls them "friends," *philoi*, a word that suggests a close tie of kinship or love. Odysseus is a smart talker, who knows the best words to use for a particular audience. But the narrator instead calls these men *hetairoi*, "companions" or "servants," a term that can suggest a much more hierarchical relationship. Of the troops Odysseus rounded up to take with him to Troy, some fell in battle, and all the rest die in various horrible ways in the course of their leader's journey home.

The first lines of the poem invite us to see these deaths in terms of the dead men's own folly or childish naïveté, because they chose to eat the Cattle of the Sun. They were "poor fools" (*nepioi*), a term that suggests childish thoughtlessness. This foolishness is sharply contrasted with Odysseus' own characteristic qualities of scheming intelligence, quick planning, and forward thinking (*metis*). But this prologue does not hint at the numerous other deaths suffered by the men in Odysseus' crew—including those who are eaten alive by the sea-monster Scylla when Odysseus chooses to sail past her island; those who are devoured by the Cyclops, thanks to Odysseus' insistence on visiting his cave; or those who are skewered from their ships and eaten by the man-eating giants, the Laestrygonians, when Odysseus docks the fleet at their island and moors only his own ship in a safe place outside the harbor. These deaths clearly have nothing to do with the men's cognitive or moral qualities. The prophet Tiresias predicts that, if Odysseus hurts the Cattle of the Sun, he will arrive home only "late and exhausted, in a stranger's boat, / having destroyed [his] men," and a similar prophecy is made by the goddess Circe. The participle here translated as "having destroyed" can also mean "having lost." The ambiguous phrasing matters, because the ultimate responsibility for all these deaths remains an open question.

Endings

The traditional poetic stories of archaic Greece included tales of how the heroes came home from the Trojan War—the *Nostoi*, as they were known. *The Odyssey* is obviously a story of *nostos*, meaning "homecoming" (the word from which we get "nostalgia," the pain of missing home). But the poem suggests that it may not be entirely easy to see what a homecoming is, and when exactly it happens. Coming home means more than simply reaching a particular spatial or geographical location. The hero reaches his home country of Ithaca when the poem is almost exactly halfway through. The remaining books trace a series of journeys across a tiny geographical area: from the port of Ithaca to the loyal swineherd's hut; back and forth between the hut and the palace; from the hallway to the marriage bed, and back again; out from the palace to the orchard, and back again to slaughter his fellow countrymen who are assembled in front of his house. Each of these locations seems to offer a different version of home, and one can wonder when and where Odysseus feels most fully that he has arrived.

Thanks to Athena's magic, Odysseus initially does not recognize Ithaca; it seems like yet another unfamiliar and probably dangerous place. Once the divine mist disperses, Odysseus knows that he is on Ithaca, but we can also see that his initial suspicions were in many ways correct: Ithaca is indeed a dangerous and unfamiliar place, and there are real questions about how and when Odysseus might be able to transform it again into the home that he left behind.

A key part of his strategy for doing so is to test the loyalty and behavior of various members of his household. He appears in disguise to the key players, each in turn, and tests their responses to his own persona as a homeless migrant. Those who pass the test are to be incorporated into Odysseus' plan and restored into the household; those who fail are killed. Thanks to the long process by which Odysseus gradually infiltrates his way into the community of Ithaca, he is able to assess who will help him, and whom he must destroy in order to reassert his own power over his home.

But it is unclear when Odysseus finally achieves his ends and reaches his home, if indeed this moment ever comes. Odysseus is reunited with Penelope, but the poem continues. We see the ghosts of the suitors travel down to the underworld and meet the spirits of Achilles and Agamemnon, which might have been a kind of ending; but the poem continues. We see Odysseus reunite with his old father, Laertes; but the poem continues. Fighting breaks out on Ithaca between Odysseus and his supporters, and the friends and family members of the dead suitors. The battle grows intense, and Odysseus is wild with martial rage; only thanks to the intervention of Athena does it stop. And there the poem ends.

Scholars since antiquity have been puzzled by the ending of *The Odyssey*. Two Homeric scholars of the Library of Alexandria in the third and second centuries BCE, Aristarchus of Samothrace and Aristophanes of Byzantium (not the comic playwright), argued that the poem really ended at the moment when Odysseus and Penelope go to bed together; on this model, the real ending is in Book 23, when the narrator tells us,

Finally, at last,
with joy the husband and the wife arrived
back in the rites of their old marriage bed. (23.293–95)

We do not know what grounds were given by these ancient scholars for treating the end of Book 23 and the whole of 24 as extraneous. Eustathius, a twelfth-century critic, tried to defend Book 24 on literary and semantic grounds, arguing that the recognition scene between Odysseus and his father is an essential element in the story.

Modern scholars have also argued about the "correct" or "original" place for the poem to end. Linguistic arguments have been made against Book 24, but these are highly debatable; Homer's language, as we have seen, is always a mixture of words and phrases from many different dialects and periods. The episode involving the ghosts of the dead suitors is unusual—

but the situation is also unusual. The encounter between Laertes and Odysseus seems cruel to some readers, since Odysseus has no need to "test" his father, now that the suitors are already dead; yet it is arguably not out of character for Odysseus, a person "addicted to deceit," to keep spinning his lies even when they seem to serve no particular purpose.

Perhaps there are two related reasons that many readers have felt unsatisfied with the ending of *The Odyssey*. First, it feels less than definitive as a place to stop the story. More events will clearly happen after this conflict between the Ithacans and Odysseus, which is stopped only thanks to the convenient intervention of the goddess. Moreover, a curtailed battle does not feel like the proper culmination of a story of homecoming—unless Odysseus feels most at home when he is killing his fellow countrymen.

Both of these "problems" are perhaps precisely the point. The poem refuses to offer us a definitive moment at which home and peace are achieved, once and for all. Odysseus never sets aside his desire to fight and kill his fellow men, or his yearning to wander and be absent. According to the prophecy given by the dead spirit of the prophet Tiresias in Book 11, Odysseus will not remain and settle in Ithaca. He has at least one more journey to complete, to a land that is, from the perspective of the Greek islands, the strangest of all: where nobody knows the sea, where people eat food without salt, and nobody has even seen a boat. He will know he has arrived when he meets "someone who calls the object on my back / a winnowing fan" (a tool used in preindustrial agriculture to separate wheat from chaff). Only in this utterly alien location, Tiresias suggests, can Odysseus finally put to rest the anger of Poseidon, the Lord of the Sea.

But even if he were ever to return from this obviously mythical location, one might wonder whether Odysseus would be able to settle down in peace and comfort in Ithaca—the land that would still be populated by the families of those Odysseus has killed. In antiquity, there were a number of legends about what happened to the protagonist after the poem ends—alternatives that may reflect ancient recognition of how little the last book wraps things up. One story tells that this criminally aggressive hero was sent into exile for killing the suitors. Other ancient stories express discomfort with Odysseus' habit of committing adultery. We are told that he had a son by Circe, named Telegonus, who sailed in search of him and eventually killed him with a poisoned spear. Several stories provide alternative futures for Penelope: either she was killed by Odysseus himself for sleeping with Antinous the suitor; or, creepily, she married Odysseus' son Telegonus; or she was spirited to Arcadia and seduced by the god Hermes, and became the mother of the god Pan. All of these stories seem to suggest dissatisfaction with the state of Odysseus and Penelope's marriage, which is defined in the poem primarily by absence, pain, economic dependence, and mutual mistrust.

The Odyssey is in some ways like a fairy tale. "Bad" people are killed, and the "good" hero triumphs. But the poem is surprisingly clear-sighted about both the problematic tendencies of its own hero and its own dominant fantasy. Everybody likes the idea of a radical reversal of fortune, a surprising and long-delayed final victory, a settled, forever home. This is a text that allows us to explore our desire for power and for permanence, in the world of imagination, while also showing us the darker side of these deep human dreams, hopes, and fears.

Reception

In antiquity, Homer was traditionally said to have been a blind man from the Greek island of Chios. This popular idea is expressed in a poem from the sixth century BCE called the "Homeric Hymn to Delian Apollo," which tells how Apollo and his twin sister, Artemis, were born. Their mother, Leto, was pregnant with the twins by Zeus, and had to find a place to give birth: a hard task, since Zeus' jealous wife, Hera, had made all lands on earth reject her. Finally Leto reached Delos, which was supposedly a floating island, unattached to the sea floor. Since this was a space unattached to the earth, the island welcomed the laboring goddess. Delos was rewarded with a special sanctuary to the god Apollo, who felt deep attachment to the island as the place of his birth. The poem ends by instructing the girls who worship Apollo on Delos to remember the poet who composed the present song:

Bless me, Apollo, bless me, Artemis;
and greetings, all you girls! Remember me
whenever any poor and homeless stranger
comes here and asks you, "Girls, who is to you
the sweetest of all singers? Which one gives you
most pleasure?" All of you must answer him,
"He is a blind man and he makes his home
in rocky Chios; all his songs will be
the best forever."

The historian Thucydides, writing in the late fifth century BCE, confidently quotes the passage as evidence that Homer was a blind man from Chios. Often seen as the father of modern or "scientific" historiography, Thucydides prides himself on his skeptical attitude towards implausible traditional myths. But it is extremely unlikely that the person who composed these lines had any hand in creating the Homeric epics. The hymn was probably composed by a member of a family or professional organization who lived on Chios in the sixth century, calling themselves the Homeridae—the children of Homer. These people gave performances of *The Iliad* and *Odyssey* (or portions from them) and also created their own poetic compositions, which they presented as also "Homeric." This particular hymn may have been composed by an active member of this clan to honor an unusual double festival to Apollo of Delos and Delphi in 522 BCE—far later than the composition of the Homeric poems themselves.

The testimony about the "blind man from Chios," then, does not tell us anything about the composition of *The Iliad* and *Odyssey* themselves—which probably originated a good two hundred years earlier. But the "Homeric Hymn" does bring into sharp relief the fact that already in archaic, preclassical Greece, the Homeric poems had a place at the absolute top of the poetic canon: they were the "sweetest," the "best forever." Moreover, the notion that "Homer" is a poet who celebrates a birth on a floating island may express an awareness that these poems had evolved out of a long oral history, from multiple different local traditions. Homer, like the god of poetry, emerges from an ambiguous or floating origin.

Everybody in the Greek-speaking world wanted to claim and remake Homer for themselves—a process that continues to this day.

The Odyssey was, along with *The Iliad,* the foundation of Greek and Roman elite education. Sections from the poems were also performed by rhapsodes to adults, for entertainment. All upper-class men in the Graeco-Roman world knew the Homeric poems well. Aeschylus is said to have called his tragedies "slices from the banquet of Homer." Homer (and the rest of the archaic epic tradition) provided the basis for much of classical literature: tragedy, but also history, later forms of epic, pastoral, and the novel.

But Greek and Roman writers often struggled with the legacy of Homer. Plato's character Socrates in the *Republic* famously insists that Homer, along with the Athenian tragedians, must be excluded from the ideal city, because his work provides a false image of reality, and stirs up emotions that are better repressed and controlled. Plato and others criticized the depiction of the gods in the poems, for their lack of morality. Odysseus himself is often a problematic character in later Greek and Roman literature, characterized by his abuse of cleverness for self-interested goals. In Sophocles' *Ajax,* he is a commonsensical realist, but in the same author's *Philoctetes,* as well as in Euripides' *Hecuba,* he is a scheming sophist, willing to say or do anything (including murder children) in order to achieve his own military ends. In Virgil's *Aeneid,* Odysseus becomes "cruel Odysseus," the unscrupulous destroyer of Troy, which was the home of the poem's hero. But Aeneas himself becomes a new kind of Odysseus, in his search for a home that exists only in the future: the city of Rome itself.

The canonical status of Homer, combined with the philosophical and ethical challenges involved in treating these poems as a source of "truth," led to a tradition of allegorizing the various adventures of Odysseus. We have, for example, an extensive Neoplatonic interpretation by Porphyry (third century CE) of the episode in Book 13 when Odysseus reaches Ithaca and comes to the cave of the Nymphs. Porphyry notes the fact that there is apparently no such cave on Ithaca, and that the details of the description are extremely implausible. The passage must therefore, he suggests, be read as an extended metaphor for the soul's place inside the material, terrestrial world.

The Odyssey continued to be read and studied, alongside *The Iliad*, throughout classical antiquity. But knowledge of Greek became extremely rare in the Western world after the fall of the western Roman Empire, in the fifth century CE. Dante had no access to the original *Odyssey*, though he knew the story of Odysseus. In his *Inferno*, he places Ulysses (the Romanized name for Odysseus) low down in Hell (the eighth circle out of nine, the circle of Fraud), because he leads his people by deceit into destruction. Dante's silver-tongued, self-serving, and falsely inspiring Ulysses gives his men a rousing, deceitful speech urging them to continue their adventures for "virtue and knowledge"; he is urging them on, yet again, to shipwreck, on the Mountain of Purgatory. This rhetorically gifted version of Odysseus is not entirely alien to the character we meet in Homer.

Texts of Homer were preserved in Arabic translation and in the Byzantine (eastern) Empire. We still have hundreds of important Homeric manuscripts from the eastern empire, dating from the ninth to the fifteenth centuries CE. When Byzantium fell in 1453, refugees from Constantinople brought their knowledge of Greek with them to Italy. The Italian humanists of the fifteenth century learned Greek, read Homer, and began to spread their knowledge through Europe, by means of printed editions and translations of the Homeric poems. The poems were translated first into Latin, and then into all the vernacular languages of Europe.

The first complete *Odyssey* in English was that of George Chapman, in 1615. Chapman's *Odyssey*, in rhyming pentameter couplets, presents the hero as a true soldier and gentleman, a proto-Christian and proto-Stoic whose greatest virtue is his ability to endure suffering and control his impulses. But not everybody in seventeenth-century England was so optimistic about the possibility of claiming Odysseus as a Christian hero. In John Milton's *Paradise Lost* (1667), Odysseus' clever, deceptively inspiring rhetoric and tendency to get lost on a long journey to a homeland from which he has been excluded by divine power are now the characteristics of Satan—the epic antihero who shows us what is wrong with classical notions of heroism from Milton's perspective.

In the eighteenth century, Alexander Pope, along with a team of collaborators, produced translations of *The Iliad* and *The Odyssey* that dominated the market and transformed interpretation of the poems for several generations to come. Pope makes *The Odyssey* into a text about those essentially eighteenth-century preoccupations: proper manners and good government. In Pope's version, Odysseus is the ultimate hero of politeness and tact, the man who always has the appropriate response to every social challenge. He is also a just monarch, whose knowledge of suffering informs his exertion of power over the "nations" whom he governs.

John Keats, who knew no Greek, wrote "On First Looking into Chapman's Homer" in 1816; the appeal of Chapman, imagined in the sonnet like the discovery of the New World, comes partly from the fact that Chapman offered a glimpse of a Homer that was different from the familiar, normalized Homer of Pope. Dipping into Chapman's Homer makes him feel like an astronomer, "when a new planet swims into his ken." As we have seen, scholars in the nineteenth and then twentieth century discovered "new" versions of Homer by searching for the real places that might lie behind the texts, and also by reconstructing the conditions in which these poems were created. But *The Odyssey* could also be used as a way of thinking about what might be old and worn out in the Western cultural tradition. Tennyson's "Ulysses" imagines the protagonist as a weary but compulsive imperial explorer, whose restless boredom makes it impossible for him ever to settle at home: he insists on pushing onward to the western stars, "made weak by time and fate, but strong in will / To strive, to seek, to find, and not to yield."

The stubborn persistence of interest in *The Odyssey* in modern times makes it impossible to mention more than a tiny fraction of the adaptations that it has inspired. New versions of Odysseus' story were created in the literary world, perhaps most famously by James Joyce in *Ulysses* (1922), which uses the book structure of *The Odyssey* for a stylistically virtuosic narrative of one ordinary man's day wandering around Dublin before returning to his wife. In *Omeros* (1990), Derek Walcott used some of the characters from *The Odyssey* as the basis for his poetic account of life on the Caribbean island of St. Lucia. *The Odyssey* has been adapted numerous times in film, television, comic books, music, and visual art, as well as in poetry and novels.

Children often encounter stories from *The Odyssey* as their first exposure to ancient Greek culture. *The Odyssey* is also often used in college literature classes, as the starting point for studying Western or world literature. It is a poem that has the power to speak to people from many different social backgrounds in the contemporary Anglo-American world. Reading *The Odyssey* with fresh, curious, and critical eyes may help us not only rethink our assumptions about people in the past, but also break down some of our modern distinctions and assumptions. Odysseus is a migrant, but he is also a political and military leader, a strategist, a poet, a loving husband and father, an adulterer, a homeless person, an athlete, a disabled cripple, a soldier with a traumatic past, a pirate, thief and liar, a fugitive, a colonial invader, a home owner, a sailor, a construction worker, a mass murderer, and a war hero. Immersing ourselves in his story, and considering how these categories can exist in the same imaginative space, may help us reconsider both the origins of Western literature, and our infinitely complex contemporary world.

TRANSLATOR'S NOTE

When I was eight years old, my primary school put on a production of a (much-shortened) *Odyssey,* complete with costumes, song, and dance. The play starred the cute troublemaker in my class as Odysseus, the headmaster of the school as Polyphemus (the one-eyed monster outwitted by his tiny opponents), and me in pigtails as the goddess Athena.

It was a turning point in my life. I was enthralled by the production, not only because we could pretend to gouge out the headmaster's eye (thrilling though that was), or just because I was cast to play a goddess (ditto), but because of the story and the atmosphere it evoked: a world of magic and adventure, of diverse cultures (both human and nonhuman, welcoming and murderous, foreign and familiar), and of an individual's struggle to survive and return home. After this experience, I was inspired to read as many Greek myths as I could find, including versions of *The Odyssey* itself. I went on to learn Latin and Greek, to read classics at Oxford, and to become a professional classicist. Over the decades since my eight-year-old performance, *The Odyssey* has always been with me.

In planning to translate the poem into English, my first thoughts were of style. The original is written in a highly rhythmical form of verse. It reads nothing like prose and nothing like any spoken or nonpoetic kinds of discourse. Many modern poets in the Anglo-American tradition write free verse, and modern British and American readers are not usually accustomed to reading long narratives with a regular metrical beat, except for earlier literature like Shakespeare. Most contemporary translators of Homer have not attempted to create anything like a regular line beat, though they often lay out their text as if it were verse. But *The Odyssey* is a poem, and it needs to have a predictable and distinctive rhythm that can be easily heard when the text is read out loud. The original is in six-footed lines (dactylic hexameters), the conventional meter for archaic Greek narrative verse. I used iambic pentameter, because it is the conventional meter for regular English narrative verse—the rhythm of Chaucer, Shakespeare, Milton, Byron, Keats, and plenty of more recent anglophone poets. I have spent many hours reading aloud, both the Greek original and my own work in progress. Homer's music is quite different from mine, but my translation sings to its own regular and distinctive beat.

My version is the same length as the original, with exactly the same number of lines. I chose to write within this difficult constraint because any translation without such limitations will tend to be longer than the original, and I wanted a narrative pace that could match its stride to Homer's nimble gallop. Moreover, in reading the original, one is constantly aware of the rhythms and the units that make up elements of every line, as well as of the ongoing movement of the narrative—like a large, elaborate piece of embroidery made of tiny, still visible stitches. I wanted my translation to mark its own nature as a web of poetic language, with a sentence structure that is, like that of Homer, audibly built up out of smaller units of sense. There is often a notion, especially in the Anglo-American world, that a translation is good insofar as it disguises its own existence as a translation; translations are praised for being "natural." I hope that my translation is readable and fluent, but that its literary artifice is clearly apparent.

Matthew Arnold famously claimed that translators of Homer must convey four supposedly essential qualities of Homeric style: rapidity, directness of expression, plainness of thought, and nobility. I have worked hard to capture Homer's rapidity and to achieve, for the most part, a stylistic simplicity that I hope echoes the original. But I am also aware that Homeric style is often redundant and very often repetitious, not always simple or direct. Homer's style is also not "noble" in the sense we may imagine from the later history of epic. The language is not colloquial, and it avoids obscenity, but it is not bombastic or grandiloquent. The notion that Homeric epic must be rendered in grand, ornate, rhetorically elevated English has been with us since the time of Alexander Pope. It is past time, I believe, to reject this assumption. Homer's language is markedly rhythmical, but it is not difficult or ostentatious. *The Odyssey* relies on coordinated, not subordinated syntax ("and then this, and then this, and then this," rather than "although this, because of that, when this, which was this, on account of that"). I have frequently aimed for a certain level of simplicity, often using fairly ordinary, straightforward, and readable English. In using language that is largely simple, my goal is not to make Homer sound "primitive," but to mark the fact that stylistic pomposity is entirely un-Homeric. I also hope to invite readers to respond more actively with the text. Impressive displays of rhetoric and linguistic force are a good way to seem important and invite a particular kind of admiration, but they tend to silence dissent and discourage deeper modes of engagement. A consistently elevated style can make it harder for readers to keep track of what is at stake in the story. My translation is, I hope, recognizable as an epic poem, but it is one that avoids trumpeting its own status with bright, noisy linguistic fireworks, in order to invite a more thoughtful consideration of what the narrative means, and the ways it matters.

I have also tried to break up the plainness with phrases and passages in quite different registers. Sometimes the metaphors and similes are surprising, as when the women of Phaeacia work the wool "with fingers quick as rustling poplar leaves." I echo the oddness of Homeric color terms (with terms such as "purple" waves), and the Homeric eye for things that sparkle (like dancing boys, whose legs were "bright with speed"). Sometimes there are slightly strange phrases or metaphors which have their own kind of resonance—as when Odysseus, having survived shipwreck, hides under a pile of leaves, and is compared to a glowing torch, used by a farmer in the outback "to save the seed of fire and keep a source."

The formulaic elements in Homer, especially the repeated epithets, pose a particular challenge. The epithets applied to Dawn, Athena, Hermes, Zeus, Penelope, Telemachus, Odysseus, and the suitors repeat over and over in the original. But in my version, I have chosen deliberately to interpret these epithets in several different ways, depending on the demands of the scene at hand. I do not want to deceive the unsuspecting reader about the nature of the original poem; rather, I hope to be truthful about my own text—its relationships with its readers and with the original. In an oral or semiliterate culture, repeated epithets give a listener an anchor in a quick-moving story. In a highly literate society such as our own, repetitions are likely to feel like moments to skip. They can be a mark of writerly laziness or unwillingness to acknowledge one's own interpretative position, and can send a reader to sleep. I have used the opportunity offered by the repetitions to explore the multiple different connotations of each epithet. The enduring Odysseus can be a "veteran" or "resilient" or "stoical," while the wily Odysseus can be a "trickster" or speak "deceitfully," depending on the needs of a particular passage. I have tried to bring out the beauty in the formulaic scenes that repeat, as normalized cultural practices, actions that will be alien to every modern reader—as when the people of Pylos are sacrificing "black bulls for blue Poseidon, Lord of Earthquakes," or in the many moments when black ships, equipped with oars and sails, travel across the water from one island to another: "A fair wind whistled and our ships sped on / across the journey-ways of fish."

I hope there is in my translation, as in the original, a wide range of stylistic registers. There are descriptive passages that should combine the simple with the sublime, as in the evocation of Mount Olympus, the home of the gods:

The place is never shaken by the wind,
or wet with rain or blanketed by snow.
A cloudless sky is spread above the mountain,
white radiance all round. The blessed gods
live there in happiness forevermore. (6:42–46)

In Homer, there is something marvelous not only in descriptions of the gods, but even in the most ordinary experiences, like spending a warm summer night outside, "surrounded by the rustling of the porch," or when Queen Arete of Phaeacia is sitting at home working the wool with her women, and we are told that she "sat beside the hearth and spun / sea-purpled yarn." There are moments that are strange and beautiful at the same time, as when Menelaus has to hide among the smelly seals to wait for the old Sea God Proteus:

Around him sleep the clustering seals, the daughters
of lovely Lady Brine. Their breath smells sour
from gray seawater, pungent salty depths. (4.402–4)

Sometimes there is a horrible, paradoxical kind of beauty to be found even in moments of terrible violence—as when Odysseus looks round his hall at the corpses of the boys whom he has slaughtered:

He saw them fallen, all of them, so many,
lying in blood and dust, like fish hauled up
out of the dark-gray sea in fine-mesh nets. . . .
The sun shines down and takes their life away. (22.383–88)

Other moments should arouse a sense of curiosity or excitement or horror or comedy. I wanted to bring out the particular ways in which Homer can be funny—in, for example, Nausicaa's obvious, supposedly concealed desire for Odysseus ("I hope I get a man like this as husband," she innocently remarks), or in Athena's almost convincing role-playing as a little girl:

Divine Athena winked at him and said,
"Here, Mr. Foreigner, this is the house." (7.47–48)

Simple language sometimes helps convey simple but intense, consuming feelings—as when Odysseus says, "I miss my family. I have been gone / so long it hurts." Simplicity of diction can also make clear feelings that are far from simple—as in the scene when Penelope and Odysseus meet for the first time after he kills her suitors, when she has not yet recognized him as her husband:

He sat beside the pillar,
and kept his eyes down, waiting to find out
whether the woman who once shared his bed
would speak to him. She sat in silence, stunned. (23.90–93)

I have tried to make sure that a reader can feel inside the characters in the poem, to convey the ways that each character in the poem has her or his own distinctive point of view—the immaturity and vulnerability of Telemachus, for example, when he tries to speak out against the suitors, but ends up bursting into tears: "He stopped, frustrated, flung the scepter down / and burst out crying." I hope readers can see each character, even the minor ones, as people with a rounded, complete perspective on their lives. For instance, in my version of the hanging of the slave women, I aim to invite genuine empathy rather than an objectifying thrill; while other translators call their death "piteous" or "pitiful," in my version we glimpse their pain, not the feelings of a spectator: it is "an agony"—"They gasped / feet twitching for a while, but not for long."

It is traditional in statements like this Translator's Note to bewail one's own inadequacy when trying to be faithful to the original. Like many contemporary translation theorists, I believe that we need to rethink the terms in which we talk about translation. My translation is, like all translations, an entirely different text from the original poem. Translation always, necessarily, involves interpretation; there is no such thing as a translation that provides anything like a transparent window through which a reader can see the original. The gendered metaphor of the "faithful" translation, whose worth is always secondary to that of a male-authored original, acquires a particular edge in the context of a translation by a woman of *The Odyssey,* a poem that is deeply invested in female fidelity and male dominance. I have taken very seriously the task of understanding the language of the original text as deeply as I can, and working through what Homer may have meant in archaic and classical Greece. I have also taken seriously the task of creating a new and coherent English text, which conveys something of that understanding but operates within an entirely different cultural context. The Homeric text grows inside my translation, like Athena's olive tree inside the bed made by Odysseus, "with delicate long leaves, full-grown and green, / as sturdy as a pillar."

My translation is written in a style that echoes the rhythms and phrases of contemporary anglophone speech. It may be tempting to imagine that a translation of a very ancient poem would be somehow better if it used the language of an earlier era. Mild stylistic archaism is often accepted without question in translations of ancient texts and can be presented as if it were a mark of authenticity. But of course, the English of the nineteenth or early twentieth century is no closer to Homeric Greek than the language of today. The use of a noncolloquial or archaizing linguistic register can blind readers to the real, inevitable, and vast gap between the Greek original and any modern translation. My use of contemporary language—rather than the English of a generation or two ago—is meant to remind readers that this text can engage us in a direct way, and also that it is genuinely ancient. My Homer does not speak in your grandparents' English, since that language is no closer to the wine-dark sea than your own. I have tried to keep to a register that is recognizably speakable and readable, while skirting between the Charybdis of artifice and the Scylla of slang.

All modern translations of ancient texts exist in a time, a place, and a language that are entirely alien from those of the original. All modern translations are equally modern. The question facing translators and their readers is whether to try to disguise this fact, through stylistic tricks such as archaism and an elevated, artificially "literary" register, or to underline it, and thereby encourage readers to be aware that the text exists in two different temporal and spatial moments at once. I have tried to make my translation sound markedly poetic and sometimes linguistically distinctive, even odd. But I have also aimed for a fresh and contemporary register. The shock of encountering an ancient author speaking in largely recognizable language can make him seem more strange, and newly strange. I would like to invite readers to experience a sense of connection to this ancient text, while also recognizing its vast distance from our own place and time. Homer is, and is not, our contemporary.

A translator has a responsibility to acknowledge her own agency and to wrestle, in explicit and conscious ways, not only with the multiple meanings of the original in its own culture but also with what her own text may mean, and the effects it may have on its readers. Because *The Odyssey* has become such a foundational text in our educational system and in our imagination of Western history, I believe it is particularly important for the translator to think through and tease out its values, and to allow the reader to see the cracks and fissures in its constructed fantasy. I see this process not as a denial or abandonment of the original text, but as a way to pay deep attention to the original, most especially in the moments when it may contradict itself.

For example, *The Odyssey* is a poem that may seem to normalize or valorize the treatment of non-Western people as monsters. I have made clear, especially in my version of the Polyphemus episode, that this is not entirely true: the text allows for a certain amount of sympathy and even admiration for this maimed non-Greek person. Unlike many modern translators, I have avoided describing the Cyclops with words such as "savage," which carry with them the legacy of early modern and modern forms of colonialism—a legacy that is, of course, anachronistic in the world of *The Odyssey*.

The elite households represented in *The Odyssey* all include a large staff of domestic slaves to work in the house, preparing and serving food and taking care of their masters' clothes, and field slaves to work the estate and tend the animals. The language used to describe these people poses a particular challenge to the translator. To translate a domestic female slave, called in the original a *dmoe* ("female-house-slave"), as a "maid" or "domestic servant" would imply that she was free. I have often used "slave," although it is less specific than many of the terms for types of slaves in the original. The need to acknowledge the fact and the horror of slavery, and to mark the fact that the idealized society depicted in the poem is one where slavery is shockingly taken for granted, seems to me to outweigh the need to specify, in every instance, the type of slave. I have also used the terms "house girl" and "house boy." The analogy with a slave-owning plantation in the antebellum American South is certainly not exact, but it is at least a little closer than the alternative analogies—of a Victorian stately home or a modern nightclub.

I try to avoid importing contemporary types of sexism into this ancient poem, instead shining a clear light on the particular forms of sexism and patriarchy that do exist in the text, which are only partly familiar from our world. For instance, in the scene where Telemachus oversees the hanging of the slaves who have been sleeping with the suitors, most translations introduce derogatory language ("sluts" or "whores"), suggesting that these women are being punished for a genuinely objectionable pattern of behavior, as if their sexual history actually justified their deaths. The original Greek does not label these slaves with any derogatory language. Many contemporary translators render Helen's "dog-face" as if it were equivalent to "shameless Helen" (or "Helen the bitch"). I have kept the metaphor ("hounded"), and have also made sure that my Helen, like that of the original, refrains from blaming herself for what men have done in her name.

In the difficult case of Penelope, I have tried to maintain what I see as the most important feature of her characterization, which is opacity. But I have also done my best to bring out her pain, her courage, her intelligence, and her strength. One important tiny detail will illustrate some of the challenges involved in the depiction of Penelope, as well as suggest the kind of linguistic challenges with which I have wrestled throughout the poem. It comes at the start of Book 21, when Penelope goes to the storeroom to fetch the bow and axes and initiate the contest. Whether or not she has recognized her husband at this point, and whatever her motives in setting up the contest, her action of picking up the key in the door of the weaponry is momentous and consequential: it is what enables the whole denouement of the poem. Milton echoes this episode in *Paradise Lost*, when Sin turns the "fatal key" of Hell, to enable Satan to ascend and invade Earth. Homer describes Penelope's hand at this moment with the epithet *pachus*, which means "thick." It is often used elsewhere in Homer to describe hands, but always, in other contexts, the hands of male warriors; Penelope is the only woman whose hand is "thick." There is a problem here, since in our culture, women are not supposed to have big, thick, or fat hands—and yet Penelope is clearly being presented in a positive light. Translators have tended to normalize the text by skipping the epithet, or by substituting the kind of word one might expect ("steady hand"). But the use of an epithet in an exceptional way signals the uniqueness and importance of this action. To call her hand "clenched," "swollen," or "fumbling" would risk suggesting that she might be incompetent, which is clearly not the point of the passage. A "heavy" hand might suggest that Penelope is reluctant to open the storeroom (as if she might also have a heavy heart); this would be a confusing signal to send, given that she proposed the contest herself. "Strong" seems too neutral, and not thick enough. So I used "muscular":

Her muscular, firm hand
picked up the ivory handle of the key. (21.7–8)

Weaving does in fact make a person's hands more muscular. I wanted to ensure that my translation, like the original, underlines Penelope's physical competence, which marks her as a character who plays a crucial part in the action—whether or not she knows what she is doing.

Throughout my work on this translation, I have thought hard about my different responsibilities: to the original text; to my readers; to the need to make sense; to the urge to question everything; to fiction, myth, and truth; to the demands of rhythm and the rumble of sound; to the feet that need to step in five carefully trotting paces, and the story that needs to canter on its way. I have been aware, constantly, of gaps and impossibilities in providing escort to Homer from archaic Greece to the contemporary anglophone world, as I have woven, unwoven, and woven up again the fabric of this complex web.

The Odyssey is a very ancient and very foreign text, although its long-standing prominence in Anglo-American and European cultures may mask its strangeness. Homer's concerns—with loyalty, families, migrants, consumerism, violence, war, poverty, identity, rhetoric, and lies—are in many ways deeply familiar, but we see them here in unfamiliar guises. The poem is concerned, above all, with the duties and dangers involved in welcoming foreigners into one's home. I hope my translation will enable contemporary readers to welcome and host this foreign poem, with all the right degrees of warmth, curiosity, openness, and suspicion.

There is a stranger outside your house. He is old, ragged, and dirty. He is tired. He has been wandering, homeless, for a long time, perhaps many years. Invite him inside. You do not know his name. He may be a thief. He may be a murderer. He may be a god. He may remind you of your husband, your father, or yourself. Do not ask questions. Wait. Let him sit on a comfortable chair and warm himself beside your fire. Bring him some food, the best you have, and a cup of wine. Let him eat and drink until he is satisfied. Be patient. When he is finished, he will tell his story. Listen carefully. It may not be as you expect.

MAPS

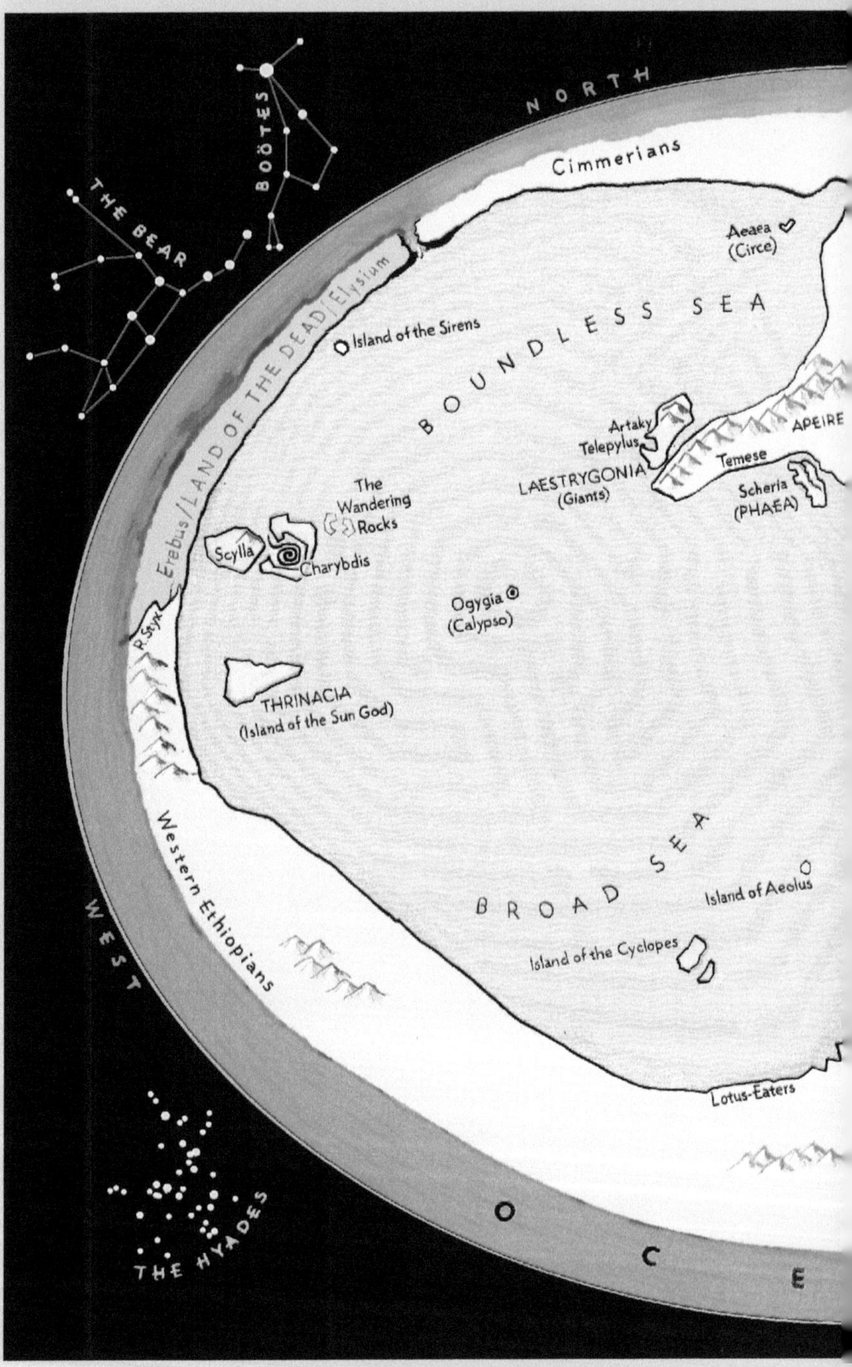

NORTH
Cimmerians
BOÖTES
THE BEAR
Aeaea
(Circe)
BOUNDLESS SEA
Elysium
LAND OF THE DEAD
Erebus
Island of the Sirens
Artaky
Telepylus
APEIRE
Temese
LAESTRYGONIA
(Giants)
Scheria
(PHAEA)
The
Wandering
Rocks
Scylla
Charybdis
Ogygia
(Calypso)
R. Styx
THRINACIA
(Island of the Sun God)
Western Ethiopians
WEST
BROAD SEA
Island of Aeolus
Island of the Cyclopes
Lotus-Eaters
THE HYADES
O C E

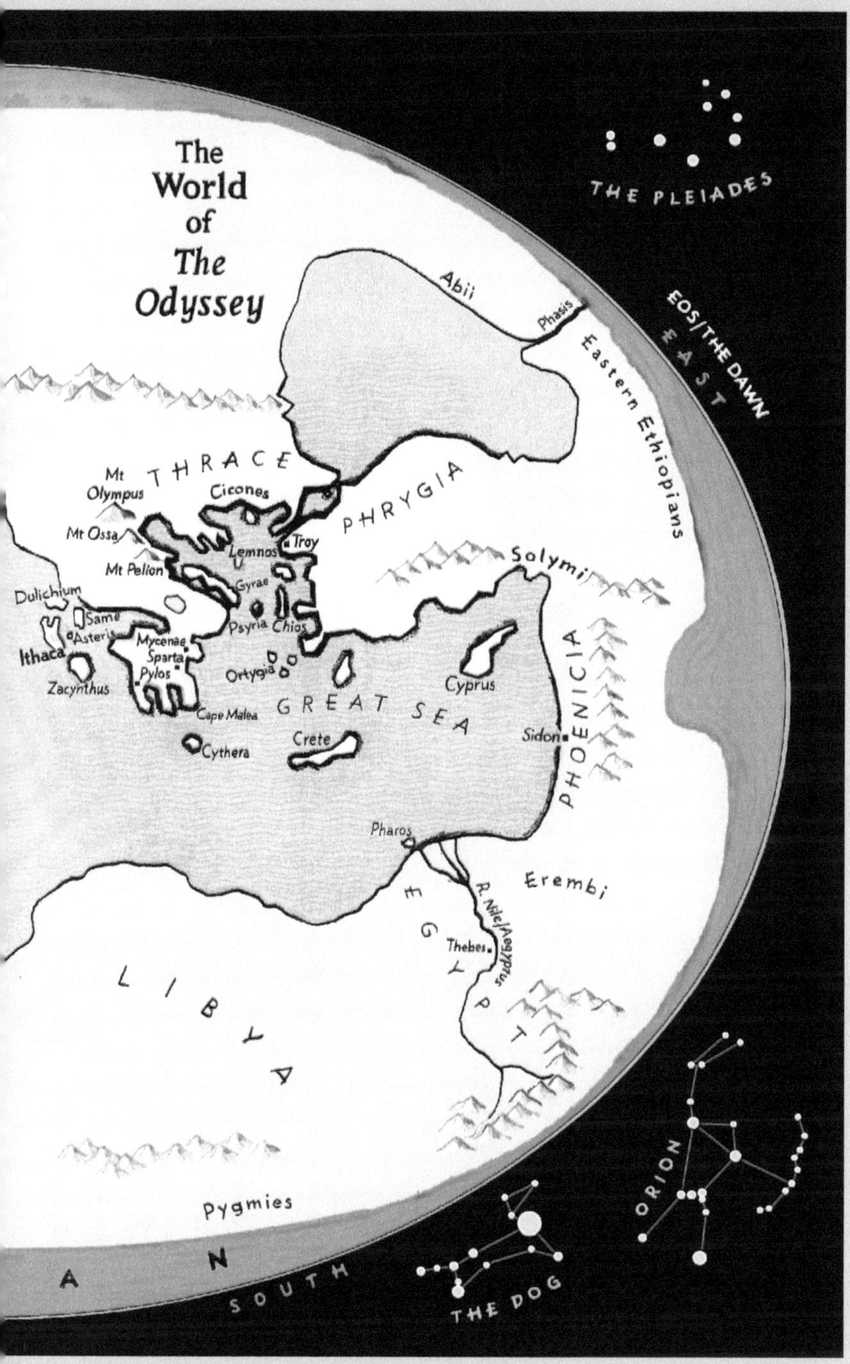

The World of The Odyssey
THE PLEIADES
EOS/THE DAWN
EAST
Abii
Phasis
Eastern Ethiopians
THRACE
Mt Olympus
Cicones
PHRYGIA
Mt Ossa
Troy
Lemnos
Mt Pelion
Solymi
Gyrae
Dulichium
Same
Asteris
Psyria
Chios
Ithaca
Mycenae
Sparta
Pylos
Ortygia
Zacynthus
Cyprus
PHOENICIA
GREAT SEA
Cape Malea
Sidon
Crete
Cythera
Pharos
Erembi
EGYPT
R. Nile/Aegyptus
Thebes
LIBYA
Pygmies
ORION
THE DOG
SOUTH

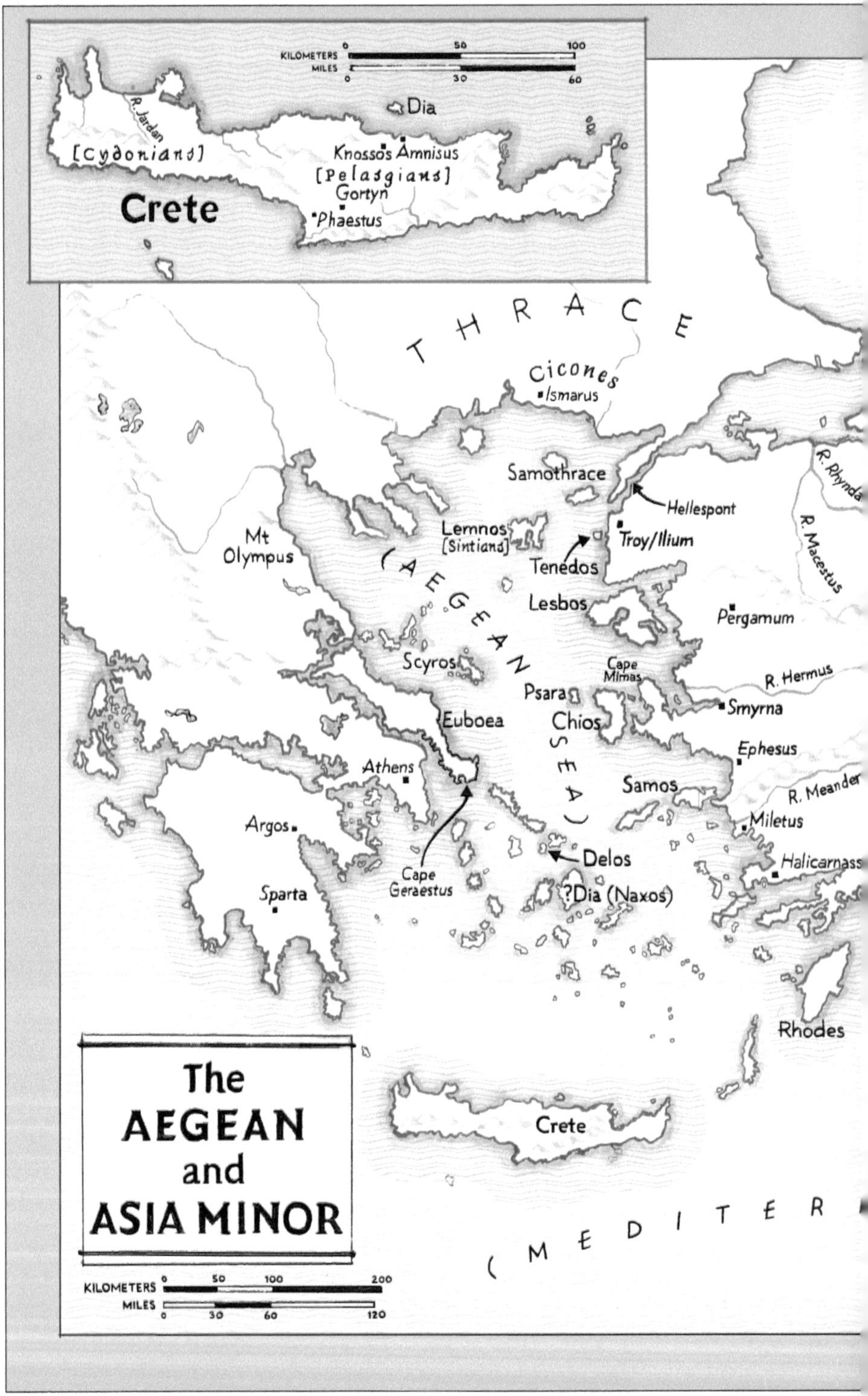
KILOMETERS 0 50 100
MILES 0 30 60
Dia
R. Jardan
[Cydonians]
Knossos
Amnisus
[Pelasgians]
Gortyn
Phaestus
Crete
THRACE
Cicones
Ismarus
Samothrace
Hellespont
Lemnos
[Sintians]
Troy/Ilium
Mt Olympus
(AEGEAN SEA)
Tenedos
Lesbos
R. Rhyndacus
R. Macestus
Pergamum
Scyros
Cape Mimas
R. Hermus
Psara
Smyrna
Chios
Euboea
Ephesus
Athens
Samos
R. Meander
Argos
Miletus
Delos
Cape Geraestus
Halicarnass
Sparta
?Dia (Naxos)
Rhodes
Crete
The AEGEAN and ASIA MINOR
(MEDITERR
KILOMETERS 0 50 100 200
MILES 0 30 60 120

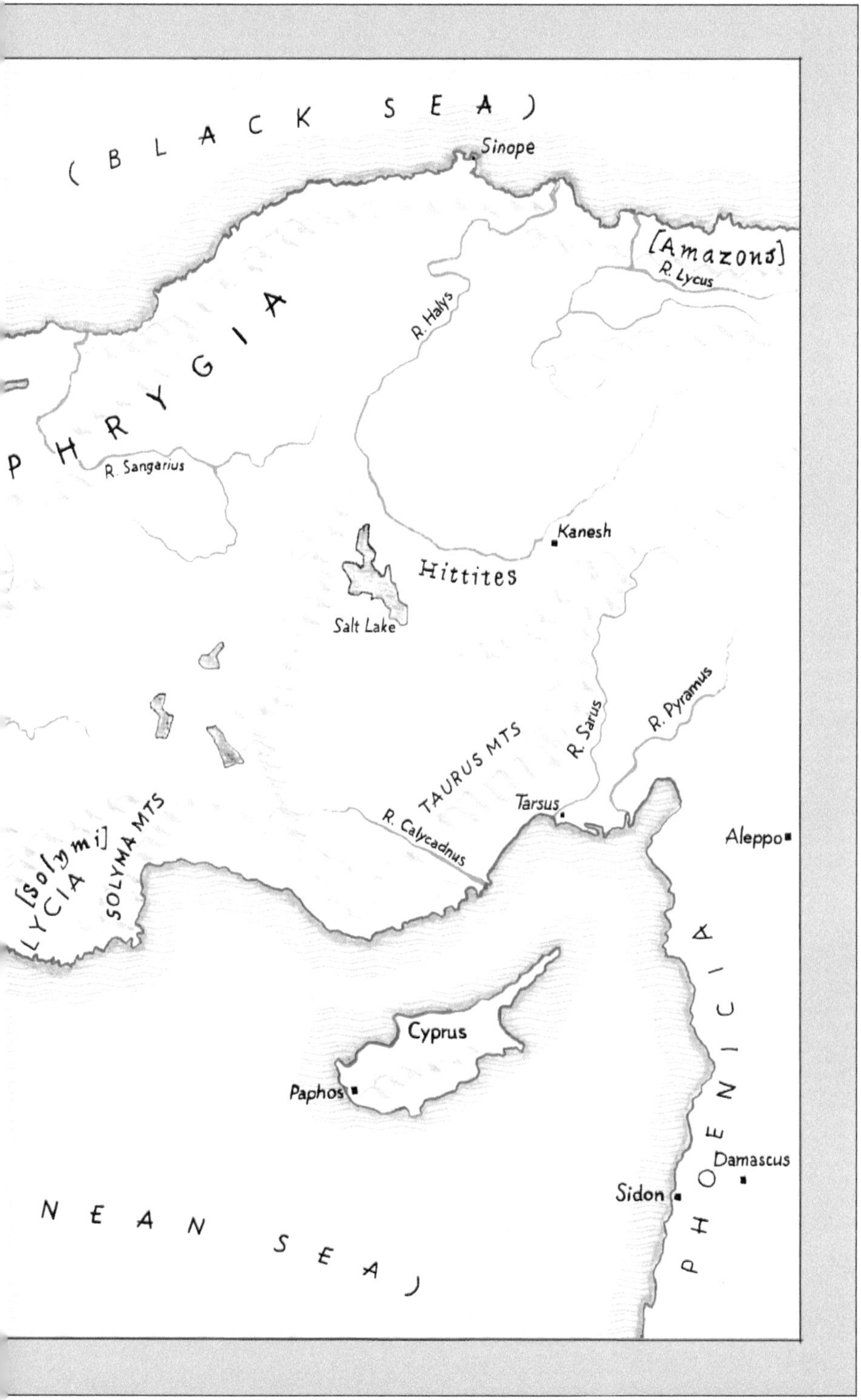

(BLACK SEA)
Sinope
[Amazons]
R. Lycus
R. Halys
PHRYGIA
R. Sangarius
Kanesh
Hittites
Salt Lake
R. Pyramus
R. Sarus
TAURUS MTS
Tarsus
R. Calycadnus
Aleppo
[Solymi]
LYCIA
SOLYMA MTS
Cyprus
Paphos
PHOENICIA
Damascus
Sidon
NEAN SEA)

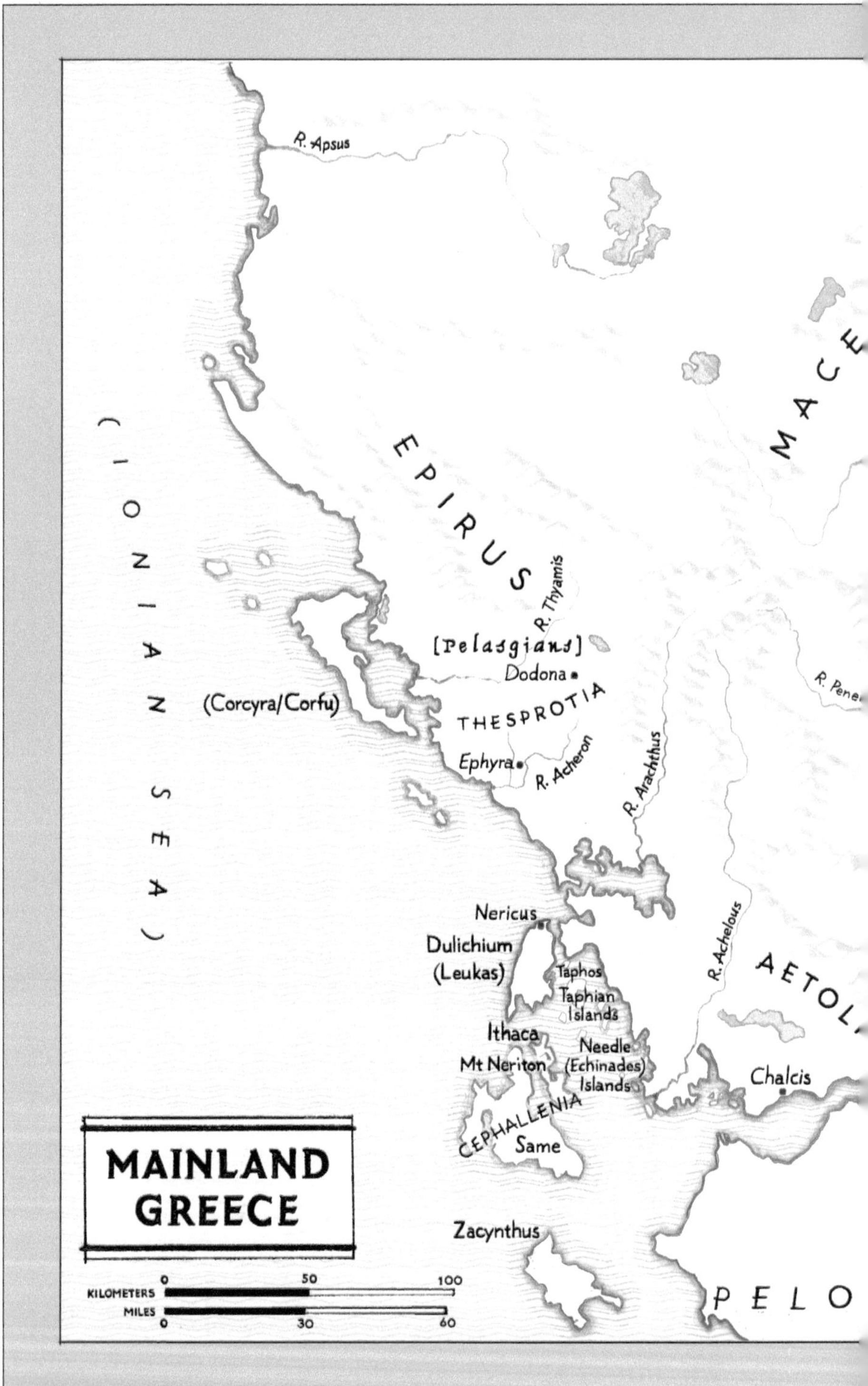

R. Apsus
EPIRUS
MACE
(IONIAN SEA)
R. Thyamis
[Pelasgians]
Dodona
(Corcyra/Corfu)
THESPROTIA
R. Pene
Ephyra
R. Acheron
R. Arachthus
Nericus
Dulichium
(Leukas)
Taphos
Taphian
Islands
R. Achelous
AETOL
Ithaca
Mt Neriton
Needle
(Echinades)
Islands
Chalcis
CEPHALLENIA
Same
MAINLAND
GREECE
Zacynthus
PELO
KILOMETERS
0
50
100
MILES
0
30
60

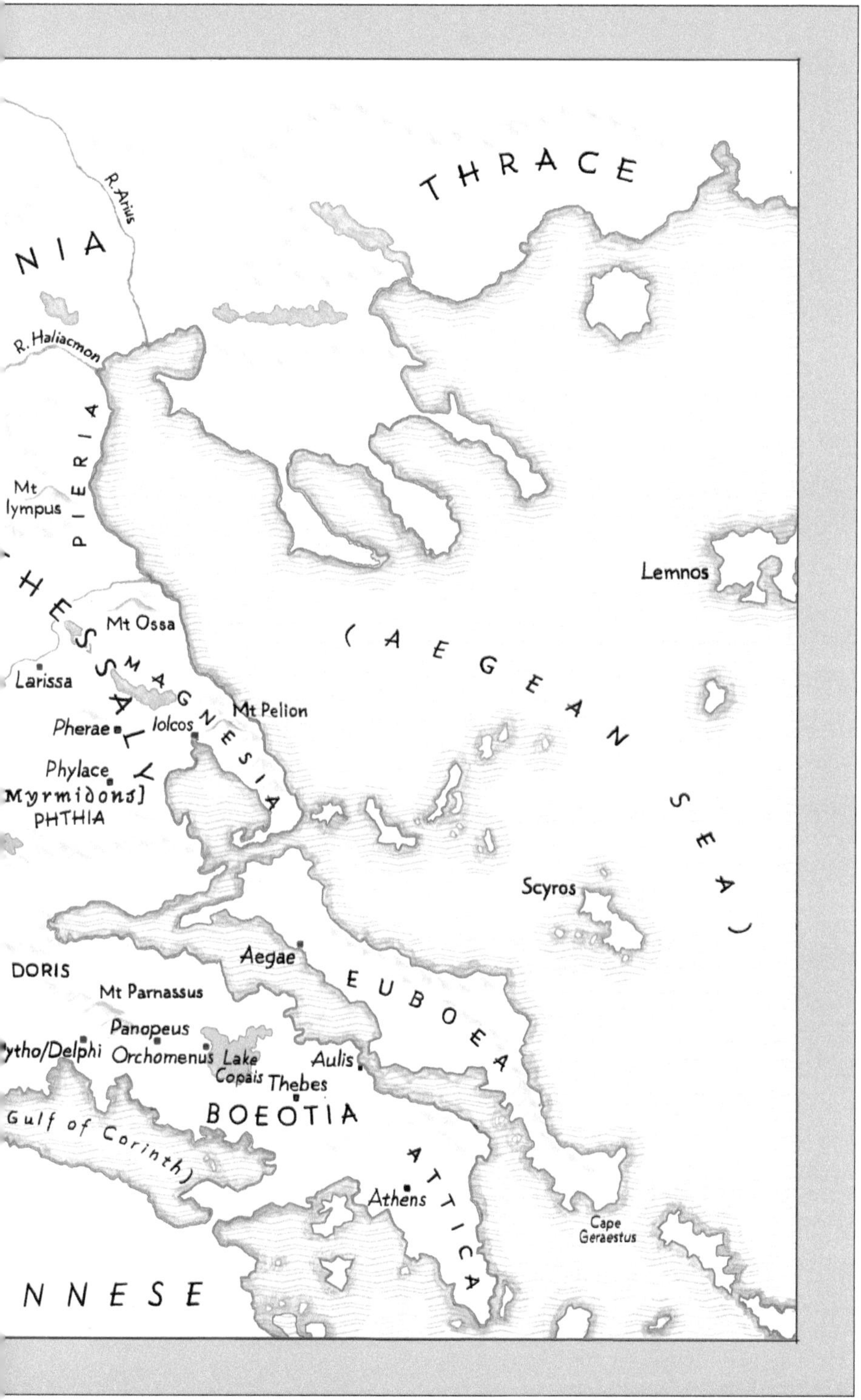
THRACE
NIA
R. Arius
R. Haliacmon
PIERIA
Mt
lympus
THESSALY
Mt Ossa
Larissa
MAGNESIA
Mt Pelion
Pherae
Iolcos
Phylace
Myrmidons]
PHTHIA
Lemnos
(AEGEAN SEA)
Scyros
Aegae
EUBOEA
DORIS
Mt Parnassus
Panopeus
ytho/Delphi
Orchomenus
Lake
Copais
Aulis
Thebes
BOEOTIA
Gulf of Corinth)
ATTICA
Athens
Cape
Geraestus
NNESE

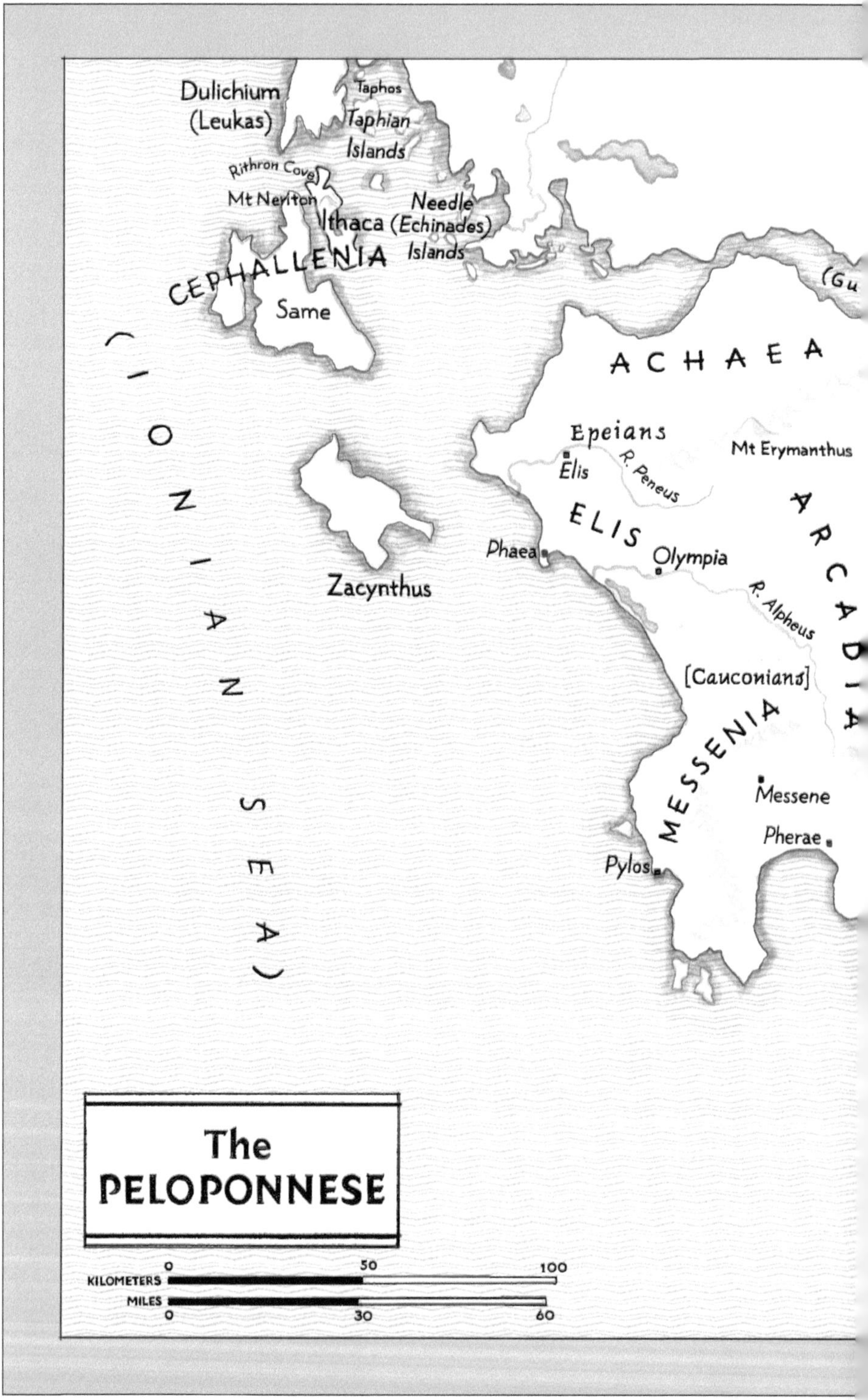

Dulichium (Leukas)
Taphos
Taphian Islands
Rithron Cove
Mt Neriton
Needle (Echinades) Islands
Ithaca
CEPHALLENIA
Same
(IONIAN SEA)
(Gu
ACHAEA
Epeians
Elis
R. Peneus
Mt Erymanthus
ELIS
ARCADIA
Phaea
Olympia
Zacynthus
R. Alpheus
[Cauconians]
MESSENIA
Messene
Pherae
Pylos
The PELOPONNESE
KILOMETERS
0
50
100
MILES
0
30
60

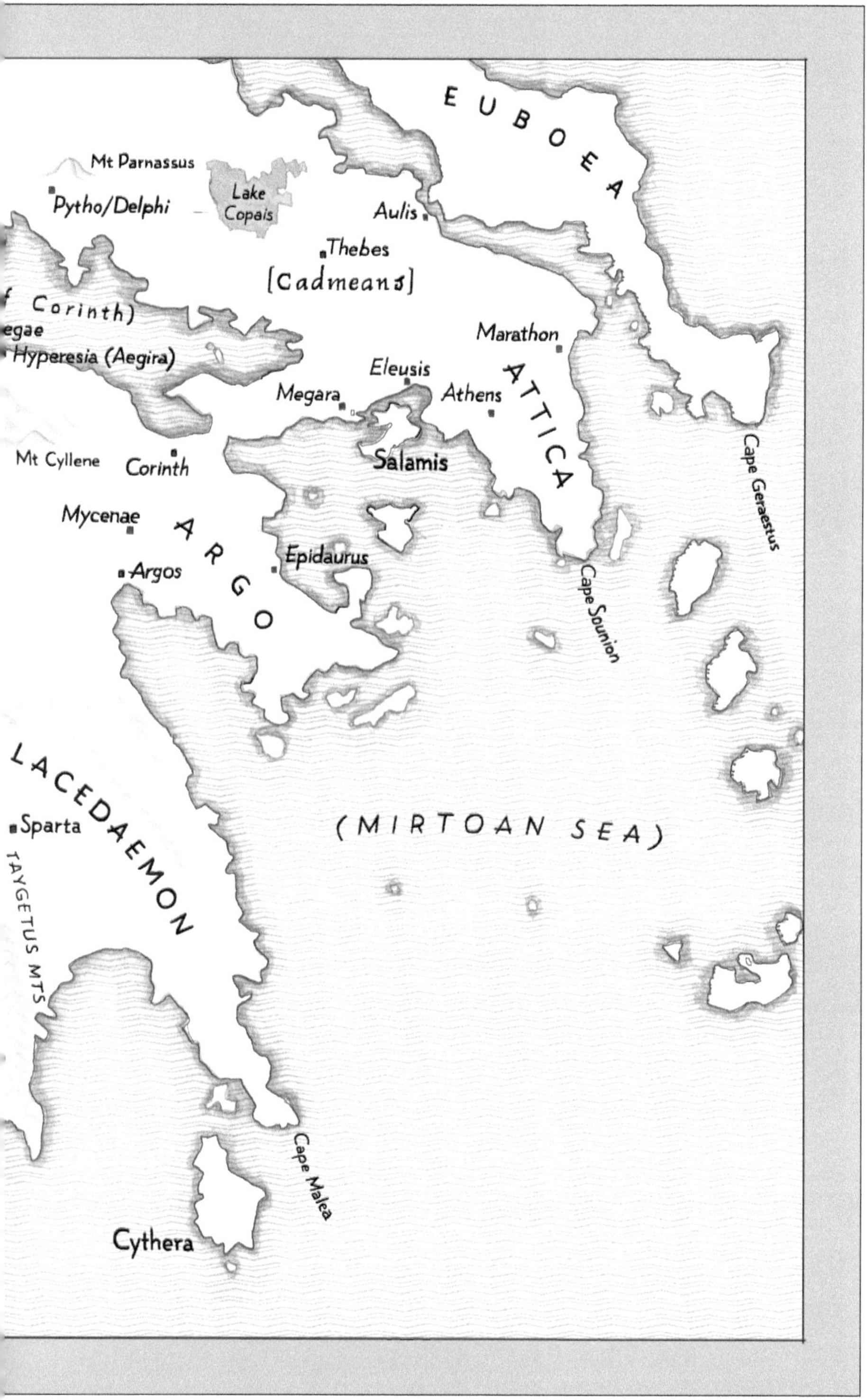
EUBOEA
Mt Parnassus
Pytho/Delphi
Lake Copais
Aulis
Thebes
[Cadmeans]
Corinth)
egae
Hyperesia (Aegira)
Marathon
Eleusis
Megara
Athens
ATTICA
Salamis
Mt Cyllene
Corinth
Mycenae
ARGO
Epidaurus
Argos
Cape Geraestus
Cape Sounion
LACEDAEMON
Sparta
TAYGETUS MTS
(MIRTOAN SEA)
Cape Malea
Cythera

THE ODYSSEY

BOOK 1

The Boy and the Goddess

Tell me about a complicated man.
Muse, tell me how he wandered and was lost
when he had wrecked the holy town of Troy,
and where he went, and who he met, the pain
he suffered on the sea, and how he worked
to save his life and bring his men back home.
He failed, and for their own mistakes, they died.
They ate the Sun God's cattle, and the god
kept them from home. Now goddess, child of Zeus,
tell the old story for our modern times.
Find the beginning.

All the other Greeks
who had survived the brutal sack of Troy
sailed safely home to their own wives—except
this man alone. Calypso, a great goddess,
had trapped him in her cave; she wanted him
to be her husband. When the year rolled round
in which the gods decreed he should go home
to Ithaca, his troubles still went on.

The man was friendless. All the gods took pity,
except Poseidon's anger never ended
until Odysseus was back at home.
But now the distant Ethiopians,
who live between the sunset and the dawn,
were worshipping the Sea God with a feast,
a hundred cattle and a hundred rams.
There sat the god, delighting in his banquet.
The other gods were gathered on Olympus,
in Father Zeus' palace. He was thinking
of fine, well-born Aegisthus, who was killed
by Agamemnon's famous son Orestes.
He told the deathless gods,

"This is absurd,
that mortals blame the gods! They say we cause
their suffering, but they themselves increase it
by folly. So Aegisthus overstepped:
he took the legal wife of Agamemnon,
then killed the husband when he came back home,
although he knew that it would doom them all.
We gods had warned Aegisthus; we sent down
perceptive Hermes, who flashed into sight
and told him not to murder Agamemnon
or court his wife; Orestes would grow up
and come back to his home to take revenge.
Aegisthus would not hear that good advice.
But now his death has paid all debts."

Athena
looked at him steadily and answered, "Father,
he did deserve to die. Bring death to all
who act like him! But I am agonizing
about Odysseus and his bad luck.
For too long he has suffered, with no friends,

sea all around him, sea on every side,
out on an island where a goddess lives,
daughter of fearful Atlas, who holds up
the pillars of the sea, and knows its depths—
those pillars keep the heaven and earth apart.
His daughter holds that poor unhappy man,
and tries beguiling him with gentle words
to cease all thoughts of Ithaca; but he
longs to see even just the smoke that rises
from his own homeland, and he wants to die.
You do not even care, Olympian!
Remember how he sacrificed to you
on the broad plain of Troy beside his ships?
So why do you dismiss Odysseus?"

"Daughter!" the Cloud God said, "You must be joking,
since how could I forget Odysseus?
He is more sensible than other humans,
and makes more sacrifices to the gods.
But Lord Poseidon rages, unrelenting,
because Odysseus destroyed the eye
of godlike Polyphemus, his own son,
the strongest of the Cyclopes—whose mother,
Thoösa, is a sea-nymph, child of Phorcys,
the sea king; and she lay beside Poseidon
inside a hollow cave. The Lord of Earthquakes
prevents Odysseus from reaching home
but does not kill him. Come then, we must plan:
how can he get back home? Poseidon must
give up his anger, since he cannot fight
alone against the will of all the gods."

Athena's eyes lit up and she replied,

"Great Father, if the blessed gods at last
will let Odysseus return back home,
then hurry, we must send our messenger,
Hermes the giant-slayer. He must swoop
down to Ogygia right away and tell
the beautiful Calypso we have formed
a firm decision that Odysseus
has waited long enough. He must go home.
And I will go to Ithaca to rouse
the courage of his son, and make him call
a meeting, and speak out against the suitors
who kill his flocks of sheep and longhorn cattle
unstoppably. Then I will send him off
to Pylos and to Sparta, to seek news
about his father's journey home, and gain
a noble reputation for himself."

With that, she tied her sandals on her feet,
the marvelous golden sandals that she wears
to travel sea and land, as fast as wind.
She took the heavy bronze-tipped spear she uses
to tame the ranks of warriors with whom
she is enraged. Then from the mountain down
she sped to Ithaca, and stopped outside
Odysseus' court, bronze spear in hand.
She looked like Mentes now, the Taphian leader,
a guest-friend. There she found the lordly suitors
sitting on hides—they killed the cows themselves—
and playing checkers. Quick, attentive house slaves
were waiting on them. Some were mixing wine
with water in the bowls, and others brought
the tables out and wiped them off with sponges,
and others carved up heaping plates of meat.
Telemachus was sitting with them, feeling

dejected. In his mind he saw his father
coming from somewhere, scattering the suitors,
and gaining back his honor, and control
of all his property. With this in mind,
he was the first to see Athena there.
He disapproved of leaving strangers stranded,
so he went straight to meet her at the gate,
and shook her hand, and took her spear of bronze,
and let his words fly out to her.

"Good evening,
stranger, and welcome. Be our guest, come share
our dinner, and then tell us what you need."

He led her in, and Pallas followed him.
Inside the high-roofed hall, he set her spear
beside a pillar in a polished stand,
in which Odysseus kept stores of weapons.
And then he led her to a chair and spread
a smooth embroidered cloth across the seat,
and pulled a footstool up to it. He sat
beside her on a chair of inlaid wood,
a distance from the suitors, so their shouting
would not upset the stranger during dinner;
also to ask about his absent father.
A girl brought washing water in a jug
of gold, and poured it on their hands and into
a silver bowl, and set a table by them.
A deferential slave brought bread and laid
a wide array of food, a generous spread.
The carver set beside them plates of meat
of every kind, and gave them golden cups.
The cup boy kept on topping up the wine.
The suitors sauntered in and sat on chairs,

observing proper order, and the slaves
poured water on their hands. The house girls brought
baskets of bread and heaped it up beside them,
and house boys filled their wine-bowls up with drink.
They reached to take the good things set before them.
Once they were satisfied with food and drink,
the suitors turned their minds to other things—
singing and dancing, glories of the feast.
A slave brought out a well-tuned lyre and gave it
to Phemius, the man the suitors forced
to sing for them. He struck the chords to start
his lovely song.

Telemachus leaned in
close to Athena, so they would not hear,
and said,

"Dear guest—excuse my saying this—
these men are only interested in music,
a life of ease. They make no contribution.
This food belongs to someone else, a man
whose white bones may be lying in the rain
or sunk beneath the waves. If they saw him
return to Ithaca, they would all pray
for faster feet, instead of wealth and gold
and fancy clothes. In fact, he must have died.
We have no hope. He will not come back home.
If someone says so, we do not believe it.
But come now, tell me this and tell the truth.
Who are you? From what city, and what parents?
What kind of ship did you arrive here on?
What sailors brought you here, and by what route?
You surely did not travel here on foot!
Here is the thing I really want to know:

have you been here before? Are you a friend
who visited my father? Many men
came to his house. He traveled many places."

Athena's clear bright eyes met his. She said,
"Yes, I will tell you everything. I am
Mentes, the son of wise Anchialus,
lord of the Taphians, who love the oar.
I traveled with my ship and my companions
over the wine-dark sea to foreign lands,
with iron that I hope to trade for copper
in Temese. My ship is in the harbor
far from the town, beneath the woody hill.
And you and I are guest-friends through our fathers,
from long ago—Laertes can confirm it.
I hear that fine old man no longer comes
to town, but lives out in the countryside,
stricken by grief, with only one old slave,
who gives him food and drink when he trails back
leg-weary from his orchard, rich in vines.
I came because they told me that your father
was here—but now it seems that gods have blocked
his path back home. But I am sure that he
is not yet dead. The wide sea keeps him trapped
upon some island, captured by fierce men
who will not let him go. Now I will make
a prophecy the gods have given me,
and I think it will all come true, although
I am no prophet. He will not be gone
much longer from his own dear native land,
even if chains of iron hold him fast.
He will devise a means of getting home.
He is resourceful. Tell me now—are you
Odysseus' son? You are so tall!

Your handsome face and eyes resemble his.
We often met and knew each other well,
before he went to Troy, where all the best
leaders of Argos sailed in hollow ships.
From that time on, we have not seen each other."

Telemachus was careful as he answered.
"Dear guest, I will be frank with you. My mother
says that I am his son, but I cannot
be sure, since no one knows his own begetting.
I wish I were the son of someone lucky,
who could grow old at home with all his wealth.
Instead, the most unlucky man alive
is said to be my father—since you ask."

Athena looked at him with sparkling eyes.
"Son of Penelope, you and your sons
will make a name in history, since you are
so clever. But now tell me this. Who are
these banqueters? And what is the occasion?
A drinking party, or a wedding feast?
They look so arrogant and self-indulgent,
making themselves at home. A wise observer
would surely disapprove of how they act."

Telemachus said moodily, "My friend,
since you have raised the subject, there was once
a time when this house here was doing well,
our future bright, when he was still at home.
But now the gods have changed their plans and cursed us,
and cast my father into utter darkness.
If he had died it would not be this bad—
if he had fallen with his friends at Troy,
or in his loved ones' arms, when he had wound

the threads of war to end. The Greeks would then
have built a tomb for him; he would have won
fame for his son. But now, the winds have seized him,
and he is nameless and unknown. He left
nothing but tears for me. I do not weep
only for him. The gods have given me
so many other troubles. All the chiefs
of Same, Zacynthus, Dulichium,
and local lords from rocky Ithaca,
are courting Mother, wasting our whole house.
She does not turn these awful suitors down,
nor can she end the courting. They keep eating,
spoiling my house—and soon, they will kill me!"

Athena said in outrage, "This is monstrous!
You need Odysseus to come back home
and lay his hands on all those shameless suitors!
If only he would come here now and stand
right at the gates, with two spears in his hands,
in shield and helmet, as when I first saw him!
Odysseus was visiting our house,
drinking and having fun on his way back
from sailing in swift ships to Ephyra
to visit Ilus. He had gone there looking
for deadly poison to anoint his arrows.
Ilus refused, because he feared the gods.
My father gave Odysseus the poison,
loving him blindly. May Odysseus
come meet the suitors with that urge to kill!
A bitter courtship and short life for them!
But whether he comes home to take revenge,
or not, is with the gods. You must consider
how best to drive these suitors from your house.
Come, listen carefully to what I say.

Tomorrow call the Achaean chiefs to meeting,
and tell the suitors—let the gods be witness—
'All of you, go away! To your own homes!'
As for your mother, if she wants to marry,
let her return to her great father's home.
They will make her a wedding and prepare
abundant gifts to show her father's love.
Now here is some advice from me for you.
Fit out a ship with twenty oars, the best,
and go find out about your long-lost father.
Someone may tell you news, or you may hear
a voice from Zeus, best source of information.
First go to Pylos, question godlike Nestor;
from there, to Sparta; visit Menelaus.
He came home last of all the Achaean heroes.
If you should hear that he is still alive
and coming home, put up with this abuse
for one more year. But if you hear that he
is dead, go home, and build a tomb for him,
and hold a lavish funeral to show
the honor he deserves, and give your mother
in marriage to a man. When this is done,
consider deeply how you might be able
to kill the suitors in your halls—by tricks
or openly. You must not stick to childhood;
you are no longer just a little boy.
You surely heard how everybody praised
Orestes when he killed the man who killed
his famous father—devious Aegisthus?
Dear boy, I see how big and tall you are.
Be brave, and win yourself a lasting name.
But I must go now, on my nimble ship;
my friends are getting tired of waiting for me.
Remember what I said and heed my words."

Telemachus was brooding on her words,
and said, "Dear guest, you were so kind to give me
this fatherly advice. I will remember.
I know that you are eager to be off,
but please enjoy a bath before you go,
and take a gift with you. I want to give you
a precious, pretty treasure as a keepsake
to mark our special friendship."

But the goddess
Athena met his gaze and said, "Do not
hold me back now. I must be on my way.
As for the gift you feel inspired to give me,
save it for when I come on my way home
and let me give you presents then as well
in fair exchange."

With that, the owl-eyed goddess
flew away like a bird, up through the smoke.
She left him feeling braver, more determined,
and with his father even more in mind.
Watching her go, he was amazed and saw
she was a god. Then godlike, he went off
to meet the suitors.

They were sitting calmly,
listening to the poet, who sang how
Athena cursed the journey of the Greeks
as they were sailing home from Troy. Upstairs,
Penelope had heard the marvelous song.
She clambered down the steep steps of her house,
not by herself—two slave girls came with her.
She reached the suitors looking like a goddess,
then stopped and stood beside a sturdy pillar,
holding a gauzy veil before her face.

Her slave girls stood, one on each side of her.
In tears, she told the holy singer,

"Stop,
please, Phemius! You know so many songs,
enchanting tales of things that gods and men
have done, the deeds that singers publicize.
Sing something else, and let them drink in peace.
Stop this upsetting song that always breaks
my heart, so I can hardly bear my grief.
I miss him all the time—that man, my husband,
whose story is so famous throughout Greece."

Sullen Telemachus said, "Mother, no,
you must not criticize the loyal bard
for singing as it pleases him to sing.
Poets are not to blame for how things are;
Zeus is; he gives to each as is his will.
Do not blame Phemius because he told
about the Greek disasters. You must know
the newest song is always praised the most.
So steel your heart and listen to the song.
Odysseus was not the only one
who did not come back home again from Troy.
Many were lost. Go in and do your work.
Stick to the loom and distaff. Tell your slaves
to do their chores as well. It is for men
to talk, especially me. I am the master."

That startled her. She went back to her room,
and took to heart her son's deliberate scolding.
She went upstairs, along with both her slaves,
and wept there for her dear Odysseus,
until Athena gave her eyes sweet sleep.

Throughout the shadowy hall the suitors clamored,
praying to lie beside her in her bed.
Telemachus inhaled, then started speaking.

"You suitors, you are taking this too far.
Let us enjoy the feast in peace. It is
a lovely thing to listen to a bard,
especially one with such a godlike voice.
At dawn, let us assemble in the square.
I have to tell you this—it is an order.
You have to leave my halls. Go dine elsewhere!
Eat your own food, or share between your houses.
Or if you think it easier and better
to ruin one man's wealth, and if you think
that you can get away with it—go on!
I call upon the gods; Zeus will grant vengeance.
You will be punished and destroyed, right here!"

He spoke, and they began to bite their lips,
shocked that Telemachus would dare to speak
so boldly. But Antinous replied,

"Telemachus, the gods themselves have taught you
such pride, to talk so big and brash in public!
May Zeus the son of Cronus never grant you
your true inheritance, which is the throne
of Ithaca."

His mind alert and focused,
Telemachus replied, "Antinous,
you will not like this, but I have to say,
I hope Zeus does give me the throne. Do you
deny it is an honorable thing
to be a king? It brings the household wealth,
and honor to the man. But there are many

other great chiefs in sea-girt Ithaca,
both old and young. I know that. One of them
may seize the throne, now that Odysseus
has died. But I shall be at least the lord
of my own house and of the slaves that he
seized for my benefit."

Eurymachus
replied, "Telemachus, the gods must choose
which of us will be king of Ithaca.
But still, I hope you keep your own possessions,
and rule your house. May no man drive you out,
and seize your wealth, while Ithaca survives.
Now, friend, I want to ask about the stranger.
Where was he from, what country? Did he say?
Where is his place of birth, his native soil?
Does he bring news your father will come home?
Or did he come here for some other purpose?
How suddenly he darted off, not waiting
for us to meet him. Yet he looked important."

The boy said soberly, "Eurymachus,
my father is not ever coming home.
I do not listen now to any gossip,
or forecasts from the psychics whom my mother
invites to visit us. The stranger was
my father's guest-friend Mentes, son of wise
Anchialus, who rules the Taphians,
the people of the oar."

Those were his words,
but in his mind he knew she was a god.
They danced to music and enjoyed themselves
till evening, then they went back home to sleep.

Telemachus' bedroom had been built
above the courtyard, so it had a view.
He went upstairs, preoccupied by thought.
A loyal slave went with him, Eurycleia,
daughter of Ops; she brought the burning torches.
Laertes bought her many years before
when she was very young, for twenty oxen.
He gave her status in the household, equal
to his own wife, but never slept with her,
avoiding bitter feelings in his marriage.
She brought the torches now; she was the slave
who loved him most, since she had cared for him
when he was tiny. Entering the room,
he sat down on the bed, took off his tunic,
and gave it to the vigilant old woman.
She smoothed it out and folded it, then hung it
up on a hook beside his wooden bed,
and left the room. She used the silver latch
to close the door; the strap pulled tight the bolt.
He slept the night there, wrapped in woolen blankets,
planning the journey told him by Athena.

BOOK 2

A Dangerous Journey

The early Dawn was born; her fingers bloomed.
Odysseus' well-beloved son
jumped up, put on his clothes, and strapped his sword
across his back, and tied his handsome sandals
onto his well-oiled feet. He left the room
looking just like a god.

He quickly told
the clear-voiced heralds they must call the Greeks
to council. Soon the men, their long hair flowing,
were gathered all together in the square.
Telemachus arrived, bronze sword in hand,
not by himself—two swift dogs came with him.
Athena poured a heavenly grace upon him.
The elders let him join them, and he sat
upon his father's throne. The first to speak
was wise Aegyptius, a bent old soldier.
His darling son, the spear-man Antiphus,
had sailed with Lord Odysseus to Troy;
the Cyclops killed him in his cave and made him
his final course at dinner. This old father

had three sons left. One teamed up with the suitors—
Eurynomus. The others spent their time
working the farm. But still the father mourned
the son whom he had lost. He spoke in tears.

"People of Ithaca, now hear my words.
We have not met in council since the day
Odysseus departed with his ships.
Who called us? Someone old or young? And why?
Has he found out an army is approaching?
Or does he have some other piece of news
which he would like to share with all of us?
I think he is a helpful, decent man.
I hope that Zeus rewards his good intentions!"

Odysseus' loving son felt glad,
and eagerly got up to speak and stood
among them, in the center of the group.
The competent official, named Pisenor,
passed him the speaking-stick; he held it up,
and first addressed Aegyptius.

"Here, sir!
Now look no further for the man you seek.
I called the meeting. I am in deep trouble.
I have no information of an army
that might attack us, nor do I have news
of any other danger to our people.
I need help for myself. My family
has suffered two disasters. First I lost
my father, who was kind to you as if
you also were his sons. Now, even worse,
my house is being ripped apart; my wealth
will soon be gone! The sons of all the nobles
have shoved inside my house to court my mother,

against her wishes. They should go and ask
Icarius her father to provide
a dowry, and choose who should be her husband.
They are too scared. Instead, they haunt our house
day after day, and kill our cows and pigs
and good fat goats. They feast and drink red wine,
not caring if they waste it all. There is
no man to save the house—no man like him,
Odysseus. I cannot fight against them;
I would be useless. I have had no training.
But if I had the power, I would do it!
It is unbearable, what they have done!
They ruined my whole house! It is not fair!
You suitors all should feel ashamed! Consider
what others in the neighborhood will think!
And also be afraid! The angry gods
will turn on you in rage; they will be shocked
at all this criminal behavior!
I beg you, by Olympian Zeus, and by
the goddess who presides in human meetings:
Justice! But never mind. Friends, leave me be,
and let me cry and suffer by myself.
Or did Odysseus, my warlike father,
deliberately do harm to our own side?
Is that why you seem set on hurting me,
encouraging these suitors? Oh, if only
you Ithacans would eat my stock yourselves!
If you did that, I soon would get revenge;
I would come through the town and keep demanding,
until it all got given back. But now,
you make me so unhappy! This is pointless!"

He stopped, frustrated, flung the scepter down,
and burst out crying. Everyone was seized

by pity. No one spoke; they hesitated
to answer him unkindly. Then at last
Antinous began.

"Telemachus,
you stuck-up, wilful little boy! How dare you
try to embarrass us and put the blame
on us? We suitors have not done you wrong.
Go blame your precious mother! She is cunning.
It is the third year, soon it will be four,
that she has cheated us of what we want.
She offers hope to all, sends signs to each,
but all the while her mind moves somewhere else.
She came up with a special trick: she fixed
a mighty loom inside the palace hall.
Weaving her fine long cloth, she said to us,
'Young men, you are my suitors. Since my husband,
the brave Odysseus, is dead, I know
you want to marry me. You must be patient;
I have worked hard to weave this winding-sheet
to bury good Laertes when he dies.
He gained such wealth, the women would reproach me
if he were buried with no shroud. Please let me
finish it!' And her words made sense to us.
So every day she wove the mighty cloth,
and then at night by torchlight, she unwove it.
For three long years her trick beguiled the Greeks.
But when the fourth year's seasons rolled around,
a woman slave who knew the truth told us.
We caught her there, unraveling the cloth,
and made her finish it. This is our answer,
so you and all the Greeks may understand.
Dismiss your mother, let her father tell her
to marry anyone his heart desires.

Athena blessed her with intelligence,
great artistry and skill, a finer mind
than anyone has ever had before,
even the braided girls of ancient Greece,
Tyro, Alcmene, garlanded Mycene—
none of them had Penelope's understanding.
But if she wants to go on hurting us,
her plans are contrary to destiny.
We suitors will keep eating up your wealth,
and livelihood, as long as she pursues
this plan the gods have put inside her heart.
For her it may be glory, but for you,
pure loss. We will not go back to our farms
or anywhere, until she picks a husband."

Telemachus insisted, breathing hard,
"Antinous, I cannot force my mother
out of the house. She gave me birth and raised me.
My father is elsewhere—alive or dead.
If I insist my mother has to leave,
Icarius will make me pay the price,
and gods will send more trouble; if she goes,
Mother will rouse up Furies full of hate
to take revenge, and everyone will curse me.
I will not. If you feel upset, you go!
Out of my house! Stop eating all my food!
Devour each other's property, not mine!
Or do you really think it right to waste
one person's means of life, and go scot-free?
Then try it! I will call the deathless gods!
May Zeus give recompense some day for this!
You will die here, and nobody will care!"

Then Zeus, whose voice resounds around the world,
sent down two eagles from the mountain peak.

At first they hovered on the breath of wind,
close by each other, balanced on their wings.
Reaching the noisy middle of the crowd,
they wheeled and whirred and flapped their mighty wings,
swooping at each man's head with eyes like death,
and with their talons ripped each face and neck.
Then to the right they flew, across the town.
Everyone was astonished at the sight;
they wondered in their hearts what this could mean.
Old Halitherses, son of Mastor, spoke.
More than the other elders, this old leader
excelled at prophecy and knew the birds.
He gave them good advice.

"Now Ithacans,
listen! I speak especially for the suitors.
Disaster rolls their way! Odysseus
will not be absent from his friends for long;
already he is near and sows the seeds
of death for all of them, and more disaster
for many others in bright Ithaca.
We have to form a plan to make them stop.
That would be best for them as well by far.
I am experienced at prophecy;
my words came true for him, that mastermind,
Odysseus. I told him when he left
for Troy with all the Argives, he would suffer
most terribly, and all his men would die,
but in the twentieth year he would come home,
unrecognized. Now it is coming true."

Eurymachus, the son of Polybus,
replied, "Old man, be off! Go home and spout
your portents to your children, or it will
be worse for them. But I can read these omens

better than you can. Many birds go flying
in sunlight, and not all are meaningful.
Odysseus is dead, away from home.
I wish that you had died with him, to stop
your forecasts! You are making this boy angry,
hoping that he will give your household gifts.
But let me tell you this, which will come true.
You may know many ancient forms of wisdom,
but if you tease this boy and stir his rage,
he will be hurt, and never get to act
on any of these prophecies of yours.
And, old man, we will make you pay so much
your heart will break, your pain will cut so deep.
I will advise Telemachus myself,
in front of everyone, to send his mother
back to her father's family, to fix
her wedding, and the gifts a well-loved daughter
should have. Unless he does that, we will never
cease from this torturous courtship. We are not
afraid of anyone, much less this boy
with his long speeches, nor your pointless portents.
They will not come to pass and they will make you
hated. His house will be devoured, and payback
will never come, as long as she frustrates
our wish for marriage. Meanwhile, we will wait
in daily hope, competing for the prize,
not seeking other women as our wives."

Telemachus, his mind made up, replied,
"All right, Eurymachus, and all of you.
I will not talk about this anymore.
The gods and all of you already know.
Just let me have a ship and twenty men
to make a journey with me, out and back,

to Sparta and to sandy Pylos, seeking
news about when my father may come home.
I may hear it from somebody, or from
a voice from Zeus—it often happens so.
If I find out my father is alive
and coming home, I will endure this pain
for one more year. But if I hear that he
is dead, I will come home to my own land,
and build a tomb and hold the funeral rites
as he deserves, and I will give my mother
to a new husband."

He sat down, and up
stood Mentor. When Odysseus sailed off,
this was the friend he asked to guard his house
and told the slaves to look to him as master.
Mentor addressed the crowd.

"Now Ithacans!
Listen! This changes everything! Now kings
should never try to judge with righteousness
or rule their people gently. Kings should always
be cruel, since the people whom he ruled
as kindly as a father, have forgotten
their King Odysseus. I do not blame
the suitors' overconfidence, rough ways
and violence, in eating up his household;
they risk their lives, supposing that the master
will never come back home. But I do blame
you others, sitting passive, never speaking
against them, though you far outnumber them."

Leocritus, Euenor's son, replied,

"Mentor, for shame! You must have lost your mind!
Fool, telling us to stop our banqueting!
You could not fight us; we outnumber you.
Even if Ithacan Odysseus
came back and found us feasting in his house,
and tried to drive us out, his wife would get
no joy of his return, no matter how
she misses him. If he tried fighting solo
against us, he would die a cruel death.
So what you said was nonsense. Anyway,
we must disperse, and everyone get busy.
Mentor and Halitherses, since you are
old comrades of his father, you can guide
Telemachus' journey. I suspect
he will not manage to go anywhere;
he will just wait in Ithaca for news."

The crowd broke up; the Ithacans went home;
the suitors, to Odysseus' house.

Telemachus slipped out and at the beach
he dipped his hands in salty gray seawater,
and asked Athena,

"Goddess, hear my prayer!
Just yesterday you came and ordered me
to sail the hazy sea and find out news
of my long-absent father's journey home.
The Greeks are wasting everything, especially
these bullying, mean suitors."

Then Athena
came near him with the voice and guise of Mentor,
and spoke to him with words that flew like birds.

"Telemachus, you will be brave and thoughtful,
if your own father's forcefulness runs through you.
How capable he was, in word and deed!
Your journey will succeed, if you are his.
If you're not his son by Penelope,
I doubt you can achieve what you desire.
And it is rare for sons to be like fathers;
only a few are better, most are worse.
But you will be no coward and no fool.
You do possess your father's cunning mind,
so there is hope you will do all these things.
Forget about those foolish suitors' plans.
They have no brains and no morality.
They do not know black doom will kill them all,
and some day soon: their death is near at hand.
You will achieve the journey that you seek,
since I will go with you, just like a father.
I will equip a good swift ship for you.
Now go back home to where those suitors are,
and get provisions. Pack them in containers:
some wine in jars, and grain, the strength of men,
in sturdy skins. And I will go through town,
calling for volunteers to come with us.
This island, Ithaca, has many ships
both new and old. I will select the best one;
we will equip her quickly and sail fast,
far off across the sea."

So spoke the goddess,
daughter of Zeus. Telemachus obeyed.
His heart was troubled as he went back home.
He found the arrogant suitors in the hall,
skinning some goats and charring hogs for dinner.
Antinous began to laugh. He called him,
and seized his hand and spoke these words to him.

"Telemachus, you are being so pigheaded!
Why not put all your troubles from your heart?
Come eat and drink with me, just as before.
You know the Greeks will fix it all for you.
They will select a ship and crew, and soon
you will reach Pylos, where you hope to hear
word of your father."

But the boy was wary,
and said, "Antinous, I cannot eat;
I have no peace or joy when I am with
you selfish suitors. Is it not enough
that you destroyed my rich inheritance
when I was just a little boy? But now
I have grown bigger, and I got advice
from other people, and my heart wells up
with courage. I will try to bring down doom
on your heads here at home or when I go
to Pylos. Yes, I really will go there,
as passenger, although I do not own
a ship or have a crew—because of you!"

He snatched his hand away. But as they feasted,
the suitors started mocking him and jeering.
With sneers they said,

"Oh no! Telemachus
is going to kill us! He will bring supporters
from Pylos or from Sparta—he is quite
determined! Or indeed he may be fetching
some lethal poisons from the fertile fields
of Ephyra, to mix up in our wine-bowl
and kill us all!"

Another proud young man
said, "Well, who knows, perhaps he will get lost
in that curved ship, and die, so far away
from all his family—just like his father.
And what a pity that would be for us!
Then we would have to share out all his wealth,
and give away the house itself to her—
his mother, and the man who marries her."

The boy went downstairs, to his father's storeroom,
wide and high-roofed, piled high with gold and bronze
and clothes in chests and fragrant olive oil.
Down there the jars of vintage wine were stored,
which held the sweet, unmixed and godlike drink,
lined in a row against the wall, in case
weary Odysseus came home at last.
The double doors were locked and closely fitted.
A woman checked the contents, night and day,
guarding it all with great intelligence,
and that was Eurycleia, child of Ops.
He called her to the chamber and addressed her.

"Nanny, please pour sweet wine in jugs for me,
the second best one, not the one you keep
for when the poor unlucky king escapes
from evil fate and death, and comes back home.
Fill up twelve jugs with wine for me, and pour me
some twenty pounds of fine-milled barley-groats,
all packed in sturdy leather bags. Load up
all these provisions secretly. At nightfall,
I will come here and get them, when my mother
has gone upstairs to go to sleep. I am
leaving for Sparta and for sandy Pylos,
to learn about my father's journey home."

At that his loving nurse began to wail,
and sobbed,

"Sweet child! What gave you this idea?
Why do you want to go so far? You are
an only child, and dearly loved! The king,
Odysseus, is gone, lost, far from home,
and they will plot against you when you leave,
scheming to murder you and share this wealth.
Stay with us, we who love you! Do not go
searching for danger out on restless seas!"

Telemachus decisively replied,
"Nanny, you need not worry. Gods have blessed
this plan. But promise me you will not tell
Mother, until she notices me gone.
Say nothing for twelve days, so she will not
start crying; it would spoil her pretty skin."

At that the old nurse swore a mighty oath
by all the gods that she would keep the secret,
and then she drew the wine for him in jars,
and poured the barley-groats in well-stitched bags.
Telemachus returned to see the suitors.

Meanwhile, bright-eyed Athena had a plan.
Resembling Telemachus, she went
all through the city, standing by each man,
and urged them to assemble by the ship
at night, and asked the son of Phronius,
Noëmon, for his speedy ship; he promised
to give it gladly. Then the sun went down
and all the streets grew dark. The goddess dragged
the ship into the water, and she loaded

the necessary tackle for a journey.
Right at the beach's farthest end the goddess
stood and assembled good strong men as crew;
she coached each one. Then, eyes ablaze with plans,
she went back to Odysseus' house,
and poured sweet sleep upon the drunken suitors.
She struck them and their cups fell from their hands.
Disguised as Mentor both in looks and voice,
she called the boy out from the mighty hall,
and looked intently in his face, and said,

"Telemachus, your crew of armored men
is ready at the oar for your departure.
Come on! No time to waste! We must be gone!"

So speaking, Pallas quickly led the boy;
he followed in the footsteps of the goddess.
They went down to the seashore and the ship,
and found the long-haired sailors on the beach.
Inspired and confident, Telemachus
called out,

"My friends! Come on, let us go fetch
the rations; they are ready in the hall.
But quietly—my mother does not know,
nor do the other women, except one."

And so he led them, and they followed him.
They loaded everything upon the decks;
Odysseus' son instructed them,
and then embarked—Athena led the way.
She sat down in the stern, and next to her
Telemachus was sitting. Then the crew
released the ropes and boarded, each at oar.

Athena called a favorable wind,
pure Zephyr whistling on wine-dark sea.
Telemachus commanded his companions
to seize the rigging; so they did, and raised
the pine-wood mast inside the rounded block,
and bound it down with forestays round about,
and raised the bright white sails with leather ropes.
Wind blew the middle sail; the purple wave
was splashing loudly round the moving keel.
The goddess rode the waves and smoothed the way.
The quick black ship held steady, so they fastened
the tackle down, and filled their cups with wine.
They poured libations to the deathless gods,
especially to the bright-eyed child of Zeus.
All through the night till dawn the ship sailed on.

BOOK 3

An Old King Remembers

Leaving the Ocean's streams, the Sun leapt up
into the sky of bronze, to shine his light
for gods and mortals on the fertile earth.
Telemachus arrived in Pylos, where
the Pylians were bringing to the beach
black bulls for blue Poseidon, Lord of Earthquakes.
There were nine pews, five hundred men on each,
and each group had nine bulls to sacrifice.
They burned the thigh-bones for the god, and ate
the innards. Then the Ithacans arrived,
took down their sails, dropped anchor and alighted.
The goddess with the flashing eyes, Athena,
first led Telemachus onshore, then spoke.

"Do not be shy, Telemachus. You sailed
over the sea to ask about your father,
where the earth hides him, what his fate might be.
So hurry now to Nestor, lord of horses.
Learn what advice he has in mind for you.
Supplicate him yourself, and he will tell you
the truth; he is not one to tell a lie."

Telemachus replied, "But Mentor, how
can I approach and talk to him? I am
quite inexperienced at making speeches,
and as a young man, I feel awkward talking
to elders."

She looked straight into his eyes,
and answered, "You will work out what to do,
through your own wits and with divine assistance.
The gods have blessed you in your life so far."

So Pallas spoke and quickly led him on;
he followed in the footsteps of the goddess.

They reached the center of the town, where Nestor
was sitting with his sons and his companions,
putting the meat on spits and roasting it
for dinner. When they saw the strangers coming,
they all stood up with open arms to greet them,
inviting them to join them. Nestor's son,
Pisistratus, shook hands and sat them down,
spreading soft fleeces on the sand beside
his father and his brother, Thrasymedes.
He served them giblets and he poured some wine
into a golden cup, and raised a toast
to Pallas, child of Zeus the Aegis-Lord.

"Now guest, give prayers of thanks to Lord Poseidon,
and pour libations for the god. This feast
is in his honor; pay him proper dues.
Then give the boy the cup of honeyed wine,
so he can offer to the deathless gods
libations. Everybody needs the gods.
I give the golden chalice to you first,
because the boy is younger, more my age."

He put the cup of sweet wine in her hand.
Athena was impressed with his good manners,
because he rightly gave it first to her.
At once she made a heartfelt prayer.

"Poseidon!
O Shaker of the Earth, do not refuse
to grant our prayer; may all these things come true.
Bring fame to Nestor and his sons, and grant
gifts to the Pylians, as recompense
for this fine sacrifice. And may the quest
for which we sailed here in our swift black ship
succeed, and may we come home safe again."

She made her prayer come true all by herself.
She gave Telemachus the splendid cup
with double handle, and his prayer matched hers.
And then they cooked the outer parts of meat,
and helped themselves to pieces, sharing round
the glorious feast, till they could eat no more.
Then first Gerenian Nestor, horse-lord, spoke.

"Now that our guests are satisfied with food,
time now to talk to them and ask them questions.
Strangers, who are you? Where did you sail from?
Are you on business, or just scouting round
like pirates on the sea, who risk their lives
to ravage foreign homes?"

Telemachus
was thoughtful but not shy. Athena gave him
the confidence deep in his heart to ask
about his absent father, and to gain
a noble reputation for himself.

"Great Nestor, son of Neleus," he said,
"You ask where I am from. I will be frank.
I come from Ithaca, beneath Mount Neion:
my business here is personal, not public.
I came to gather news about my father,
long-suffering Odysseus. They say
he fought with you to sack the town of Troy.
We know the place where all the other men
who battled with the Trojans lost their lives.
But Zeus still keeps Odysseus' fate
in darkness; no one knows where he was lost.
Maybe some hostile men killed him on land,
or he was drowned in Amphitrite's waves.
I beg you, tell me, did you see him die
with your own eyes? Or have you any news
about where he may be? He must be lost.
His mother surely bore him for misfortune.
You need not sweeten what you say, in pity
or from embarrassment. Just tell me straight
what your eyes saw of him, my noble father.
If ever he made promises to you
and kept his word at Troy, in times of trouble,
remember those times now. Tell me the truth!"

Gerenian Nestor, horse-lord, answered him,
"Dear boy, you call to mind how much we suffered,
with strong, unyielding hearts, in distant lands
when we were sailing over misty seas,
led by Achilles on a hunt for spoils,
and when we fought around the mighty city
of Priam. Our best warriors were killed.
Ajax lies dead there, and there lies Achilles;
there lies his godlike friend and guide, Patroclus;
my own strong, matchless son lies dead there too,

Antilochus, who fought and ran so well.
More pain, more grief—our sufferings increased.
Who could recount so many, many losses?
If you stayed here five years and kept on asking
how many things the fighters suffered there,
you would get bored and go back home again
before the story ended. Nine long years
we schemed to bring them down, and finally
Zeus made our plots succeed. Odysseus,
your father, if you really are his son—
well, no one dared to try to equal him
in cleverness. That man was always best
at every kind of trick. And seeing you,
I am amazed at how you talk like him.
One would not think so young a man could do it.
Well, back in Troy, Odysseus and I
always agreed in councils, with one mind.
We gave the Argives all the best advice.
After we conquered Priam's lofty town,
a god dispersed the ships of the Achaeans.
Zeus planned a bitter journey home for us,
since some of us had neither sense nor morals.
Gray-eyed Athena, daughter of the Thunder,
became enraged and brought about disaster.
She set the sons of Atreus to fight
each other. Hastily, they called the people
at sunset, not observing proper norms.
The men arrived already drunk on wine;
the brothers told them why they called the meeting.
Then Menelaus said that it was time
to sail back home across the open sea.
But Agamemnon disagreed entirely.
He wanted them to stay and sacrifice
to heal the sickness of Athena's wrath—

pointless! He did not know she would not yield.
The minds of the immortals rarely change.
So those two stood and argued angrily,
and with a dreadful clash of arms the Greeks
leapt up on two opposing sides. We slept
that eerie night with hearts intent on hatred
against each other—since Zeus meant us harm.
At dawn one group of us dragged down our ships
into the sea piled high with loot and women,
while half the army still remained there, stationed
with Agamemnon, shepherd of the people.
My friends and I set sail with all good speed—
a god had made the choppy sea lie calm.
We came to Tenedos and sacrificed,
praying to get back home—but Zeus refused;
the cruel god roused yet more strife among us.
Your father's plans were always flexible:
his men turned round their prows and sailed right back
to make their peace again with Agamemnon.
But I assembled all my fleet, and fled—
I understood some god must mean us harm.
Then Diomedes roused his men to come,
and ruddy Menelaus quickly sailed
to meet with us on Lesbos, and we pondered
our long sea journey. Should we travel north,
go past the rocks of Chios to our left,
to Psyria, or under Chios, passing
blustery Mimas? So we prayed for signs.
The god told us to cross the open sea
towards Euboea, to escape disaster.
A fair wind whistled and our ships sped on
across the journey-ways of fish, and landed
at nightfall in Geraestus. To Poseidon
we offered many bulls, since we had crossed

safely across wide waters. The fourth day
the men of Diomedes moored their ships
at Argos; I kept going on, to Pylos.
The wind the god had sent kept holding strong
the whole way home. So, my dear boy, I have
no news about what happened next. I do not
know which of them has died and who is safe.
But I can tell you what I heard while sitting
here in my halls. You ought to know. They say
Achilles' son led home the Myrmidons,
and Philoctetes came back home with glory.
And Idomeneus led back his crew
to Crete; no man of his who had survived
the war was lost at sea. And Agamemnon?
You must have heard, though you live far away.
Aegisthus murdered him! But he has paid
a bitter price. How fortunate the dead man
had left a son to take revenge upon
the wicked, scheming killer, that Aegisthus,
who killed Orestes' father. My dear boy,
I see that you are tall and strong. Be brave,
so you will be remembered."

Thoughtfully
Telemachus replied, "Your Majesty,
King Nestor, yes. Orestes took revenge.
The Greeks will make him famous through the world
and into future times. I wish the gods
would grant me that much power against those men
who threaten and insult me—those cruel suitors!
The gods have not yet granted us this blessing,
my father and myself. We must endure."

Gerenian Nestor, lord of horses, answered,
"Dear boy, since you have brought the subject up,
I have been told about your mother's suitors,
how badly they are treating you at home.
But do you willingly submit to it?
Or has a god's voice led the townspeople
to hate you? Well, who knows, perhaps one day
he will come home and take revenge, alone,
or with an army of the Greeks. If only
Athena loved you, as she used to care
for glorious Odysseus at Troy
when we were doing badly. I have never
seen gods display such favor as she gave
when she stood by your father. If she helped you
with that much love, the suitors would forget
their hopes for marriage."

Then Telemachus
replied, "My lord, I doubt that this will happen.
I am surprised you have such confidence.
I would not be so hopeful, even if
the gods were willing."

Then the goddess spoke.
"Telemachus, what do you mean? A god
can easily save anyone, at will,
no matter what the distance. I would rather
suffer immensely, but then get home safe,
than die on my return like Agamemnon,
murdered by his own wife, and by Aegisthus.
But death is universal. Even gods
cannot protect the people that they love,
when fate and cruel death catch up with them."

Telemachus said apprehensively,
"Mentes, this is upsetting. Change the subject.
He has no real chance now of getting home.
The gods have fenced him round with death and darkness.
Let me ask Nestor something else—he is
wiser and more informed than anyone.
They say he ruled for three whole generations.
He looks to me like some immortal god.
So Nestor, son of Neleus, please tell me,
how did the great King Agamemnon die?
And where was Menelaus? Was he lost,
away from Greece, when that Aegisthus dared
to kill a king, a better man than him?
How did that wicked trickster's plot succeed?"

Gerenian Nestor, lord of horses, answered,
"I will tell everything—though you can guess
what would have happened if fair Menelaus
had found Aegisthus living in his halls
on his return. And even when he died,
no one would bury him; he lay upon
the open plain without a tomb and far
from town for birds and dogs to eat. No Greek
would mourn that monster. While we fought and labored
at Troy, this layabout sat safe in Argos,
seducing Clytemnestra, noble wife
of Agamemnon. For a while, she scorned
his foul suggestions, since her heart was good.
Moreover, when her husband went to Troy,
he left a poet, ordered to protect her.
But finally Fate forced the queen to yield.
Aegisthus left the poet to be eaten
by birds, abandoned on a desert island.
He led the woman back to his own house

by mutual desire, and then he made
numerous offerings on holy altars
of animals and lovely gold and cloth:
he had succeeded far beyond his hopes.

And meanwhile, I left Troy with Menelaus;
we sailed together, best of friends. We reached
the holy cape of Athens, Sounion.
There Phoebus with his gentle arrows shot
and killed the pilot, Phrontis, as he held
the ship's helm as she sped along. No man
knew better how to steer through any storm,
so Menelaus stopped to bury him
with proper rites. At last he sailed again
across the wine-dark sea; but as his ships
rushed round the craggy heights of Malea,
far-seeing Zeus sent curses on his journey,
pouring out screaming winds and giant waves
the size of mountains—splitting up the fleet.
Some ships were hurled to Crete, to River Jardan,
where the Cydonian people have their homes.
There steep rock rises sheer above the sea
near Gortyn in the misty deep; south winds
drive mighty waves towards the left-hand crag,
and push them west to Phaestus; one small rock
restrains the massive currents. All the ships
were smashed by waves against those rocks. The men
were almost drowned. Five other dark-prowed ships
were blown by wind and sea away to Egypt.
There Menelaus gathered wealth and gold
and drifted with his ships through foreign lands.

Meanwhile at home, Aegisthus had been plotting.
He killed the son of Atreus and seized

control of rich Mycenae, where he reigned
for seven years. But in the eighth, Orestes
came to destroy him. He returned from Athens,
and killed his father's murderer, then called
the Argives to a funeral, a feast
for clever, scheming, cowardly Aegisthus
whom he had killed, and his own hated mother.
That very day, rambunctious Menelaus
arrived with all his ships crammed full of treasure.
The moral is, you must not stay away
too long, dear boy, when those proud suitors lurk
inside your house. They may divide your wealth
among themselves and make your journey useless.
But I suggest you go to Menelaus.
He recently returned from lands so distant
no one would even hope to get home safe
once driven by the winds so far off course,
over such dangerous, enormous seas.
Birds migrate there and take a year or more
to travel back. Go visit him by ship
with your own crew. Or if you would prefer,
you can go there by land—here is a carriage.
My sons can guide you all the way to Sparta,
to Menelaus. Ask him for the truth.
He will not lie; he is an honest man."

The sun went down and darkness fell. The goddess,
bright-eyed Athena, spoke to them.

"King Nestor,
your speech was good and your advice was sound.
But now slice up the tongues and pour the wine
for Lord Poseidon and the other gods
before we rest—time now to go to bed.

The light is fading and it is not right
to linger at a banquet in the dark."

The people listened to Athena's words.
The house slaves poured fresh water on their hands,
and boys filled up the mixing bowls with wine,
and poured it into cups, and first prepared
the sacrifice. They threw tongues on the fire,
then sprinkled wine, then each man drank his fill.
Then Zeus' daughter and the godlike boy
both rose to go together to their ship.
But Nestor called to stop them.

"Zeus forbids it!
And all the other gods who live forever!
You cannot leave my house for your swift ship
as if I were a poor and ragged man
with so few beds and blankets in his home
that neither he nor guests can sleep in comfort.
I have soft quilts and blankets in abundance.
The darling son of great Odysseus
must not sleep on the ship's deck, while I live!
Not while my sons remain here in my house,
ready to welcome anyone who visits."

The bright-eyed goddess answered him, "Old friend,
you are quite right. Telemachus should do
just as you say. That is a better plan.
He will stay here tonight and go to sleep
in your fine palace. But I must go back
to tell the crew the news and keep them strong.
You see, I am the oldest in our party.
The rest are younger men, close friends together,
the same age as our brave Telemachus.
I will sleep there beside the hollow ship.

At dawn I have important obligations:
to visit with the great Cauconians.
The boy can be your guest. Then send him off
escorted by your son. Give him a carriage,
drawn by your strongest and most nimble horses."

Bright-eyed Athena flew away, transformed
into an ossifrage. Astonishment
seized all the people watching, even Nestor.
He seized Telemachus' hand and said,

"Dear boy, I am now sure that you will be
a hero, since the gods are on your side
at your young age. This was a god, none other
than great Athena, true-born child of Zeus,
who also glorified your noble father.
Goddess, be kind to us as well, and grant
honor to me, my good wife, and our sons.
Now I will sacrifice a yearling heifer,
broad-browed and still unyoked, and gild her horns
with gold to bless your journey."

So he spoke,
and Pallas heard his prayer. Gerenian Nestor
led them and led his sons and sons-in-law
inside his own magnificent great hall.
When they were all inside, he seated them
on benches and on chairs arranged in order,
and he himself mixed up the bowl for them
of sweet delicious wine. He had preserved it
eleven years. The slave girl opened it,
pulling the lid off. As the old man mixed,
he prayed and poured libations for Athena.

They all poured also, then they drank their fill,
then each went home to sleep in his own chamber.
Nestor the horseman made a special bed
right there for his dear friend, the warrior's son:
a camp bed on the echoing portico,
beside Pisistratus, the only son
not living with a wife but still at home.
Nestor himself slept by his wife, the queen,
in a secluded corner of the palace.

When newborn Dawn appeared with rosy fingers,
the horse-lord Nestor jumped up out of bed,
and hurried down towards the polished stones
that stood outside his palace, bright with oil.
There Neleus used to give godlike advice,
until Fate took him and he went to Hades,
and Nestor, guardian of the Greeks, took over
the scepter. From their rooms his sons arrived
to throng around him: Echephron and Stratius,
Aretus, Perseus, great Thrasymedes,
and strong Pisistratus the sixth. They brought
godlike Telemachus to sit with them.
Nestor spoke first.

"Dear sons, now hurry up,
fulfill my wishes. First we must appease
Athena, who revealed herself to me
during the holy feast. Now one of you
must run down to the fields to choose a cow;
let herdsmen drive her back here. And another,
go to Telemachus' ship and bring
the men—leave only two behind. Another
must bring Laerces here, who pours the gold,
so he can gild the heifer's horns. You others,

stay here together. Tell the girls inside
to cook a royal feast, and set out seats,
put wood around the altar, and clear water."

At that, the sons all got to work. The cow
was brought up from the field. The crew arrived
from the swift, solid ship. The goldsmith came
with all the bronze tools useful for his trade—
hammer and anvil and well-crafted tongs—
and worked the gold. Athena came to take
the sacrifice. King Nestor gave the gold;
the craftsman poured it on the horns, to make
a lovely offering to please the goddess.
Stratius and Echephron together led
the heifer by the horns. Aretus came
and brought a water bowl adorned with flowers,
and in his other hand, a box of grain.
Strong Thrasymedes stood nearby and held
a sharpened axe, prepared to strike the cow.
Perseus held the blood-bowl. Nestor started
to sprinkle barley-groats and ritual water,
and as he threw the hairs into the fire
he said prayers to Athena. When the rites
were finished, mighty Thrasymedes struck.
The axe sliced through the sinews of the neck.
The cow was paralyzed. Then Nestor's daughters
and his sons' wives, and his own loyal queen,
Eurydice, began to chant. The men
hoisted the body, and Pisistratus
sliced through her throat. Black blood poured out. The life
was gone. They butchered her, cut out the thighs,
all in the proper place, and covered them
with double fat and placed raw flesh upon them.
The old king burned the pieces on the logs,

and poured the bright red wine. The young men came
to stand beside him holding five-pronged forks.
They burned the thigh-bones thoroughly and tasted
the entrails, then carved up the rest and skewered
the meat on pointed spits, and roasted it.

Meanwhile, Telemachus was being washed
by Nestor's youngest daughter, Polycaste.
When she had washed and rubbed his skin with oil
she dressed him in a tunic and fine cloak
and he emerged; his looks were like a god's.
He sat by Nestor, shepherd of the people.

The meat was roasted and drawn off the spits.
They sat to eat, while trained slaves served the food,
pouring the wine for them in golden cups.
After their hunger and their thirst were gone,
Gerenian Nestor, horse-lord, started talking.

"My sons, now bring two horses with fine manes
and yoke them to the carriage, so our guest
can start his journey."

They obeyed at once,
and quickly latched swift horses to the carriage.
One of the house girls brought out food and wine
and delicacies fit to feed a king.
Telemachus got in the lovely carriage;
Pisistratus, the son of Nestor, followed,
and sat beside him, taking up the reins,
and whipped the horses. Eagerly they flew
off for the open plain, and left the town.
All day they ran and made the harness rattle.
At sunset when the streets grew dark, they came

to Pherae, to the home of Diocles,
son of Ortilochus; Alpheus was
his grandfather. They spent the night as guests.
When rosy-fingered Dawn came bright and early,
they yoked the horses to the painted carriage,
and drove out from the gate and echoing porch.
At a light touch of whip, the horses flew.
Swiftly they drew towards their journey's end,
on through the fields of wheat, until the sun
began to set and shadows filled the streets.

BOOK 4

What the Sea God Said

They came to Sparta, land of caves and valleys,
and drove to Menelaus' house. They found him
hosting a wedding feast for many guests
to celebrate his children's marriages.
In Troy he had declared that he would give
his daughter to Achilles' son, who ruled
the Myrmidons. Now he was sending her,
with dowry gifts of horse-drawn chariots;
the gods had made the marriage come to pass.
And he was welcoming a Spartan bride,
Alector's daughter, for his well-loved son,
strong Megapenthes, mothered by a slave.
The gods had given Helen no more children
after the beautiful Hermione,
image of Aphrodite all in gold.
Neighbors and family were feasting gladly
under the king's high roof. The bard was singing
and strumming, and two acrobats were spinning
and leading them in dance. Telemachus
and Nestor's son stopped by the palace doors

and held their horses. Menelaus' guard,
Eteoneus, ran out and saw them there,
and then hurried back inside to tell his master.

"Your Majesty, there are two men outside,
strangers who seem like sons of Zeus. Please tell me,
should we take off the harness from their horses?
Or send them off to find another host?"

Flushed Menelaus shouted angrily,
"You used to have some brains!
Now you are talking like a silly child.
We two were fed by many different hosts
before returning home. As we may hope
for Zeus to keep us safe in future times,
untack their horses! Lead them in to dine!"

So Eteoneus rushed out from the palace,
and ordered other slaves to follow him.
They freed the sweating horses from their yoke
and tied them by the manger, which they filled
with emmer that they mixed with bright white barley.
They leaned the carriage up against the wall
and led their guests inside the godlike house.
The boys looked round the palace in amazement:
the lofty halls of famous Menelaus
shone like the dazzling light of sun or moon.
When they had satisfied their eyes with staring,
they went to take a bath in polished tubs.
The slave girls helped them wash and rubbed them down
in olive oil, then dressed them in wool cloaks
and tunics, and then seated them beside
the son of Atreus, King Menelaus.
A house girl brought a basin made of silver,

and water in a golden jug. She poured it
over their hands to wash, then set a table
of polished wood beside them, and a humble
slave girl brought bread and many canapés,
a lavish spread. The carver carried platters
with every kind of meat, and set before them
cups made of gold. Then ruddy Menelaus
welcomed them both and told them,

"Help yourselves!
Enjoy the food! When you have shared our meal,
we will begin to ask you who you are.
Your fathers must be scepter-bearing kings;
the sons of peasants do not look like you."

With that, he took the dish of rich roast meat,
cut from the back, which was his special meal,
and offered it to them. They reached their hands
to take the food set out in front of them.
After their thirst and hunger had been sated,
Telemachus turned round to Nestor's son,
ducking his head so no one else could hear.

"Pisistratus! Dear friend, do you see how
these echoing halls are shining bright with bronze,
and silver, gold and ivory and amber?
It is as full of riches as the palace
of Zeus on Mount Olympus! I am struck
with awe." When Menelaus heard his words,
he spoke to them in turn—his words flew out.

"No mortal, my dear boys, can rival Zeus.
His halls and home and property are deathless.
Some man may match my wealth; or maybe not.
I suffered for it. I was lost, adrift

at sea for eight long years. I traipsed through Cyprus,
Phoenicia, Egypt, Ethiopia,
Sidon and Araby, and Libya,
where lambs are born with horns—their ewes give birth
three times a year. The master and his slave
have milk and cheese and meat; the flock provides
sweet milk year round. But while I wandered there
accumulating wealth, someone crept in
and killed my brother; his own scheming wife
betrayed him. I can take no joy in all
my wealth. Whoever they may be, your fathers
have surely told you how much I have suffered!
I lost my lovely home, and I was parted
for many years from all my splendid riches.
I wish I had stayed here, with just a third
of all the treasure I have now acquired,
if those who died at Troy, so far away
from Argive pastures, were alive and well.
I sit here in my palace, mourning all
who died, and often weeping. Sometimes tears
bring comfort to my heart, but not for long;
cold grief grows sickening. I miss them all,
but one man most. When I remember him,
I cannot eat or sleep, since no one labored
like him—Odysseus. His destiny
was suffering, and mine the endless pain
of missing him. We do not even know
if he is still alive—he has been gone
so long. His faithful wife and old Laertes
must grieve for him, and young Telemachus,
who was a newborn when he went away."

These words roused in the boy a desperate need
to mourn his father. Tears rolled down his face
and splashed down on the ground. He lifted up

his cloak to hide his eyes. But Menelaus
noticed and wondered whether he should wait
until the boy first spoke about his father,
or ask. As he was hesitating, Helen
emerged from her high-ceilinged, fragrant bedroom,
like Artemis, who carries golden arrows.
Adraste set a special chair for her,
Alcippe spread upon it soft wool blankets,
and Phylo brought a silver sewing basket,
given to her by Alcandre, the wife
of Polybus, who lived in Thebes, in Egypt,
where people have extraordinary wealth.
He gave two silver tubs to Menelaus,
a pair of tripods and ten pounds of gold.
His wife gave other lovely gifts for Helen:
a golden spindle and this silver basket
on wheels; the rims were finished off with gold.
Phylo, her girl, brought out that basket now,
packed full of yarn she had already spun.
A spindle wound around with purple wool
was laid across it. She sat down and put
her feet upon a stool, and asked her husband,

"Do we know who these men are, Menelaus,
who have arrived here in our house? Shall I
conceal my thoughts or speak? I feel compelled
to say, the sight of them amazes me.
I never saw two people so alike
as this boy and Telemachus, the son
of spirited Odysseus, the child
he left behind, a little newborn baby,
the day the Greeks marched off to Troy, their minds
fixated on the war and violence.
They made my face the cause that hounded them."

High-colored Menelaus answered, "Wife,
I saw the likeness too. Odysseus
had hands like those, those legs, that hair, that head,
that glancing gaze. And when I spoke just now
about Odysseus and all the things
he suffered for my sake, the boy grimaced,
and floods of tears were rolling down his cheeks;
he raised his purple cloak to hide his eyes."

Pisistratus, the son of Nestor, spoke.
"King Menelaus, you are right. This is
truly his son, just as you say he is.
But he is shy and feels he should not speak
too boldly in your presence right away.
Your voice is like a god's to us. Lord Nestor
sent me to guide him here. He longed to see you
to get some news from you or some advice.
A son whose father is away will suffer
intensely, if he has no man at home
to help him. In the absence of his father,
Telemachus has no one to protect him."

Then Menelaus answered, "So the son
of my dear friend, who worked so hard for me,
has come here to my house! I always thought
that I would greet that friend with warmth beyond
all other Argives, if Zeus let us sail
home with all speed across the sea. I would have
brought him from Ithaca, with all his wealth,
his son and people, and bestowed on him
a town in Argos, driving out the natives
from somewhere hereabouts under my rule.
We would have constantly spent time together.
Nothing would have divided us in love
and joy, till death's dark cloud surrounded us.

But I suppose the god begrudged our friendship,
and kept that poor, unlucky man from home."

His words made everybody want to cry.
Helen was weeping, as was Menelaus.
Pisistratus' eyes were full of tears
for irreplaceable Antilochus,
killed by the noble son of shining Dawn.
Mindful of him, he spoke with words like wings.

"King Menelaus, when we spoke of you
back home in our own halls, my father Nestor
always declared you are exceptional
for common sense. So listen now to me.
I disapprove of crying during dinner.
Dawn will soon come; weep then. There is no harm
in mourning when a person dies; it is
the only honor we can pay the dead—
to cut our hair and drench our cheeks with tears.
I had a brother named Antilochus,
one of the bravest fighters in the army,
a sprinter and a warrior. He died.
I never got to meet him or to see him.
Perhaps you did?"

King Menelaus answered,
"My friend, you speak just as a wise man should,
like somebody much older than yourself.
You show your father's wisdom in your speech.
A lineage is easy to discern
when Zeus spins out a life of happiness,
in marriage and in offspring. So he gave
good luck to Nestor all his life; he aged
at home in comfort, and his sons are wise

and skillful spear-men. Yes, we will stop crying
and turn our minds to dinner once again.
Let them pour water on our hands. At dawn,
Telemachus and I can talk at length."

At that Asphalion, the nimble house slave
of mighty Menelaus, poured the water
over their hands. They helped themselves to food
from laden tables. Then the child of Zeus,
Helen, decided she would mix the wine
with drugs to take all pain and rage away,
to bring forgetfulness of every evil.
Whoever drinks this mixture from the bowl
will shed no tears that day, not even if
her mother or her father die, nor even
if soldiers kill her brother or her darling
son with bronze spears before her very eyes.
Helen had these powerful magic drugs
from Polydamna, wife of Thon, from Egypt,
where fertile fields produce the most narcotics:
some good, some dangerous. The people there
are skillful doctors. They are the Healer's people.
She mixed the wine and told the slave to pour it,
and then she spoke again.

"Now Menelaus,
and you two noble sons of noble men,
Zeus gives us good and bad at different times;
he has the power. Sit here then and eat,
and I will entertain you with a story.
Enjoy it; it is fitting to the times.
I cannot tell of all the challenges
steadfast Odysseus has undergone.
But I will tell you what that brave man did

at Troy, when the Achaeans were in trouble.
He beat himself and bruised his body badly
and put a ragged cloak on, like a slave,
then shuffled through the enemy city streets.
In his disguise he seemed a poor old beggar,
hardly a man to sail with the Achaeans.
He crept through Troy like that, and no one knew him
except for me. I saw through his disguise
and questioned him. He was too smart to talk,
acting evasive. But I washed and scrubbed him
with oil and dressed him, and I swore an oath
that I would not reveal him to the Trojans
before he had got back to his own camp.
He told me all the things the Greeks were planning.
On his way back, he used his long bronze sword
to slaughter many Trojans, and he brought
useful intelligence to tell the Greeks.
The Trojan women keened in grief, but I
was glad—by then I wanted to go home.
I wished that Aphrodite had not made me
go crazy, when she took me from my country,
and made me leave my daughter and the bed
I shared with my fine, handsome, clever husband."

And Menelaus said,

"Yes, wife, quite right.
I have been round the world, and I have met
many heroic men and known their minds.
I never saw a man so resolute
as that Odysseus. How tough he was!
And what impressive fortitude he showed
inside the Wooden Horse! We fighters lurked
inside, to bring destruction to the Trojans.

You came there too. Some spirit who desired
to glorify the Trojans urged you on.
Godlike Deiphobus was following you.
Three times you went around the hollow belly,
touching the hiding place, and calling on
us Greeks by name; you put on different voices
for each man's wife. Then I and Diomedes
and good Odysseus, inside the horse,
heard you call out to us, and we two wanted
to go out, or to answer from in there.
Odysseus prevented us from going.
Then all the other sons of the Achaeans
were quiet; Anticlus still wished to answer.
Odysseus' hands clamped shut his mouth
and saved us all. He held him there like that,
until Athena led you far away."

Weighing these words, Telemachus replied,
"But Menelaus, all this makes it worse!
My father's courage could not save his life,
even if he had had a heart of iron.
So now, show us to bed. We need the comfort
of being lulled into a sweet deep sleep."

Then Argive Helen told her girls to spread
beds on the porch and pile on them fine rugs
of purple, and lay blankets over them,
with woolly covers on the very top.
The girls went out with torches in their hands
and made the beds. A slave led out the guests.
Telemachus and Nestor's handsome son
slept in the front room; Menelaus slept
far back inside the lofty house. Beside him
lay marvelous Helen, in her flowing gown.

Soon Dawn was born, her fingers bright with roses.
Gruff Menelaus jumped up out of bed,
got dressed and strapped his sharp sword to his shoulder,
then tied his sandals on his well-oiled feet.
He went out of his bedroom like a god,
approached Telemachus, and spoke to him.

"What need has brought you here, Telemachus,
to Sparta, over such expanse of sea?
Private or public business? Tell me truly!"

Telemachus inhaled and then replied,
"King Menelaus, son of Atreus,
I came in search of news about my father.
My house is being eaten up; our wealth
is ruined. My whole home is full of men
who mean me harm—my mother's loutish suitors.
Each day they kill more sheep, more longhorn cattle.
So I am begging you, here on my knees,
tell me the dreadful news, if he is dead!
Perhaps you saw it with your eyes, or heard
tales of his travels. He was surely born
to suffer in extraordinary ways.
Please do not try to sweeten bitter news
from pity; tell me truly if you saw him,
and how he was. If my heroic father
ever helped you at Troy when things were bad,
keep that in mind right now, and tell the truth."

Flushed, Menelaus shouted out in anger,
"Damn them! Those cowards want to steal the bed
of one whose heart is braver than their own.
As when a deer lays down two newborn fawns,

still sucklings, in the lair of some strong lion,
and goes to look for pasture, over slopes
and grassy valleys; when the lion comes back
to his own bed, he brings down doom on them—
so will Odysseus upon those men.
O Father Zeus, Athena, and Apollo,
I pray he is as strong as when he stood
to wrestle Philomeleides, on Lesbos,
and hurled him to the ground, and we all cheered.
So may Odysseus attack the suitors.
May all their lives be brief, their weddings cursed!
As for your questions, I will not deceive you.
I will not hide a single word I heard
from that old Sea God Proteus. Although
I longed to come back home, away from Egypt,
the gods prevented me, since I had failed
to offer perfect hecatombs. They always
desire obedience. There is an island
out in the sea beside the coast of Egypt,
named Pharos. If a clear wind blows your ship,
it takes all day to travel to that island.
Its harbor has good anchorage, and there
men draw dark water up, and then launch off
to sea. But I was held for twenty days
by gods. No winds appeared to guide my ships
across the water's back. All our supplies
would have been gone, and all our hope; but then
a goddess, Eidothea, pitied me—
the child of Proteus, the old sea god.
She met me pacing sadly all alone.
My men were off around the island, fishing
with hooks, as usual—hunger pinched their bellies.
She stood beside me and she spoke to me.

'Stranger, are you so foolish that you choose
to give up, and take pleasure in your pain?
There is no end in sight; you have been stuck
here on this island for so long. Your men
grow weak at heart.' I answered her and said,
'Whoever you may be—for sure a goddess—
I tell you I am trapped against my will.
I must have sinned against the deathless gods
who live in heaven. Please explain which spirit
is blocking me from going home across
the teeming sea. Gods must know everything.'
That shining goddess answered me at once,
'Stranger, I will be frank with you. A deathless
old sea god haunts this place, named Proteus
of Egypt, who can speak infallibly,
who knows the depths of seas, and serves Poseidon.
They say he is the one who fathered me.
If you can somehow lie in wait and catch him,
he will explain how you can get back home,
plotting your path where fish leap through the waters.
And if you wish it, prince, he will explain
what happened in your home, both good and bad,
while you were gone on this long, painful journey.'
Those were her words. I answered, 'Tell me, please,
how I can trap this ancient god, so he
will not see me too soon, and get away.
It is not easy for a man to catch
a god.' The goddess answered me at once,
'Stranger, I will instruct you thoroughly.
When the sun hits the midpoint of the sky,
the old god bobs above the salty water;
the breath of Zephyr hides him in dark shade.
He goes to take his nap inside the caves.
Around him sleep the clustering seals, the daughters

of lovely Lady Brine. Their breath smells sour
from gray seawater, pungent salty depths.
Select the three best men you have on board,
and when dawn breaks, I will take all of you
down to the shore, and set you in a line.
Let me explain the old god's tricks. He will
first count the seals and walk around among them.
When he has counted them and checked them all,
he lies down in the middle, like a shepherd
among his flock of sheep. When you observe
him sleeping, gather all your force and strength,
and hold him there, despite his desperate struggles.
In trying to escape, he will change shape
to every animal on earth, and then
water and holy fire. You must hold fast
unshaken, and press harder; keep him down.
At last he will assume again the form
in which he went to sleep, and he will speak
and question you. Then, warrior, release
your forceful hold on that old god, and ask him
which god is angry with you, and the way
to cross the fish-filled waters and go home.'
With that she sank beneath the deep sea waves.
I went down to the ships upon the sand.
My heart was surging in me as I walked.
Arriving at the ships and at the shore,
we made our meal. Then came immortal night;
we went to sleep beside the water's edge.
When Dawn appeared, her fingers bright with flowers,
I walked beside the spreading sea, along
the dunes, and prayed intensely to the gods.
Then I chose out my three most trusted men.
The goddess dove down deep inside the sea
and brought four sealskins up from underwater,

new-flayed—to help her plot against her father.
She scooped out hiding places in the sand,
and sat to wait. We came right up to her.
She laid us in a row, and put a skin
on each. It would have been a dismal hideout,
stinking of salt-bred seals. Who would lie down
to rest beside a creature from the sea?
But she brought sweet ambrosia to save us.
She very kindly put it in our nostrils,
to take away the stench of seal. We waited
all morning, apprehensively. And then
out of the sea there rose a pod of seals;
they lay along the shore. At noon the god
emerged above the waves. He went among
his fatted seals and counted out their number.
He counted us among the first of them,
suspecting nothing. Then he lay down too.
With a great shout we pounced on him and grabbed him.
The old god still remembered all his tricks,
and first became a lion with a mane,
then snake, then leopard, then a mighty boar,
then flowing water, then a leafy tree.
But we kept holding on: our hearts stood firm.
At last that ancient sorcerer grew tired,
and then he asked me, 'Son of Atreus!
What god devised this plan with you and taught you
to lurk and capture me against my will?
What do you want from me?' And I replied,
'Old god, why do you want to throw me off?
You know I have been trapped here on this island
for far too long, with no way out; my heart
grows faint. So tell me—gods know everything—
what spirit stops my journey? And how can I
get home across the watery shoals of fish?'

At once he answered me and told me this:
'You should have given Zeus and other gods
fine offerings, to speed your journey home
across the wine-dark sea. It is your fate
not to go home or see the ones you love
until you go again to Egypt's river,
watered by Zeus, and kill a hundred cows,
to please the deathless gods who live in heaven.
Then they will let you travel where you wish.'
I felt heartbroken that I had to cross
the misty sea and go again to Egypt:
a long and bitter journey! But I answered,
'Sir, I will do exactly as you say.
But come now, tell me this, and tell me truly,
did all the Greeks sail safely home by ship,
whom Nestor and myself left there in Troy?
Did any meet a dreadful death at sea,
on his own ship, or in familiar arms,
after the war wound up?' When I said this,
at once he answered me and said these words.
'O son of Atreus! Why ask me this?
You have no need to know or learn my mind.
When I have told you, you will not be long
able to hold back tears. So many men
were killed, and many left behind at Troy.
Just two of all the bronze-clad captains died
while traveling back home; one more perhaps
may be alive, trapped somewhere out at sea.
Ajax was drowned; his ships were sunk. Poseidon
first drove him to the rocks of Gyrae, then
rescued him from the sea; he would have lived,
despite Athena's hatred, but he made
a crazy boast—that he survived the waves
against the wishes of the gods. Poseidon

heard his rash words. At once, he seized his trident
in mighty hands, and hit the Gyran rock.
One half remained; the other, on which Ajax
sat as he boasted, cracked right off and fell
into the sea, and carried him deep down.
The boundless waves washed over him; he drank
the salty brine, and died. But Agamemnon
survived—the goddess Hera saved his fleet.
When he had almost reached the craggy mountain
of Malea, a gust of wind took hold
and bore him over waves where fish were jumping,
across the rumbling depths to where all farms
are finished, where Thyestes used to live,
and now his son Aegisthus. After that,
the route was clear: the gods made all winds fair.
Then joyfully he stepped foot in his country,
and touched and kissed the earth of his dear home.
He wept hot floods of tears, from happiness.
But from the lookout post the watchman saw him.
Scheming Aegisthus paid that man two talents
of gold to watch all year, so Agamemnon
could not slip past unseen, or summon up
his will to fight. The spy rushed off to tell
the King. Aegisthus formed a plan at once.
He chose the twenty best men in the land
to lurk in ambush, and he told the house slaves
to cook a feast. He rode out on his carriage,
and summoned Agamemnon, who suspected
nothing. Aegisthus killed him over dinner,
just as a person kills an ox at manger.
All of the men who came with him were killed,
and all those of Aegisthus; all were killed.'

His story broke my heart, and I sat down
upon the sands and wept. I did not want
to go on living or to see the sun.
I thrashed around and wailed. When I was done,
the old Sea God spoke words of truth to me.
'Now, son of Atreus, your endless weeping
has gone on long enough. It does no good.
Quickly, go home. You may still find Aegisthus
alive, or else Orestes may have come
and killed him; you can join his funeral.'
Those words made me a man again: my heart
was warmed inside, despite my grief. My words
took wings. I said, 'I know now of those two;
but name the third who may be still alive,
trapped somewhere in the wide expanse of sea,
or may be dead. I know the news may hurt,
but still I want to hear it.' And he answered,
'It is Laertes' son, the Ithacan.
I saw him crying, shedding floods of tears
upon Calypso's island, in her chambers.
She traps him there; he cannot go back home.
He has no boats with oars or crew to row him
across the sea's broad back to his own land.
But Menelaus, it is not your fate
to die in Argos. Gods will carry you
off to the world's end, to Elysium.
Those fields are ruled by tawny Rhadamanthus
and life is there the easiest for humans.
There is no snow, no heavy storms or rain,
but Ocean always sends up gentle breezes
of Zephyr to refresh the people there.
You gain these blessings as the son-in-law
of Zeus through Helen.' Then the old god sank

beneath the waves. I went back to my ships
and godlike men, and as I walked my mind
swirled with my many thoughts. Beside the fleet
we cooked and ate our meal, then holy night
came down; we slept beside the surging water.
When early Dawn appeared and touched the sky
with blossom, first we launched the balanced ships
into the salty sea, put up the masts
and fixed the sails, and then the men embarked
and sat on benches neatly, in their lines.
And then at once they struck the sea with oars.
We soon reached Egypt's holy rain-fed river.
We docked the ships and sacrificed the oxen.
When I had quenched the anger of the gods,
I built a mound to honor Agamemnon,
for his immortal fame. The gods at last
gave me fair wind, and sent me quickly home.
But come now, stay with me here in my palace,
until eleven days or twelve have passed.
Then I will send you off with precious gifts,
three horses and a gleaming chariot.
Also a lovely cup so you can pour
gifts to the gods, and always think of me."

Then tactfully Telemachus replied,
"Please do not keep me here so long, my lord.
Indeed, I would be glad to stay a year;
I would not even miss my home or parents—
I get such pleasure listening to you.
But my poor friends are surely tired of waiting
in Pylos. You have made me stay too long.
And for a gift, please only give me treasure.
You keep your lovely horses here; I cannot
transport them all the way to Ithaca.

You rule these open meadows, rich in clover,
white barley in wide rows, and wheat and grass.
In Ithaca, there are no fields or racetracks.
Though it is only fit for goats, we love it
more than horse pasture. Islands out at sea
have no good grazing—ours the least of all."

Then Menelaus smiled and clasped his hand,
and spoke to him in his loud booming voice.

"My boy, your words are proof of your good blood.
I will give different gifts, just as you ask.
I will give you the finest piece of treasure
of all the hoard I have piled up at home:
a finely crafted bowl, of purest silver,
with gold around the rim. Hephaestus made it,
and Phaedimus the king of Sidon gave it
to me, when I was visiting his house
as I was traveling home. You can have that."

Such was their conversation. Then the guests
entered the palace, bringing lamb and wine
that gives one confidence. The girls, all dressed
in pretty scarves, brought bread for them. So went
the feasting in the house of Menelaus.

Meanwhile, outside Odysseus' house,
the suitors were as arrogant as usual,
enjoying throwing discuses and spears
out on the playing field. The two chief suitors,
were sitting there: Antinous and godlike
Eurymachus. Just then Noëmon, son
of Phronius, approached and asked a question.

"So do we know, Antinous, or not,
whether Telemachus is coming back
from sandy Pylos? He left with my ship.
I need it, to cross over to the fields
of Elis, where I have twelve mares with mules
suckling their teats and not yet broken in.
I want to take and train one."

They were all
astonished, since they had not thought the boy
was gone to Pylos, but was somewhere near,
out with the sheep or pigs. Antinous
said,

"Tell me the truth, when did he go? And who
went with him? Did he choose some Ithacans,
or slaves and laborers? It could be either.
And tell me also, did he steal the ship
from you by force, or did you give it to him
freely, because he asked?"

Noëmon, son
of Phronius, replied, "I gave it freely.
What could I do, when someone so upset
was asking me? A noble boy like that?
It would have been ungracious to refuse.
The young men who were with him were high class,
the best in town except ourselves. I saw
Mentor embark as captain—or perhaps
not Mentor but a god who looked like him.
This puzzles me, that yesterday at dawn
I saw great Mentor here, though he had gone
to Pylos in the ship."

With that, Noëmon
departed for his father's house. Those leaders
were furious. At once they made the suitors
stop playing games and sit. Antinous
spoke up with eyes bright as fire, his mind
darkened with anger.

"Damn! That stuck-up boy
succeeded in his stupid trip. We thought
he would not manage it. Telemachus
has launched a ship and picked an ideal crew,
despite us all! This is the start of worse.
May Zeus destroy his strength before he reaches
manhood. Give me a ship and twenty men,
so I may watch and catch him in the strait
in between Ithaca and craggy Same.
A sad end to this journey for his father!"

All of them praised his words, endorsed his plan,
and went inside Odysseus' palace.
Penelope was soon aware of all
the suitors' secret plots. The house boy Medon
told her, since he had been outside the courtyard
and he had heard the plans they were devising.
He rushed to tell her. As he stepped inside,
across the threshold, she came up and asked him,

"Well, boy, why have those lordly suitors sent you?
To tell godlike Odysseus' girls
to stop their work and make a feast for them?
I hope this is their final meal! I hope
they never gather elsewhere to go courting!
You suitors who come crowding here are wasting
Telemachus' wealth! When you were younger

you never paid attention to your fathers
who told you of Odysseus' greatness.
He never spoke or acted without justice,
among the people. Lords are mostly biased;
they favor one person and hate another.
But he did not. He did no wrong at all.
Now you! Your wicked deeds and plans are clear.
No gratitude for favors from the past!"

Then knowledgeable Medon answered her,
"My Queen, I wish this were the worst of it.
Now they are plotting even greater ruin.
May Zeus ensure it never comes to pass!
The suitors want to kill Telemachus
with sharp bronze weapons on his journey home.
He went to sandy Pylos and to Sparta
for word about his father."

At the news,
her legs grew weak; her heart sank; she was struck
dumb for a time, her voice blocked as her eyes
filled up with tears. At last she answered him,
"But why did my son go away? There was
no need to go on those swift ships that gallop
like horses over miles of salty water.
Did he intend to lose his name as well,
and be unknown?"

And Medon said, "Perhaps
some god or his own heart nudged him to go
to Pylos to find out about his father,
if he will come back home, or if he has
already met his fate." With that, he left her.

Grief wrapped around her, eating at her heart.
The house was full of chairs but she could not
bear to sit upright. In her bedroom doorway,
collapsing on the floor, she wept and cried.
Around her all her women, young and old,
were whimpering. Voice thick with tears, she sobbed,

"Friends, listen! Zeus has cursed me more than all
the women of my family. Already
I lost my noble, lionhearted husband,
most talented and brave of all the Greeks,
whose fame is spread through Greece. And now the winds
have taken my dear son, and no one told me
that he was setting out. Shame on you all!
You knew that he was leaving in that ship!
Not one of you came here to wake me up!
If only I had known about his journey,
he would have stayed—no matter how he wanted
to leave—or else have left me dead right here.
Now call old Dolius, my gardener,
the slave who cares for all my trees. My father
gave him to me when I came here. Tell him
to hurry off and sit beside Laertes,
and tell him everything; he may decide
to go in tears to plead with those who want
to kill godlike Odysseus' son,
his grandson."

Then the loyal Eurycleia
said, "Lady, sweetheart, even if you take
a sword and kill me, I will tell the truth.
I knew all this. I gave him what he asked for,
bread and sweet wine. He made me swear an oath
not to inform you, till twelve days had passed,

or till you heard about it, and you missed him,
so that you would not cry and spoil your beauty.
Now have a bath, get changed into clean clothes,
go with your slave girls upstairs to your room.
Pray to Athena, child of Zeus the King.
She may save him from death. And do not bother
poor old Laertes; he has pain enough.
I do not think the blessed gods despise
this family; I trust that there will always
be one to rule this house and rich estate."

This soothed Penelope. She dried her tears,
and took her bath and got dressed in clean clothes,
then went up to her bedroom with her girls.
She put some barley on a tray and prayed.

"Hear me, Athena, tireless child of Zeus,
if my quick-minded husband ever gave you
fat thighs of beef or lamb here in our halls,
remember now and save the son I love.
Protect him from the abuses of those suitors!"
She wailed aloud; the goddess heard her prayer.

The suitors made a racket that resounded
all through the palace shadows. They were boasting,
"This queen whom all of us have come here courting
is ready now to marry one of us,
and does not even know her son will die!"
They spoke not knowing how things really stood.
Antinous declared to them,

"My lords,
you have to stop this bragging! Quiet down,
or those inside will hear it. Now get up

in silence. We must go and follow through
the plan we all agreed on in our hearts."

With that, he picked the twenty strongest men.
They went down to the seashore; first of all
they launched the swift black ship in deep saltwater,
set up the mast and raised the sails and fit
the oars in proper order in the straps
of leather, then spread out the bright white sails.
With confidence their slaves dealt out the weapons.
They moored high up the stream and disembarked.
They ate there, while they waited for the evening.

Penelope lay upstairs in her bedroom,
refusing food and drink, consuming nothing.
She wondered if her fine son would escape
from death, or be brought down by those proud suitors.
Her mind was like a lion caught by humans,
terrified, as they throng and circle round him,
trying to trap him; so sweet drowsiness
subdued her and she slept, her limbs relaxed.

Athena, bright-eyed goddess, had a plan.
She made a phantom looking like a woman,
Iphthime, child of great Icarius,
the wife of Eumelus who lived in Pherae.
She sent it to Odysseus' house,
to make Penelope feel less distressed
and stop her tears of grief. It traveled through
the latch's thong, and in her bedroom stood
above her head, and asked,

"Penelope,
Are you asleep? And are you still upset?

The gods who live at ease have no desire
for you to weep or worry. Know, your son
is coming home. He has not wronged the gods."

Intelligent Penelope, still sleeping
sweetly inside the gates of dreams, replied,

"Sister, why have you come? Your house is far,
and you have never visited before.
You tell me to stop grieving and not feel
the many pains that prickle at my heart.
But long ago I lost my lionhearted
husband, a man more talented than any,
famous throughout all Greece. Now my dear son
has sailed off in a ship, though he knows nothing
of hardship and the world; he is a child.
I worry for him more than for his father.
I shudder, I am scared of what may happen,
at sea, or in the country that he went to.
He has so many enemies; they plan
to murder him before he reaches home."

The misty phantom answered her, "Have courage.
Let not your heart be troubled or afraid.
He has a goddess as his guide—Athena,
a helper many men have prayed to have.
She has great power. Pitying your grief,
she sent me here to tell you all of this."

Careful Penelope replied, "If you
are actually a god, with news from gods,
tell me about my husband too, poor man!
Tell if he is alive and sees the sun,
or dead already in the house of Hades!"

The spirit said, "I cannot tell you whether
he is alive or dead. It is not good
to speak of things intangible as wind."

With that, the phantom floated through the air
into the breeze. And then Penelope
woke up from sleep, and she was glad at heart,
because she dreamed so clearly in the night.

The suitors got on board and sailed across
the water, set on murdering the boy.
There is a rocky island out at sea,
in between Ithaca and craggy Same,
called Asteris—quite small but with a harbor
to shelter ships, and there they lurked in ambush.

BOOK 5

From the Goddess to the Storm

Then Dawn rose up from bed with Lord Tithonus,
to bring the light to deathless gods and mortals.
The gods sat down for council, with the great
Thunderlord Zeus. Athena was concerned
about Odysseus' many troubles,
trapped by the nymph Calypso in her house.

"Father, and all immortal gods," she said,
"No longer let a sceptered king be kind,
or gentle, or pay heed to right and wrong.
Let every king be cruel, his acts unjust!
Odysseus ruled gently, like a father,
but no one even thinks about him now.
The wretched man is stranded on an island;
Calypso forces him to stay with her.
He cannot make his way back to his country.
He has no ships, no oars, and no companions
to help him sail across the wide-backed sea.
His son has gone for news of his lost father,

in sandy Pylos and in splendid Sparta;
they plot to kill the boy when he returns!"

Smiling at her, Lord Zeus who heaps the clouds
replied, "Ah, daughter! What a thing to say!
Did you not plan all this yourself, so that
Odysseus could come and take revenge
upon those suitors? Now use all your skill:
ensure Telemachus comes safely home,
and that the suitors fail and sail away."

Then turning to his son he said, "Dear Hermes,
you are my messenger. Go tell the goddess
our fixed intention: that Odysseus
must go back home—he has endured enough.
Without a god or human as his guide,
he will drift miserably for twenty days
upon a makeshift raft, and then arrive
at fertile Scheria. The magical
Phaeacians will respect him like a god,
and send him in a ship to his dear homeland,
with gifts of bronze and heaps of gold and clothing,
more than he would have brought with him from Troy
if he had come directly, with his share
of plunder. It is granted him to see
the ones he loves, beneath his own high roof,
in his own country."

Hermes heard these words.
At once he fastened on his feet the sandals
of everlasting gold with which he flies
on breath of air across the sea and land;
he seized the wand he uses to enchant

men's eyes to sleep or wake as he desires,
and flew. The god flashed bright in all his power.
He touched Pieria, then from the sky
he plunged into the sea and swooped between
the waves, just like a seagull catching fish,
wetting its whirring wings in tireless brine.
So Hermes scudded through the surging swell.
Then finally, he reached the distant island,
stepped from the indigo water to the shore,
and reached the cavern where the goddess lived.

There sat Calypso with her braided curls.
Beside the hearth a mighty fire was burning.
The scent of citrus and of brittle pine
suffused the island. Inside, she was singing
and weaving with a shuttle made of gold.
Her voice was beautiful. Around the cave
a luscious forest flourished: alder, poplar,
and scented cypress. It was full of wings.
Birds nested there but hunted out at sea:
the owls, the hawks, the gulls with gaping beaks.
A ripe and verdant vine, hung thick with grapes,
was stretched to coil around her cave. Four springs
spurted with sparkling water as they laced
with crisscross currents intertwined together.
The meadow softly bloomed with celery
and violets. He gazed around in wonder
and joy, at sights to please even a god.
Even the deathless god who once killed Argos
stood still, his heart amazed at all he saw.
At last he went inside the cave. Calypso,
the splendid goddess, knew the god on sight:
the deathless gods all recognize each other,
however far away their homes may be.

But Hermes did not find Odysseus,
since he was sitting by the shore as usual,
sobbing in grief and pain; his heart was breaking.
In tears he stared across the fruitless sea.

Divine Calypso told her guest to sit
upon a gleaming, glittering chair, and said,
"Dear friend, Lord Hermes of the golden wand,
why have you come? You do not often visit.
What do you have in mind? My heart inclines
to help you if I can, if it is fated.
For now, come in, and let me make you welcome."

At that the goddess led him to a table
heaped with ambrosia, and she mixed a drink:
red nectar. So swift-flashing Hermes drank
and ate till he was satisfied, and then
the diplomat explained why he had come.

"You are a goddess, I a god—and yet
you ask why I am here. Well, I will tell you.
Zeus ordered me to come—I did not want to.
Who would desire to cross such an expanse
of endless salty sea? No human town
is near here, where gods get fine sacrifices.
Still, none can sway or check the will of Zeus.
He says the most unhappy man alive
is living here—a warrior from those
who fought the town of Priam for nine years
and in the tenth they sacked it and sailed home.
But on the journey back, they wronged Athena.
She roused the wind and surging sea against them
and all his brave companions were destroyed,
while he himself was blown here by the waves.
Zeus orders you to send him on his way

at once, since it is not his destiny
to die here far away from those he loves.
It is his fate to see his family
and come back home, to his own native land."

Calypso shuddered and let fly at him.
"You cruel, jealous gods! You bear a grudge
whenever any goddess takes a man
to sleep with as a lover in her bed.
Just so the gods who live at ease were angry
when rosy-fingered Dawn took up Orion,
and from her golden throne, chaste Artemis
attacked and killed him with her gentle arrows.
Demeter with the cornrows in her hair
indulged her own desire, and she made love
with Iasion in triple-furrowed fields—
till Zeus found out, hurled flashing flame and killed him.
So now, you male gods are upset with me
for living with a man. A man I saved!
Zeus pinned his ship and with his flash of lightning
smashed it to pieces. All his friends were killed
out on the wine-dark sea. This man alone,
clutching the keel, was swept by wind and wave,
and came here, to my home. I cared for him
and loved him, and I vowed to set him free
from time and death forever. Still, I know
no other god can change the will of Zeus.
So let him go, if that is Zeus' order,
across the barren sea. I will not give
an escort for this trip across the water;
I have no ships or rowers. But I will
share what I know with him, and gladly give
useful advice so he can safely reach
his home."

The mediator, Zeus' servant,
replied, "Then send him now, avoid the wrath
of Zeus, do not enrage him, or one day
his rage will hurt you." With these words, he vanished.

Acknowledging the edict sent from Zeus,
the goddess went to find Odysseus.
She found him on the shore. His eyes were always
tearful; he wept sweet life away, in longing
to go back home, since she no longer pleased him.
He had no choice. He spent his nights with her
inside her hollow cave, not wanting her
though she still wanted him. By day he sat
out on the rocky beach, in tears and grief,
staring in heartbreak at the fruitless sea.

The goddess stood by him and said, "Poor man!
Stop grieving, please. You need not waste your life.
I am quite ready now to send you off.
Using your sword of bronze, cut trunks and build
a raft, fix decks across, and let it take you
across the misty sea. I will provide
water, red wine, and food, to stop you starving,
and I will give you clothes, and send a wind
to blow you safely home, if this is what
those sky gods want. They are more powerful
than me; they get their way."

Odysseus,
informed by many years of pain and loss,
shuddered and let his words fly out at her.
"Goddess, you have some other scheme in mind,
not my safe passage. You are telling me
to cross this vast and terrifying gulf,

in just a raft, when even stable schooners
sped on by winds from Zeus would not succeed?
No, goddess, I will not get on a raft,
unless you swear to me a mighty oath
you are not planning yet more pain for me."

At that, divine Calypso smiled at him.
She reached out and caressed him with her hand,
saying, "You scalawag! What you have said
shows that you understand how these things work.
But by this earth, and by the sky above,
and by the waters of the Styx below,
which is the strongest oath for blessed gods,
I swear I will not plot more pain for you.
I have made plans for you as I would do
for my own self, if I were in your place.
I am not made of iron; no, my heart
is kind and decent, and I pity you."

And with those words, the goddess quickly turned
and led the way; he followed in her footsteps.
They reached the cave together, man and goddess.
The chair that Hermes had been sitting on
was empty now; Odysseus sat there.
The goddess gave him human food and drink.
She sat and faced godlike Odysseus
while slave girls brought her nectar and ambrosia.
They reached to take the good things set before them,
and satisfied their hunger and their thirst.

The goddess-queen began. "Odysseus,
son of Laertes, blessed by Zeus—your plans
are always changing. Do you really want

to go back to that home you love so much?
Well then, good-bye! But if you understood
how glutted you will be with suffering
before you reach your home, you would stay here
with me and be immortal—though you might
still wish to see that wife you always pine for.
And anyway, I know my body is
better than hers is. I am taller too.
Mortals can never rival the immortals
in beauty."

So Odysseus, with tact,
said "Do not be enraged at me, great goddess.
You are quite right. I know my modest wife
Penelope could never match your beauty.
She is a human; you are deathless, ageless.
But even so, I want to go back home,
and every day I hope that day will come.
If some god strikes me on the wine-dark sea,
I will endure it. By now I am used
to suffering—I have gone through so much,
at sea and in the war. Let this come too."

The sun went down and brought the darkness on.
They went inside the hollow cave and took
the pleasure of their love, held close together.

When vernal Dawn first touched the sky with flowers,
they rose and dressed: Odysseus put on
his cloak and tunic, and Calypso wore
her fine long robe of silver. Round her waist
she wrapped a golden belt, and veiled her head.
Then she prepared the journey for the man.

She gave an axe that fitted in his grip,
its handle made of finest olive wood;
its huge bronze blade was sharp on either side.
She also gave a polished adze. She led him
out to the island's end, where tall trees grew:
black poplar, alder, fir that touched the sky,
good for a nimble boat of seasoned timber.
When she had shown him where the tall trees grew,
Calypso, queen of goddesses, went home.
Odysseus began and made good progress.
With his bronze axe he cut down twenty trunks,
polished them skillfully and planed them straight.
Calypso brought a gimlet and he drilled
through every plank and fitted them together,
fixing it firm with pegs and fastenings.
As wide as when a man who knows his trade
marks out the curving hull to fit a ship,
so wide Odysseus marked out his raft.
He notched the side decks to the close-set frame
and fixed long planks along the ribs to finish.
He set a mast inside, and joined to it
a yardarm and a rudder to steer straight.
He heaped the boat with brush, and caulked the sides
with wickerwork, to keep the water out.
Calypso brought him fabric for a sail,
and he constructed that with equal skill.
He fastened up the braces, clews and halyards,
and using levers, launched her on the sea.

The work had taken four days; on the fifth
Calypso let him go. She washed and dressed him
in clothes that smelled of incense. On the raft
she put a flask of wine, a bigger flask
of water, and a large supply of food.

She sent him off with gentle, lukewarm breezes.
Gladly Odysseus spread out his sails
to catch the wind; with skill he steered the rudder.
No sleep fell on his eyes; he watched the stars,
the Pleiades, late-setting Boötes,
and Bear, which people also call the Plow,
which circles in one place, and marks Orion—
the only star that has no share of Ocean.
Calypso, queen of goddesses, had told him
to keep the Bear on his left side while sailing.
He sailed the sea for seven days and ten,
and on the eighteenth day, a murky mountain
of the Phaeacian land appeared—it rose
up like a shield beyond the misty sea.

Returning from the Ethiopians,
and pausing on Mount Solyma, Poseidon,
Master of Earthquakes, saw the distant raft.
Enraged, he shook his head and told himself,

"This is outrageous! So it seems the gods
have changed their plans about Odysseus
while I was absent! He has almost reached
Phaeacia, where it is his destiny
to flee the rope of pain that binds him now.
But I will goad him to more misery,
till he is sick of it."

He gathered up
the clouds, and seized his trident and stirred round
the sea and roused the gusts of every wind,
and covered earth and sea with fog. Night stretched
from heaven. Eurus, Notus, blasting Zephyr
and Boreas, the child of sky, all fell

and rolled a mighty wave. Odysseus
grew weak at knees. He cried out in despair,

"More pain? How will it end? I am afraid
the goddess spoke the truth: that I will have
a sea of sufferings before I reach
my homeland. It is coming true! Zeus whirls
the air. Look at those clouds! He agitates
the waves, as winds attack from all directions.
I can hold on to one thing: certain death.
Those Greeks were lucky, three and four times over,
who died upon the plain of Troy to help
the sons of Atreus. I wish I had
died that same day the mass of Trojans hurled
their bronze-tipped spears at me around the corpse
of Peleus' son. I would have had
a funeral, and honor from the Greeks;
but now I have to die this cruel death!"

A wave crashed onto him, and overturned
the raft, and he fell out. The rudder slipped
out of his hands. The winds blew all directions
and one enormous gust snapped off the mast.
The sail and yardarm drifted out to sea.
Then for a long time rushing, crashing waves
kept him submerged: he could not reach the surface.
The clothes Calypso gave him weighed him down.
At last he rose and spat the sour saltwater
out of his mouth—it gushed forth in a torrent.
Despite his pain and weakness, he remembered
his raft, and lunged to get it through the waves;
he climbed on top of it and clung to life.
The great waves carried it this way and that.
As when the thistles, clumping close together,

are borne across the prairie by the North Wind,
so these winds swept the raft across the sea.
The South Wind hurls it, then the North Wind grabs it,
then East Wind yields and lets the West Wind drive it.
But stepping softly, Ino, the White Goddess,
Cadmus' child, once human, human-voiced,
now honored with the gods in salty depths,
noticed that he was suffering and lost,
with pity. Like a gull with wings outstretched
she rose up from the sea, sat on the raft
and said,

"Poor man! Why does enraged Poseidon
create an odyssey of pain for you?
But his hostility will not destroy you.
You seem intelligent. Do as I say.
Strip off your clothes and leave the raft behind
for winds to take away. With just your arms
swim to Phaeacia. Fate decrees that there
you will survive. Here, take my scarf and tie it
under your chest: with this immortal veil,
you need not be afraid of death or danger.
But when you reach dry earth, untie the scarf
and throw it out to sea, away from land,
and turn away." With that, the goddess gave it,
and plunged back down inside the surging sea,
just like a gull. The black wave covered her.

The hero who had suffered so much danger
was troubled and confused. He asked himself,
"Some deity has said to leave the raft.
But what if gods are weaving tricks again?
I will not trust her yet: with my own eyes
I saw the land she said I should escape to,

and it is far away. I will do this:
as long as these wood timbers hold together,
I will hang on, however hard it is.
But when the waves have smashed my raft to pieces,
then I will have no choice, and I will swim."

While he was thinking this, the Lord of Earthquakes,
Poseidon, roused a huge and dreadful wave
that arched above his head: he hurled it at him.
As when a fierce wind ruffles up a heap
of dry wheat chaff; it scatters here and there;
so were the raft's long timbers flung apart.
He climbed astride a plank and rode along
as if on horseback. He took off the clothes
Calypso gave him, but he tied the scarf
around his chest, and dove into the sea,
spreading his arms to swim. The Lord of Earthquakes
saw him and nodded, muttering, "At last
you are in pain! Go drift across the sea,
till you meet people blessed by Zeus, the Sky Lord.
But even then, I think you will not lack
for suffering." He spurred his fine-maned horses,
and went to Aegae, where he had his home.

Athena, child of Zeus, devised a plan.
She blocked the path of all the other winds,
told them to cease and made them go to sleep,
but roused swift Boreas and smoothed the waves
in front of him, so that Odysseus
could reach Phaeacia and escape from death.

Two days and nights he drifted on the waves:
each moment he expected he would die.
But when the Dawn with dazzling braids brought day

for the third time, the wind died down. No breeze,
but total calm. As he was lifted up
by an enormous wave, he scanned around,
and saw the shore nearby. As when a father
lies sick and weak for many days, tormented
by some cruel spirit, till at last the gods
restore him back to life; his children feel
great joy; Odysseus felt that same joy
when he saw land. He swam and longed to set
his feet on earth. But when he was in earshot,
he heard the boom of surf against the rocks.
The mighty waves were crashing on the shore,
a dreadful belching. Everything was covered
in salty foam. There were no sheltering harbors
for ships, just sheer crags, reefs and solid cliffs.
Odysseus' heart and legs gave way.
Shaken but purposeful, he told himself,

"Zeus went beyond my hopes and let me see
dry land! I made it, cutting the abyss!
But I see no way out from this gray sea.
There are steep cliffs offshore, and all around
the rushing water roars; the rock runs sheer;
the sea is deep near shore; there is no way
to set my feet on land without disaster.
If I attempt to scramble out, a wave
will seize and dash me on the jagged rock;
a useless effort. But if I swim on farther,
looking for bays or coves or slanting beaches,
storm winds may seize me once again and drag me,
howling with grief, towards the fish-filled sea.
A god may even send a great sea-monster,
the kind that famous Amphitrite rears.
I know Poseidon wants to do me harm."

As he was thinking this, the waves grew big
and hurled him at the craggy shore. His skin
would have been ripped away, and his bones smashed,
had not Athena given him a thought.
He grabbed a rock as he was swept along
with both hands, and clung to it, groaning, till
the wave passed by. But then the swell rushed back,
and struck him hard and hurled him out to sea.
As when an octopus, dragged from its den,
has many pebbles sticking to its suckers,
so his strong hands were skinned against the rocks.
A mighty wave rolled over him again.
He would have died too soon, in misery,
without the inspiration of Athena.
He came up from the wave that spewed to shore
and swam towards the land, in search of beaches
with gradual slopes, or inlets from the sea.
He swam until he reached a river's mouth
with gentle waters; that place seemed ideal,
smooth and not stony, sheltered from the wind.
He sensed its current; in his heart he prayed,

"Unknown god, hear me! How I longed for you!
I have escaped the salt sea and Poseidon.
Even the deathless gods respect a man
who is as lost as I am now. I have
gone through so much and reached your flowing streams.
Pity me, lord! I am your supplicant."

The current ceased; the River God restrained
the waves and made them calm. He brought him safe
into the river mouth. His legs cramped up;
the sea had broken him. His swollen body

gushed brine from mouth and nostrils. There he lay,
winded and silent, hardly fit to move.
A terrible exhaustion overcame him.
When he could breathe and think again, he took
the goddess' scarf off, and let it go
into the river flowing to the sea;
strong currents swept it down and Ino's hands
took it. He crawled on land and crouched beside
the reeds and bent to kiss life-giving earth,
and trembling, he spoke to his own heart.

"What now? What will become of me? If I
stay up all wretched night beside this river,
the cruel frost and gentle dew together
may finish me: my life is thin with weakness.
At dawn a cold breeze blows beside the river.
But if I climb the slope to those dark woods
and go to rest in that thick undergrowth,
letting sweet sleep take hold of me, and losing
my cold and weariness—wild beasts may find me
and treat me as their prey."

But he decided
to go into the woods. He found a place
beside a clearing, near the water's edge.
He crawled beneath two bushes grown together,
of olive and thorn. No strong wet wind could blow
through them, no shining sunbeam ever strike them,
no rain could penetrate them; they were growing
so thickly intertwined. Odysseus
crept under, and he scraped a bed together,
of leaves: there were enough to cover two
against the worst of winter. Seeing this,

the hero who had suffered for so long
was happy. He lay down inside and heaped
more leaves on top. As when a man who lives
out on a lonely farm that has no neighbors
buries a glowing torch inside black embers
to save the seed of fire and keep a source—
so was Odysseus concealed in leaves.
Athena poured down sleep to shut his eyes
so all his painful weariness could end.

BOOK 6

A Princess and Her Laundry

Odysseus had suffered. In exhaustion
from all his long ordeals, the hero slept.
Meanwhile, Athena went to the Phaeacians.
This people used to live in Hyperia,
a land of dancing. But their mighty neighbors,
the Cyclopes, kept looting them, and they
could not hold out. Their king, Nausithous,
brought them to Scheria, a distant place,
and built a wall around the town, and homes,
and temples to the gods, and plots of land.
He went to Hades. Then Alcinous,
who has god-given wisdom, came to power.
Bright-eyed Athena traveled to his palace,
to help Odysseus' journey home.
She went inside the decorated bedroom
where the young princess, Nausicaa, was sleeping,
as lovely as a goddess. Slaves were sleeping
outside her doorway, one on either side;
two charming girls with all the Graces' gifts.
The shining doors were shut, but like the wind

the goddess reached the bed of Nausicaa,
disguised as her best friend, a girl her age,
the daughter of the famous sailor Dymas.
Sharp-eyed Athena said,

"Oh, Nausicaa!
So lazy! But your mother should have taught you!
Your clothes are lying there in dirty heaps,
though you will soon be married, and you need
a pretty dress to wear, and clothes to give
to all your bridesmaids. That impresses people,
and makes the parents happy. When day comes,
we have to do the laundry. I will come
and help you, so the work will soon be done.
Surely you will not long remain unmarried.
The best young men here in your native land
already want to court you. So at dawn
go ask your father for the cart with mules,
to carry dresses, scarves, and sheets. You should
ride there, not walk; the washing pools are far
from town."

The goddess looked into her eyes,
then went back to Olympus, which they say
is where the gods will have their home forever.
The place is never shaken by the wind,
or wet with rain or blanketed by snow.
A cloudless sky is spread above the mountain,
white radiance all round. The blessed gods
live there in happiness forevermore.

Then Dawn came from her lovely throne, and woke
the girl. She was amazed, remembering
her dream, and in a fine dress, went to tell
her parents, whom she found inside the hall.

Her mother sat beside the hearth and spun
sea-purpled yarn, her house girls all around her.
Her father was just heading out to council
with his renowned advisors, since his people
had called him to a meeting. She stood near him
and said,

"Dear Daddy, please would you set up
the wagon with the big smooth wheels for me,
so I can take my fine clothes to the river
to wash them? They are dirty. And you too
should wear clean clothes for meeting your advisors,
dressed in your best to make important plans.
Your five sons also—two of whom are married,
but three are strapping single men—they always
want to wear nice fresh-laundered clothes when they
are going dancing. This is on my mind."

She said this since she felt too shy to talk
of marriage to her father. But he knew,
and answered, "Child, I would not grudge the mules
or anything you want. Go on! The slaves
can fit the wagon with its cargo rack."

He called the household slaves, and they obeyed.
They made the wagon ready and inspected
its wheels, led up the mules, and yoked them to it.
The girl brought out the multicolored clothes,
and put them on the cart, while in a basket
her mother packed nutritious food for her—
a varied meal, with olives, cheese, and wine,
stored in a goatskin. Then the girl got in.
Her mother handed her a golden flask
of oil, to use when she had had her bath.

Then Nausicaa took up the whip and reins,
and cracked the whip. The mules were on their way,
eager to go and rattling the harness,
bringing the clothes and girl and all her slaves.
They reached the lovely river where the pools
are always full—the water flows in streams
and bubbles up from underneath, to wash
even the dirtiest of laundry. There
they freed the mules and drove them to the river
to graze on honeyed grass beside the stream.
The girls brought out the laundry from the cart,
and brought it to the washing pools and trod it,
competing with each other. When the dirt
was gone, they spread the clothes along the shore,
where salt sea washes pebbles to the beach.
They bathed and rubbed themselves with olive oil.
Then they sat on the riverbank and ate,
and waited for the sun to dry the clothes.
But when they finished eating, they took off
their head-scarves to play ball. The white-armed princess
led them in play—like Artemis the archer,
running across the heights of Taygetus
and Erymanthus; she is glad to run
with boars and fleet-foot deer. The rustic daughters
of Zeus the Aegis King play round about her,
while Leto is delighted in her heart,
seeing her daughter far above the rest,
though all are beautiful. So Nausicaa
stood out above them all. But when the girl
was thinking she should head for home and yoke
the mules, and pack the laundry up again,
Athena's eyes flashed bright. Odysseus
must wake up, see the pretty girl, and have
an escort to the town of the Phaeacians.

The princess threw the ball towards a slave girl,
who missed the catch. It fell down in an eddy;
the girls all started screaming, very loudly.
Odysseus woke up, and thought things over.

"What is this country I have come to now?
Are all the people wild and violent,
or good, hospitable, and god-fearing?
I heard the sound of female voices. Is it
nymphs, who frequent the craggy mountaintops,
and river streams and meadows lush with grass?
Or could this noise I hear be human voices?
I have to try to find out who they are."

Odysseus jumped up from out the bushes.
Grasping a leafy branch he broke it off
to cover up his manly private parts.
Just as a mountain lion trusts its strength,
and beaten by the rain and wind, its eyes
burn bright as it attacks the cows or sheep,
or wild deer, and hunger drives it on
to try the sturdy pens of sheep—so need
impelled Odysseus to come upon
the girls with pretty hair, though he was naked.
All caked with salt, he looked a dreadful sight.
They ran along the shore quite terrified,
some here, some there. But Nausicaa stayed still.
Athena made her legs stop trembling
and gave her courage in her heart. She stood there.
He wondered, should he touch her knees, or keep
some distance and use charming words, to beg
the pretty girl to show him to the town,
and give him clothes. At last he thought it best
to keep some distance and use words to beg her.

The girl might be alarmed at being touched.
His words were calculated flattery.

"My lady, please! Are you divine or human?
If you are some great goddess from the sky,
you look like Zeus' daughter Artemis—
you are as tall and beautiful as she.
But if you live on earth and are a human,
your mother and your father must be lucky,
your brothers also—lucky three times over.
Their hearts must be delighted, seeing you,
their flourishing new sprout, the dancers' leader.
And that man will be luckiest by far,
who takes you home with dowry, as his bride.
I have seen no one like you. Never, no one.
My eyes are dazzled when I look at you.
I traveled once to Delos, on my way
to war and suffering; my troops marched with me.
Beside Apollo's altar sprang a sapling,
a fresh young palm. I gazed at it and marveled.
I never saw so magical a tree.
My lady, you transfix me that same way.
I am in awe of you, afraid to touch
your knees. But I am desperate. I came from
Ogygia, and for twenty days storm winds
and waves were driving me, adrift until
yesterday some god washed me up right here,
perhaps to meet more suffering. I think
my troubles will not end until the gods
have done their all. My lady, pity me.
Battered and wrecked, I come to you, you first—
and I know no one else in this whole country.
Show me the town, give me some rags to wear,
if you brought any clothes when you came here.

So may the gods grant all your heart's desires,
a home and husband, somebody like-minded.
For nothing could be better than when two
live in one house, their minds in harmony,
husband and wife. Their enemies are jealous,
their friends delighted, and they have great honor."

Then white-armed Nausicaa replied, "Well, stranger,
you seem a brave and clever man; you know
that Zeus apportions happiness to people,
to good and bad, each one as he decides.
Your troubles come from him, and you must bear them.
But since you have arrived here in our land,
you will not lack for clothes or anything
a person needs in times of desperation.
I will show you the town. The people here
are called Phaeacians, and I am the daughter
of the great King Alcinous, on whom
depends the strength and power of our people."

And then she called her slaves with braided hair.
"Wait, girls! Why are you running from this man?
Do you believe he is an enemy?
No living person ever born would come
to our Phaeacia with a hostile mind,
since we are much beloved by the gods.
Our island is remote, washed round by sea;
we have no human contact. But this man
is lost, poor thing. We must look after him.
All foreigners and beggars come from Zeus,
and any act of kindness is a blessing.
So give the stranger food and drink, and wash him
down in the river, sheltered from the wind."

They stopped, and egged each other on to take
Odysseus to shelter, as the princess,
the daughter of Alcinous, had told them.
They gave him clothes, a tunic and a cloak,
the olive oil in the golden flask,
and led him down to wash beside the river.
Odysseus politely said,

"Now, girls,
wait at a distance here, so I can wash
my grimy back, and rub myself with oil—
it has been quite a while since I have done it.
Please let me wash in private. I am shy
of being naked with you—pretty girls
with lovely hair."

So they withdrew, and told
their mistress. Then he used the river water
to scrub the brine off from his back and shoulders,
and wash the crusty sea salt from his hair.
But when he was all clean and richly oiled,
dressed in the clothes the young unmarried girl
had given him, Athena made him look
bigger and sturdier, and made his hair
grow curling tendrils like a hyacinth.
As when Athena and Hephaestus teach
a knowledgeable craftsman every art,
and he pours gold on silver, making objects
more beautiful—just so Athena poured
attractiveness across his head and shoulders.
Then he went off and sat beside the sea;
his handsomeness was dazzling. The girl
was shocked. She told her slaves with tidy hair,

"Now listen to me, girls! The gods who live
on Mount Olympus must have wished this man
to come in contact with my godlike people.
Before, he looked so poor and unrefined;
now he is like a god that lives in heaven.
I hope I get a man like this as husband,
a man that lives here and would like to stay.
But, girls, now give the stranger food and drink!"

She gave her orders and the girls obeyed—
they gave Odysseus some food and drink.
He wolfed the food and drank. He was half starved;
it had been ages since he tasted food.
Then white-armed Nausicaa had formed a plan.
Folding the clothes, she packed them in the wagon,
and yoked the mules, and then she climbed inside.
She gave Odysseus some clear instructions.

"Stranger, get ready; you must go to town,
and I will have you meet the best of all
our people. You seem smart; do as I say.
While we are passing through the fields and farmlands,
you have to follow quickly with the girls
behind the mules, and let me lead the way.
Then we will reach the lofty city wall,
which has a scenic port on either side,
and one slim gate, where curved ships are drawn up
along the road: a special spot for each.
The meeting place surrounds Poseidon's shrine,
fitted with heavy stones set deep in earth.
And there the workers make the ships' equipment—
cables and sails—and there they plane the oars.
Phaeacians do not care for archery;
their passion is for sails and oars and ships,

on which they love to cross the dark-gray ocean.
The people in the town are proud; I worry
that they may speak against me. Someone rude
may say, 'Who is that big strong man with her?
Where did she find that stranger? Will he be
her husband? She has got him from a ship,
a foreigner, since no one lives near here,
or else a god, the answer to her prayers,
descended from the sky to hold her tight.
Better if she has found herself a man
from elsewhere, since she scorns the people here,
although she has so many noble suitors.'
So they will shame me. I myself would blame
a girl who got too intimate with men
before her marriage, and who went against
her loving parents' rules. But listen, stranger,
I will explain the quickest way to gain
my father's help to make your way back home.
Beside the road there is a grove of poplars;
it has a fountain, and a meadow round it.
It is Athena's place, where Father has
his orchard and estate, as far from town
as human voice can carry. Sit down there
and wait until I reach my father's house
in town. But when you think I have arrived,
walk on and ask directions for the palace
of King Alcinous, my mighty father.
It will be very easy finding it;
a tiny child could guide you there. It is
unlike the other houses in Phaeacia.
Go through the courtyard, in the house and on
straight to the Great Hall. You will find my mother
sitting beside the hearth by firelight,
and spinning her amazing purple wool.

She leans against a pillar, slaves behind her.
My father has a throne right next to hers;
he sits and sips his wine, just like a god.
But pass him by, embrace my mother's knees
to supplicate. If you do this, you quickly
will reach your home, however far it is,
in happiness. If she is good to you,
and looks upon you kindly in her heart,
you can be sure of getting to your house,
back to your family and native land."

With that, she used her shining whip to urge
the mules to go. They left the river streams,
and trotted well and clipped their hooves along.
She drove an easy pace to let her slaves
and great Odysseus keep up on foot.
The sun was setting when they reached the grove,
the famous sanctuary of Athena.
Odysseus sat in it, and at once
he prayed to mighty Zeus' daughter.

"Hear me,
daughter of Zeus! Unvanquished Queen! If ever,
when that earth-shaker god was wrecking me,
you helped me—may they pity me and give me
kind welcome in Phaeacia." And Athena
heard him but did not yet appear to him,
respecting her own uncle in his fury
against Odysseus till he reached home.

BOOK 7

A Magical Kingdom

Odysseus sat patiently and prayed.
Meanwhile, the fine strong mules conveyed the girl
to town; she reached her father's palace gate.
Her brothers gathered round her like immortals.
They took the harness off the mules and brought
the clothes inside. She went to her own room.
Eurymedusa, her old slave, had lit
a fire for her. This woman had been brought
from Apeire by ship, long years before.
The people chose to give her to the king,
because they bowed before him like a god.
She used to babysit young Nausicaa,
and now she lit her fire and cooked her meal.

Odysseus walked briskly to the town.
Athena helpfully surrounded him
with mist that kept him safe from rude remarks
from people who might ask him who he was.
When he had almost reached the lovely city,
bright-eyed Athena met him, like a girl,
young and unmarried, with a water pitcher.

She stopped in front of him. Odysseus
said,

"Child, would you escort me to the house
of King Alcinous, who rules this land?
I have been through hard times. I traveled here
from far away; I am a foreigner,
and I know no one who lives here in town
or anywhere round here."

With twinkling eyes
the goddess answered, "Mr. Foreigner,
I will take you to where you want to go.
The king lives near my father's home. But you
must walk in silence. Do not look at people,
and ask no questions. People here are not
too keen on strangers coming from abroad,
although they like to cross the sea themselves.
They know their ships go very fast. Poseidon
gave them this gift. Their boats can fly like wings,
or quick as thoughts."

The goddess led him there.
He followed closely in her skipping steps.
The seafaring Phaeacians did not see him
as he passed through the town, since that great goddess,
pigtailed Athena, in her care for him
made him invisible with magic mist.
He was amazed to see the ships and harbors
and meeting places of the noblemen,
and high walls set with stakes on top—a wonder!
They reached the splendid palace of the king.
Divine Athena winked at him and said,

"Here, Mr. Foreigner, this is the house
you wanted me to take you to. You will
find them, the king and queen, inside at dinner.
Do not be scared; go in. The brave succeed
in all adventures, even those who come
from countries far away. First greet the queen.
Arete is her name. The king and queen
have common ancestry—Nausithous.
Eurymedon was long ago the king
over the Giants, who were proud and bad.
He killed them, his own people, and then he
got killed as well. His youngest daughter was
named Periboea. She was very pretty.
Poseidon slept with her. She had a child,
Nausithous, and he became the king
here in Phaeacia, and he had two sons,
our King Alcinous, and Rhexenor.
Apollo shot that Rhexenor when he
was newly married, with no son. He left
a daughter, our Arete, and her uncle,
Alcinous, made her his wife. No woman
is honored as he honors her. She is
precious to him, her children, and the people.
We look at her as if she were a goddess,
and point her out when she walks through our town.
She is extremely clever and perceptive;
she solves disputes to help the men she likes.
If she looks on you kindly in her heart,
you have a chance of seeing those you love,
and getting back again to your big house
and homeland."

So bright-eyed Athena left him.
She went from lovely Scheria, across

the tireless sea, to Marathon and Athens,
and went inside Erechtheus' palace.

Odysseus approached the royal house,
and stood there by the threshold made of bronze.
His heart was mulling over many things.
The palace of the mighty king was high,
and shone like rays of sunlight or of moonlight.
The walls were bronze all over, from the entrance
back to the bedrooms, and along them ran
a frieze of blue. Gold doors held safe the house.
Pillars of silver rose up from the threshold,
the lintel silver, and the handle, gold.
Silver and golden dogs stood at each side,
made by Hephaestus with great artistry,
to guard the home of brave Alcinous—
immortal dogs, unaging for all time.
At intervals were seats set in the walls,
right from the doorway to the inner rooms,
with delicate fine throws, the work of women.
Phaeacian lords and ladies sat upon them,
eating and drinking, since they lacked for nothing.
Boys made of gold were set on pedestals,
and they held burning torches in their hands,
lighting the hall at night for those at dinner.
The King had fifty slave girls in his house;
some ground the yellow grain upon the millstone,
others wove cloth and sat there spinning yarn,
with fingers quick as rustling poplar leaves,
and oil was dripping from the woven fabric.
Just as Phaeacian men have special talent
for launching ships to sea, the women there
are expert weavers, since Athena gave them
fine minds and skill to make most lovely things.

Outside the courtyard by the doors there grows
an orchard of four acres, hedged around.
The trees are tall, luxuriant with fruit:
bright-colored apples, pears and pomegranate,
sweet figs and fertile olives, and the crop
never runs out or withers in the winter,
nor in the summer. Fruit grows all year round.
The West Wind always blows and makes it swell
and ripen: mellowing pear on mellowing pear,
apple on apple, grapes on grapes, and figs.
A fertile vineyard too is planted there.
They use the warmer side, a flattened slope,
for drying grapes in sunshine. They pick bunches
and trample them, while unripe clusters open
and shed their blooms, and others turn to purple.
There are two springs: one flows all through the garden,
the other gushes from the courtyard threshold,
towards the palace, and the people draw
freshwater. So the gods had blessed the house
of King Alcinous with lovely gifts.
Hardened, long-suffering Odysseus
stood there and stared, astonished in his heart,
then quickly strode across the palace threshold.
He found the lordly leaders of Phaeacia
pouring drink offerings for sharp-eyed Hermes,
to whom they give libations before bed.
Odysseus went in the house disguised
in mist with which Athena covered him,
until he reached Arete and the king.
He threw his arms around Arete's knees,
and all at once, the magic mist dispersed.
They were astonished when they saw the man,
and all fell silent. Then Odysseus
said,

"Queen Arete, child of Rhexenor,
I have had many years of pain and loss.
I beg you, and your husband, and these men
who feast here—may the gods bless you in life,
and may you leave your children wealth and honor.
Now help me, please, to get back home, and quickly!
I miss my family. I have been gone
so long it hurts."

He sat down by the hearth
among the ashes of the fire. They all
were silent till Echeneus spoke up.
He was an elder statesman of Phaeacia,
a skillful orator and learned man.
Wanting to help, he said,

"Alcinous,
you know it is not right to leave a stranger
sitting there on the floor beside the hearth
among the cinders. Everyone is waiting
for you to give the word. Make him get up,
and seat him on a silver chair, and order
wine to be poured, so we may make libations
to Zeus the Thunderlord, who loves the needy.
The house girl ought to bring the stranger food
out from the storeroom."

So Alcinous
reached for Odysseus' hand, and raised
the many-minded hero from the ashes.
He made Laodamas, his favorite son,
vacate his chair so he could sit beside him.
The slave girl brought him water in a pitcher
of gold to wash his hands, and poured it out
over a silver bowl, and fetched a table

of polished wood; a humble slave brought out
bread and an ample plateful of the meat.
Half-starved and weak, the hero ate and drank.
Majestic King Alcinous addressed
Pontonous, the wine boy.

"Go and mix
a bowl and serve the wine to all our guests,
so we may offer drink to thundering Zeus
who blesses those in need." The boy mixed up
the sweet, delicious wine, and filled the cups
for everyone, with first pour for the gods.
They made the offerings and drank as much
as they desired, and then Alcinous
said,

"Listen, lords. Hear what my heart commands.
The feast is over; go home, go to bed.
At dawn, we will call more of our best men,
and host the stranger in our halls, and offer
fine sacrifices to the gods, then plan
how we may help his journey, so our guest
may travel quickly, without pain or trouble,
encountering no trouble on the way,
however far away it is, until
he reaches home. Once there, he must endure
whatever was spun out when he was born
by Fate and by the heavy ones, the Spinners.
But if he is immortal, come from heaven,
the gods have changed their ways, since in the past
they used to show themselves to us directly
whenever we would give them hecatombs.
They sit and eat among us. Even if
just one of us meets them alone, out walking,

they do not hide from us; we are close friends,
as are the Giants and Cyclopic peoples."

Odysseus, with careful calculation,
said,

"No, Alcinous, please think again.
I am not like the deathless gods in heaven.
My height is normal. I look like a human.
In pain I am a match for any man,
whoever you may know that suffers most.
I could tell many stories of the dangers
that I have suffered through; gods willed it so.
But let me have my meal, despite my grief.
The belly is just like a whining dog:
it begs and forces one to notice it,
despite exhaustion or the depths of sorrow.
My heart is full of sorrow, but my stomach
is always telling me to eat and drink.
It tells me to forget what I have suffered,
and fill it up. At dawn tomorrow, help me
to reach my homeland, after all this pain.
May I live out my final days in sight
of my own property and slaves and home."

They all agreed the stranger's words made sense,
and that he should be sent back home. They poured
drink offerings to the gods, and drank as much
as they desired, then all went home to bed.
Odysseus was left there in the hall,
sitting beside Arete and the godlike
Alcinous. The dishes from the feast
were cleaned up by the slaves. White-armed Arete
had noticed his fine clothes, the cloak and shirt

she wove herself, with help from her slave girls.
Her words flew out to him as if on wings.

"Stranger, let me be first to speak to you.
Where are you from? And who gave you those clothes?
I thought you said you drifted here by sea?"

Planning his words with careful skill, he answered,
"It would be difficult, Your Majesty,
to tell it all; the gods have given me
so many troubles. I will tell you this.
There is an island, far out in the sea,
Ogygia, where the child of Atlas lives,
the mighty goddess with smooth braids, the crafty
Calypso, friend to neither gods nor mortals.
A spirit brought me to her hearth, alone,
when Zeus scooped up my ship and with bright lightning
split it apart across the wine-dark sea.
All of my comrades, my brave friends, were killed.
I wrapped my arms around the keel and floated
for ten days. On the tenth black night, the gods
carried me till I reached Ogygia,
home of the beautiful and mighty goddess
Calypso. Lovingly she cared for me,
vowing to set me free from death and time
forever. But she never swayed my heart.
I stayed for seven years; she gave me clothes
like those of gods, but they were always wet
with tears. At last the eighth year rolled around,
and word came down from Zeus that I must go,
and finally her mind was changed. She sent me
upon a well-bound wooden raft, equipped
with food, sweet wine, and clothes as if for gods,

and sent a fair warm wind. I sailed the sea
for seventeen long days; on day eighteen,
the murky mountains of your land appeared,
and I was overjoyed, but more bad luck
was hurled at me. Poseidon roused the winds
to block me, and he stirred the sea. I sobbed,
and clung there, going nowhere, till my raft
was smashed to pieces by the massive storm.
But I swam through this gulf of water till
the current brought me here. If I had tried
to land at once, I would have been swept back
against the crags. I swam a way away,
until I reached a river mouth, which seemed
a perfect spot for landing: it was sheltered
from wind, and smooth, quite free from rocks. So there
I flopped and tried to gather up my strength
until the holy nightfall. Then I crawled
out of the rain-fed river to the bank,
and hid inside the bushes, and I heaped
some leaves to cover me. Some god poured down
deep sleep. With heavy heart I slept all night
and through the dawn to noon, beneath the leaves.
Then in the afternoon, when sleep released me,
I woke, and saw girls playing on the beach—
your daughter, like a goddess, and her slaves.
I prayed to her. One would not think a girl
as young as her would have so much good sense;
young people are not usually so thoughtful.
She was so kind to me; she gave me food
and wine, and had them wash me in the river,
and let me have these clothes. Now I have told you
the truth, no matter what."

Alcinous
said, "Just one of these things that my daughter did
was not correct: she should have brought you here
to us herself, escorted by her slave girls,
since you had supplicated first to her."

With careful tact Odysseus replied,
"Your daughter is quite wonderful, great king.
Please do not blame her. She told me to come
here with her slaves, but I was too embarrassed,
and nervous. I thought you might get annoyed
at seeing me. We humans on this earth
are apt to be suspicious."

And the king
replied, "My heart is not the type to feel
anger for no good reason. Moderation
is always best. Athena, Zeus, Apollo,
what a congenial man you are! I wish
you would stay here, and marry my own daughter,
and be my son. I would give you a home
and wealth if you would like to stay. If not,
we will not keep you here against your will.
May Zeus not have it so! As for your journey,
I give my word that you can go tomorrow.
Lying down, lulled to sleep, you will be rowed
across the peaceful sea until you reach
your land and home, or anywhere you want,
even beyond Euboea, which our people
saw when they carried fair-haired Rhadamanthus
to visit Tityus, the son of Gaia.
It is supposed to be the farthest shore
on earth, but they were there and back that day,
not even tired. That shows just how fine

my ships are, and my men who stir the sea
with oars."

At that Odysseus, who had
endured so much, was happy, and he prayed,

"O Father Zeus, may everything come true,
just as Alcinous has said. So may
his fame burn bright forever on the earth,
and may I reach my home."

Then at these words,
white-armed Arete called to her attendants
to put a bed out on the porch and lay
fine purple blankets on it and to spread
covers and woolly quilts across the top.
With torches in their hands they bustled out.
They made the bed up neatly, very fast,
then came and called Odysseus.

"Now guest,
get up and come outside, your bed is ready."

Odysseus was glad to go to sleep
after his long adventures, on that bed
surrounded by the rustling of the porch.
Alcinous was sleeping in his room,
beside his wife, who made their bed and shared it.

BOOK 8

The Songs of a Poet

Soon Dawn appeared and touched the sky with roses.
Majestic, holy King Alcinous
leapt out of bed, as did Odysseus,
the city-sacker. Then the blessed king,
mighty Alcinous, led out his guest
to the Phaeacian council by the ships.
They sat there side by side on polished stones.
Meanwhile, Athena walked all through the town,
appearing like the royal messenger.
To help Odysseus' journey home,
she stood beside each man in turn and said,

"My lord, come to the meeting place, to learn
about the visitor to our king's home.
Despite his wanderings by sea, he looks
like an immortal god."

So she roused up
the hearts and minds of each, and soon the seats
of council were filled up; the men assembled.
Seeing Laertes' clever son, the crowd

marveled. Athena poured unearthly charm
upon his head and shoulders, and she made him
taller and sturdier, so these Phaeacians
would welcome and respect him, when he managed
the many trials of skill that they would set
to test him. When the people were assembled,
Alcinous addressed them.

"Hear me, leaders
and chieftains of Phaeacia. I will tell you
the promptings of my heart. This foreigner—
I do not know his name—came wandering
from west or east and showed up at my house.
He begs and prays for help to travel on.
Let us assist him, as we have before
with other guests: no visitor has ever
been forced to linger in my house. We always
give them safe passage home. Now let us launch
a ship for her maiden voyage on the water,
and choose a crew of fifty-two, the men
selected as the best, and lash the oars
beside the benches. Then return to shore,
and come to my house. Let the young men hurry
to cook a feast. I will provide supplies,
plenty for everyone. And I invite
you also, lords, to welcome him with me.
Do not refuse! We also must invite
Demodocus, the poet. Gods inspire him,
so any song he chooses to perform
is wonderful to hear."

He led the way.
The lords went with him, and the house boy fetched
the bard. The fifty-two select young men
went to the shore, just as the king commanded.

They reached the restless salty sea, and launched
the black ship on the depths, set up the mast
and sails, and fastened in the oars, by tying
each to its leather thole-strap, all in order.
They spread the white sails wide, and moored the ship
out in the water. Then the men walked up
towards the mighty palace of the king.
The halls and porticoes were thronged with people,
both old and young. To feed his many guests
Alcinous killed twelve sheep, and eight boars
with silver tusks, and two slow-lumbering cows.
Skinning the animals, they cooked a feast.
The house boy brought the poet, whom the Muse
adored. She gave him two gifts, good and bad:
she took his sight away, but gave sweet song.
The wine boy brought a silver-studded chair
and propped it by a pillar, in the middle
of all the guests, and by a peg he hung
the poet's lyre above his head and helped him
to reach it, and he set a table by him,
and a bread basket and a cup of wine
to drink whenever he desired. They all
took food. When they were satisfied, the Muse
prompted the bard to sing of famous actions,
an episode whose fame has touched the sky:
Achilles' and Odysseus' quarrel—
how at a splendid sacrificial feast,
they argued bitterly, and Agamemnon
was glad because the best of the Achaeans
were quarreling, since when he had consulted
the oracle at Pytho, crossing over
the entry stone, Apollo had foretold
that this would be the start of suffering
for Greeks and Trojans, through the plans of Zeus.
So sang the famous bard. Odysseus

with his strong hands picked up his heavy cloak
of purple, and he covered up his face.
He was ashamed to let them see him cry.
Each time the singer paused, Odysseus
wiped tears, drew down the cloak and poured a splash
of wine out of his goblet, for the gods.
But each time, the Phaeacian nobles urged
the bard to sing again—they loved his songs.
So he would start again; Odysseus
would moan and hide his head beneath his cloak.
Only Alcinous could see his tears,
since he was sitting next to him, and heard
his sobbing. So he quickly spoke.

"My lords!
We have already satisfied our wish
for feasting, and the lyre, the feast's companion.
Now let us go outside and set up contests
in every sport, so when our guest goes home
he can tell all his friends we are the best
at boxing, wrestling, high-jumping, and sprinting."

With that he led the way; the others followed.
The boy took down the lyre from its peg
and took Demodocus' hand to lead him
out with the crowd who went to watch the games.
Many young athletes stood there: Acroneüs,
Ocyalus, Elatreus, Nauteus,
Thoön, Anchialus, Eretmeus,
Anabesineus and Ponteus,
Prymneus, Proreus, Amphialus,
the son of Polynaus, son of Tecton,
and Naubolus' son, Euryalus,
like Ares, cause of ruin. In his looks
and strength, he was the best in all Phaeacia,

after Laodamas. Three sons of great
Alcinous stood up: Laodamas,
godlike Clytoneus, and Halius.
First came the footrace. They lined up, then dashed
all in an instant, right around the track
so fast they raised the dust up from the field.
Clytoneus was the best by far at sprinting:
he raced past all the others by the length
of a field plowed by mules, and reached the crowd.
Next came the brutal sport of wrestling,
in which Euryalus was best. In jumping,
Amphialus excelled. And at the discus,
by far the best of all was Elatreus.
The prince Laodamas excelled at boxing.
They all enjoyed the games. When they were over,
Laodamas, Alcinous' son,
said,

"Now my friends, we ought to ask the stranger
if he plays any sports. His build is strong;
his legs and arms and neck are very sturdy,
and he is in his prime, though he has been
broken by suffering. No pain can shake
a man as badly as the sea, however
strong he once was."

Euryalus replied,
"You are quite right, Laodamas. Why not
call out to challenge him yourself?"

The noble
son of Alcinous agreed with him.
He stood up in the middle of them all
and called Odysseus.

"Come here!" he said.
"Now you, sir! You should try our games as well,
if you know any sports; it seems you would.
Nothing can be more glorious for a man,
in a whole lifetime, than what he achieves
with hands and feet. So try, set care aside.
Soon you will travel, since your ship is launched.
The crew is standing by."

Odysseus
thought carefully—he had a plan. He answered,
"Laodamas, why mock me with this challenge?
My heart is set on sorrow, not on games,
since I have suffered and endured so much
that now I only want to get back home.
I sit here praying to your king and people
to grant my wish."

Euryalus responded
with outright taunting.

"Stranger, I suppose
you must be ignorant of all athletics.
I know your type. The captain of a crew
of merchant sailors, you roam round at sea
and only care about your freight and cargo,
keeping close watch on your ill-gotten gains.
You are no athlete."

With a scowl, he answered,
"What crazy arrogance from you, you stranger!
The gods do not bless everyone the same,
with equal gifts of body, mind, or speech.
One man is weak, but gods may crown his words
with loveliness. Men gladly look to him;

his speech is steady, with calm dignity.
He stands out from his audience, and when
he walks through town, the people look at him
as if he were a god. Another man
has godlike looks but no grace in his words.
Like you—you look impressive, and a god
could not improve your body. But your mind
is crippled. You have stirred my heart to anger
with these outrageous comments. I am not
lacking experience of sports and games.
When I was young, I trusted my strong arms
and was among the first. Now pain has crushed me.
I have endured the agonies of war,
and struggled through the dangers of the sea.
But you have challenged me and stung my heart.
Despite my suffering, I will compete."

With that he leapt up, cloak and all, and seized
a massive discus, heavier than that
used by the others. He spun around, drew back
his arm and from his brawny hand he hurled.
The stone went humming. The Phaeacians, known
for rowing, ducked down cowering beneath
its arc; it flew beyond the other pegs.
Athena marked the spot. In human guise
she spoke.

"A blind man, stranger, could discern
this mark by groping. It is far ahead
of all the others. You can celebrate!
You won this round, and none of them will ever
throw further—or as far!"

Odysseus
was thrilled to realize he had a friend

to take his side, and with a lighter heart,
he told the young Phaeacians,

"Try to match this!
If you can do it, I will throw another,
as far or farther. You have made me angry,
so I will take you on in any sport.
Come on! In boxing, wrestling, or sprinting,
I will compete with anyone, except
Laodamas: he is my host. Who would
fight with a friend? A man who challenges
those who have welcomed him in a strange land
is worthless and a fool; he spites himself.
But I will challenge any of you others.
Test my ability, let me know yours.
I am not weak at any sport men practice.
I know the way to hold a polished bow.
I always was the first to hit my man
out of a horde of enemies, though many
comrades stood by me, arrows taking aim.
At Troy, when the Achaeans shot their bows,
the only one superior to me
was Philoctetes. Other men who eat
their bread on earth are all worse shots than me.
But I will not compete with super-archers,
with Heracles or Eurytus, who risked
competing with the gods at archery.
Apollo was enraged at him and killed him
as soon as he proposed it. He died young
and did not reach old age in his own home.
And I can throw a spear beyond the shots
that others reach with arrows. I am only
concerned that one of you may win the footrace:

I lost my stamina and my legs weakened
during my time at sea, upon the raft;
I could not do my exercise routine."

The crowd was silent, but Alcinous
said, "Sir, you have expressed, with fine good manners,
your wish to show your talents, and your anger
at that man who stood up in this arena
and mocked you, as no one who understands
how to speak properly would ever do.
Now listen carefully, so you may tell
your own fine friends at home when you are feasting
beside your wife and children, and remember
our skill in all the deeds we have accomplished
from our forefathers' time till now. We are
not brilliant at wrestling or boxing,
but we are quick at sprinting, and with ships
we are the best. We love the feast, the lyre,
dancing and varied clothes, hot baths and bed.
But now let the best dancers of Phaeacia
perform, so that our guest may tell his friends
when he gets home, how excellent we are
at seafaring, at running, and at dancing
and song. Let someone bring the well-tuned lyre
from inside for Demodocus—go quickly!"

So spoke the king. The house boy brought the lyre.
The people chose nine referees to check
the games were fair. They leveled out a floor
for dancing, with a fine wide ring around.
The house boy gave Demodocus the lyre.
He walked into the middle, flanked by boys,
young and well trained, who tapped their feet performing
the holy dance, their quick legs bright with speed.
Odysseus was wonder-struck to see it.

The poet strummed and sang a charming song
about the love of fair-crowned Aphrodite
for Ares, who gave lavish gifts to her
and shamed the bed of Lord Hephaestus, where
they secretly had sex. The Sun God saw them,
and told Hephaestus—bitter news for him.
He marched into his forge to get revenge,
and set the mighty anvil on its block,
and hammered chains so strong that they could never
be broken or undone. He was so angry
at Ares. When his trap was made, he went
inside the room of his beloved bed,
and twined the mass of cables all around
the bedposts, and then hung them from the ceiling,
like slender spiderwebs, so finely made
that nobody could see them, even gods:
the craftsmanship was so ingenious.
When he had set that trap across the bed,
he traveled to the cultured town of Lemnos,
which was his favorite place in all the world.
Ares the golden rider had kept watch.
He saw Hephaestus, famous wonder-worker,
leaving his house, and went inside himself;
he wanted to make love with Aphrodite.
She had returned from visiting her father,
the mighty son of Cronus; there she sat.
Then Ares took her hand and said to her,

"My darling, let us go to bed. Hephaestus
is out of town; he must have gone to Lemnos
to see the Sintians whose speech is strange."

She was excited to lie down with him;
they went to bed together. But the chains
ingenious Hephaestus had created

wrapped tight around them, so they could not move
or get up. Then they knew that they were trapped.
The limping god drew near—before he reached
the land of Lemnos, he had turned back home.
Troubled at heart, he came towards his house.
Standing there in the doorway, he was seized
by savage rage. He gave a mighty shout,
calling to all the gods,

"O Father Zeus,
and all you blessed gods who live forever,
look! It is funny—and unbearable.
See how my Aphrodite, child of Zeus,
is disrespecting me for being lame.
She loves destructive Ares, who is strong
and handsome. I am weak. I blame my parents.
If only I had not been born! But come,
see where those two are sleeping in my bed,
as lovers. I am horrified to see it.
But I predict they will not want to lie
longer like that, however great their love.
Soon they will want to wake up, but my trap
and chains will hold them fast, until her father
pays back the price I gave him for his daughter.
Her eyes stare at me like a dog. She is
so beautiful, but lacking self-control."

The gods assembled at his house: Poseidon,
Earth-Shaker, helpful Hermes, and Apollo.
The goddesses stayed home, from modesty.
The blessed gods who give good things were standing
inside the doorway, and they burst out laughing,
at what a clever trap Hephaestus set.
And as they looked, they said to one another,

"Crime does not pay! The slow can beat the quick,
as now Hephaestus, who is lame and slow,
has used his skill to catch the fastest sprinter
of all those on Olympus. Ares owes
the price for his adultery." They gossiped.

Apollo, son of Zeus, then said to Hermes,
"Hermes my brother, would you like to sleep
with golden Aphrodite, in her bed,
even weighed down by mighty chains?"

And Hermes
the sharp-eyed messenger replied, "Ah, brother,
Apollo lord of archery: if only!
I would be bound three times as tight or more
and let you gods and all your wives look on,
if only I could sleep with Aphrodite."

Then laughter rose among the deathless gods.
Only Poseidon did not laugh. He begged
and pleaded with Hephaestus to release
Ares. He told the wonder-working god,

"Now let him go! I promise he will pay
the penalty in full among the gods,
just as you ask."

The famous limping god
replied, "Poseidon, do not ask me this.
It is disgusting, bailing scoundrels out.
How could I bind you, while the gods look on,
if Ares should escape his bonds and debts?"

Poseidon, Lord of Earthquakes, answered him,
"Hephaestus, if he tries to dodge this debt,
I promise I will pay."

The limping god
said, "Then, in courtesy to you, I must
do as you ask." So using all his strength,
Hephaestus loosed the chains. The pair of lovers
were free from their constraints, and both jumped up.
Ares went off to Thrace, while Aphrodite
smiled as she went to Cyprus, to the island
of Paphos, where she had a fragrant altar
and sanctuary. The Graces washed her there,
and rubbed her with the magic oil that glows
upon immortals, and they dressed her up
in gorgeous clothes. She looked astonishing.

That was the poet's song. Odysseus
was happy listening; so were they all.
And then Alcinous told Halius
to dance with Laodamas; no one danced
as well as them. They took a purple ball
which Polybus the artisan had made them.
One boy would leap and toss it to the clouds;
the other would jump up, feet off the ground,
and catch it easily before he landed.
After they practiced throwing it straight upwards,
they danced across the fertile earth, crisscrossing,
constantly trading places. Other boys
who stood around the field were beating time
with noisy stomping. Then Odysseus
said,

"King of many citizens, great lord,
you boasted that your dancers are the best,

and it is true. I feel amazed to see
this marvelous show."

That pleased the reverend king.
He spoke at once to his seafaring people.
"Hear me, Phaeacian leaders, lords and nobles.
The stranger seems extremely wise to me.
So let us give him gifts, as hosts should do
to guests in friendship. Twelve lords rule our people,
with me as thirteenth lord. Let us each bring
a pound of precious gold and laundered clothes,
a tunic and a cloak. Then pile them up,
and let our guest take all these gifts, and go
to dinner with them, happy in his heart.
Euryalus should tell him he is sorry,
and give a special gift, since what he said
was inappropriate."

They all agreed,
and each sent back a deputy to fetch
the presents. And Euryalus spoke out.

"My lord Alcinous, great king of kings,
I will apologize, as you command.
And I will give him this bronze sword which has
a silver handle, and a scabbard carved
of ivory—a precious gift for him."
With that he put the silver-studded sword
into Odysseus' hands; his words
flew out.

"I welcome you, sir. Be our guest.
If something rude of any kind was said,
let the winds take it. May the gods allow you
to reach your home and see your wife again,

since you have suffered so long, far away
from those who love you."

And Odysseus
said, "Friend, I wish you well. May gods protect you,
and may you never miss the sword you gave me."

With that, he strapped the silver-studded sword
across his back, and as the sun went down
the precious gifts were brought to him. The slaves
took them inside Alcinous' house.
The princes piled the lovely things beside
the queen, their mother. King Alcinous
led everyone inside and had them sit
on upright chairs. He told Arete,

"Wife,
bring out our finest chest, and put inside it
a tunic and a freshly laundered cloak.
Set a bronze cauldron on the fire to boil,
so he can take a bath. Then let him see
the precious gifts our noblemen have brought,
and then enjoy the banquet and the song.
I also have a gift: a splendid cup
of gold. I hope he always thinks of me
whenever he pours offerings to Zeus
and other gods."

Arete told her slaves
to quickly set a mighty pot to warm,
for washing. So upon the blazing flames
they set the cauldron and poured water in,
and heaped up wood. The fire licked around
the belly of the tub and warmed the water.

Arete brought from her own room a chest
to give the guest, and packed the gifts inside—
the clothes and gold that they had given him;
and she herself put in a cloak and tunic.
She told him,

"Watch the lid, and tie it closed,
so nobody can rob you as you travel,
when you are lulled to sleep on your black ship."

Odysseus, experienced in loss,
took careful note. He shut the lid and tied
a cunning knot that he had learned from Circe.
Then right away the slave girl led him off
towards the bath to wash. He was delighted
to see hot water. He had not been bathed
since he had left the home of curly-haired
Calypso, who had taken care of him
as if he were a god. The slave girls washed him,
rubbed oil on him and dressed him in a tunic
and fine wool mantle. Freshly bathed, he joined
the men at wine. And there stood Nausicaa,
divinely beautiful, beside a pillar
that held the palace roof. She was amazed
to see Odysseus. Her words flew fast.

"Good-bye then, stranger, but remember me
when you reach home, because you owe your life
to me. I helped you first."

Odysseus
replied politely, "Nausicaa, may Zeus,
husband of Hera, mighty Lord of Thunder,
allow me to go back and see my home.

There I shall pray to you as to a god,
forever, princess, since you saved my life."
With that he went to sit beside the king.

Now they were serving out the food and pouring
wine, and the steward led out to the center
Demodocus, the well-respected poet.
He sat him in the middle of the banquet,
against a pillar. Then Odysseus
thought fast, and sliced a helping from the pig,
all richly laced with fat. The plate of meat
had plenty left. He told the boy,

"Go take
this meat and give it to Demodocus.
Despite my grief, I would be glad to meet him.
Poets are honored by all those who live
on earth. The Muse has taught them how to sing;
she loves the race of poets."

So the house boy
handed it to Demodocus. He took it
gladly; and everybody took their food.
When they had had enough to eat and drink,
the clever mastermind of many schemes
said,

"You are wonderful, Demodocus!
I praise you more than anyone; Apollo,
or else the Muse, the child of Zeus, has taught you.
You tell so accurately what the Greeks
achieved, and what they suffered, there at Troy,
as if you had been there, or heard about it
from somebody who was. So sing the story

about the Wooden Horse, which Epeius
built with Athena's help. Odysseus
dragged it inside and to the citadel,
filled up with men to sack the town. If you
can tell that as it happened, I will say
that you truly are blessed with inspiration."

A god inspired the bard to sing. He started
with how the Greeks set fire to their camp
and then embarked and sailed away. Meanwhile,
Odysseus brought in a gang of men
into the heart of Troy, inside the horse.
The Trojans pulled the thing up to the summit,
and sat around discussing what to do.
Some said, "We ought to strike the wood with swords!"
Others said, "Drag it higher up and hurl it
down from the rocks!" But some said they should leave it
to pacify the gods. So it would be.
The town was doomed to ruin when it took
that horse, chock-full of fighters bringing death
to Trojans. And he sang how the Achaeans
poured from the horse, in ambush from the hollow,
and sacked the city; how they scattered out,
destroying every neighborhood. Like Ares,
Odysseus, with Menelaus, rushed
to find Deiphobus' house, and there
he won at last, through dreadful violence,
thanks to Athena. So the poet sang.

Odysseus was melting into tears;
his cheeks were wet with weeping, as a woman
weeps, as she falls to wrap her arms around
her husband, fallen fighting for his home
and children. She is watching as he gasps

and dies. She shrieks, a clear high wail, collapsing
upon his corpse. The men are right behind.
They hit her shoulders with their spears and lead her
to slavery, hard labor, and a life
of pain. Her face is marked with her despair.
In that same desperate way, Odysseus
was crying. No one noticed that his eyes
were wet with tears, except Alcinous,
who sat right next to him and heard his sobs.
Quickly he spoke to his seafaring people.

"Listen, my lords and nobles of Phaeacia!
Demodocus should stop and set aside
the lyre, since what he sings does not give pleasure
to everyone. Throughout this heavenly song,
since dinnertime, our guest has been in pain,
grieving. A heavy burden weighs his heart.
Let the song end, so we can all be happy,
both guest and hosts. That would be best by far.
This send-off party and these precious gifts,
which we give out of friendship, are for him,
our guest of honor. Any man of sense
will treat a guest in need like his own brother.
Stranger, now answer all my questions clearly,
not with evasion; frankness would be best.
What did your parents name you? With what name
are you known to your people? Surely no one
in all the world is nameless, poor or noble,
since parents give a name to every child
at birth. And also tell me of your country,
your people, and your city, so our ships,
steered by their own good sense, may take you there.
Phaeacians have no need of men at helm
nor rudders, as in other ships. Our boats

intuit what is in the minds of men,
and know all human towns and fertile fields.
They rush at full tilt right across the gulf
of salty sea, concealed in mist and clouds.
They have no fear of damages or loss.
But once I heard Nausithous, my father,
say that Poseidon hates us for the help
we give to take our guests across the sea,
and that one day a ship of ours would suffer
shipwreck on its return; a mighty mountain
would block our town from sight. So Father said.
Perhaps the god will bring these things to pass
or not, as is his will. But come now, tell me
about your wanderings: describe the places,
the people, and the cities you have seen.
Which ones were wild and cruel, unwelcoming,
and which were kind to visitors, respecting
the gods? And please explain why you were crying,
sobbing your heart out when you heard him sing
what happened to the Greeks at Troy. The gods
devised and measured out this devastation,
to make a song for those in times to come.
Did you lose somebody at Troy? A man
from your wife's family, perhaps her father
or brother? Ties of marriage are the closest
after the bonds of blood. Or else perhaps
you lost the friend who knew you best of all?
A friend can be as close as any brother."

BOOK 9

A Pirate in a Shepherd's Cave

Wily Odysseus, the lord of lies,
answered,

"My lord Alcinous, great king,
it is a splendid thing to hear a poet
as talented as this. His voice is godlike.
I think that there can be no greater pleasure
than when the whole community enjoys
a banquet, as we sit inside the house,
and listen to the singer, and the tables
are heaped with bread and meat; the wine boy ladles
drink from the bowl and pours it into cups.
To me this seems ideal, a thing of beauty.
Now something prompted you to ask about
my own sad story. I will tell you, though
the memory increases my despair.
Where shall I start? Where can I end? The gods
have given me so much to cry about.
First I will tell my name, so we will be
acquainted and if I survive, you can
be my guest in my distant home one day.

I am Odysseus, Laertes' son,
known for my many clever tricks and lies.
My fame extends to heaven, but I live
in Ithaca, where shaking forest hides
Mount Neriton. Close by are other islands:
Dulichium, and wooded Zacynthus
and Same. All the others face the dawn;
my Ithaca is set apart, most distant,
facing the dark. It is a rugged land,
but good at raising children. To my eyes
no country could be sweeter. As you know,
divine Calypso held me in her cave,
wanting to marry me; and likewise Circe,
the trickster, trapped me, and she wanted me
to be her husband. But she never swayed
my heart, since when a man is far from home,
living abroad, there is no sweeter thing
than his own native land and family.
Now let me tell you all the trouble Zeus
has caused me on my journey home from Troy.
A blast of wind pushed me off course towards
the Cicones in Ismarus. I sacked
the town and killed the men. We took their wives
and shared their riches equally among us.
Then I said we must run away. Those fools
refused to listen. They were drinking wine
excessively, and killing sheep and cattle
along the beach. The Cicones called out
to neighbors on the mainland, who were strong
and numerous, and skilled at horseback fighting,
and if need be, on foot. They came like leaves
and blossoms in the spring at dawn. Then Zeus
gave us bad luck. Poor us! The enemy
assembled round the ships and fought with swords
of bronze. And while the holy morning light

was bright and strong, we held them off, though they
outnumbered us. But when the sun turned round
and dipped, the hour when oxen are released,
the Cicones began to overpower
us Greeks. Six well-armed members of my crew
died from each ship. The rest of us survived,
and we escaped the danger. We prepared
to sail away with heavy hearts, relieved
to be alive, but grieving for our friends.
Before we launched the ships, we called aloud
three times to each of our poor lost companions,
slaughtered at the hands of the Cicones.

The Cloud Lord Zeus hurled North Wind at our ships,
a terrible typhoon, and covered up
the sea and earth with fog. Night fell from heaven
and seized us and our ships keeled over sideways;
the sails were ripped three times by blasting wind.
Scared for our lives, we hoisted down the sails
and rowed with all our might towards the shore.
We stayed there for two days and nights, exhausted,
eating our hearts with pain. When bright-haired Dawn
brought the third morning, we set up our masts,
unfurled the shining sails, and climbed aboard.
The wind blew straight, the pilots steered, and I
would have come safely home, to my own land,
but as I rounded Malea, a current
and blast of wind pushed me off course, away
from Cythera. For nine days I was swept
by stormy winds across the fish-filled sea.
On the tenth day, I landed on the island
of those who live on food from luscious lotus.
We gathered water, and my crew prepared
a meal. We picnicked by the ships, then I

chose two men, and one slave to make the third,
to go and scout. We needed to find out
what kind of people lived there on that island.
The scouts encountered humans, Lotus-Eaters,
who did not hurt them. They just shared with them
their sweet delicious fruit. But as they ate it,
they lost the will to come back and bring news
to me. They wanted only to stay there,
feeding on lotus with the Lotus-Eaters.
They had forgotten home. I dragged them back
in tears, forced them on board the hollow ships,
pushed them below the decks, and tied them up.
I told the other men, the loyal ones,
to get back in the ships, so no one else
would taste the lotus and forget about
our destination. They embarked and sat
along the rowing benches, side by side,
and struck the grayish water with their oars.

With heavy hearts we sailed along and reached
the country of the reckless Cyclopes,
lacking in customs. They put trust in gods,
and do not plant their food from seed, nor plow,
and yet the barley, grain, and clustering wine-grapes
all flourish there, increased by rain from Zeus.
They hold no councils, have no common laws,
but live in caves on lofty mountaintops,
and each makes laws for his own wife and children,
without concern for what the others think.
A distance from this island is another,
across the water, slantways from the harbor,
level and thickly wooded. Countless goats
live there but people never visit it.
No hunters labor through its woods to scale

its hilly peaks. There are no flocks of sheep,
no fields of plowland—it is all untilled,
unsown and uninhabited by humans.
Only the bleating goats live there and graze.
Cyclopic people have no red-cheeked ships
and no shipwright among them who could build
boats, to enable them to row across
to other cities, as most people do,
crossing the sea to visit one another.
With boats they could have turned this island into
a fertile colony, with proper harvests.
By the gray shore there lie well-watered meadows,
where vines would never fail. There is flat land
for plowing, and abundant crops would grow
in the autumn; there is richness underground.
The harbor has good anchorage; there is
no need of anchor stones or ropes or cables.
The ships that come to shore there can remain
beached safely till the sailors wish to leave
and fair winds blow. Up by the harbor head
freshwater gushes down beneath the caves.
The poplars grow around it. There we sailed:
the gods were guiding us all through the darkness.
Thick fog wrapped round our ships and in the sky
the moon was dark and clothed in clouds, so we
saw nothing of the island. None of us
could see the great waves rolling in towards
the land, until we rowed right to the beach.
We lowered all the sails and disembarked
onto the shore, and there we fell asleep.

When early Dawn shone forth with rosy fingers,
we roamed around that island full of wonders.
The daughters of the great King Zeus, the nymphs,
drove out the mountain goats so that my crew

could eat. On seeing them, we dashed to fetch
our javelins and bows from on board ship.
We split into three groups, took aim and shot.
Some god gave us good hunting. All twelve crews
had nine goats each, and ten for mine. We sat there
all day till sunset, eating meat and drinking
our strong red wine. The ships' supply of that
had not run out; when we had sacked the holy
citadel of the Cicones, we all
took gallons of it, poured in great big pitchers.
We looked across the narrow strip of water
at the Cyclopic island, saw their smoke,
and heard the baaing of their sheep and goats.
The sun went down and in the hours of darkness
we lay and slept on shore beside the sea.
But when the rosy hands of Dawn appeared,
I called my men together and addressed them.

'My loyal friends! Stay here, the rest of you,
while with my boat and crew I go to check
who those men are, find out if they are wild,
lawless aggressors, or the type to welcome
strangers, and fear the gods.'

With that, I climbed
on board and told my crew to come with me
and then untie the cables of the ship.
Quickly they did so, sat along the benches,
and struck the whitening water with their oars.
The journey was not long. Upon arrival,
right at the edge of land, beside the sea,
we saw a high cave overhung with laurel,
the home of several herds of sheep and goats.
Around that cave was built a lofty courtyard,
of deep-set stones, with tall pines rising up,

and leafy oaks. There lived a massive man
who shepherded his flocks all by himself.
He did not go to visit other people,
but kept apart, and did not know the ways
of custom. In his build he was a wonder,
a giant, not like men who live on bread,
but like a wooded peak in airy mountains,
rising alone above the rest.

I told
my loyal crew to guard the ship, while I
would go with just twelve chosen men, my favorites.
I took a goatskin full of dark sweet wine
that I was given by Apollo's priest,
Maron the son of Euanthes, who lived
inside the shady grove on Ismarus.
In reverence to the god, I came to help him,
and save his wife and son. He gave me gifts:
a silver bowl and seven pounds of gold,
well wrought, and siphoned off some sweet strong wine,
and filled twelve jars for me—a godlike drink.
The slaves knew nothing of this wine; it was
known just to him, his wife, and one house girl.
Whenever he was drinking it, he poured
a single shot into a cup, and added
twenty of water, and a marvelous smell
rose from the bowl, and all would long to taste it.
I filled a big skin up with it, and packed
provisions in a bag—my heart suspected
that I might meet a man of courage, wild,
and lacking knowledge of the normal customs.

We soon were at the cave, but did not find
the Cyclops; he was pasturing his flocks.
We went inside and looked at everything.

We saw his crates weighed down with cheese, and pens
crammed full of lambs divided up by age:
the newborns, middlings, and those just weaned.
There were well-crafted bowls and pails for milking,
all full of whey. My crew begged, 'Let us grab
some cheese and quickly drive the kids and lambs
out of their pens and down to our swift ships,
and sail away across the salty water!'
That would have been the better choice. But I
refused. I hoped to see him, and find out
if he would give us gifts. In fact he brought
no joy to my companions. Then we lit
a fire, and made a sacrifice, and ate
some cheese, and sat to wait inside the cave
until he brought his flocks back home. He came
at dinnertime, and brought a load of wood
to make a fire. He hurled it noisily
into the cave. We were afraid, and cowered
towards the back. He drove his ewes and nannies
inside to milk them, but he left the rams
and he-goats in the spacious yard outside.
He lifted up the heavy stone and set it
to block the entrance of the cave. It was
a rock so huge and massive, twenty-two
strong carts could not have dragged it from the threshold.
He sat, and all in order milked his ewes
and she-goats, then he set the lambs to suck
beside each bleating mother. Then he curdled
half of the fresh white milk, set that aside
in wicker baskets, and the rest he stored
in pails so he could drink it with his dinner.
When he had carefully performed his chores,
he lit a fire, then looked around and saw us.

'Strangers! Who are you? Where did you come from
across the watery depths? Are you on business,
or roaming round without a goal, like pirates,
who risk their lives at sea to bring disaster
to other people?'

So he spoke. His voice,
so deep and booming, and his giant size,
made our hearts sink in terror. Even so,
I answered,

'We are Greeks, come here from Troy.
The winds have swept us off in all directions
across the vast expanse of sea, off course
from our planned route back home. Zeus willed it so.
We are proud to be the men of Agamemnon,
the son of Atreus, whose fame is greatest
under the sky, for sacking that vast city
and killing many people. Now we beg you,
here at your knees, to grant a gift, as is
the norm for hosts and guests. Please sir, my lord:
respect the gods. We are your suppliants,
and Zeus is on our side, since he takes care
of visitors, guest-friends, and those in need.'

Unmoved he said, 'Well, foreigner, you are
a fool, or from some very distant country.
You order me to fear the gods! My people
think nothing of that Zeus with his big scepter,
nor any god; our strength is more than theirs.
If I spare you or spare your friends, it will not
be out of fear of Zeus. I do the bidding
of my own heart. But are you going far
in that fine ship of yours, or somewhere near?'

He spoke to test me, but I saw right through him.
I know how these things work. I answered him
deceitfully.

'Poseidon, the Earth-Shaker,
shipwrecked me at the far end of your island.
He pushed us in; wind dashed us on the rocks.
We barely managed to survive.'

But he
made no reply and showed no mercy. Leaping
up high, he reached his hands towards my men,
seized two, and knocked them hard against the ground
like puppies, and the floor was wet with brains.
He ripped them limb by limb to make his meal,
then ate them like a lion on the mountains,
devouring flesh, entrails, and marrow bones,
and leaving nothing. Watching this disaster,
we wept and lifted up our hands in prayer
to Zeus. We felt so helpless. When the Cyclops
had filled his massive belly with his meal
of human meat and unmixed milk, he lay
stretched out among his flocks. Then thinking like
a military man, I thought I should
get out my sword, go up to him and thrust
right through his torso, feeling for his liver.
That would have doomed us all. On second thoughts,
I realized we were too weak to move
the mighty stone he set in the high doorway.
So we stayed there in misery till dawn.

Early the Dawn appeared, pink fingers blooming,
and then he lit his fire and milked his ewes
in turn, and set a lamb by every one.
When he had diligently done his chores,

he grabbed two men and made a meal of them.
After he ate, he drove his fat flock out.
He rolled the boulder out and back with ease,
as one would set the lid upon a quiver.
Then whistling merrily, the Cyclops drove
his fat flocks to the mountain. I was left,
scheming to take revenge on him and hurt him,
and gain the glory, if Athena let me.
I made my plan. Beside the pen there stood
a great big club, green olive wood, which he
had cut to dry, to be his walking stick.
It was so massive that it looked to us
like a ship's mast, a twenty-oared black freighter
that sails across the vast sea full of cargo.
I went and cut from it about a fathom,
and gave it to the men, and ordered them
to scrape it down. They made it smooth and I
stood by and sharpened up the tip, and made it
hard in the blazing flame. The cave was full
of dung; I hid the club beneath a pile.
Then I gave orders that the men cast lots
for who would lift the stake with me and press it
into his eye, when sweet sleep overtook him.
The lots fell on the men I would have chosen:
four men, and I was fifth among their number.

At evening he drove back his woolly flocks
into the spacious cave, both male and female,
and left none in the yard outside—perhaps
suspecting something, or perhaps a god
told him to do it. He picked up and placed
the stone to form a door, and sat to milk
the sheep and bleating goats in turn, then put
the little ones to suck. His chores were done;
he grabbed two men for dinner. I approached

and offered him a cup of ivy wood,
filled full of wine. I said,

'Here, Cyclops! You
have eaten human meat; now drink some wine,
sample the merchandise our ship contains.
I brought it as a holy offering,
so you might pity me and send me home.
But you are in a cruel rage, beyond
what anyone could bear. Do you expect
more guests, when you have treated us so rudely?'

He took and drank the sweet delicious wine;
he loved it, and demanded more.

'Another!
And now tell me your name, so I can give you
a present as my guest, one you will like.
My people do have wine; grape clusters grow
from our rich earth, fed well by rain from Zeus.
But this is nectar, god food!'

So I gave him
another cup of wine, and then two more.
He drank them all, unwisely. With the wine
gone to his head, I told him, all politeness,

'Cyclops, you asked my name. I will reveal it;
then you must give the gift you promised me,
of hospitality. My name is Noman.
My family and friends all call me Noman.'

He answered with no pity in his heart,
'I will eat Noman last; first I will eat
the other men. That is my gift to you.'

Then he collapsed, fell on his back, and lay there,
his massive neck askew. All-conquering sleep
took him. In drunken heaviness, he spewed
wine from his throat, and chunks of human flesh.
And then I drove the spear into the embers
to heat it up, and told my men, 'Be brave!'
I wanted none of them to shrink in fear.
The fire soon had seized the olive spear,
green though it was, and terribly it glowed.
I quickly snatched it from the fire. My crew
stood firm: some god was breathing courage in us.
They took the olive spear, its tip all sharp,
and shoved it in his eye. I leaned on top
and twisted it, as when a man drills wood
for shipbuilding. Below, the workers spin
the drill with straps, stretched out from either end.
So round and round it goes, and so we whirled
the fire-sharp weapon in his eye. His blood
poured out around the stake, and blazing fire
sizzled his lids and brows, and fried the roots.
As when a blacksmith dips an axe or adze
to temper it in ice-cold water; loudly
it shrieks. From this, the iron takes on its power.
So did his eyeball crackle on the spear.
Horribly then he howled, the rocks resounded,
and we shrank back in fear. He tugged the spear
out of his eye, all soaked with gushing blood.
Desperately with both hands he hurled it from him,
and shouted to the Cyclopes who lived
in caves high up on windy cliffs around.
They heard and came from every side, and stood
near to the cave, and called out, 'Polyphemus!
What is the matter? Are you badly hurt?
Why are you screaming through the holy night

and keeping us awake? Is someone stealing
your herds, or trying to kill you, by some trick
or force?'

Strong Polyphemus from inside
replied, 'My friends! Noman is killing me
by tricks, not force.'

Their words flew back to him:
'If no one hurts you, you are all alone:
Great Zeus has made you sick; no help for that.
Pray to your father, mighty Lord Poseidon.'

Then off they went, and I laughed to myself,
at how my name, the 'no man' maneuver, tricked him.
The Cyclops groaned and labored in his pain,
felt with blind hands and took the door-stone out,
and sat there at the entrance, arms outstretched,
to catch whoever went out with the sheep.
Maybe he thought I was a total fool.
But I was strategizing, hatching plans,
so that my men and I could all survive.
I wove all kinds of wiles and cunning schemes;
danger was near and it was life or death.
The best idea I formed was this: there were
those well-fed sturdy rams with good thick fleece,
wool as dark as violets—all fine big creatures.
So silently I tied them with the rope
used by the giant Cyclops as a bed.
I bound the rams in sets of three and set
a man beneath each middle sheep, with one
on either side, and so my men were saved.
One ram was best of all the flock; I grabbed
his back and curled myself up underneath

his furry belly, clinging to his fleece;
by force of will I kept on hanging there.
And then we waited miserably for day.

When early Dawn revealed her rose-red hands,
the rams jumped up, all eager for the grass.
The ewes were bleating in their pens, unmilked,
their udders full to bursting. Though their master
was weak and worn with pain, he felt the back
of each ram as he lined them up—but missed
the men tied up beneath their woolly bellies.
Last of them all, the big ram went outside,
heavy with wool and me—the clever trickster.
Strong Polyphemus stroked his back and asked him,

'Sweet ram, why are you last today to leave
the cave? You are not normally so slow.
You are the first to eat the tender flowers,
leaping across the meadow, first to drink,
and first to want to go back to the sheepfold
at evening time. But now you are the last.
You grieve for Master's eye; that wicked man,
helped by his nasty henchmen, got me drunk
and blinded me. Noman will not escape!
If only you could talk like me, and tell me
where he is skulking in his fear of me.
Then I would dash his brains out on the rocks,
and make them spatter all across the cave,
to ease the pain that no-good Noman brought.'

With that, he nudged the ram away outside.
We rode a short way from the cave, then I
first freed myself and then untied my men.
We stole his nice fat animals, and ran,
constantly glancing all around and back

until we reached the ship. The other men
were glad to see us, their surviving friends,
but wept for those who died. I ordered them
to stop their crying, scowling hard at each.
I made them shove the fleecy flock on board,
and row the boat out into salty water.
So they embarked, sat on their rowing benches,
and struck their oar blades in the whitening sea.
When I had gone as far as shouts can carry,
I jeered back,

'Hey, you, Cyclops! Idiot!
The crew trapped in your cave did not belong
to some poor weakling. Well, you had it coming!
You had no shame at eating your own guests!
So Zeus and other gods have paid you back.'

My taunting made him angrier. He ripped
a rock out of the hill and hurled it at us.
It landed right in front of our dark prow,
and almost crushed the tip of the steering oar.
The stone sank in the water; waves surged up.
The backflow all at once propelled the ship
landwards; the swollen water pushed us with it.
I grabbed a big long pole, and shoved us off.
I told my men, 'Row fast, to save your lives!'
and gestured with my head to make them hurry.
They bent down to their oars and started rowing.
We got out twice as far across the sea,
and then I called to him again. My crew
begged me to stop, and pleaded with me.

'Please!
Calm down! Why are you being so insistent
and taunting this wild man? He hurled that stone

and drove our ship right back to land. We thought
that we were going to die. If he had heard us,
he would have hurled a jagged rock and crushed
our heads and wooden ship. He throws so hard!

But my tough heart was not convinced; I was
still furious, and shouted back again,

'Cyclops! If any mortal asks you how
your eye was mutilated and made blind,
say that Odysseus, the city-sacker,
Laertes' son, who lives in Ithaca,
destroyed your sight.'

He groaned, 'The prophecy!
It has come true at last! There was a tall
and handsome man named Telemus, the son
of Eurymus, who lived among my people;
he spent his life here, soothsaying for us.
He told me that Odysseus' hands
would make me lose my sight. I always thought
somebody tall and handsome, strong and brave
would come to me. But now this little weakling,
this little nobody, has blinded me;
by wine he got the best of me. Come on,
Odysseus, and let me give you gifts,
and ask Poseidon's help to get you home.
I am his son; the god is proud to be
my father. He will heal me, if he wants,
though no one else, not god nor man, can do it.'

After he said these words, I answered him,
'If only I could steal your life from you,
and send you down to Hades' house below,

as sure as nobody will ever heal you,
even the god of earthquakes.'

But he prayed
holding his arms towards the starry sky,
'Listen, Earth-Shaker, Blue-Haired Lord Poseidon:
acknowledge me your son, and be my father.
Grant that Odysseus, the city-sacker,
will never go back home. Or if it is
fated that he will see his family,
then let him get there late and with no honor,
in pain and lacking ships, and having caused
the death of all his men, and let him find
more trouble in his own house.'

Blue Poseidon
granted his son's prayer. Polyphemus raised
a rock far bigger than the last, and swung,
then hurled it with immeasurable force.
It fell a little short, beside our rudder,
and splashed into the sea; the waves surged up,
and pushed the boat ahead, to the other shore.
We reached the island where our ships were docked.
The men were sitting waiting for us, weeping.
We beached our ship and disembarked, then took
the sheep that we had stolen from the Cyclops
out of the ship's hold, and we shared them out
fairly, so all the men got equal portions.
But in dividing up the flock, my crew
gave me alone the ram, the Cyclops' favorite.
There on the shore, I slaughtered him for Zeus,
the son of Cronus, god of Dark Clouds, Lord
of all the world. I burned the thighs. The god
ignored my offering, and planned to ruin

all of my ships and all my loyal men.
So all day long till sunset we were sitting,
feasting on meat and drinking sweet strong wine.
But when the sun went down and darkness fell,
we went to sleep beside the breaking waves.
Then when rose-fingered Dawn came, bright and early,
I roused my men and told them to embark
and loose the cables. Quickly they obeyed,
sat at their rowing benches, all in order,
and struck the gray saltwater with their oars.
So we sailed on, with sorrow in our hearts,
glad to survive, but grieving for our friends."

BOOK 10

The Winds and the Witch

"We reached the floating island of Aeolus,
who is well loved by all the deathless gods.
Around it, on sheer cliffs, there runs a wall
of solid bronze, impregnable. Twelve children
live with him in his palace: six strong boys,
and six girls. He arranged their marriages,
one sister to each brother. They are always
feasting there with their parents, at a banquet
that never ends. By day, the savor fills
the house; the court reverberates with sound.
At night they sleep beside the wives they love
on rope beds piled with blankets.

We arrived
at that fine citadel. He welcomed me
and made me stay a month, and asked for news
of Troy, the Argive ships, and how the Greeks
went home. I told him everything. At last
I told him he should send me on my way.
So he agreed to help me, and he gave me

a bag of oxhide leather and he tied
the gusty winds inside it. Zeus, the son
of Cronus, made him steward of the winds,
and he can stop or rouse them as he wishes.
He bound the bag with shining silver wire
to my curved ship, so no gust could escape,
however small, and he made Zephyr blow
so that the breath could carry home our ships
and us. But it was not to be. Our folly
ruined us. For nine days and nights we sailed,
and on the tenth, our native land appeared.
We were so near, we saw men tending fires.
Exhausted, I let sweet sleep overcome me.
I had been doing all the steering, hoping
that we would get home sooner if I did.
But while I slept my men began to mutter,
saying the great Aeolus gave me gifts—
silver and gold that I was taking home.
With glances to his neighbor, each complained,

'It seems that everybody loves this man,
and honors him, in every place we sail to.
He also has that loot from sacking Troy.
We shared the journey with him, yet we come
back home with empty hands. And now Aeolus
has made this friendly gift to him. So hurry,
we should look in the bag, and see how much
is in there—how much silver, how much gold.'

That bad idea took hold of them; they did it.
They opened up the bag, and all the winds
rushed out at once. A sudden buffet seized us
and hurled us back to sea, the wrong direction,
far from our home. They screamed and I woke up,

and wondered if I should jump off the ship
and drown, or bite my lip, be stoical,
and stay among the living. I endured it,
covered my face, and lay on deck. A blast
of storm wind whooshed the ships back to the island
of great Aeolus. They began to weep.
We disembarked and filled our jars with water,
and hungrily the men devoured their dinner.
When they were done, I took one slave with me
and one crew member, back to see Aeolus.
He was at dinner with his wife and children.
We entered and sat down beside the doorposts.
Startled, they asked,

'Why are you here again?
You had bad luck? What happened? Surely we
helped you go on your way, and meant for you
to reach your homeland, where you wished to go.'

I answered sadly, 'Blame my men, and blame
my stubborn urge to sleep, which ruined us.
Dear friends, you have the power to put things right.'

I hoped these words would soften them, but they
were silent. Then the father yelled, 'Get out!
You nasty creature, leave my island! Now!
It is not right for me to help convey
a man so deeply hated by the gods.
You godforsaken thing, how dare you come here?
Get out!'

He roared and drove us from his palace.
Dispirited, we sailed away. The men
grew worn out with the agony of rowing;

our folly had deprived us of fair winds.
We rowed six days and nights; the seventh day
we came to Laestrygonia—the town
of Telepylus upon the cliffs of Lamos.
A herdsman there, returning to his home,
can greet another herdsman going out.
A sleepless man could earn a double wage
by herding cows, then pasturing white sheep—
the paths of day and night are close together.
We reached the famous harbor, all surrounded
by sheer rock cliffs. On each side, strips of shore
jut out and almost meet, a narrow mouth.
No waves rear up in there, not even small ones.
White calm is everywhere. So all the others
harbored their ships inside, crammed close together.
I was the only one who chose to moor
my ship outside the harbor, fastening
the cables to a rock a way away.
I disembarked and climbed a crag to scout.
I saw no sign of cattle or of humans,
except some smoke that rose up from the earth.
I picked two men, and one slave as the third,
and sent them to find out what people lived
and ate bread in this land. They disembarked
and walked along a smooth path, where the wagons
brought wood down from the mountains to the city.
They met a girl in front of town, out fetching
some water. She was heading for the fountain
of Artaky, the whole town's water source.
She was the strapping child of Antiphates,
king of the Laestrygonians. They asked her
about the king and people of the country.
She promptly took them to the high-roofed palace
of her own father. When they went inside

they found a woman, mountain-high. They were
appalled and shocked. The giantess at once
summoned the king her husband from the council;
he tried to kill my men, and grabbing one
he ate him up. The other two escaped,
back to the ship. The king's shout boomed through town.
Hearing, the mighty Laestrygonians
thronged from all sides, not humanlike, but giants.
With boulders bigger than a man could lift
they pelted at us from the cliffs. We heard
the dreadful uproar of ships being broken
and dying men. They speared them there like fish.
A gruesome meal! While they were killing them
inside the harbor, I drew out my sword
and cut the ropes that moored my dark-cheeked ship,
and yelling to my men, I told them, 'Row
as fast as possible away from danger!'
They rowed at double time, afraid to die.
My ship was lucky and we reached the sea
beyond the overhanging cliffs. The rest,
trapped in the bay together, were destroyed.
We sailed off sadly, happy to survive,
but with our good friends lost. We reached Aeaea,
home of the beautiful, dreadful goddess Circe,
who speaks in human languages—the sister
of Aeetes whose mind is set on ruin.
Those two are children of the Sun who shines
on mortals, and of Perse, child of Ocean.
Under the guidance of some god we drifted
silently to the harbor, and we moored there.
For two days and two nights we lay onshore,
exhausted and our hearts consumed with grief.
On the third morning brought by braided Dawn,
I took my spear and sharp sword, and I ran

up from the ship to higher ground, to look
for signs of humans, listening for voices.
I climbed up to a crag, and I saw smoke
rising from Circe's palace, from the earth
up through the woods and thickets. I considered
if I should go down and investigate,
since I had seen the smoke. But I decided
to go back down first, to the beach and ship
and feed my men, and then set out to scout.
When I had almost reached my ship, some god
took pity on me in my loneliness,
and sent a mighty stag with great tall antlers
to cross my path. He ran down from the forest
to drink out of the river; it was hot.
I struck him in the middle of his back;
my bronze spear pierced him. With a moan, he fell
onto the dust; his spirit flew away.
I stepped on him and tugged my bronze spear out,
and left it on the ground, while I plucked twigs
and twines, and wove a rope, a fathom's length,
well knotted all the way along, and bound
the hooves of that huge animal. I went
down to my dark ship with him on my back.
I used my spear to lean on, since the stag
was too big to be lugged across one shoulder.
I dumped him down before the ship and made
a comforting pep talk to cheer my men.

'My friends! We will not yet go down to Hades,
sad though we are, before our fated day.
Come on, since we have food and drink on board,
let us not starve ourselves; now time to eat!'

They quickly heeded my commands, and took
their cloaks down from their faces, and they marveled

to see the big stag lying on the beach.
It was enormous. When they finished staring,
they washed their hands and cooked a splendid meal.
So all that day till sunset we sat eating
the meat aplenty and the strong sweet wine.
When darkness fell, we went to sleep beside
the seashore. Then the roses of Dawn's fingers
appeared again; I called my men and told them,

'Listen to me, my friends, despite your grief.
We do not know where darkness lives, nor dawn,
nor where the sun that shines upon the world
goes underneath the earth, nor where it rises.
We need a way to fix our current plight,
but I do not know how. I climbed the rocks
to higher ground to look around. This is
an island, wreathed about by boundless sea.
The land lies low. I saw smoke in the middle,
rising up through the forest and thick bush.'

At that, their hearts sank, since they all remembered
what happened with the Laestrygonians,
their King Antiphates, and how the mighty
Cyclops devoured the men. They wept and wailed,
and shed great floods of tears. But all that grieving
could do no good. I made them wear their armor,
and split them in two groups. I led one,
and made Eurylochus command the other.
We shook the lots in a helmet made of bronze;
Eurylochus' lot jumped out. So he
went with his band of twenty-two, all weeping.
Those left behind with me were crying too.
Inside the glade they found the house of Circe
built out of polished stones, on high foundations.
Round it were mountain wolves and lions, which

she tamed with drugs. They did not rush on them,
but gathered around them in a friendly way,
their long tails wagging, as dogs nuzzle round
their master when he comes back home from dinner
with treats for them. Just so, those sharp-clawed wolves
and lions, mighty beasts, came snuggling up.
The men were terrified. They stood outside
and heard some lovely singing. It was Circe,
the goddess. She was weaving as she sang,
an intricate, enchanting piece of work,
the kind a goddess fashions. Then Polites,
my most devoted and most loyal man,
a leader to his peers, said,

'Friends, inside
someone is weaving on that massive loom,
and singing so the floor resounds. Perhaps
a woman, or a goddess. Let us call her.'

They shouted out to her. She came at once,
opened the shining doors, and asked them in.
So thinking nothing of it, in they went.
Eurylochus alone remained outside,
suspecting trickery. She led them in,
sat them on chairs, and blended them a potion
of barley, cheese, and golden honey, mixed
with Pramnian wine. She added potent drugs
to make them totally forget their home.
They took and drank the mixture. Then she struck them,
using her magic wand, and penned them in
the pigsty. They were turned to pigs in body
and voice and hair; their minds remained the same.
They squealed at their imprisonment, and Circe
threw them some mast and cornel cherries—food
that pigs like rooting for in muddy ground.

Eurylochus ran back to our black ship,
to tell us of the terrible disaster
that happened to his friends. He tried to speak,
but could not, overwhelmed by grief. His eyes
were full of tears, his heart was pierced with sorrow.
Astonished, we all questioned him. At last
he spoke about what happened to the others.

'Odysseus, we went off through the woods,
as you commanded. In the glade we found
a beautiful tall house of polished stone.
We heard a voice: a woman or a goddess
was singing as she worked her loom. My friends
called out to her. She opened up the doors,
inviting them inside. Suspecting nothing,
they followed her. But I stayed there outside,
fearing some trick. Then all at once, they vanished.
I sat there for a while to watch and wait,
but none of them came back.'

At this, I strapped
my silver-studded sword across my back,
took up my bow, and told him, 'Take me there.'
He grasped my knees and begged me tearfully,

'No no, my lord! Please do not make me go!
Let me stay here! You cannot bring them back,
and you will not return here if you try.
Hurry, we must escape with these men here!
We have a chance to save our lives!'

I said,
'You can stay here beside the ship and eat
and drink. But I will go. I must do this.'

I left the ship and shore, and walked on up,
crossing the sacred glades, and I had almost
reached the great house of the enchantress Circe,
when I met Hermes, carrying his wand
of gold. He seemed an adolescent boy,
the cutest age, when beards first start to grow.
He took my hand and said,

'Why have you come
across these hills alone? You do not know
this place, poor man. Your men were turned to pigs
in Circe's house, and crammed in pens. Do you
imagine you can set them free? You cannot.
If you try that, you will not get back home.
You will stay here with them. But I can help you.
Here, take this antidote to keep you safe
when you go into Circe's house. Now I
will tell you all her lethal spells and tricks.
She will make you a potion mixed with poison.
Its magic will not work on you because
you have the herb I gave you. When she strikes you
with her long wand, then draw your sharpened sword
and rush at her as if you mean to kill her.
She will be frightened of you, and will tell you
to sleep with her. Do not hold out against her—
she is a goddess. If you sleep with her,
you will set free your friends and save yourself.
Tell her to swear an oath by all the gods
that she will not plot further harm for you—
or while you have your clothes off, she may hurt you,
unmanning you.'

The bright mercurial god
pulled from the ground a plant and showed me how

its root is black, its flower white as milk.
The gods call this plant Moly. It is hard
for mortal men to dig it up, but gods
are able to do everything. Then Hermes
flew through the wooded island, back towards
high Mount Olympus. I went in the house
of Circe. My heart pounded as I walked.
I stood there at the doorway, and I saw her,
the lovely Circe with her braided hair.
I called; she heard and opened up the doors
and asked me in. I followed nervously.
She led me to a silver-studded chair,
all finely crafted, with a footstool under.
In a gold cup she mixed a drink for me,
adding the drug—she hoped to do me harm.
I sipped it, but the magic did not work.
She struck me with her wand and said,

'Now go!
Out to the sty, and lie there with your men!'
But I drew my sharp sword from by my thigh
and leapt at her as if I meant to kill her.
She screamed and ducked beneath the sword, and grasped
my knees, and wailing asked me,

'Who are you?
Where is your city? And who are your parents?
I am amazed that you could drink my potion
and yet not be bewitched. No other man
has drunk it and withstood the magic charm.
But you are different. Your mind is not
enchanted. You must be Odysseus,
the man who can adapt to anything.
Bright flashing Hermes of the golden wand

has often told me that you would sail here
from Troy in your swift ship. Now sheathe your sword
and come to bed with me. Through making love
we may begin to trust each other more.'

I answered, 'Circe! How can you command me
to treat you gently, when you turned my men
to pigs, and you are planning to play tricks
in telling me to come to bed with you,
so you can take my courage and my manhood
when you have got me naked? I refuse
to come to bed with you, unless you swear
a mighty oath that you will not form plans
to hurt me anymore.'

When I said that,
at once she made the oath as I had asked.
She vowed and formed the oath, and then at last
I went up to the dazzling bed of Circe.

Meanwhile, four slaves, her house girls, were at work
around the palace. They were nymphs, the daughters
of fountains and of groves and holy rivers
that flow into the sea. One set fine cloths
of purple on the chairs, with stones beneath them.
Beside each chair, another pulled up tables
of silver and set golden baskets on them.
The third mixed up inside a silver bowl
sweet, cheering wine, and poured it in gold cups.
The fourth brought water, and she lit a fire
beneath a mighty tripod, till it boiled.
It started bubbling in the copper cauldron;
she took me to the bathtub, and began
to wash my head and shoulders, using water
mixed to the perfect temperature, to take

my deep soul-crushing weariness away.
After the bath, she oiled my skin and dressed me
in fine wool cloak and tunic, and she led me
to a silver-studded well-carved chair, and set
a footstool underneath. Another slave
brought water for my hands, in a gold pitcher,
and poured it over them, to a silver bowl.
She set a polished table near. The cook
brought bread and laid a generous feast, and Circe
told me to eat. But my heart was unwilling.
I sat there with my mind on other things;
I had forebodings. Circe noticed me
sitting, not touching food, and weighed by grief.
She stood near me and asked, 'Odysseus!
why are you sitting there so silently,
like someone mute, eating your heart, not touching
the banquet or the wine? You need not fear.
Remember, I already swore an oath.'

But I said, 'Circe, no! What decent man
could bear to taste his food or sip his wine
before he saw his men with his own eyes,
and set them free? If you are so insistent
on telling me to eat and drink, then free them,
so I may see with my own eyes my crew
of loyal men.'

So Circe left the hall
holding her wand, and opened up the pigsty
and drove them out, still looking like fat boars,
large and full grown. They stood in front of her.
Majestic Lady Circe walked among them,
anointing each with some new drug. The potion
had made thick hog-hairs sprout out on their bodies.
Those bristles all flew off and they were men,

but younger than before, and much more handsome,
and taller. Then they recognized me. Each
embraced me tightly in his arms, and started
sobbing in desperation. So the house
rang loud with noise, and even she herself
pitied them. She came near to me and said,

'Odysseus, you always find solutions.
Go now to your swift ship beside the sea.
First drag the ship to land, and bring your stores
and all your gear inside the caves. Then come
back with your loyal men.'

My heart agreed;
I went down to my swift ship on the shore.
I found my loyal men beside the ship,
weeping and shedding floods of tears. As when
a herd of cows is coming back from pasture
into the yard; and all the little heifers
jump from their pens to skip and run towards
their mothers, and they cluster round them, mooing;
just so my men, as soon as they saw me,
began to weep, and in their minds it seemed
as if they had arrived in their own home,
the land of rugged Ithaca, where they
were born and raised. Still sobbing, they cried out,

'Oh, Master! We are glad to see you back!
It is as if we had come home ourselves,
to Ithaca, our fatherland. But tell us
about how all our other friends were killed.'

I reassured them, saying, 'First we must
drag up the ship to land, and put the stores

and all our gear inside the caves; then hurry,
all of you, come with me, and see your friends
inside the goddess Circe's holy house,
eating and drinking; they have food enough
to last forever.'

They believed my story,
with the exception of Eurylochus,
who warned them,

'Fools! Why would you go up there?
Why would you choose to take on so much danger,
to enter Circe's house, where she will turn us
to pigs or wolves or lions, all of us,
forced to protect her mighty house for her?
Remember what the Cyclops did? Our friends
went to his home with this rash lord of ours.
Because of his bad choices, they all died.'

At that, I thought of drawing my long sword
from by my sturdy thigh, to cut his head off
and let it fall down to the ground—although
he was close family. My men restrained me,
saying to me, 'No, king, please let him go!
Let him stay here and guard the ship, and we
will follow you to Circe's holy house.'

So they went up, away from ship and shore.
Eurylochus did not stay there; he came,
fearing my angry scolding.

Meanwhile Circe
had freed the other men, and in her house
she gently bathed them, rubbing them with oil.

She had them dressed in woolen cloaks and tunics.
We found them feasting in the hall. The men,
seeing each other face-to-face again,
began to weep; their sobbing filled the hall.
The goddess stood beside me and said,

'King,
clever Odysseus, Laertes' son,
now stop encouraging this lamentation.
I know you and your men have suffered greatly,
out on the fish-filled sea, and on dry land
from hostile men. But it is time to eat
and drink some wine. You must get back the drive
you had when you set out from Ithaca.
You are worn down and brokenhearted, always
dwelling on pain and wandering. You never
feel joy at heart. You have endured too much.'

We did as she had said. Then every day
for a whole year we feasted there on meat
and sweet strong wine. But when the year was over,
when months had waned and seasons turned, and each
long day had passed its course, my loyal men
called me and said,

'Be guided by the gods.
Now it is time to think of our own country,
if you are fated to survive and reach
your high-roofed house and your forefathers' land.'

My warrior soul agreed. So all day long
till sunset we kept sitting at the feast
of meat and sweet strong wine. But when the sun
set, and the darkness came, they went to bed
all through the shadowy palace. I went up

to Circe's splendid bed, and touched her knees
in supplication, and the goddess listened.

'Circe,' I said, 'Fulfill the vow you made
to send me home. My heart now longs to go.
My men are also desperate to leave.
Whenever you are absent, they exhaust me
with constant lamentation.'

And she answered,
'Laertes' son, great King Odysseus,
master of every challenge, you need not
remain here in my house against your will.
But first you must complete another journey.
Go to the house of Hades and the dreadful
Persephone, and ask the Theban prophet,
the blind Tiresias, for his advice.
Persephone has given him alone
full understanding, even now in death.
The other spirits flit around as shadows.'

That broke my heart, and sitting on the bed
I wept, and lost all will to live and see
the shining sun. When I was done with sobbing
and rolling round in grief, I said to her,

'But Circe, who can guide us on this journey?
No one before has ever sailed to Hades
by ship.'

And right away the goddess answered,
'You are resourceful, King Odysseus.
You need not worry that you have no pilot
to steer your ship. Set up your mast, let fly
your white sails, and sit down. The North Wind's breath

will blow the ship. When you have crossed the stream
of Ocean, you will reach the shore, where willows
let fall their dying fruit, and towering poplars
grow in the forest of Persephone.
Tie up your ship in the deep-eddying Ocean,
and go into the spacious home of Hades.
The Pyriphlegethon and Cocytus,
a tributary of the Styx, both run
into the Acheron. The flowing water
resounds beside the rock. Brave man, go there,
and dig a hole a cubit wide and long,
and round it pour libations for the dead:
first honey-mix, then sweet wine, and the third
of water. Sprinkle barley, and beseech
the spirits of the dead. Vow if you reach
the barren land of Ithaca, to kill
a heifer in your halls, the best you have,
uncalved, and you will heap the fire with meat,
and offer to Tiresias alone
a ram, pure black, the best of all your flock.
When you have prayed to all the famous dead,
slaughter one ram and one black ewe, directing
the animals to Erebus, but turn
yourself away, towards the gushing river.
Many will come. Then tell your men to skin
the sheep that lie there killed by ruthless bronze,
and burn them, with a prayer to mighty Hades
and terrible Persephone. Then draw
your sword and sit. Do not let them come near
the blood, until you hear Tiresias.
The prophet will soon come, and he will tell you
about your journey, measured out across
the fish-filled sea, and how you will get home.'

Dawn on her golden throne began to shine,
and Circe dressed me in my cloak and tunic.
The goddess wore a long white dress, of fine
and delicate fabric, with a golden belt,
and on her head, a veil. Then I walked round,
all through the house, and called my men. I stood
beside each one, and roused them with my words.

'Wake up! Now no more dozing in sweet sleep.
We have to go. The goddess gave instructions.'

They did as I had said. But even then
I could not lead my men away unharmed.
The youngest one—Elpenor was his name—
not very brave in war, nor very smart,
was lying high up in the home of Circe,
apart from his companions, seeking coolness
since he was drunk. He heard the noise and bustle,
the movements of his friends, and jumped up quickly,
forgetting to climb down the lofty ladder.
He fell down crashing headlong from the roof,
and broke his neck, right at the spine. His spirit
went down to Hades.

Then I told the others,
'Perhaps you think that you are going home.
But Circe says we have to go towards
the house of Hades and Persephone,
to meet Tiresias, the Theban spirit.'

At that, their hearts were broken. They sat down
right there and wept and tore their clothes. But all
their lamentation did no good. We went
down to our speedy ship beside the sea,

despite our grief. We shed abundant tears.
Then Circe came and tied up one black ewe
and one ram by the ship, and slipped away,
easily; who can see the gods go by
unless they wish to show themselves to us?"

BOOK 11

The Dead

"We reached the sea and first of all we launched
the ship into the sparkling salty water,
set up the mast and sails, and brought the sheep
on board with us. We were still grieving, weeping,
in floods of tears. But beautiful, dread Circe,
the goddess who can speak in human tongues,
sent us a wind to fill our sails, fair wind
befriending us behind the dark blue prow.
We made our tackle shipshape, then sat down.
The wind and pilot guided straight our course.
The sun set. It was dark in all directions.

We reached the limits of deep-flowing Ocean,
where the Cimmerians live and have their city.
Their land is covered up in mist and cloud;
the shining Sun God never looks on them
with his bright beams—not when he rises up
into the starry sky, nor when he turns
back from the heavens to earth. Destructive night
blankets the world for all poor mortals there.

We beached our ship, drove out the sheep, and went
to seek the stream of Ocean where the goddess
had told us we must go. Eurylochus
and Perimedes made the sacrifice.
I drew my sword and dug a hole, a cubit
widthways and lengthways, and I poured libations
for all the dead: first honey-mix, sweet wine,
and lastly, water. On the top, I sprinkled
barley, and made a solemn vow that if
I reached my homeland, I would sacrifice
my best young heifer, still uncalved, and pile
the altar high with offerings for the dead.
I promised for Tiresias as well
a pure black sheep, the best in all my flock.
So with these vows, I called upon the dead.
I took the sheep and slit their throats above
the pit. Black blood flowed out. The spirits came
up out of Erebus and gathered round.
Teenagers, girls and boys, the old who suffered
for many years, and fresh young brides whom labor
destroyed in youth; and many men cut down
in battle by bronze spears, still dressed in armor
stained with their blood. From every side they crowded
around the pit, with eerie cries. Pale fear
took hold of me. I roused my men and told them
to flay the sheep that I had killed, and burn them,
and pray to Hades and Persephone.
I drew my sword and sat on guard, preventing
the spirits of the dead from coming near
the blood, till I had met Tiresias.

First came the spirit of my man Elpenor,
who had not yet been buried in the earth.
We left his body in the house of Circe
without a funeral or burial;

we were too occupied with other things.
On sight of him, I wept in pity, saying,

'Elpenor, how did you come here, in darkness?
You came on foot more quickly than I sailed.'

He groaned in answer, 'Lord Odysseus,
you master every circumstance. But I
had bad luck from some god, and too much wine
befuddled me. In Circe's house I lay
upstairs, and I forgot to use the ladder
to climb down from the roof. I fell headfirst;
my neck was broken from my spine. My spirit
came down to Hades. By the men you left,
the absent ones! And by your wife! And father,
who brought you up from babyhood! And by
your son, Telemachus, whom you abandoned
alone at home, I beg you! When you sail
from Hades and you dock your ship again
at Aeaea, please, my lord, remember me.
Do not go on and leave me there unburied,
abandoned, without tears or lamentation—
or you will make the gods enraged at you.
Burn me with all my arms, and heap a mound
beside the gray salt sea, so in the future
people will know of me and my misfortune.
And fix into the tomb the oar I used
to row with my companions while I lived.'

'Poor man!' I answered, 'I will do all this.'

We sat there talking sadly—I on one side
held firm my sword in blood, while on the other
the ghost of my crew member made his speech.

Then came the spirit of my own dead mother,
Autolycus' daughter Anticleia,
whom I had left alive when I went off
to holy Troy. On seeing her, I wept
in pity. But despite my bitter grief,
I would not let her near the blood till I
talked to Tiresias. The prophet came
holding a golden scepter, and he knew me,
and said,

'King under Zeus, Odysseus,
adept survivor, why did you abandon
the sun, poor man, to see the dead, and this
place without joy? Step back now from the pit,
hold up your sharp sword so that I may drink
the blood and speak to you.'

At that, I sheathed
my silver-studded sword. When he had drunk
the murky blood, the famous prophet spoke.

'Odysseus, you think of going home
as honey-sweet, but gods will make it bitter.
I think Poseidon will not cease to feel
incensed because you blinded his dear son.
You have to suffer, but you can get home,
if you control your urges and your men.
Turn from the purple depths and sail your ship
towards the island of Thrinacia; there
you will find grazing cows and fine fat sheep,
belonging to the god who sees and hears
all things—the Sun God. If you leave them be,
keeping your mind fixed on your journey home,
you may still get to Ithaca, despite

great losses. But if you hurt those cows, I see
disaster for your ship and for your men.
If you yourself escape, you will come home
late and exhausted, in a stranger's boat,
having destroyed your men. And you will find
invaders eating your supplies at home,
courting your wife with gifts. Then you will match
the suitors' violence and kill them all,
inside your halls, through tricks or in the open,
with sharp bronze weapons. When those men are dead,
you have to go away and take an oar
to people with no knowledge of the sea,
who do not salt their food. They never saw
a ship's red prow, nor oars, the wings of boats.
I prophesy the signs of things to come.
When you meet somebody, a traveler,
who calls the thing you carry on your back
a winnowing fan, then fix that oar in earth
and make fine sacrifices to Poseidon—
a bull and stud-boar. Then you will go home
and offer holy hecatombs to all
the deathless gods who live in heaven, each
in order. Gentle death will come to you,
far from the sea, of comfortable old age,
your people flourishing. So it will be.'

I said, 'Tiresias, I hope the gods
spin out this fate for me. But tell me this,
and tell the truth. I saw my mother's spirit,
sitting in silence near the blood, refusing
even to talk to me, or meet my eyes!
My lord, how can I make her recognize
that it is me?'

At once he made his answer.
'That is an easy matter to explain.
Whenever you allow one of these spirits
to come here near the blood, it will be able
to speak the truth to you. As soon as you
push them away, they have to leave again.'

With that, Tiresias, the prophet spirit,
was finished; he departed to the house
of Hades. I stayed rooted there in place
until my mother came and drank the blood.
She knew me then and spoke in tones of grief.

'My child! How did you come here through the darkness
while you were still alive? This place is hard
for living men to see. There are great rivers
and dreadful gulfs, including the great Ocean
which none can cross on foot; one needs a ship.
Have you come wandering here, so far from Troy,
with ship and crew? Have you not yet arrived
in Ithaca, nor seen your wife at home?'

I answered, 'Mother, I was forced to come
to Hades to consult the prophet spirit,
Theban Tiresias. I have not yet
come near to Greece, nor reached my own home country.
I have been lost and wretchedly unhappy
since I first followed mighty Agamemnon
to Troy, the land of horses, to make war
upon the people there. But tell me, how
was sad death brought upon you? By long illness?
Or did the archer Artemis destroy you
with gentle arrows? Tell me too about
my father and the son I left behind.

Are they still honored as the kings? Or has
another taken over, saying I
will not return? And tell me what my wife
is thinking, and her plans. Does she stay with
our son and focus on his care, or has
the best of the Achaeans married her?'

My mother answered, 'She stays firm. Her heart
is strong. She is still in your house. And all
her nights are passed in misery, and days
in tears. But no one has usurped your throne.
Telemachus still tends the whole estate
unharmed and feasts in style, as lords should do,
and he is always asked to council meetings.
Your father stays out in the countryside.
He will not come to town. He does not sleep
on a real bed with blankets and fresh sheets.
In winter he sleeps inside, by the fire,
just lying in the ashes with the slaves;
his clothes are rags. In summer and at harvest,
the piles of fallen leaves are beds for him.
He lies there grieving, full of sorrow, longing
for your return. His old age is not easy.
And that is why I met my fate and died.
The goddess did not shoot me in my home,
aiming with gentle arrows. Nor did sickness
suck all the strength out from my limbs, with long
and cruel wasting. No, it was missing you,
Odysseus, my sunshine; your sharp mind,
and your kind heart. That took sweet life from me.'

Then in my heart I wanted to embrace
the spirit of my mother. She was dead,
and I did not know how. Three times I tried,

longing to touch her. But three times her ghost
flew from my arms, like shadows or like dreams.
Sharp pain pierced deeper in me as I cried,

'No, Mother! Why do you not stay for me,
and let me hold you, even here in Hades?
Let us wrap loving arms around each other
and find a frigid comfort in shared tears!
But is this really you? Or has the Queen
sent me a phantom, to increase my grief?'

She answered, 'Oh, my child! You are the most
unlucky man alive. Persephone
is not deceiving you. This is the rule
for mortals when we die. Our muscles cease
to hold the flesh and skeleton together;
as soon as life departs from our white bones,
the force of blazing fire destroys the corpse.
The spirit flies away and soon is gone,
just like a dream. Now hurry to the light;
remember all these things, so you may tell
your wife in times to come.'

As we were talking,
some women came, sent by Persephone—
the daughters and the wives of warriors.
They thronged and clustered round the blood. I wanted
to speak to each of them, and made a plan.
I drew my sword and would not let them come
together in a group to drink the blood.
They took turns coming forward, and each told
her history; I questioned each. The first
was well-born Tyro, child of Salmoneus,
and wife of Cretheus, Aeolus' son.
She fell in love with River Enipeus,

most handsome of all rivers that pour water
over the earth. She often went to visit
his lovely streams. Poseidon took his form,
and at the river mouth he lay with her.
Around them arched a dark-blue wave that stood
high as a mountain, and it hid the god
and mortal woman. There he loosed her belt
and made her sleep. The god made love to her,
and afterwards, he took her hand and spoke.

'Woman, be glad about this love. You will
bear glorious children in the coming year.
Affairs with gods always result in offspring.
Look after them and raise them. Now go home;
tell no one who I am. But I will tell you.
I am Poseidon, Shaker of the Earth.'
With that he sank beneath the ocean waves.

She brought two sons to term, named Pelias
and Neleus, both sturdy boys who served
almighty Zeus; and Pelias' home
was on the spacious dancing fields of Iolcus,
where sheep are plentiful; his brother lived
in sandy Pylos. And she bore more sons,
to Cretheus: Aeson, Pheres, Amythaeon
who loved war chariots.

And after her
I saw Antiope, who said she slept
in Zeus' arms and bore two sons: Amphion
and Zethus, the first settlers of Thebes,
city of seven gates. Strong though they were,
they could not live there on the open plain
without defenses.

Then I saw Alcmene,
wife of Amphitryon, who by great Zeus
conceived the lionhearted Heracles.
And I saw Megara, proud Creon's child,
the wife of tireless Heracles. I saw
fine Epicaste, Oedipus' mother,
who did a dreadful thing in ignorance:
she married her own son. He killed his father,
and married her. The gods revealed the truth
to humans; through their deadly plans, he ruled
the Cadmeans in Thebes, despite his pain.
But Epicaste crossed the gates of Hades;
she tied a noose and hung it from the ceiling,
and hanged herself for sorrow, leaving him
the agonies a mother's Furies bring.

Then I saw Chloris, who was youngest daughter
of Amphion, who ruled the Minyans
in Orchomenus. She was beautiful,
and Neleus paid rich bride-gifts for her.
She was the queen in Pylos, and she bore
Chromius, Nestor, Periclymenus,
and mighty Pyro, who was such a marvel
that all the men desired to marry her.
But Neleus would only let her marry
a man who could drive off the stubborn cattle
of Iphicles from Phylace. The prophet
Melampus was the only one who tried,
but gods restrained him, cursing him; the herdsmen
shackled him. Days and months went by, the seasons
changed as the year went by, until at last
Iphicles set him free as his reward
for prophecy. The will of Zeus was done.

And then I saw Tyndareus' wife,
Leda, who bore him two strong sons: the horseman
Castor, and Polydeuces, skillful boxer.
Life-giving earth contains them, still alive.
Zeus honors them even in the underworld.
They live and die alternately, and they
are honored like the gods.

And then I saw
Iphimedeia, wife of Aloeus,
who proudly said Poseidon slept with her.
She had two sons whose lives were both cut short:
Otus and famous Ephialtes, whom
the fertile earth raised up as the tallest heroes
after renowned Orion. At nine years,
they were nine cubits wide, nine fathoms high.
They brought the din of dreadful raging war
to the immortal gods and tried to set
Ossa and Pelion—trees, leaves and all—
on Mount Olympus, high up in the sky.
They might have managed it, if they had reached
full adulthood. Apollo, son of Zeus
by braided Leto, killed them: they were both
dead before down could grow on their young chins,
dead before beards could wreathe their naked faces.

Then I saw Phaedra, Procris, and the lovely
daughter of dangerous Minos, Ariadne.
Theseus tried to bring her back from Crete
to Athens, but could not succeed; the goddess
Artemis killed her on the isle of Día,
when Dionysus spoke against her. Then
came Maera, Clymene and Eriphyle:
accepting golden bribes, she killed her husband.

I cannot name each famous wife and daughter
I saw there; holy night would pass away
before I finished. I must go to sleep
on board the ship beside my crew, or else
right here. I know the gods and you will help
my onward journey."

They were silent, spellbound,
listening in the shadowy hall. White-armed
Arete spoke.

"Phaeacians! Look at him!
What a tall, handsome man! And what a mind!
He is my special guest, but all of you
share in our rank as lords; so do not send him
away too fast, and when he leaves, you must
be generous. He is in need, and you
are rich in treasure, through the will of gods."

The veteran Echeneus, the oldest
man in their company, said, "Our wise queen
has hit the mark, my friends. Do as she says.
But first Alcinous must speak and act."

The king said, "Let it be as she has spoken,
as long as I am ruler of this nation
of seafarers. I know our guest is keen
to go back home, but let him stay till morning.
I will give all his presents then. You men
will all help him, but I will help the most,
since I hold power here."

Odysseus
answered with careful tact, "Alcinous,

king over all the people, if you urged me
to stay here for a year before you gave
the parting gifts and sent me on my way,
I would be happy. It would be far better
to reach my own dear home with hands filled full
of treasure. So all men would honor me
and welcome me back home in Ithaca."

Alcinous replied, "Odysseus,
the earth sustains all different kinds of people.
Many are cheats and thieves, who fashion lies
out of thin air. But when I look at you,
I know you are not in that category.
Your story has both grace and wisdom in it.
You sounded like a skillful poet, telling
the sufferings of all the Greeks, including
what you endured yourself. But come now, tell me
if you saw any spirits of your friends,
who went with you to Troy and undertook
the grief and pain of war. The night is long;
it is not time to sleep yet. Tell me more
amazing deeds! I would keep listening
until bright daybreak, if you kept on telling
the dangers you have passed."

Odysseus
answered politely, "King Alcinous,
there is a time for many tales, but also
a time for sleep. If you still want to hear,
I will not grudge you stories. I will tell you
some even more distressing ones, about
my friend who managed to escape the shrieks
and battle din at Troy but perished later,
killed in his own home by an evil wife.

Holy Persephone dispersed the ghosts
of women and they went their separate ways.
The ghost of Agamemnon came in sorrow
with all the rest who met their fate with him
inside Aegisthus' house. He recognized me
when he had drunk the blood. He wept out loud,
and tearfully reached out his hands towards me,
desperate to touch. His energy and strength
and all the suppleness his limbs once had
were gone. I wept and my heart pitied him.
I cried out,

'Lord of men, King Agamemnon!
How did you die? What bad luck brought you down?
Was it Poseidon rousing up a blast
of cruel wind to wreck your ships? Or were you
killed on dry land by enemies as you
were poaching their fat flocks of sheep or cattle,
or fighting for their city and their wives?'

He answered right away, 'King under Zeus,
Odysseus—survivor! No, Poseidon
did not rouse up a dreadful blast of wind
to wreck my ship. No hostile men on land
killed me in self-defense. It was Aegisthus
who planned my death and murdered me, with help
from my own wife. He called me to his house
to dinner and he killed me, as one slaughters
an ox at manger. What a dreadful death!
My men were systematically slaughtered
like pigs in a rich lord's house for some feast,
a wedding or a banquet. You have seen
many cut down in war in thick of battle,
or slaughtered in a combat hand to hand;

but you would grieve with even deeper pity
if you could see us lying dead beneath
the tables piled with food and wine. The floor
swam thick with blood. I heard the desperate voice
of Priam's daughter, poor Cassandra, whom
deceitful Clytemnestra killed beside me.
As I lay dying, struck through by the sword,
I tried to lift my arms up from the ground.
That she-dog turned away. I went to Hades.
She did not even shut my eyes or close
my mouth. There is no more disgusting act
than when a wife betrays a man like that.
That woman formed a plot to murder me!
Her husband! When I got back home, I thought
I would be welcomed, at least by my slaves
and children. She has such an evil mind
that she has poured down shame on her own head
and on all other women, even good ones.'

I cried out, 'Curse her! Zeus has always brought
disaster to the house of Atreus
through women. Many men were lost for Helen,
and Clytemnestra formed this plot against you
when you were far away.'

At once he answered,
'So you must never treat your wife too well.
Do not let her know everything you know.
Tell her some things, hide others. But your wife
will not kill you, Odysseus. The wise
Penelope is much too sensible
to do such things. Your bride was very young
when we went off to war. She had a baby
still at her breast, who must be now a man.

He will be glad when you come home and see him,
and he will throw his arms around his father.
That is how things should go. My wife prevented
my eager eyes from gazing at my son.
She killed me first. I have a final piece
of sound advice for you—take heed of it.
When you arrive in your own land, do not
anchor your ship in full view; move in secret.
There is no trusting women any longer.
But have you any news about my son?
Is he alive? Is he in Orchomenus,
or sandy Pylos, or with Menelaus
in Sparta? Surely my fine son Orestes
is not yet dead.'

I answered, 'Agamemnon,
why ask me this? I do not even know
whether he is alive or dead. It is
pointless to talk of hypotheticals.'

Both of us wept profusely, deeply grieving
over the bitter words we spoke. Then came
the spirits of Achilles and Patroclus
and of Antilochus and Ajax, who
was handsomest and had the best physique,
of all the Greeks, next only to Achilles
the sprinter. And Achilles recognized me
and spoke in tears.

'My lord Odysseus,
you fox! What will you think of next? How could you
bear to come down to Hades? Numb dead people
live here, the shades of poor exhausted mortals.'

I said, 'Achilles, greatest of Greek heroes,
I came down here to meet Tiresias,
in case he had advice for my return
to rocky Ithaca. I have not even
returned to Greece, my homeland. I have had
bad luck. But no one's luck was ever better
than yours, nor ever will be. In your life
we Greeks respected you as we do gods,
and now that you are here, you have great power
among the dead. Achilles, you should not
be bitter at your death.'

But he replied,
'Odysseus, you must not comfort me
for death. I would prefer to be a workman,
hired by a poor man on a peasant farm,
than rule as king of all the dead. But come,
tell me about my son. Do you have news?
Did he march off to war to be a leader?
And what about my father Peleus?
Does he still have good standing among all
the Myrmidons? Or do they treat him badly
in Phthia and Greece, since he is old
and frail? Now I have left the light of day,
and am not there to help, as on the plains
of Troy when I was killing the best Trojans,
to help the Greeks. If I could go for even
a little while, with all that strength I had,
up to my father's house, I would make those
who hurt and disrespect him wish my hands
were not invincible.'

I answered him,
'I have no news to tell about your father,

but I can tell you all about your son,
dear Neoptolemus. I brought him from
Scyros by ship, with other well-armed Greeks.
When we were strategizing about Troy,
he always spoke up first and to the purpose,
unmatched except by Nestor and myself.
And when we fought at Troy, he never paused
in the great throng of battle; he was always
fearlessly running forward, and he slaughtered
enormous numbers in the clash of war.
I cannot name all those he killed for us.
But with his bronze he cut down Eurypylus,
the son of Telephus, most handsome man
I ever saw, next only to great Memnon.
The multitude of Cetians he brought
were also killed, since Priam bribed his mother.
When we, the Argive leaders, were preparing
to climb inside the Wooden Horse, it was
my task to open up and close the door.
The other Greek commanders were in tears;
their legs were shaking. Not your handsome boy!
I never saw his face grow pale; he had
no tears to wipe away. Inside the horse,
he begged me to allow him to jump out.
He gripped his sword hilt and his heavy spear,
so desperate to go hurt the Trojans.
At last, when we had sacked the lofty city
of Priam, he embarked weighed down with spoils.
No sharp bronze spear had wounded him at all;
he was unhurt by all the skirmishes
endured in war when Ares rages blind.'

After I told him this, Achilles' ghost
took great swift-footed strides across the fields

of asphodel, delighted to have heard
about the glorious prowess of his son.

Other dead souls were gathering, all sad;
each told the story of his sorrow. Only
Ajax kept back, enraged because I won
Achilles' armor, when the case was judged
beside the ships. The hero's mother, Thetis,
and sons of Troy, and Pallas, gave the arms
to me. I wish I had not won this contest!
For those arms Ajax lies beneath the earth,
whose looks and deeds were best of all the Greeks
after Achilles, son of Peleus.
I spoke to him to try to make it up.

'Please, Ajax, son of mighty Telamon,
can you not set aside your rage at me
about those cursed arms? Not even now,
in death? The gods made them to ruin us.
You were our tower; what a loss you were!
We Greeks were struck by grief when you were gone;
we mourned as long for you as for Achilles.
Blame nobody but Zeus. He ruined us,
in hatred for the army of the Greeks;
and that was why he brought this doom on you.
But listen now, my lord. Subdue your anger.'
He did not answer. He went off and followed
the spirits of the dead to Erebus.

Despite his rage, we might have spoken longer
if I had not felt in my heart an urge
to see more spirits. I saw Minos there,
the son of Zeus, who holds the golden scepter
and sits in judgment on the dead. They ask

their king to arbitrate disputes, inside
the house of Hades, where the doors are always
wide open. I saw great Orion, chasing
across the fields of asphodel the beasts
he killed when living high in lonely mountains,
holding his indestructible bronze club.
And I saw Tityus, the son of Gaia,
stretched out nine miles. When Leto, Zeus' lover,
was traveling to Pytho, through the fields
of beautiful Panopeus, he raped her.
Two vultures sit on either side of him,
ripping his liver, plunging in his bowels;
he fails to push them off. I saw the pain
of Tantalus, in water to his chin,
so parched, no way to drink. When that old man
bent down towards the water, it was gone;
some god had dried it up, and at his feet
dark earth appeared. Tall leafy trees hung fruit
above his head: sweet figs and pomegranates
and brightly shining apples and ripe olives.
But when he grasped them with his hands, the wind
hurled them away towards the shadowy clouds.
And I saw Sisyphus in torment, pushing
a giant rock with both hands, leaning on it
with all his might to shove it up towards
a hilltop; when he almost reached the peak,
its weight would swerve, and it would roll back down,
heedlessly. But he kept on straining, pushing,
his body drenched in sweat, his head all dusty.
I saw a phantom of great Heracles.
The man himself is with the deathless gods,
happy and feasting, with fine-ankled Hebe,
the child of mighty Zeus and golden Hera.
Around his ghost, the dead souls shrieked like birds,

all panic-struck. He walked like gloomy night,
holding his bow uncased and with an arrow
held on the string. He glowered terribly,
poised for a shot. Around his chest was strapped
a terrifying baldric made of gold,
fashioned with marvelous images of bears,
wild boars, and lions with fierce staring eyes,
and battles and the slaughtering of men.
I hope the craftsman who designed this scene
will never make another work like this.
This Heracles at once knew who I was,
and full of grief he cried,

'Odysseus!
Master of every circumstance, so you
are also tortured by the weight of fortune
as I was while I lived beneath the sun?
I was a son of Zeus, and yet my pain
was infinite. I was enslaved to someone
far less heroic than myself, who laid
harsh labors on me. Once he sent me here
to bring back Cerberus, since he could think
of no worse task for me. I brought the Dog
up out of Hades, with the help of Hermes,
and flashing-eyed Athena.'

He went back
to Hades' house. I stayed, in case more heroes
who died in ancient times should come to me.
I would have seen the noble men I hoped for,
Pirithous and Theseus, god-born.
But masses of the dead came thronging round
with eerie cries, and cold fear seized me, lest
the dreadful Queen Persephone might send

the monster's head, the Gorgon, out of Hades.
So then I hurried back and told my men
to climb on board the ship and loose the cables.
They did so, and sat down along the benches.
The current bore the ship down River Ocean,
first with the help of oars, and then fair wind."

BOOK 12

Difficult Choices

"Our ship sailed out beyond the stream of Ocean,
across the waves of open sea, and came
to Aeaea, home of newborn Dawn, who dances
in meadows with the beams of Helius.
We beached the ship upon the sandy shore,
and disembarked, and there we fell asleep
while waiting for bright morning. When Dawn came,
born early, with her fingertips like petals,
I sent my men to Circe's house, to bring
the body of the dead Elpenor. Quickly
we chopped the wood and at the farthest headland
we held a funeral for him, and wept
profusely, crying out in grief. We burned
his body and his gear, and built a mound,
and dragged a pillar onto it, and fixed
his oar on top—each ritual step in turn.
Circe, the well-groomed goddess, was aware
that we were back from Hades, and she hurried
to meet us with her slaves. They carried bread
and meat and bright red wine. She stood among us,
and said,

'This is amazing! You all went
alive to Hades—you will be twice-dead,
when other people only die one time!
Eat now, and stay here drinking wine all day.
At dawn, sail on. I will explain your route
in detail, so no evil thing can stitch
a means to hurt you, on the land or sea.'

I am a stubborn man, but I agreed,
so there we sat and feasted on the meat
and strong sweet wine until the sun went down.
When darkness fell, the men slept by the ship.
Then Circe took my hand, and led me off
apart from them, and questioned me in detail.
I told her everything. The lady Circe
replied at last,

'That quest is over now.
So listen, I will give you good instructions;
another god will make sure you remember.
First you will reach the Sirens, who bewitch
all passersby. If anyone goes near them
in ignorance, and listens to their voices,
that man will never travel to his home,
and never make his wife and children happy
to have him back with them again. The Sirens
who sit there in their meadow will seduce him
with piercing songs. Around about them lie
great heaps of men, flesh rotting from their bones,
their skin all shriveled up. Use wax to plug
your sailors' ears as you row past, so they
are deaf to them. But if you wish to hear them,
your men must fasten you to your ship's mast
by hand and foot, straight upright, with tight ropes.

So bound, you can enjoy the Sirens' song.
But if you beg your men to set you free,
they have to tie you down with firmer knots.
I will not give you definite instructions
about which route to take when you have sailed
beyond the Sirens. Let your heart decide.
There are two choices, and the first goes through
vast overhanging rocks, which Amphitrite
batters aggressively with mighty waves.
The blessed gods call these the Wandering Rocks.
No birds can fly through safe, not even doves,
who bring ambrosia to Zeus. One dove
is always lost in that sheer gulf of stone
and Zeus must send another to restore
the number of the flock. No human ship
has ever passed there. When one tries to enter,
the waves and raging gusts of fire engulf
ship timbers and the bodies of the men.
Only the famous *Argo* sailed through there
returning from the visit with Aeetes.
The current hurled the ship towards the rocks,
but Hera, who loved Jason, led them safe.
Taking the second way, you meet two rocks:
one reaches up to heaven with its peak,
surrounded by blue fog that never clears.
No light comes through there, even in the summer.
No man could climb it or set foot upon it,
even if he had twenty hands and feet.
The rock is sheer, as if it had been polished.
Right in the middle lies a murky cave
that faces west, towards dark Erebus.
Steer your ship past it, great Odysseus.
The hollow cave is so high up, no man
could shoot it with an arrow. There lives Scylla,

howling and barking horribly; her voice
is puppylike, but she is dangerous;
even a god would be afraid of her.
She has twelve dangling legs and six long necks
with a gruesome head on each, and in each face
three rows of crowded teeth, pregnant with death.
Her belly slumps inside the hollow cave;
she keeps her heads above the yawning chasm
and scopes around the rock, and hunts for fish.
She catches dolphins, seals, and sometimes even
enormous whales—Queen Amphitrite, ruler
of roaring waters, nurtures many creatures.
No sailors ever pass that way unharmed.
She snatches one man with each mouth from off
each dark-prowed ship. The other rock is near,
enough to shoot an arrow right across.
This second rock is lower down, and on it
there grows a fig tree with thick leaves. Beneath,
divine Charybdis sucks black water down.
Three times a day she spurts it up; three times
she glugs it down. Avoid that place when she
is swallowing the water. No one could
save you from death then, even great Poseidon.
Row fast, and steer your ship alongside Scylla,
since it is better if you lose six men
than all of them.'

I answered, 'Goddess, please,
tell me the truth: is there no other way?
Or can I somehow circumvent Charybdis
and stop that Scylla when she tries to kill
my men?'

The goddess answered, 'No, you fool!
Your mind is still obsessed with deeds of war.
But now you must surrender to the gods.
She is not mortal. She is deathless evil,
terrible, wild and cruel. You cannot fight her.
The best solution and the only way
is flight. I am afraid if you take time
to arm beside the rock, she will attack
again with all six heads and take six more.
So row away with all your might, and call
on Scylla's mother, Cratais, Great Force,
who bore her as a blight on humankind.
Go fast, before the goddess strikes again.
Then you will reach the island called Thrinacia,
where Helius keeps sheep and many cattle:
fifty per herd, with seven herds in all.
They never reproduce or die, and those
who tend them are the smooth-haired goddesses,
Phaethousa and Lampetia, the shining
daughters of Helius by bright Neaira.
She brought them up, then sent them off to live
there in remote Thrinacia, to guard
their father's sheep and cattle. If you can
remember home and leave the cows unharmed,
you will at last arrive in Ithaca.
But if you damage them, I must foretell
disaster for your ship and for your crew.
Even if you survive, you will return
late and humiliated, having caused
the death of all your men.'

The golden throne
of Dawn was riding up the sky as Circe
concluded, and she strode across her island.

I went back to my ship and roused the men
to get on board and loose the sternward cables.
Embarking, they sat down, each in his place,
and struck the gray saltwater with their oars.
Behind our dark-prowed ship, the dreadful goddess
Circe sent friendly wind to fill the sails.
We worked efficiently to organize
the rigging, and the breeze and pilot steered.
Then with an anxious heart I told the crew,

'My friends, the revelations Circe shared
with me should not be kept a secret, known
to me alone. I will share them with you,
and we can die in knowledge of the truth,
or else escape. She said we must avoid
the voices of the otherworldly Sirens;
steer past their flowering meadow. And she says
that I alone should hear their singing. Bind me,
to keep me upright at the mast, wound round
with rope. If I beseech you and command you
to set me free, you must increase my bonds
and chain me even tighter.'

So I told them
each detail. Soon our well-built ship, blown fast
by fair winds, neared the island of the Sirens,
and suddenly, the wind died down. Calm came.
Some spirit lulled the waves to sleep. The men
got up, pulled down the sails, and stowed them in
the hollow hold. They sat at oar and made
the water whiten, struck by polished wood.
I gripped a wheel of wax between my hands
and cut it small. Firm kneading and the sunlight
warmed it, and then I rubbed it in the ears

of each man in his turn. They bound my hands
and feet, straight upright at the mast. They sat
and hit the sea with oars. We traveled fast,
and when we were in earshot of the Sirens,
they knew our ship was near, and started singing.

'Odysseus! Come here! You are well-known
from many stories! Glory of the Greeks!
Now stop your ship and listen to our voices.
All those who pass this way hear honeyed song,
poured from our mouths. The music brings them joy,
and they go on their way with greater knowledge,
since we know everything the Greeks and Trojans
suffered in Troy, by gods' will; and we know
whatever happens anywhere on earth.'

Their song was so melodious, I longed
to listen more. I told my men to free me.
I scowled at them, but they kept rowing on.
Eurylochus and Perimedes stood
and tied me even tighter, with more knots.
But when we were well past them and I could
no longer hear the singing of the Sirens,
I nodded to my men, and they removed
the wax that I had used to plug their ears,
and untied me. When we had left that island,
I saw a mighty wave and smoke, and heard
a roar. The men were terrified; their hands
let fall the oars—they splashed down in the water.
The ship stayed still, since no one now was pulling
the slender blades. I strode along the deck
pausing to cheer each man, then gave a speech
to rally all of them.

'Dear friends! We are
experienced in danger. This is not
worse than the time the Cyclops captured us,
and forced us to remain inside his cave.
We got away that time, thanks to my skill
and brains and strategy. Remember that.
Come on then, all of you, and trust my words.
Sit on your benches, strike the swelling deep
with oars, since Zeus may grant us a way out
from this disaster also. Pilot, listen:
these are your orders. As you hold the rudder,
direct the ship away from that dark smoke
and rising wave, and head towards the rock;
if the ship veers the other way, you will
endanger us.'

They promptly followed orders.
I did not mention Scylla, since she meant
inevitable death, and if they knew,
the men would drop the oars and go and huddle
down in the hold in fear. Then I ignored
Circe's advice that I should not bear arms;
it was too hard for me. I dressed myself
in glorious armor; in my hands I took
two long spears, and I climbed up on the forecastle.
I thought that rocky Scylla would appear
from that direction, to destroy my men.
So we rowed through the narrow strait in tears.
On one side, Scylla; on the other, shining
Charybdis with a dreadful gurgling noise
sucked down the water. When she spewed it out,
she seethed, all churning like a boiling cauldron
on a huge fire. The froth flew high, to spatter
the topmost rocks on either side. But when
she swallowed back the sea, she seemed all stirred

from inside, and the rock around was roaring
dreadfully, and the dark-blue sand below
was visible. The men were seized by fear.
But while our frightened gaze was on Charybdis,
Scylla snatched six men from the ship—my strongest,
best fighters. Looking back from down below,
I saw their feet and hands up high, as they
were carried off. In agony they cried
to me and called my name—their final words.
As when a fisherman out on a cliff
casts his long rod and line set round with oxhorn
to trick the little fishes with his bait;
when one is caught, he flings it gasping back
onto the shore—so those men gasped as Scylla
lifted them up high to her rocky cave
and at the entrance ate them up—still screaming,
still reaching out to me in their death throes.
That was the most heartrending sight I saw
in all the time I suffered on the sea.

Free from the rocks of Scylla and Charybdis
we quickly reached the island of the god,
Hyperion's son Helius, the Sun God.
There were his cattle, with their fine broad faces,
and many flocks of well-fed sheep. While still
out on the sea in my black ship, I heard
the lowing of the cattle in their pens,
and bleating of the sheep. I kept in mind
the words of blind Tiresias the prophet
and Circe. Both had given strict instructions
that we avoid the island of the Sun,
the god of human joy. I told the men
with heavy heart,

'My friends, I know how much
you have endured. But listen to me now.
Tiresias and Circe both insisted
we must avoid the island of the Sun,
the joy of mortals. They said dreadful danger
lurks there for us. We have to steer our ship
around it.'

They were quite downcast by this.
Eurylochus said angrily to me,
'You are unfair to us, Odysseus.
You may be strong; you never seem to tire;
you must be made of iron. But we men
have had no rest or sleep; we are exhausted.
And you refuse to let us disembark
and cook our tasty dinner on this island.
You order us to drift around all night
in our swift ship across the misty sea.
At night, fierce storms rise up and wreck men's ships,
and how can anyone escape disaster
if sudden gusts of wind from north or west
bring cruel blasts to break the ship, despite
the wishes of the gods? Let us submit
to evening. Let us stay here, and cook food
beside the ship. At dawn we can embark
and sail the open sea.'

That was his speech.
The other men agreed, and then I saw
a spirit must be plotting our destruction.
My words flew out.

'Eurylochus! You force me
to yield, since I am one and you are many.
But all of you, swear me a mighty oath:

if we find any herd of cows, or flock
of sheep, do not be fool enough to kill
a single animal. Stay clear, and eat
the food provided by immortal Circe.'

They swore as I commanded. When they finished
making the oath, we set our well-built ship
inside the curving harbor, near freshwater.
The men got out and skillfully cooked dinner.
When they were satisfied with food and drink,
they wept, remembering their dear companions,
whom Scylla captured from the ship and ate.
Sweet sleep came down upon them as they cried.
When night was over, when the stars were gone,
Zeus roused a blast of wind, an eerie storm.
He covered earth and sea with fog, and darkness
fell down from heaven. When rose-fingered Dawn
appeared, we dragged the ship inside a cave,
a place Nymphs danced in, and we moored it there.
I gave a speech to my assembled men.

'My friends, we have supplies on board. Let us
not touch the cattle, or we will regret it.
Those cows and fat sheep are the property
of Helius, the great Sun God, who sees
all things, and hears all things.' I told them this.
Reluctantly they yielded. But that month
the South Wind blew and never stopped. No other
was ever blowing, only South and East.
While the men still had food and wine, they kept
clear of the cows. They hoped to save their lives.
But when our ship's supplies ran out, the men
were forced to hunt; they used their hooks to catch
both fish and birds, whatever they could get,
since hunger gnawed their bellies. I strode off

to pray, in case some god would show me how
to get back home. I left my men behind,
and crossed the island, washed my hands, in shelter
out of the wind, and prayed to all the gods.
They poured sweet sleep upon my eyes.

Meanwhile,
Eurylochus proposed a foolish plan.
'Listen, my friends! You have already suffered
too much. All human deaths are hard to bear.
But starving is most miserable of all.
So let us poach the finest of these cattle,
and sacrifice them to the deathless gods.
If we get home to Ithaca, at once
we will construct a temple to the Sun God,
with treasure in it. If he is so angry
about these cows that he decides to wreck
our ship, and if the other gods agree—
I would prefer to drink the sea and die
at once, than perish slowly, shriveled up
here on this desert island.'

All the others
agreed with him. They went to poach the best
of Helius' cattle, which were grazing
beside the ship. The men surrounded them,
and called upon the gods. They had plucked leaves
from oak trees—on the ship there was no barley.
They prayed, then killed them, skinned them, and cut off
the thighs, and covered up the bones with fat,
a double layer, with raw meat on top.
They had no wine to pour libations over
the burning offering, but they made do
with water, and they roasted all the innards.
And when the thighs were burned, the entrails sprinkled,

they cut the other meat up into chunks
for skewers.

Sweet sleep melted from my eyes;
I rushed back to the ship beside the shore.
When I was close, the meaty smell of cooking
enfolded me. I groaned, and told the gods,

'O Zeus, and all you deathless gods! You blinded
my mind with that infernal sleep. My men
did dreadful things while I was gone.'

Meanwhile,
Lampetia in flowing skirts ran off
to tell the Sun God we had killed his cows.
Enraged, he called the other gods.

'Great Zeus,
and all you other deathless gods, you must
punish Odysseus' men. They killed
my cattle! I delighted in those cows
all through each day, when I went up to heaven
and when I turned to earth. If they do not
repay me, I will sink down into Hades
and bring my bright light only to the dead.'

Zeus answered, 'Helius! Please shine with us
and shine for mortals on life-giving earth.
I will immediately smite their ship
with my bright thunderbolt, and smash it up
in fragments, all across the wine-dark sea.'

I heard this from the beautiful Calypso,
who had been told by Hermes.

Back on shore
beside my ship, I scolded each of them.
It did no good; the cows were dead already.
The gods sent signs—the hides began to twitch,
the meat on skewers started mooing, raw
and cooked. There was the sound of cattle lowing.
For six days my men banqueted on beef
from Helius. When Zeus, the son of Cronus,
led in the seventh day, the wind became
less stormy, and we quickly went on board.
We set the mast up and unfurled the sails
and set out on the open sea.

When we
had left that island, we could see no other,
only the sky and sea. Zeus made a mass
of dark-blue storm cloud hang above our ship.
The sea grew dark beneath it. For a moment
the ship moved on, but then came Zephyr, shrieking,
noisily rushing, with torrential tempest.
A mighty gust of wind broke off both forestays;
the tacking was all scattered in the hold.
The mast was broken backwards, and it struck
the pilot in the stern; it smashed his skull.
His bones were crushed, his skeleton was smashed.
He fell down like a diver from the deck;
his spirit left his body. At that instant,
Zeus thundered and hurled bolts to strike the ship;
shaken, it filled with sulfur. All the men
fell overboard, and they were swept away
like seagulls on the waves beside the ship.
The gods prevented them from reaching home.

I paced on board until the current ripped
the ship's side from the keel. The waves bore off

the husk, and snapped the mast. But thrown across it
there was a backstay cable, oxhide leather.
With this I lashed the keel and mast together,
and rode them, carried on by fearsome winds.
At last the tempest ceased, the West Wind lulled.
I worried that the South Wind might compel me
to backtrack, to the terrible Charybdis.
All night I was swept backwards and at sunrise
I came back to the dreadful rocks of Scylla
and of Charybdis, gulping salty water,
and overshadowed by the fig tree's branches.
I jumped and clutched its trunk, batlike—unable
to plant my feet, or climb. The roots were down
too low; the tall long branches were too high.
So I kept clinging on; I hoped Charybdis
would belch my mast and keel back up. She did!
As one who spends the whole day judging quarrels
between young men, at last goes home to eat—
at that same hour, the planks came bobbing up
out of Charybdis. I let go my hands
and feet and dropped myself way down to splash
into the sea below, beside the timbers
of floating wood. I clambered onto them,
and used my hands to row myself away,
and Zeus ensured that Scylla did not see me,
or else I could not have survived. I drifted
for nine days. On the evening of the tenth,
the gods helped me to reach the island of
the dreadful, beautiful, divine Calypso.
She loved and cared for me. Why should I tell
the story that I told you and your wife
yesterday in your house? It is annoying,
repeating tales that have been told before."

BOOK 13

Two Tricksters

After he finished, all were silent, spellbound,
sitting inside the shadowy hall. At last,
Alcinous said,

"Now, Odysseus,
since you have been my guest, beneath my roof,
you need not wander anymore. You have
endured enough; you will get home again.
And all you regulars, my honored friends
who always drink red wine here in my house
and listen to my singer: heed my words.
Our guest has clothes packed up inside a trunk,
and other gifts that we have given him.
Each of us now should add a mighty tripod
and cauldron. I will make the people pay
a levy, so that none of us will suffer
from unrewarded generosity."

The king's words pleased them all. They went back home
to rest. Then Dawn was born again; her fingers

bloomed, and they hurried back towards the ship
bringing heroic gifts of bronze. The king
embarked and stowed them underneath the beams,
to leave room for the crew when they were rowing.
Then all the men went back with him to eat.
The holy king killed sacrificial meat—
a cow to Zeus of dark clouds, son of Cronus,
who rules the world. They burned the thighs and feasted
in happiness. The well-respected singer
Demodocus made music in their midst.
But all the while Odysseus kept turning
his head towards the shining sun, impatient
for it to set. He longed to leave. As when
a man is desperate for dinnertime
after he spends the whole day with his oxen
dragging the jointed plow across the field,
and welcomes sunset, when he can go home
to eat; his legs are aching on the way—
just so Odysseus was glad of sunset.
At once he told the seafaring Phaeacians,
especially Alcinous,

"Great king,
and all of you, please send me safely home
with offerings, and thank you. I am grateful
to you for giving me my heart's desire:
a passage home, with gifts. I hope the gods
maintain my luck. When I am home, I pray
to find my wife still faultless, and my loved ones
safe. And may you Phaeacians live to bring
joy to your wives and children—every blessing.
I pray there is no trouble for your people."

They praised his words and said that they must help
their guest go home, since he had spoken well.
Alcinous addressed his right-hand man.

"Pontonous, now mix a bowl of wine;
serve drinks to everybody in the hall,
so we may pray to Zeus and help our guest
back to his homeland."

So the steward mixed
a cheering bowl of wine and served them all
in turn. Still in their seats, they poured libations
to all the blessed gods that live in heaven.
Godlike Odysseus stood up and put
a double-handled cup into the hands
of Arete. His words flew out to her.

"Bless you forever, queen, until old age
and death arrive for you, as for us all.
I will leave now. Be happy in your home
and children, and your people, and your king."

With that, the noble hero crossed the threshold.
Alcinous sent out his steward with him
to guide him to the swift ship on the shore.
Arete sent some slave girls too. One brought
a freshly laundered cloak and tunic; one
carried the well-carved chest; the third brought bread
and red wine. When they reached the ship, the guides
took all the food and drink and packed it neatly
inside the hold. They spread a sheet and blanket
out on the stern-deck of the hollow ship
so he could sleep there soundly. Climbing on,

he lay there quietly. The rowers sat
down on the benches calmly, and then loosed
the cable from the mooring stone. They pulled,
leaning back hard; the oar blades splashed the water.
A sound sweet sleep fell on his eyes, like death;
he did not stir. As four fine stallions
rush at the whip and race their chariot
across the track, heads high, an easy canter—
so was the ship's prow raised. The seething waves
of sounding purple sea rushed round the stern
as she sped straight ahead. The swiftest bird,
a hawk, could never overtake; she sailed
so fast, and cleaved the waves. She bore a man
whose mind was like the gods', who had endured
many heartbreaking losses, and the pain
of war and shipwreck. Now he slept in peace,
and he remembered nothing of his pain.

But when the brightest star that carries news
about the coming Dawn rose up the sky,
the seaborne ship neared land. There is a harbor
of Phorcys, ancient sea god, in the district
of Ithaca. On either side of it
there are sheer cliffs that jut across the bay;
they shelter it and keep big waves outside
when storm winds blow. The ships remain in harbor
without a tether, once they cross its bounds.
At the bay's head there grows a long-leafed olive,
and near it is a beautiful dark cave,
a holy place of sea-nymphs—Nereids.
Inside are bowls and amphorae of stone,
and buzzing bees bring honey. There are looms,
also of stone; the Nymphs weave purple cloth,

sea-purple—it is marvelous to see.
Water is always flowing through. There are
two entrances. The north one is for humans;
the south is sacred. People cannot enter
that way—it is the path of the immortals.

They rowed inside the bay; they knew the place
of old. Their arms were pulling at top speed;
the ship was traveling so fast that when
she reached dry land, she beached for half her length.
They disembarked, and lifted from the ship
Odysseus, wrapped up in sheets and blankets.
They set him on the sand, still fast asleep.
They unpacked all the presents he was given
by the Phaeacian lords to take back home,
thanks to Athena's care. They heaped the things
beside the olive tree, so no one passing
would do them any damage while their owner
was sleeping. Then they rowed away, back home.

Poseidon, Lord of Earthquakes, still remembered
his hatred of Odysseus; he asked
Zeus what he meant to do.

"O Father Zeus!
I will lose all my standing with the gods,
since mortals fail to honor me, though these
Phaeacians are my very own descendants!
I always said Odysseus would reach
home in the end. I did not take away
that privilege from him, no, not at all,
since you had promised it with your own nod.
Their swift ship carried him across the ocean,
and they have set him down in Ithaca

with a magnificent array of gifts:
bronze, heaps of gold and fine-spun clothes, far more
spoils than he ever would have won at Troy
if he had got out safely."

Storm God Zeus
exclaimed, "Earth-Shaker! How absurd! The gods
do not dishonor you; it would be hard
to disrespect an elder so high-ranking.
If willful humans fail to show respect,
then punish them; you always have that power.
Do as you wish!"

Poseidon answered, "Lord
of Dark Clouds, I have always wanted to.
I held back out of deference to you.
But now, when that fine ship of those Phaeacians
comes back from helping him across, I want
to smash it in the sea, and overwhelm
their city with a mountain, to prevent them
from ever guiding travelers again."

The Cloud Lord Zeus said, "Brother, I suggest
that while the people in the city watch,
you turn the ship arriving into stone,
still looking like a ship. They will all
be shocked. Then you can surround their town
with a huge mountain."

Hearing this, Poseidon
went to Phaeacian Scheria, and waited.
As the ship sped towards the shore, the god
moved near it, turned it all to stone, and slapped
his palm to make it rooted to the seabed.

He vanished, and the people of Phaeacia,
known for their oars and famous ships, began
to ask each other,

"What? Who fixed that ship
firm in the sea as she was rushing home?
We saw it all!" They could not understand it.
Alcinous addressed the crowd and spoke.

"So it is true! My father long ago
said that Poseidon hates us for our habit
of helping travelers get home again;
we got away with it, but he foretold
that one day great Poseidon would destroy
a ship on her return from such a journey;
the god would hide our city with a mountain.
And now the old man's words are coming true.
So all of you must listen to me now.
Stop helping visitors to travel onward.
We have to sacrifice twelve bulls, handpicked
for Lord Poseidon, so he may show mercy,
and not enfold our city in a mountain."

At this, they were afraid, and they prepared
the bulls, and all the leaders of Phaeacia
prayed to Poseidon, standing round the altar.

Meanwhile Odysseus, who had been sleeping
in his own native land of Ithaca
woke up, but did not recognize the place
from which he had been absent for so long.
Pallas Athena cast a mist upon it,
so she could tell him how things stood, and make him
unrecognizable to his own wife

and family and neighbors, till he paid
the suitors back for how they misbehaved.
The friendly harbors and the winding paths
and leafy trees were all quite unfamiliar
to their own king. He leapt up to his feet
and looking at his native land, he groaned
and smacked his thighs, and sobbed,

"Where am I now?
Are those who live here violent and cruel?
Or are they kind to strangers, folks who fear
the gods? Where can I carry all my treasure?
And where can I go wandering? If only
I had remained there in Phaeacia, till
I went on to some other mighty king
who might have been my friend and helped me home.
Where can I leave my things? Not here for sure;
they will be stolen. Those Phaeacian lords
were not so trustworthy! They promised me
that they would bring me home to Ithaca.
They broke their word and brought me somewhere else.
May Zeus who helps the needy make them pay!
Zeus watches everyone, and punishes
the sinner. Let me count my treasure now—
they may have stolen some when they sailed off."

He counted all the tripods, cauldrons, gold
and cloth, but none was missing. Then he paced
beside the loud resounding sea, hunched up
with homesickness and sobbing in his grief.
Athena came towards him; she looked like
a shepherd, young and soft-skinned as a prince,
wearing a folded mantle of fine cloth
across her shoulders; on her tender feet

were sandals, and she held a javelin.
Odysseus was overjoyed to see her.
He cried,

"Oh, friend! You are the very first
person that I have met here. Greetings! Please,
be kind, protect my treasure and myself.
I pray to you and supplicate, as if
you were a god. I touch your knees; please help me!
And tell me, please, what is this place? An island?
Or is it a peninsula that slopes
towards the sea from fertile mainland fields?
Who lives here?"

And with twinkling eyes the goddess
said, "Stranger, you must be a foreigner
from distant parts, or foolish, since you ask
about this famous country. Many people
know it, from those who live towards the east
under the rising sun, to those out west
in lands of gloomy dusk. This is rough country,
not fit for grazing horses, and not spacious,
but not infertile; grain and wine abound here.
The land is always wet with rain and dew.
There are fine water holes, and it is good
for raising goats and cattle, and the trees
are varied. Foreigner, I think the name
of Ithaca is even known in Troy,
a land they say is far away from Greece."

Odysseus, who had endured so much,
so long, was overjoyed, to hear from her
that he was in his own dear native land.

His words took wings and flew, but he did not
tell her the truth; he bit his story back.
His mind was always full of clever schemes.

"Yes, I have heard of Ithaca, although
I come from distant Crete. Now I am here
with all this wealth; I left an equal share
of riches for my children back at home.
I am in exile. On the fields of Crete
I killed Orsilochus, the speedy sprinter,
the son of Idomeneus, the king.
I had refused to serve or help his father
at Troy; I led my own men. So the son
wanted to steal the Trojan spoils for which
I worked so hard, in war and long sea journeys.
I hid beside the road with one companion,
and as he came back from the countryside,
I ambushed him, and hit him with my spear.
The sky was dark that night, and no one saw me
kill him with my sharp sword of bronze. And after
I murdered him, I quickly rowed away
to visit the Phoenicians, and I gave them
a share of loot, which made them very glad.
I told them they should transport me to Pylos,
or famous Elis, ruled by the Epeians.
But storm winds drove them off away from there
against their will: they did not mean to trick me.
So swept off course, we came here in the night.
We rowed at top speed into harbor, hungry,
but none of us took any thought of dinner.
We disembarked and all lay down right there.
Sweet sleep enfolded me. I was exhausted.
They took my treasure from the ship and set it

beside me as I slept upon the sand.
And then they sailed away to well-built Sidon,
and I was left here grieving."

At his words,
Athena smiled into his eyes. She took
his hand, and changed her body to a woman's:
beautiful, tall, and skilled in all the arts.
Her words were light as feathers.

"To outwit you
in all your tricks, a person or a god
would need to be an expert at deceit.
You clever rascal! So duplicitous,
so talented at lying! You love fiction
and tricks so deeply, you refuse to stop
even in your own land. Yes, both of us
are smart. No man can plan and talk like you,
and I am known among the gods for insight
and craftiness. You failed to recognize me:
I am Athena, child of Zeus. I always
stand near you and take care of you, in all
your hardships. I made sure that you were welcomed
by the Phaeacians. I have come here now
to weave a plan with you and hide the treasure
which, thanks to me, they gave you to take home.
I will reveal the challenges you face
at home. This is your fate, and you must bear it
bravely, not telling any man or woman
that you have finished wandering and come back.
Suffer in silence, bear their brutal treatment."

Odysseus, still wary, answered, "Goddess,
even the smartest man may find it hard

to recognize you. You disguise yourself
so many ways. I do know that you helped me
during the Trojan War, so long ago.
But when we Greeks had sacked the town of Priam,
and we embarked, and gods dispersed our fleet,
I did not see you there on board my ship,
daughter of Zeus. You gave me no protection.
Lost and confused, I waited for the gods
to free me from my pain. I met you later,
in rich Phaeacia, and you spoke to me
comforting words, and led me to the city.
Please, by your father Zeus! I cannot think
that this is Ithaca. I must be elsewhere.
You want to fool me and make fun of me.
Tell me the truth! Is this my own dear home?"

With glowing eyes she said, "You always have
such keen intelligence, and that is why
I cannot leave you when you need my help.
You have such intuition and such focus.
An ordinary man would rush straight home
to see his wife and children when he reached
his country, after such a journey. You
decided not to even ask about them,
until you test your wife. She sits at home,
passing each night in misery, each day
in tears. For my part, I have never doubted.
I felt sure in my heart you would get home,
after the loss of all your men. But I
did not want conflict with my father's brother,
Poseidon, who resented you because
you blinded his beloved son. Now I
will show you Ithaca, so you believe.
This is the bay of Phorcys, ancient sea god,

and at the head there is an olive tree
with long leaves, and nearby, the shady cave
sacred to nymphs called Nereids, to whom
you sacrificed so many hundred cattle.
And here is Neriton, the wooded mountain."

With that, the goddess made the mist disperse.
The land was visible. Odysseus,
after so long a wait and so much pain,
was filled with happiness at last. In joy
he kissed the fertile earth of his own country,
then lifted high his arms and prayed,

"O Nymphs!
I never thought I would come back to you,
daughters of Zeus. Accept my loving prayers,
and I will give you gifts, as in the past,
if my commander, child of Zeus, is kind
and lets me live and raise my son."

Athena
looked straight into his eyes and said, "Be brave.
You need not worry. Let us hurry now
to hide the treasure safely in the cave.
And then we must make plans."

The goddess went
down in the murky cave, and looked around
for hiding spots. Odysseus brought in
the presents the Phaeacians gave him—gold,
and tireless bronze and finely woven cloth.
Athena set them all inside, and fixed
the door-stone up, and then the two sat down
against the sacred olive and they planned

how to destroy the suitors. Eyes aglow,
Athena said,

"Great king, Laertes' son,
master of plots and plans, Odysseus,
think how to strike the suitors. For three years
they have been lording in your house and courting
your godlike wife with gifts. She always longs
for your return, and grieves. She leads them on
with promises and messages to each,
but her mind moves elsewhere."

Odysseus
cried, "Oh! I would have died like Agamemnon
in my own house, if you had not explained
exactly how things stand. So, goddess, now
weave me a strategy to pay them back.
Stand by me, give me courage and the drive
to fight as when I broke the shining crown
of Troy. If you will join me with that zeal
and help me, goddess-queen, I could do battle
against three hundred men at once."

Athena
looked straight at him, clear-eyed. She said, "I will
be with you, truly. Know I stand beside you
as we begin our work. I do believe
the suitors who devour your livelihood
will spatter your broad floors with blood and brains.
But now I will disguise you, so no human
can recognize you. I will shrivel up
the fine skin of your supple arms and legs,
ruin your hair, and dress you up in rags,
so everyone will shudder, seeing you.

And I will cloud your eyes, to make you seem
ugly to all the suitors, and your wife
and to the son you left at home. Now visit
the swineherd who, though he is just a slave,
adores your son and wise Penelope
and is your friend. Go look for him among
the sows who root beside the Corax rock
and near the spring of Arethusa, drinking
black water, eating good nutritious acorns,
which fatten pigs. Stay there and sit with him,
and ask him everything. And I will go
to Sparta, where the girls are beautiful,
to fetch Telemachus, the boy you love.
He went to Menelaus, to find out
if you are still alive."

He asked her sharply,
"But why did you not tell him? You must know
everything. Did you want him suffering
like me, lost out at sea, while others eat
his whole inheritance?"

With shining eyes
Athena answered, "Come now, do not worry
about the boy. I guided him myself
so that he might win glory by his journey.
He is not suffering. He is away,
sitting and banqueting with Menelaus.
The suitors do indeed desire to kill him,
and wait in ambush for him in their ship.
But they will not succeed, I think. The earth
will cover one or more of those who eat
your property."

Then with her wand Athena
tapped him; his handsome body withered up;
his limbs became arthritic. She bleached out
his hair, and made his skin look old and wrinkled,
and dimmed his fine bright eyes. She turned his clothes
into a tattered cloak and ragged tunic,
dirty with soot. She wrapped around his shoulders
a massive leather deerskin, and she gave him
a threadbare satchel and a walking stick.
Their plans were set; they parted. She went off
to Sparta, to go fetch Telemachus.

BOOK 14

A Loyal Slave

Leaving the bay, he hiked the rugged path
through woodland and across the cliffs; Athena
had shown him where to go to find the swineherd.
Of all those in Odysseus' household,
this noble slave cared most about preserving
the master's property. Odysseus
found him as he was sitting out on his porch.
His yard was high and visible for miles,
of fieldstones topped with twigs of thorny pear.
He built it in the absence of his master,
with no help from Laertes or the mistress.
Around the yard, he set a ring of stakes,
of wood with bark stripped off. Inside the yard,
he made twelve sties all next to one another,
for breeding sows, with fifty in each one.
The boars slept outside; there were fewer of them,
because the suitors kept on eating them.
The swineherd let them have the fattest boars;
just three hundred and sixty still remained.
Their captain kept four fierce half-wild dogs
to guard the gate. Now he was cutting oxhide

to make himself some sandals. Of his men,
three herded up the pigs, and ran around
in all directions; he had sent the fourth
to town to take a pig to those proud suitors.
He had no choice; he had to satisfy
their cravings for fresh meat.

Then suddenly
the guard dogs saw Odysseus, and rushed
towards him with loud barks. He kept his head,
and sank down to the ground and dropped his stick.
They would have hurt him terribly, and shamed him
on his own property—but acting fast
the swineherd dropped his leatherwork and rushed
to chase the dogs away. He yelled at them
and pelted them with stones to make them scatter.
And then he told his master,

"My dogs almost
ripped you apart, old man! You would have brought me
shame, when the gods are hurting me already.
I am in mourning for an absent master,
raising his pigs for other men to eat.
My lord is lost and maybe even hungry,
in lands where the people speak in foreign tongues—
if he is even still alive, still seeing
the sunlight. Well now, follow me, old man,
fill up on food and wine, then tell me where
you come from, and the troubles you have borne."

The noble swineherd heaped up cushy brushwood,
and spread a furry goatskin over it—his own
bed-blanket, thick and warm. Odysseus
sat down and was delighted at this welcome.
He said,

"May Zeus and all the deathless gods
reward you with your heart's desire, because
you welcomed me so willingly."

And you,
Eumaeus, answered, "One must honor guests
and foreigners and strangers, even those
much poorer than oneself. Zeus watches over
beggars and guests and strangers. What I have
to give is small, but I will give it gladly.
Life is like this for slaves: we live in fear,
when younger men have power over us.
My real lord is kept from home by gods.
He would have taken care of me, and given
what kindly owners give to loyal slaves:
a house with land, and wife whom many men
would want—as recompense for years of labor
which gods have blessed and made to prosper. Master
would have been good to me, if he had stayed
here till old age. He must be dead by now.
Damn Helen and her family! So many
have died for her sake. Master went to Troy,
to win back Agamemnon's honor, fighting
the Trojans."

Then he belted up his tunic
and hurried to the pen, and chose two piglets.
Inside he butchered them, singed off the bristles,
chopped up the meat and roasted it on skewers.
He set it, piping hot, before his guest,
sprinkling barley on the top. He mixed
wine in an ivy bowl, as sweet as honey,
and then sat down across from him, and urged,

"Now, guest, eat up! This is a poor slave's meal:
a suckling pig. The suitors eat the hogs.
Their hearts have no compassion! They ignore
the gods, who watch and hate such crimes and bless
good deeds and justice. Even cutthroat pirates,
who go to plunder other people's lands,
seizing the spoils that Zeus has granted them,
and sail home in a ship filled full of treasure—
even they feel the watchful eyes of gods.
These suitors must have heard some god's voice saying,
'Odysseus has died.' So they refuse
to go back to their own homes or to arrange
suitable marriages. Instead they sit,
wasting his wealth on feasts. Each night and day
they butcher sheep, not one but dozens of them,
and pour out yet more wine for reckless drinking.
Those selfish oafs! My lord was very rich;
no others on the mainland or back here
in Ithaca, nor twenty all combined,
possessed as much. I will list all of it.
Twelve herds of cattle on the mainland, twelve
of sheep, and twelve of pigs, and twelve of goats.
He had to hire more laborers to help us.
And out here on the far end of the island,
eleven herds of goats are grazing, watched
by good men. Every day, a herdsman takes
whichever goat seems fattest and most healthy
up to the palace. I, who watch these pigs,
must choose the best for them."

Odysseus
gratefully wolfed the meat and drank the wine
in silence. He was hatching plots to ruin
the suitors. After he had had enough

to eat, he took the wine-cup he had drunk from,
filled it again and gave it to Eumaeus,
who took it gladly. Then Odysseus
said,

"Friend, who bought you? This rich, noble man
that you describe—who is he? You say he
died in the war for Agamemnon's honor.
Perhaps I know him, since he must be famous.
Zeus and the other gods will be aware
if I have seen him and can bring you news.
He traveled widely."

But the swineherd said,
"His wife and son will not trust travelers
who claim to bring them news. Tramps always lie
to get a meal—they have no cause to tell
the truth. All those who pass through Ithaca
go to my mistress spinning foolish tales.
She welcomes them and questions them, while tears
stream from her eyes, and rightly so: a wife
should mourn for her dead husband. Sir, you also
would weave tall tales if you got clothes for it.
But in reality, my master's skin
has been ripped off his bones by birds of prey
and dogs; his life is gone. Or he has been
eaten at sea by fish; his bones are lying
upon the beach, heaped high with sand. His death
is ruin for us all, especially me,
since I will never have so kind a master,
however far I go, not even if
I go back to the home of my own parents
who gave me birth and brought me up. I wish
that I could see them, in my native land.

But I grieve less for my own family
than for Odysseus. I miss him so.
I hesitate to call him by his name,
stranger: I would prefer to call him 'brother,'
even when he is far away, because
he loved and cared for me with so much kindness."

Odysseus was self-restrained. He said,
"My friend, you are so adamant, insisting
that he will not come back. You have no faith.
But this is no tall tale: I swear to you
Odysseus is on his way. And when
he is in his own house, then I will claim
my prize as messenger—some better clothes.
Till then, I will take nothing, though I need them.
I hate like Hades' gates the man who caves
to poverty, and starts to lie. I swear
by Zeus, and by the welcome that you gave me,
and by the hearth of great Odysseus,
where I am going: all this will turn out
as I say now. Odysseus will come,
within this very cycle of the moon:
between the waning and the waxing time,
he will come home, and pay back all those here
who disrespect his wife and noble son."

You answered him, swineherd Eumaeus, "Sir,
I will not give you this reward, since he
will not come home. Relax and drink. Let us
think about other things. Do not remind me.
My heart is troubled when a person mentions
my faithful master. Never mind your oath.
I hope he comes, as do Penelope
and old Laertes and Telemachus.

May it come true. But I cannot forget
my grief for that poor boy, my master's son.
Thanks to the gods, he grew up like a tree,
handsome and strong, as if to match his father
when he becomes a man. But somebody
or some god ruined his good sense. He went
to Pylos, seeking news about his father.
The suitors lie in wait for when he comes
back home, and soon Arcesius' line
will be wiped out on Ithaca. No more.
They may catch him, or he may get away,
kept safe by Zeus. Now tell me, sir, the truth
about your own adventures. Where are you from?
Where do your parents live? Where is your town?
On what boat did you sail here? How did sailors
bring you to Ithaca? And who were they?
I know you did not reach this land by foot."

Odysseus said cunningly, "I will
tell you the truth, the whole truth. How I wish
we two could sit at ease here in this cottage,
and we had food and sweet strong wine to last
as long as we desired, while all the work
was done by others! Even if I talked
a whole year, I would not complete the story
of everything the gods have made me suffer.
Proudly I say, I come from spacious Crete,
the son of wealthy Castor Hylacides,
whose sons by his main wife were numerous,
raised in his house. My mother was a slave,
bought as a concubine, and yet my father
respected me like all his other sons.
The Cretan people held him in high honor
as if he were a god, since he was rich

and had such noble sons. But fate arrived
to take him down to Hades. Then my brothers
selfishly seized his property, and gave
only a tiny part to me, with barely
a place to live. But I was not a weakling,
or cowardly in fighting. My great skill
and talent helped me win a wife who had
a decent dowry—all lost now. But you
can see in stubble how the grain once grew,
though I am crushed by grief. I have the gift
of courage from Athena and from Ares.
Whenever I chose warriors to ambush
our enemies, I never thought of death.
I leapt out far in front, and ran to catch them
and spear them. That was how I was in war.
I did not like farmwork or housekeeping,
or raising children. I liked sailing better,
and war with spears and arrows, deadly weapons.
Others may shudder at such things, but gods
made my heart love them. People's preferences
are different. Before the Greeks went off
to march on Troy, I led my troops and fleet
on nine forays, with great success. I had
my pick of all the spoils, and got much more
when we shared out the winnings. Soon my house
grew rich; I was a fine, important man
among the Cretans. But far-seeing Zeus
arranged that expedition of disaster,
which made so many men collapse and fall.
The people wanted me to sail to Troy
with Idomeneus. We had no choice;
their will was strong, constraining us. We Greeks
fought for nine years, and in the tenth we sacked
the town of Priam, and sailed home. Some god

scattered the Greeks, and I was cursed by Zeus.
I stayed for just one month at home, enjoying
my children and my wife and my possessions.
Some impulse made me want to sail to Egypt,
with nine ships and a godlike crew. I rushed
to get the fleet prepared and gather up
the men. I paid for many animals,
to kill as sacrifices for the gods
and for the men to cook and eat. We feasted
six days, then on the seventh we embarked
and sailed from Crete. A fair north wind was blowing
so we could drift on easily, like floating
downstream. No one got sick, and all our ships
came through undamaged. We sat tight, and let
the wind and pilot guide us over seas.
In five days we had reached the river valley
of Egypt; my fleet docked inside the Nile.
I told the loyal men to wait and guard
the ships while I sent scouts to check around
from points of higher ground. But they indulged
their own aggressive impulses, and started
willfully doing damage to the fields
of Egypt and enslaved the little children
and women, and they killed the men. The news
soon reached the city; people heard the screaming,
and right away at dawn, they all arrived.
The plain was filled with warriors on foot,
and chariots and gleaming bronze, and Zeus,
the Lord of Lightning, caused my men to panic.
They dared not keep on fighting; danger lurked
on every side. Then many of my men
were killed with sharp bronze spears; the rest were taken
as slaves to work for them. I wish I too
had died in Egypt! But more pain remained.

Zeus put another plan into my mind.
I took my helmet off my head and dropped
my shield and sword, and unarmed I approached
the king. Beside his chariot I grasped
his knees and kissed them. He was merciful;
he kept me safe, and took me home with him,
riding his chariot. My eyes were wet.
Many Egyptians were enraged with me,
and tried to kill me with their spears; the king
protected me—he feared the wrath of Zeus,
the god of strangers, who hates wickedness.
I stayed there seven years and gained great wealth;
all the Egyptian people gave me gifts.
But in the eighth, an avaricious man
came from Phoenicia. He was good at lying,
skilled and well practiced at exploiting people.
He tricked me into going off with him
back to Phoenicia, where he lived. I stayed
a year, but when the hours and days and months
had rolled around again, he made me sail
over the seas to Libya, pretending
that I would go with him to do some trading.
His true plan was to sell me for a profit.
I had suspicions, but I climbed on board.
The ship sailed out with fair north wind behind her
from Crete out into open sea. But Zeus
planned to destroy the crew. On leaving Crete,
no other land was visible, but only
the sea and sky. Zeus set a dark-blue cloud
across our ship that cast a shadow over
the sea. He thundered and then hurled a bolt
of lightning at the ship. The impact whirled
the ship right round and filled her up with sulfur.
The men fell overboard and all were swept

away by waves, like cormorants beside
the dark ship, and gods took away their chance
of getting home. But in my desperation
Zeus rescued me. He put the sturdy mast
into my hands. I clung to it and drifted,
propelled by storm winds for nine days. And on
the tenth black night, the rolling waters swept me
towards Thesprotia. There the king, named Pheidon,
helped me without expecting recompense
because his son had found me all worn out,
chilled by the morning air. He took my hand,
raised me and led me to his father's house,
and dressed me. That was where I heard about
Odysseus—the king said he had been
a guest there on his journey home. The king
showed me the treasure that Odysseus
had gathered: gold and bronze and hard-worked iron.
The royal stores contained enough to feed
his family for ten more generations.
Odysseus, the king said, had gone off
to Dodona, to ask the holy oak
what Zeus intended. He had been too long
away from fertile Ithaca. He wondered
how best to get back home—in some disguise
or openly. The king then swore to me,
pouring libations, that he had a boat
prepared and crew picked out, to take him back
to his dear homeland. But he sent me first;
it happened some Thesprotians were already
sailing towards grain-rich Dulichium.
The king told them to treat me well and take me
to King Acastus. But their hearts preferred
to bring me once again to misery.
After the ship was out upon the sea,

they plotted to enslave me. They stripped off
my cloak and tunic, and tossed me these rags
in which you see me now. And when night fell
they came to Ithaca's bright fields, and tied me
tightly with rope and left me on the ship,
and quickly went ashore to get some dinner.
The gods themselves unloosed my bonds; they slipped
easily off. I pulled my ragged clothes
over my head, slid down the smooth ship's plank
and plunged chest-forward in the sea. I swam
fast with both arms, and quickly got away.
I came ashore beside a flowering thicket
and huddled there in fear. They stomped around,
shouting, but in a while they gave up looking,
and got back on the ship. The gods themselves
hid me with ease, and brought me to this cottage—
a wise man's home—because it is my fate
to stay alive."

Eumaeus, you replied,
"Poor guest! Your tale of woe is very moving,
but pointless; I will not believe a word
about Odysseus. Why did you stoop
to tell those silly lies? I know about
my master's homecoming. The gods detest him;
they loathe him, since they did not let him die
at Troy or in his friends' arms, when the war
was winding up, so that the Greeks could build
a mound to glorify him and his son
in times to come. The robber-winds have snatched him.
He has no glory now. I am a loner;
I live here with the pigs, and do not go
to town, except when wise Penelope
calls me to share some news. The people cluster

around her, asking questions—some in sorrow
about their absent master; others glad
to eat at his expense. I ask no questions,
since an Aetolian fooled me with his lies.
He came to my house, saying he had killed
a man in distant parts and run away.
I welcomed him. He said that he had seen
Odysseus with Idomeneus
in Crete, repairing ships that storms had wrecked.
He promised that my lord would come in summer
or harvesttime, made rich by heaps of treasure,
his crew complete. A god has brought you here;
but do not try to trick me or make nice
with lies. I will be kind to you, old man,
not for your stories, but in fear of Zeus,
the god of strangers, and because I feel
pity for you."

But sly Odysseus
answered, "You are too skeptical! Despite
my oath, I see you will not trust me. May
the gods of Mount Olympus be our witness
that if your master ever comes back home
to this house, you will give me clothes to wear,
and help me to Dulichium—I want
to go there. But if he does not arrive,
and I am wrong, your slaves can drive me over
the cliff tops, so no other beggar tries
to trick you."

But the upright swineherd answered,
"Yes, guest, I would be praised enormously
among all men, now and in times to come,
if I took you inside and welcomed you,

then murdered you! And doing this,
with what clean conscience could I pray to Zeus?
In any case, now it is dinnertime.
My men should come inside, so we can cook
delicious food."

That was their conversation.
In came the herdsmen, and they drove the pigs
into their usual pens to rest; there rose
a mighty din of grunting pigs. The noble
swineherd addressed his men.

"Bring out the best
pig for our guest, who comes from distant lands.
And let us all enjoy ourselves. We suffer
in bitter toil for these white-tusked pigs,
while others eat the food we labor for,
and give us nothing."

With a keen bronze axe
he chopped the wood. They brought a fattened pig
of five years old and put it on the altar.
The swineherd's heart was good: he kept in mind
the gods. He shaved the bristles off its head,
and threw them in the fire, and prayed to all
the gods, that through his ingenuity,
his master would come home. He stretched up
tall, and used a piece of oaken firewood
to strike. The life departed, and they slit
the throat and singed the hide, and chopped it up.
The swineherd made an offering of meat,
laid flesh across the fine rich fat, and put it
upon the fire with barley-grain on top,
and sliced the rest and put it all on skewers,

and roasted it with care, then drew the meat off
and heaped it high on platters. Next he stood
and served it out in seven equal parts,
the first with prayers, for Hermes and the Nymphs,
and then he served the others to the men.
He gave Odysseus the piece of honor,
cut from the spine. His master was delighted,
and said,

"Eumaeus, may Zeus bless and love you
as I do, since you give me such good things."

You answered him, swineherd Eumaeus, "Eat,
dear guest; enjoy it, simple though it is.
Gods give, gods take away, as is their will;
to gods all things are possible."

With that,
he made the sacrifices to the gods,
poured a libation from the bright red wine,
then gave Odysseus, the city-sacker,
the cup. At last the swineherd sat to eat.
Mesaulius served the food—that was the slave
bought by Eumaeus in his master's absence,
with no help from his mistress or Laertes.
He traded him from Taphians. They all
reached out to take the good things set before them.
When they had had enough of food and drink,
Mesaulius cleared things away; the men
were full of bread and meat, and wanting sleep.
Night fell, a moonless, bitter night. Zeus rained
continually; wet Zephyr blew his hardest.
Odysseus—to test out if Eumaeus

was kind enough to take his own cloak off,
or tell another man to do it—said,

"Eumaeus and you others, all of you.
I want to brag a little. I am dizzy,
under the influence of wine, which makes
even the wisest people sing and giggle,
and dance, and say things best not spoken. Since
I have begun this blabbering, here goes,
I will be honest. I wish I was young
and strong again! As when we planned an ambush
under the walls of Troy—the leading men
were Menelaus and Odysseus,
and I was chosen as the third commander.
When we had reached the city wall, we lay
in bushes, reeds, and marshes, hiding under
our shields. Night fell, harsh and icy cold,
with North Wind and a sleetlike snow, so cold
the ice grew on our weapons. All the others
had cloaks; they slept in comfort, tucked beneath
their shields. But I had foolishly forgotten
my cloak and left it, not expecting cold.
I carried just my shield and shining belt.
In the last part of night, as stars were setting,
I went near to Odysseus and nudged him.
He listened to me carefully. I said,
'Your Majesty, Odysseus, great general,
I am about to die from this cold weather!
I have no cloak. Some spirit tricked me into
wearing my tunic only; now there is
no way to fix it.' Instantly he thought
of this solution. What a strategist
and fighter! Very quietly he whispered,

'Hush now, do not let any of the others
hear you.' He propped his head up on his elbow,
and told them, 'Listen, friends. I had a dream
sent by the gods. We moved too far away
from where the ships are. Someone needs to speak
to Agamemnon, shepherd of the people,
and tell him to send more troops here.' At that,
Thoas the son of Andraimon leapt up,
took off his purple cloak and sprinted down
towards the ships. I snuggled down in comfort
under his cloak till golden Dawn shone bright.
If only I was young and strong again!
Then one of these pig-keepers on this farm
would give a cloak to me, both from respect
and friendship. As it is, they all despise me
for wearing dirty rags."

Eumaeus, you
replied, "That was a splendid tale, old man!
It worked. You will get all the clothes and things
a poor old beggar needs—at least for now.
But in the morning, you will have to put
your old rags on again. We only have
one outfit each, no spares. My master's son
will give you clothes when he arrives, and help you
to travel on wherever you desire."

With that, he stood and set a bed for him
beside the fire, and threw on it some skins
of sheep and goats. Odysseus lay down.
Eumaeus tucked him in a big thick cloak,
his extra one, for really bitter weather.
Odysseus went to sleep; the young men slept
beside him. But the swineherd did not like

to sleep so distant from the pigs; he started
to leave. Odysseus was glad the slave
took good care of his absent master's things.
Eumaeus slung his sharp sword belt across
his well-toned back, and wrapped around himself
his windproof cloak and fine big furry goatskin.
He took a sharpened knife to ward away
humans or dogs, and he went off to sleep
out where the pigs with silver tusks were sleeping;
a hanging rock protected them from wind.

BOOK 15

The Prince Returns

Athena went to Sparta, to ensure
the safe return of Prince Telemachus.
She found him with Pisistratus, both lying
on Menelaus' porch, and Nestor's son
was fast asleep, but no sweet slumber held
Telemachus. His worries for his father
kept him awake all through god-given night.
Owl-eyed Athena stood by him and said,

"Telemachus, you should no longer travel
so far from home, abandoning your wealth,
with greedy men at home. You must watch out;
They may divide and eat up all your wealth,
and make your journey useless. Quickly ask
for help from Menelaus to get home,
so you may find your mother safe and blameless.
Her father and her brothers are already
telling her she should wed Eurymachus.
He is the one most generous with gifts
to her and to her father. Do not let her

take any items from the house, without
your full consent. You know how women are—
they want to help the house of any man
they marry. When one darling husband dies,
his wife forgets him, and her children by him.
She does not even ask how they are doing.
Let your best slave girl watch your property,
until the gods give you your own wife. Also,
I have more news: take note. There is a gang
of suitors lurking in the stream between
your Ithaca and rocky Same, who
have plans to kill you on your journey home.
But I suspect that some of those who waste
your wealth will soon be lying under earth.
Now steer your ship far distant from the islands,
and sail both day and night. Some god who guards
and watches over you will send fair wind
behind your sails. When you first reach the shore
of Ithaca, your men must drag the ship
up to the town, while you first go and visit
the swineherd, who is better than most slaves.
Spend the night there. Tell him to go to town
to tell Penelope that you have come
safely back home from Pylos."

With these words
the goddess went back up to Mount Olympus.
He woke the son of Nestor with a kick,
and said to him,

"Pisistratus! Go fetch
the horses, get them harnessed to the carriage,
and let us hurry on our way."

He answered,
"Telemachus, this is impossible,
for us to drive when it is pitch-black night,
however eager we may be to travel.
Dawn will come soon. Wait till great Menelaus
comes out to bring us presents in his carriage,
and sends us on our way with friendly words.
A generous host is sure to be remembered
as long as his guests live."

Then all at once
Dawn on her golden throne lit up the sky.
King Menelaus got up from the bed
he shared with fair-haired Helen and approached them.
Seeing him on his way, Telemachus
put on his bright white tunic, and then slung
his mighty sword across his sturdy shoulders.
So in a warlike guise, the well-loved son
of godlike King Odysseus stood near
and spoke to Menelaus.

"Royal son
of Atreus, now, please, send me home now,
to my beloved country. My heart yearns
to go back home."

And Menelaus answered,
"Telemachus, I will not keep you here
if you are truly desperate for home.
I disapprove of too much friendliness
and of too much standoffishness. A balance
is best. To force a visitor to stay
is just as bad as pushing him to go.
Be kind to guests while they are visiting,

then help them on their way. So friend, remain
just till I fetch some splendid gifts to pile
onto your carriage. Wait till you see them!
I will instruct the women to prepare
a banquet in the hall from our rich stores.
Feasting before a long trip brings you honor;
it also makes good sense. And if you want
to have me travel with you all through Greece,
I shall yoke up my horses and escort you
through every town, and everywhere we go
we will be given gifts—a fine bronze tripod,
a cauldron, or two mules, or golden cups."

Telemachus replied, "King Menelaus,
I want to go home right away. I have
no one back there to watch my property.
I would not want to die while I am searching
for Father, or to lose my wealth at home."

So General Menelaus shouted out
to tell his wife and female slaves to make
a feast from his rich stores. Eteoneus
got out of bed and came—he lived nearby.
The general boomed out orders: "Light the fire
and roast the meat!" The slave obeyed. Meanwhile,
his master went inside the fragrant room
containing treasures. Helen went with him,
and Megapenthes. There he took a goblet,
two-handled, and he told his son to bring
a silver bowl. And Helen stood beside
the chests in which she kept the special clothes
that she had worked with her own hands. She lifted
the most elaborate and largest robe
that shone like starlight under all the rest.

Then they went through the palace till they reached
Telemachus. And fair-haired Menelaus
said to him,

"May great Zeus, the Lord of Thunder,
husband of Hera, make your wish come true—
may you go back home safely. I will give you
the best of all my treasure, as a mark
of deep respect: a bowl of solid silver,
circled with gold; Hephaestus fashioned it.
The King of Sidon, Phaedimus, bestowed it
on me when I was at his house, en route
for home. Now take it; it is yours."

He gave
the goblet first, and Megapenthes brought
the shining silver bowl and put it down
in front of him. Then Helen's lovely cheeks
flushed as she moved in close. She held the robe
and said,

"Sweet boy, I also have a gift,
crafted by my own hands. Remember Helen
when your own wedding day at last arrives,
and let your bride wear this. Until that time,
your mother should take care of it. I wish you
great joy. I hope you reach your well-built home,
and fatherland."

She handed it to him;
he took it gladly. Prince Pisistratus
took all the gifts and packed them in the luggage,
and marveled at them in his heart.

The king
led them inside; they sat on chairs. A slave girl
brought out a beautiful gold water pitcher
and silver bowl so she could wash their hands.
She set a polished table at their side.
Another lowly girl brought bread and food
of all kinds, and Eteoneus started
to carve and serve the meat. The king's son poured
the wine for everyone. They helped themselves
to all the delicacies spread before them.
When they were satisfied, Telemachus
and Nestor's son strapped on the horses' harness,
and yoked them to the chariot and drove
off from the echoing portico and gate.
But Menelaus ran up just behind them,
holding a golden cup of honeyed wine
in his right hand, so they could pour libations
before they left. He stopped in front of them
and spreading wide his arms said,

"Boys, good luck!
Give Nestor my best wishes—he was always
as kind as any father while we Greeks
were making war in Troy."

Telemachus
said carefully, "Yes, king, when we go there
we will pass on what you have said. I hope
I may go back to Ithaca and meet
Odysseus—good luck to match my fortune
in all your generosity and kindness."

Then on the right an eagle flew; it held
a big white goose clutched in its claws—a tame one,

caught from the yard. The people, men and women,
were running round and yelling after it.
It darted on the right beside the boys,
and flew before their horses. They were all
delighted. Nestor's son was first to speak.

"My lord, King Menelaus, what do you think?
Was this a sign sent by some god for us?
Or sent for you?"

And Menelaus, favorite
of Ares, wondered how he ought to answer.

But Helen cut in first and said, "Now listen,
and I will make a prophecy. The gods
have put it in my heart and I believe
it will come true. Just as the eagle flew
down from the mountains where he has his home
with chicks and parents, seizing this tame goose—
so will Odysseus, who has been gone
so long and has endured so much, come back
and take revenge. Indeed, he is already
at home and planting ruin for the suitors."

Telemachus replied, "May thundering Zeus
fulfill your prophecy at once! If so,
I would bow down to you as to a goddess."

He whipped the horses and they galloped off
through the town center to the open plain.
All day the harness rattled as they ran.
But when the sun went down and it grew dark,
they came to Pherae, home of Diocles,
son of Ortilochus, who was the son
of Alpheus. He welcomed them and there

they spent the night. When rosy-fingered Dawn
the early-born appeared, they yoked the horses,
climbed in the chariot, and drove away
from the resounding portico and gate.
The horses flew with gusto at the whip.
Soon they were near the rocky town of Pylos.
Telemachus then asked Pisistratus,

"Would you do me a favor? We are friends
because our fathers have been friends forever,
and we are age-mates, and this trip has made us
even more intimate. Please do not bring me
beyond my ship, but leave me here, in case
the old man forces me to visit him
and be his guest. I long to get back home.
I have to go, and fast."

The son of Nestor
wondered how he should best respond. He thought
upon reflection he should turn the horses
back to the ship and shore beside the sea.
There he took out the splendid gifts and clothes
and gold from Menelaus, and he packed them
inside the stern, and told Telemachus,

"Hurry! Embark now! Get your crew in too,
before I get back home and tell my father
that you are here. I know him; he is stubborn.
He will not let you go; he will come here
to fetch you, and he surely will not leave
without you. He will be in such a rage!"

With that, he spurred the horses. Long manes flowing,
they galloped to the citadel of Pylos.
Telemachus gave orders: "Make it all

shipshape, my friends, and get on board, so we
can start our journey."

Quickly they obeyed
and sat along the benches. As he worked,
with prayers and sacrifices to Athena,
a foreigner approached him, who had killed
a man in Argos and had run away.
He was a prophet and descended from
Melampus, who once lived in Pylos, land
of sheep. Melampus had been rich, and owned
a palace, but he left his home, escaping
from Neleus, a proud, important man,
who seized all his great wealth while he was trapped
and tortured in the house of Phylacus,
because a Fury put inside his mind
a dangerous obsession with the daughter
of Neleus. He managed to escape,
and drove the cattle, lowing loudly, off
from Phylace to Pylos. He avenged
the wrong that Neleus had done to him,
and brought the woman to his brother's house
as wife, then went to Argos, home of horses,
since there it was his destiny to rule
the multitude of Argives, and he had
two strong sons: Mantius, and Antiphates,
who fathered the heroic Oïcles,
whose son was Amphiaraus, the warlord,
whom Zeus who holds the aegis and Apollo
adored wholeheartedly. But he did not
live to old age, since he was killed at Thebes,
because his wife took bribes. He had two sons,
Amphilochus and Alcmaeon. The sons
of Mantius were Clitus, snatched by Dawn
to join the gods, because he was so handsome,

and Polypheides, whom Apollo gave
the best prophetic skill of any mortal
after Amphiaraus had died. This prophet
grew angry with his father, and migrated
to Hyperisia, and there he told
fortunes for everyone. It was his son,
named Theoclymenus, who had approached
Telemachus while he was pouring wine
and praying to the gods. The stranger said,

"My friend, I find you making sacrifices.
I beg you, by religion, by the gods,
and by your life and your men's lives: who are you?
Who are your parents? What is your home town?"

Telemachus said, "Stranger, I will tell you.
I come from Ithaca; my father is
Odysseus—he was. He must have died
some dreadful death by now. It was for him
I got this ship and crew. I sailed to seek
news of my absent father."

And the stranger
replied, "I too am far from home. I killed
a man of my own tribe, and I have many
brothers and kinsmen, powerful in Argos,
so I am on the run. They want to kill me.
I have been doomed to homelessness. But please,
let me on board your ship. I come to you
in desperation—otherwise I will
surely be killed. Those men are after me."

Telemachus said, "Yes, you can join us
on board our ship. And what we have is yours;
you are our guest."

He took the stranger's spear,
laid it on deck, then climbed on board himself,
sat at the stern, and had his guest sit down
beside him at the stern. They loosed the ropes.
Telemachus gave orders to the men
to seize the tackle; promptly they obeyed,
and raised the wooden mast and fastened it
into the socket, binding it with forestays,
and hauled the white sail up with leather cables.
Sharp-eyed Athena sent fair wind that gusted
a wild explosive breath through bright clear sky;
the ship began to race across the sea,
past Crouni and the lovely streams of Chalcis.
The sun went down and all the world was dark.
Impelled by wind from Zeus, the ship sped on
past Phaea and they came to famous Elis
ruled by the Epeians; from there they steered
towards the Needle Islands, still unsure
if they would die.

Meanwhile, Odysseus
was having dinner with the noble swineherd
inside the cottage, and the other men
were eating with them. After they were done,
Odysseus began to test the swineherd,
to see if he would be hospitable,
and ask him to stay there, out on the farm,
or send him into town. He said,

"Eumaeus,
listen, and listen all of you. At dawn
I plan to go to town to beg—I have
no wish to be a burden to you all.

I only need directions and a guide
who can go with me. I will roam around
the city on my own, in search of drink
and crusts of bread—so it must be. And if
I reach the house of King Odysseus,
I plan to tell Penelope my news,
and mingle with the high and mighty suitors;
they may give me some food from their rich stores.
I could do anything they want at once.
I have the capability, you see.
Hermes the messenger, the god who gives
favor and glorifies all human labor,
has blessed me with unrivaled skill in all
domestic tasks: fire-laying, splitting logs,
carving and roasting meat, and pouring wine—
I can do all the chores poor people do
to serve the rich."

But angrily you said,
Eumaeus, "No! Why would you think of this?
You would be killed if you set foot among
that horde of suitors; their aggression reaches
the iron sky. And those who wait on them
are not like you. They are young men, well dressed,
with bright clean hair and handsome faces, serving
the bread and wine and meat, piled high upon
their polished tables. Stay here. No one minds
your presence—not myself, nor my companions.
And when Odysseus' son arrives,
he will provide a proper cloak and tunic,
and help you travel where your heart desires."

Odysseus, experienced in pain,
answered, "I hope Zeus loves you as I do,

since you have saved me from the agonies
of wandering. The worst thing humans suffer
is homelessness; we must endure this life
because of desperate hunger; we endure,
as migrants with no home. But since you now
want me to stay and wait for your young master,
tell me about Odysseus' parents.
His father, when he left, was on the threshold
of age. Are they alive still? Have they died?"

He answered, "Stranger, I will tell you truly.
Laertes is alive, but he is always
praying to Zeus to let him pass away
in his own home. He feels such desperate grief
about his son and his beloved wife,
whose death made him so heartbroken, he aged
before his time. She died a dreadful death,
a death I would not wish for any friend—
grieving her absent son, the famous hero.
While she was still alive, despite her sadness,
she used to like to talk and chat with me—
she brought me up herself with her own daughter,
strong, pretty Ctimene, her youngest child.
She raised us both together, treating me
almost as equal, just a little less.
And when we came of age, they sent the girl
to Same, for a hefty bridal-price.
The mother dressed me in fine clothes, a cloak
and tunic, tying sandals on my feet,
and sent me to the country. But she still
loved me with all her heart. I miss them both.
The blessed gods have made my work here prosper,
so I have had enough to eat and drink
and give to guests. But I hear no good news
about my mistress. Ruin has befallen

the house from those invaders. All her slaves
miss talking to their owner, getting gossip,
sharing some food and drink with her, and taking
scraps to the fields with them—the kind of thing
that makes slaves happy."

And Odysseus
exclaimed, "Eumaeus! What a little child
you were when you were taken far from home
and from your parents! Tell me more. Did they
live in a city that was sacked? Or was it
bandits that found you, herding sheep or cows
alone? Did they seize hold of you and put you
onto their ship, and sell you for a profit
in this man's house?"

The swineherd answered him,
"Since you have asked this question, stranger, listen;
enjoy my story, sitting quietly,
drinking your wine. These nights are magical,
with time enough to sleep and to enjoy
hearing a tale. You need not sleep too early;
it is unhealthy. Any other man
who feels the need of sleep should go lie down,
get up at dawn, have breakfast, and go herd
the master's pigs. But let us, you and I,
sit in my cottage over food and wine,
and take some joy in hearing how much pain
we each have suffered. After many years
of agony and absence from one's home,
a person can begin enjoying grief.
I will tell you my story as you ask.
There is an island—you may know it—called
Syria, where the sun turns round, above
Ortygia. It has few inhabitants,

but it is good land, rich in sheep and wine
and grain; no famine ever hurts those there,
nor any deadly sickness. They grow old,
and with their gentle arrows, Artemis
and silver-bowed Apollo cause their death.
The land is split into two provinces;
my father Ctesius was king of both.
Then avaricious merchants came—Phoenicians,
skilled sailors, with great piles of treasure stored
in their black ship. And in my father's house
there was a woman from Phoenicia—tall
and beautiful and skilled in many arts.
Those clever rascals tricked her. One of them
first found her washing clothes beside the ship
and lay with her. Sex sways all women's minds,
even the best of them. And then he asked her
where she was from and who she was; she showed him
my father's palace, and she said, 'I am
from Sidon, rich in bronze. I am the daughter
of wealthy Arybas; as I was walking
back from the fields one day, some Taphian pirates
kidnapped me, brought me here to this man's house,
and sold me to him, for a tidy sum.'
Her secret lover said, 'Then would you like
to go back home with us, and see your parents
and your fine home again? They are alive
and quite rich now.' The woman said, 'Oh, yes,
I would! If all you sailors swear an oath
to bring me safely home.' At that, they swore
as she had asked, and made their solemn vows.
And then the woman said, 'You must keep mum,
and none of you can even speak to me
if you bump into me beside the road
or at the water fountain—otherwise
someone might tell the old man at the house.

Then he would get suspicious, chain me up,
and plan to have you killed. Remember this,
bear it in mind and do your trading quickly,
and when your ship is full of stores to take
back home with you, send news to me, and fast.
I will bring gold with me as well, whatever
wealth I can find to hand. I also want
to give another gift to pay my fare.
I take care of my master's clever son—
who always runs around outside with me.
I will bring him on board and he will fetch
a pretty price from foreigners.' With that,
she went back to the palace. For a year
they stayed with us accumulating wealth
by trading, and they filled their ship's hold up.
When it was time to go, they sent a man
to tell the woman at my father's house.
He was a very cunning man. He wore
a golden necklace strung with amber beads;
the slave girls in the palace and my mother
stared and began to finger it and ask
how much it cost; he nodded to the woman
in silence, and then went back to the ship.
She took me by the hand and led me out
into the forecourt, where she found some cups
left on the tables by my father's men
who had been banqueting, and now had gone
to council—they were having a debate.
She took three cups and hid them in her dress
and carried them away with her. I followed,
knowing no better. As the sun went down,
we hurried through the dark streets to the harbor.
There was the swift Phoenician ship. They all
embarked, put us on board as well, and sailed
over the watery waves; Zeus sent fair wind.

For seven days we sailed and on the eighth,
Artemis struck the woman with her arrows.
She crashed into the ship's hold like a seagull.
They threw her overboard to feed the fish
and seals, and I was left there, brokenhearted.
The current carried them to Ithaca,
and then Laertes bought me with his wealth.
That was the way my eyes first saw this land."

Odysseus replied, "My heart is touched
to hear the story of your sufferings,
Eumaeus. In the end, though, Zeus has blessed you,
since after going through all that, you came
to live with someone kind, a man who gives you
plenty to eat and drink. Your life is good.
But as for me, I am still lost; I trekked
through many towns before I wandered here."

So went their conversation; then they slept
for just a little while; Dawn soon arrived
upon her throne.

Meanwhile, Telemachus
drew near the mainland. Lowering the sail
nimbly, his men took down the mast and rowed
to anchorage. They cast the mooring stones,
and tied the cables from the stern, then climbed
out in the surf, and waded into shore.
There they made dinner, mixing bright red wine.
When they had had enough to eat and drink,
the boy said sensibly,

"You all should drag
the ship towards the town, while I go visit

the herdsmen in the fields of my estate.
Then I will come to town, at evening time.
At dawn, I will provide a feast for you
of meat and wine."

Then Theoclymenus
asked him, "But where shall I go, my dear boy?
To whose house? One of those who rule this land?
Or should I go at once to your own mother
in your house?"

And Telemachus replied,
"Well, ordinarily I would invite you.
We are good hosts. But as it is—best not,
for your own sake. I will not be at home,
and Mother will not see you; she is weaving
upstairs upon her loom—she does not want
the suitors seeing her. So I suggest
you go to someone else's house: the son
of skillful Polybus, Eurymachus.
The Ithacans look at him as a god.
He is the dominant suitor and the keenest
on marrying my mother and acquiring
the riches of Odysseus. Zeus knows
the future, he alone. Eurymachus
may die a dreadful death before that marriage."

As he said this, a bird flew on his right:
a hawk, Apollo's messenger. It clutched
a pigeon in its talons; feathers scattered
between the ship and young Telemachus.
Then Theoclymenus called him aside
and grasped him by the hand, and said to him,

"Telemachus! Some god has sent this bird
to fly on your right hand. I knew at once
it was a sign. No family in all
of Ithaca has greater power; you are
the kings forever."

He replied, "Oh, stranger!
I hope your words come true! If so, I would
give you so many gifts to show my friendship
that everyone you met would be impressed."

And then he told his faithful man, "Piraeus,
you were most trustworthy of those who came
with me to Pylos. Let this stranger come
to your own house, be kind to him and give him
a cordial welcome till I come."

Piraeus
answered, "However long you are away,
I will take care of him."

And then he climbed
aboard and told the men to come as well,
and loose the cables, which they did, and sat
down on the benches. Then Telemachus
tied on his sandals, and took from the deck
his sharp bronze spear. The men untied the ropes
and sailed towards the town, just as the son
of great Odysseus had ordered them.
The boy walked quickly till he reached the farmyard.
Hundreds of pigs were there and with them slept
the swineherd who knew how to help his masters.

BOOK 16

Father and Son

At dawn the swineherd and Odysseus
made breakfast, lit the fire, and sent the herdsmen
out with the pigs that they had rounded up.
The dogs, that as a rule would bark at strangers,
were quiet when they saw Telemachus;
they panted at him. When Odysseus
saw how they acted, and heard footsteps coming,
he said,

"Eumaeus, someone must be coming—
a friend or somebody you know—the dogs
are friendly, with no barking. I can hear
footsteps."

He hardly finished, when his son,
his own dear son, was there inside the gate.
Amazed, the swineherd jumped up, letting fall
the cups in which he had been mixing wine;
it spilled. He ran towards his master, kissed

his face and shining eyes and both his hands,
and wept. Just as a father, when he sees
his own dear son, his only son, his dear
most precious boy, returned from foreign lands
after ten years of grieving for his loss,
welcomes him; so the swineherd wrapped his arms
around godlike Telemachus and kissed him,
as if he were returning from the dead.
With tears still in his eyes he said,

"Sweet light!
You have come back, Telemachus. I thought
that I would never see you anymore,
after you sailed to Pylos. My dear child,
come in, let me enjoy the sight of you
now you are back. Come in! You do not often
come to the countryside to see us herders;
you stay in town to watch that evil horde
of suitors."

And Telemachus replied
warily, "Grandpa, yes, I will come in.
I came to see you here with my own eyes,
and hear if Mother still stays in the house,
or if some other man has married her
already, and Odysseus' bed
is empty, full of ugly spiderwebs."

The swineherd, the commander, said, "Indeed,
her heart is loyal. She is in your house,
weeping by night and sad by day."

He took
Telemachus' sword; the boy came in,
crossing the stony threshold, and his father

offered his seat. Telemachus refused,
saying, "You sit there, stranger. I can find
a chair around my hut. The slave can help."

Odysseus went back and sat back down.
The swineherd spread fresh brushwood and a fleece
on top, so that Telemachus could sit.
He set the bread in baskets and brought meat,
left over from the meal the day before.
He mixed some wine up in a wooden bowl,
and sat down opposite Odysseus.
They reached to take the good things set before them.
When they were satisfied, Telemachus
turned to the noble swineherd.

"Tell me, Grandpa,
where did this stranger come from? By what route
did sailors bring him here? And who were they?
He surely did not walk to Ithaca!"

Eumaeus answered, "I will tell you, child.
He is from Crete. He says he wandered, lost
through many towns—so some god spun his fate.
Now he has run away from the Thesprotians
who brought him, and arrived here on my farm.
He is all yours, your suppliant, to treat
however you desire."

Telemachus
said anxiously, "This news of yours, Eumaeus,
is very worrying to me. How can I
invite him to my house? I am too young
to fight back with my fists if someone picks
a fight with me. My mother is unsure
if she should stay with me and show respect

towards her husband's bed and public gossip,
and keep on taking care of things at home,
or marry one of them, whichever suitor
asserts himself, and brings most lavish gifts.
But since this man has come here, to your house,
I will dress him in fine clothes, cloak and tunic,
and sandals for his feet, and give a sword,
and help him on his way. If you are willing,
keep him here in the farmhouse; care for him.
I will send you some clothes and all his food,
so he will be no bother to these men
or you. I will not let him go to meet
the suitors; they are much too violent.
I would be mortified if they abused him.
It would be difficult for one man, even
a strong one, to do anything to them.
They are too many."

Then Odysseus,
frustrated, said, "My friend, it is my duty
to speak out when I hear the dreadful things
those suitors have been doing in your house,
against your will; it breaks my heart. You are
a good man. Tell me, did you choose to let them
bully you? Have the Ithacans been turned
against you by some god? Or do you blame
your brothers, who should be a man's supporters
when conflict comes? If only I had youth
to match my will! I wish I were the son
of great Odysseus—or that I were
the man himself come home from wandering.
We can still hope. Let someone chop my head off,
if I would not destroy them when I came
inside the palace of Odysseus!

And if I lost—since I am only one
against so many—I would rather die
in my own house, than watch such crimes committed!
Strangers dishonored! Slave girls dragged around,
raped in my lovely home! Men wasting wine
and bread—for nothing! For this waiting game!"

Telemachus said soberly, "I will
explain the situation to you, stranger.
The Ithacans are not my enemies,
and I do not have brothers I can blame.
Zeus gave my family a single line:
Arcesius had just one son, Laertes,
who had Odysseus, his only son,
and he had me, his only son, whom he
left back at home; he had no joy of me.
And now there are so many cruel invaders,
since all the toughest men from all the islands—
from Same and Dulichium and wooded
Zacynthus, and all those who hold command
in rocky Ithaca, have come to court
my mother, wasting all my wealth. She does not
refuse the awful prospect of remarriage,
nor can she end the courtship. They keep eating,
consuming my whole house, and soon they may
destroy me too. These things lie with the gods.
Now Grandpa, you must hurry to the queen,
and tell her I am safe back home from Pylos.
I will stay here while you tell her—just her;
do not let any others hear the news,
since many people want to plot my death."

Eumaeus, you replied, "I understand.
But tell me, on this same trip, should I go

and tell poor old Laertes? For a while
he used to watch the fields and join the slaves
for dinner at the house, when in the mood,
despite his grief for lost Odysseus.
But since your ship set sail away to Pylos,
they say he has stopped eating, will not drink,
and does not go to check the fields. He sits,
weeping and sobbing, worn to skin and bone."

Telemachus said calmly, "That is sad;
distressing news. But no, leave him alone.
If human wishes could come true, my first
would be to have my father come back home.
Take her your message, hurry back, and do not
trail round the countryside to look for him.
Tell Mother she should send a girl in secret
to run to old Laertes with the news."

At that, the swineherd tied his sandals on,
and started off towards the town. Athena
noticed him leaving from the yard, and stood
beside him as a woman, tall and skillful,
and beautiful. Odysseus could see her,
standing beside the entrance to the cottage.
Telemachus could not; the gods are not
equally visible to everyone.
The dogs could see her but they did not bark.
They whimpered and slunk back across the room
in fear. She raised her eyebrows, with a nod;
he understood and came out, past the wall,
and stood beside her. Then Athena told him,

"Odysseus, great strategist, it is
time for your son to know the truth; together
you have to plan how you will kill the suitors.

Then both of you go into town. I will
join you there soon myself; indeed I am
itching to fight."

And then Athena touched him,
using a golden wand, and dressed him up
in fine clean cloak and tunic, and she made him
taller and younger-looking. He became
black-skinned, his cheeks filled out, and on his chin
the beard grew dark. And so her work was done,
and off she flew. Odysseus went in.
His son was startled and looked down, afraid
in case it was a god. His words flew out.

"Stranger, you look so different from before.
Your clothes, your skin—I think that you must be
some god who has descended from the sky.
Be kind to us, and we will sacrifice,
and give you golden treasures. Pity us!"

Long-suffering Odysseus replied,
"I am no god. Why would you think such things?
I am your father, that same man you mourn.
It is because of me these brutal men
are hurting you so badly."

Then he kissed
his son and cried, tears pouring down his cheeks;
he had been holding back till then. The boy
did not yet trust it really was his father,
and said,

"No, you are not Odysseus,
my father; some god must have cast a spell,
to cause me further pain. No mortal man

could manage such a thing by his own wits,
becoming old and young again—unless
some god appeared and did it all with ease.
You certainly were old just now, and wearing
those dirty rags. Now you look like a god."

Artful Odysseus said sharply, "No,
Telemachus, you should not be surprised
to see your father. It is me; no other
is on his way. I am Odysseus.
I suffered terribly, and I was lost,
but after twenty years, I have come home.
As for the way I look—Athena did it.
The goddess can transform me as she likes;
sometimes a homeless beggar, then she makes me
look like a young man, wearing princely clothes.
For heavenly gods it is not difficult
to make a mortal beautiful or ugly."

With that, he sat back down. Telemachus
hurled his arms round his father, and he wept.
They both felt deep desire for lamentation,
and wailed with cries as shrill as birds, like eagles
or vultures, when the hunters have deprived them
of fledglings who have not yet learned to fly.
That was how bitterly they wept. Their grieving
would have continued till the sun went down,
but suddenly Telemachus said,

"Father,
by what route did the sailors bring you here,
to Ithaca? And who were they? I know
you did not walk."

Odysseus replied,
"Son, I will tell you everything. Phaeacians,
famous for navigation, brought me here.
They always help their guests travel onward.
I slept as their ship sped across the ocean;
they set me down on Ithaca, still sleeping.
They brought me marvelous gifts of gold and bronze
and clothing, which are lying in a cave,
since gods have willed it so. Athena told me
to come here and make plans with you to kill
our enemies. How many suitors are there?
What kind of men are they? I am well-known
for my intelligence, and I will plot
to work out if we two alone can fight them,
or if we might need others helping us."

Telemachus considered, then said, "Father,
I always heard how excellent you are,
at fighting with a spear, and making plans.
But what you said just now—it is too much.
We cannot fight, the two of us, against
such strong men, and so many—there are dozens,
not just a handful. Let me tell you quickly
the number of the suitors. Fifty-two
came from Dulichium, all top-notch fighters,
who brought six henchmen. Twenty-four men came
from Same, twenty more from Zacynthus,
and from right here on Ithaca came twelve,
all strong young men. They have a herald with them,
named Medon, and a poet, and two slaves
well trained in carving meat. If we attack
when all those men are crowded in the house,
I am afraid you will be paying back
their violence at all too high a price.

Think harder: can we find some kind of helper,
willing to fight for us?"

Odysseus
said, "Do you think Athena and her father,
Zeus, would be strong enough to keep us safe?
Would any other help be necessary?"

Telemachus replied, "The ones you mention
are good defenders. They sit high among
the clouds, and they control both men and gods."

The veteran Odysseus replied,
"Those two will quickly join the heat of battle
when we begin to grapple with the suitors,
when in my house the god of war is testing
our fighting force and theirs. Go back at dawn,
and join those overconfident young men.
The swineherd will escort me into town.
I will again be looking like a beggar.
If they abuse me and you see me suffer,
you must restrain yourself, repress your feelings,
even if they are pelting me with weapons,
and even if they grab me by the foot
to hurl me out. Just watch, and keep your temper.
Politely tell them they should stop this folly.
They will ignore you. Truly now their day
of doom is near at hand. Now listen hard.
Athena, my best co-conspirator,
will nudge my heart, and I will nod to you.
Then you must find all weapons in the house
that could be used for fighting; go and hide them
away inside the upstairs storage room.
And when the suitors ask where they have gone,
fob them off, saying, 'They were near the fire,

so I removed them from the breath of smoke,
since they were getting damaged; they were losing
the luster that they used to have, before
Odysseus went off to Troy. Praise Zeus!
I thought of something even more important:
if you get drunk you may start quarreling,
and hurt each other. Then your lovely dinners
and courtship will be ruined. Arms themselves
can prompt a man to use them.' Tell them that.
Leave out two swords, two spears, and two thick shields
for you and me to grab before we rush
to ambush them. Athena will bewitch them,
helped by sharp-witted Zeus. And one more thing:
if you are my true son, of my own blood,
let no one know that I am in the house.
Laertes and the swineherd must not know,
nor any of the slave girls, and not even
Penelope, until we have determined
the women's attitude. We also must
test the male slaves, and see who has respect
and fears me in his heart, and who does not,
and who looks up to you as you deserve."

His glowing son said, "Father, you will see
my courage in the moment. I am tough.
But it would take too long to go around
and test each man like that, and all the while,
the suitors would be sitting in your house,
wasting your wealth with heedless partying.
So reconsider. I agree you should
find out about the women—which of them
are innocent, and which dishonor you.
However, I have no desire to traipse
around to test the men; we can do that
later, if Zeus reveals a sign to you."

Such was their conversation. Then the ship
in which Telemachus had gone to Pylos
docked in the bay of Ithaca's main town.
They disembarked and dragged the ship onto shore.
The slaves brought out the splendid gifts and weapons
and took them to the house of Clytius.
A messenger was sent to tell the queen
Telemachus was back in Ithaca,
and that he said that they must come to town,
dragging the ship, in case she had been weeping
in her anxiety about her son.
The swineherd and this messenger met up,
on the same mission, to inform the queen.
When both of them arrived, the slave girls clustered
around the messenger. He said,

"Great queen,
your dear son has come home!"

And then the swineherd
took her aside and told her what her son
had ordered him to say. When he was done,
he walked out through the hall and out the courtyard,
leaving the palace hall to join his pigs.

The suitors were upset and down at heart.
Eurymachus the son of Polybus
said, "Friends, the journey of this upstart boy
succeeded! We were sure that he would fail.
We must launch our best ship, equipped with rowers,
to cross the salty sea and find the others
and tell them to come home at once."

His words
were hardly finished when Amphinomus
spotted a ship inside the harbor, pointed
away from land; the sails were being furled,
the men were carrying the oars. He laughed
triumphantly and said,

"No need to send
a messenger! They are already back!
Some god has told them, or they saw his ship
approaching, but could not catch up with it."

So leaping up, they went down to the seashore,
and dragged the black ship up onto dry land,
and servants proudly brought the weapons out.
They all went crowding to the marketplace,
together, and banned any other men
from joining them, both young and old. And then
Antinous addressed them.

"How amazing!
The gods have saved this man from death! For days
our scouts took turns to watch from windy cliffs.
And when the sun went down, we never spent
a night on shore, but sailed to wait till Dawn
at sea in ambush for Telemachus,
to make sure we would catch him. Now some god
has brought him home. We need to make new plans
to murder him. He must not get away.
He will obstruct our courtship if he lives,
since he is wise to us, and he will plot,
and now the people will be turned against us.
Telemachus will gather them; he must
be furious, and he will not postpone

action. He will stand up and tell them how
we planned to murder him, but failed to do so.
When they hear of our crimes, they will condemn us.
We may get hurt or driven from our land,
to foreign territories; we must stop it!
Catch him out in the countryside, away
from town, or on the road. Let us rob him,
and share his wealth and property among us—
and let his mother, and whichever man
marries her, keep the house. But if you think
it would be better if we let him live,
and keep his father's riches for himself,
we should stop flocking here to waste the wealth
inside his house. We should each go and court her
from home, by sending gifts. One day, the lady
will marry, and the lucky man will be
the one who sends the most gifts."

They were silent.
But then Amphinomus, the famous son
of Nisus, spoke. He had come from the wheat fields
and pastures of Dulichium, with others.
He was intelligent; Penelope
preferred his speeches over other men's.
Wisely he said,

"My friends, I for my part
have no desire to kill Telemachus.
It is a dreadful thing to kill a person
of royal blood. So first we must discover
the gods' intentions. If great Zeus decrees it,
I will kill him myself, and urge you all
to join me. If the gods do not approve,
I say we must not do it."

So he spoke,
and they agreed with what he said. They stood,
and went back to Odysseus' house,
and sat on polished chairs.

Penelope
decided she must show herself to these
ungentlemanly suitors, since she had
found out about the plot to kill her son—
Medon had heard their plans, and he told her.
Her women at her side, she went downstairs,
into the hall, approached them and then stopped,
standing beside the doorpost with a veil
across her face. She told Antinous,

"You are a brute! A sneak! A criminal!
The people say you are the smartest boy
of all those your own age on Ithaca.
It is not true. You are insane! How could you
devise a plan to kill Telemachus?
Do you have no respect for ties created
by supplication, which Zeus watches over?
Have you forgotten that your father came here,
running in terror from the Ithacans,
who were enraged because he joined the pirates
of Taphos, and was hounding the Thesprotians,
our allies? So the Ithacans were eager
to kill him, rip his heart out, and devour
his wealth. Odysseus protected him!
Now you consume your benefactor's wealth,
and court his wife, and try to kill his son,
and you are hurting me! I tell you, stop!
And make the other suitors stop as well."

Eurymachus said, "Wise Penelope,
you need not worry; put this from your mind.
No man will ever, ever hurt your boy
while I am still alive upon this earth.
I swear to you, if someone tries, my sword
will spill his blood! Your city-sacking husband
often would take me on his lap, and give me
tidbits of meat with his own hands, and sips
of red wine. So Telemachus is now
the man I love the most in all the world.
The boy is in no danger, not from us—
there is no help for death brought by the gods."

He spoke to mollify her; all the while
he was devising plans to kill her son.
She went up to her light and airy bedroom,
and wept for dear Odysseus, her husband,
until Athena gave her eyes sweet sleep.

As evening fell, the swineherd came back home
to find Odysseus. He and his son
had killed a year-old pig and made a meal.
Athena came beside Odysseus
and touched him with her wand again to make him
ragged and old, to make sure when the swineherd
came in, he would not recognize his master,
in case he told Penelope the secret.

He came inside. Telemachus spoke first.
"Eumaeus, you are back! What is the news
in town? Are those proud suitors in my house,
back from the ambush, or still lurking there
to catch me on my way back home?"

———

Eumaeus
answered, "I did not want to trek through town
asking that question. I preferred to share
my news as fast as possible and then
come back. One of your own men went with me,
a messenger; he told your mother first.
I saw one more thing: as I passed the hill
of Hermes, right above the town I saw
a ship draw into harbor, full of men
and loaded up with shields and spears. I thought
it could be them, but I cannot be sure."

Then Prince Telemachus began to smile
and met his father's eyes; he did not let
Eumaeus see. When they were finished cooking,
they shared the dinner equally, and all
had plenty, then they took the gift of sleep.

BOOK 17

Insults and Abuse

When newborn Dawn appeared with hands of flowers,
Telemachus, Odysseus' son,
fastened his handsome sandals on his feet,
took up his sturdy spear that fit his hand,
and headed out. He told the swineherd,

"Grandpa,
I must go into town, to see my mother.
Until we meet, I think she will not stop
her lamentations, tears, and bitter sobbing.
Now I need you to take this poor old stranger
to town to beg his supper; any man
who feels like it can feed him. I cannot
put up with everyone right now; I have
too many worries. If he gets annoyed,
the worse for him. I always like to tell
the honest truth."

Odysseus replied,
"My friend, I do not even want to stay.
Beggars should wander round the town and country.

I will get food from charitable people.
I am too old to stay here as a farmhand,
obeying orders from an overseer.
This man will take me, as you told him to,
as soon as I have warmed up by the fire.
I only have these rags; the morning frost
may do me in—you say the town is far."

At that, Telemachus strode quickly out,
thinking about his plan to hurt the suitors.
And when he reached the royal house, he propped
his spear against a pillar, and went in,
across the stony threshold.

Eurycleia
the nurse, was first to notice his arrival,
as she was laying fleeces on the chairs.
Weeping, she rushed at him. The other women
owned by strong-willed Odysseus assembled
and kissed Telemachus' head and shoulders
to welcome him. Then wise Penelope
came from her bedroom, looking like a goddess,
like Artemis or golden Aphrodite,
and flung her arms around her darling son,
and wept. She kissed his face and shining eyes,
and through her tears her words flew out.

"You came!
Telemachus! Sweet light! I was so sure
that I would never see you anymore
after you sailed to Pylos secretly,
not telling me, to get news of your father.
Tell me, what have you seen?"

                                        Telemachus
said calmly, "Mother, do not try to make me
upset, or stir my feelings. I survived
the danger. Go upstairs and take your bath,
put on clean clothes and take your women with you
into your bedroom. Sacrifice and pray
to all the gods, that one day Zeus may grant
revenge. Now I am going into town.
I will invite the stranger who arrived
right after me on Ithaca. I sent him
ahead, with my brave men, and told Piraeus
to take him home and treat him with all kindness
until I come."

                        His flying words hit home.
She washed, put on clean clothes, and prayed to all
the gods, and made them lavish sacrifices,
asking that one day Zeus would bring revenge.

Telemachus took up his spear and marched
out through the hall, two swift dogs at his side.
Athena poured unearthly grace upon him.
Everyone was amazed to see him coming.
The suitors gathered round and spoke to him
in friendly tones; at heart, they meant him harm.
Keeping away from most of them, he joined
Mentor and Antiphus and Halitherses,
who were his father's friends from long ago.
They questioned him in detail. Then Piraeus
approached with Theoclymenus, the stranger
whom he had brought through town towards the center.
At once Telemachus set out and rushed
to stand beside the stranger. And Piraeus
spoke first.

"Telemachus, send women quickly
to my house, so I may give back the gifts
that Menelaus gave you."

But with caution
Telemachus replied,

"Piraeus, no.
We do not know exactly what will happen,
and if the suitors in my house by stealth
should kill me and divide my father's wealth
between themselves, I would prefer that you
enjoy the gifts than any of those men.
And if I kill them, planting doom among them,
bring me the gifts, and we will both be happy."

With this, he led the weary stranger back
to his house, where he laid their cloaks across
chairs; they went to bathe. The slave girls washed them,
rubbed them with oil, and dressed them in wool cloaks
and tunics. Then they left the baths and sat
on chairs. A girl brought out a golden pitcher
and poured the washing water on their hands,
over a silver bowl. She set a table
beside them, and a humble slave girl brought
a generous array from their rich stores.
Penelope was leaning on a chair
beside the door, facing Telemachus,
spinning fine strands of wool. They helped themselves
to food and drink. When they had had enough,
Penelope, preoccupied, spoke up.

"Telemachus, I will go upstairs now,
to lie down on my bed, which has become
a bed of mourning, always stained with tears,

since my Odysseus went off to Troy
with those two sons of Atreus. But you
have failed to tell me if you gathered news
about your father's journey home; now tell me,
before the suitors come."

Telemachus
answered her calmly. "Mother, I will tell you.
We went to Pylos, visiting King Nestor.
He made me very welcome in his palace,
under his roof, as if I were his son
returning after many years away.
He cared for me like one of his own sons.
But he said he had not heard anything
from anyone about Odysseus,
alive or dead. He sent me on, with horses
and carriage, to the son of Atreus,
great General Menelaus. There I saw
Helen for whose sake, by the will of gods,
the Greeks and Trojans suffered through the war.
When Menelaus asked why I had come
to glorious Sparta, I told him the truth
in detail, and he answered, 'Stupid cowards!
The bed they want to lie down in belongs
to someone truly resolute. As when
a deer lays down her newborn suckling fawns
inside the leafy den of some fierce lion,
and goes off to the slopes and grassy valleys
to graze. Then he comes back to his own bed
and cruelly destroys both little ones.
So will Odysseus destroy them all.
By Father Zeus, Athena, and Apollo,
I pray he is as strong as long ago,
on Lesbos, when he wrestled Philomedes
and hurled him to the ground, and all the Greeks

cheered. May he fight the suitors that same way,
so all of them will find their courtship ends
badly, and their lives soon. And I will answer
your questions frankly, and tell what I learned
from the old Sea God, who can tell no lies.
He said he saw him in distress: the nymph
Calypso has him trapped upon her island,
inside her house. He cannot come back home
to his own country, since he has no fleet
or crew to row across the sea's broad back.'
That was what famous Menelaus said.
My tasks accomplished, I sailed off. The gods
gave me fair wind which swiftly brought me home."

His story stirred emotions in her heart.
Then godlike Theoclymenus spoke up.

"My lady, wife of great Odysseus,
this news is incomplete. I will reveal
the whole truth with a prophecy. I swear
by Zeus and hospitality and by
the hearth of great Odysseus, the place
where I have come: he is already here
in Ithaca—at rest or on his way.
He must have learned what bad things they are doing,
and he is plotting ruin for them all.
I know because I saw a sign while sitting
on board the ship—I told Telemachus."

Penelope said carefully, "Well, stranger,
I hope this does come true. I would reward you
with so much warmth and generosity
that everyone you met would see your luck."

Meanwhile, outside Odysseus' house,
the suitors relished games of darts and discus,
playing outside as usual, with no thought
of others. Then at dinnertime, when flocks
of sheep were trekking home from every field,
led by their shepherds, Medon spoke. He was
the suitors' favorite herald, whom they always
brought to their feasts.

"My lords, you have enjoyed
your games. Now come inside to eat. There is
no harm in having meals at proper times."

They followed his advice, stood up and went
inside the palace. They spread out their cloaks
over the chairs, and killed plump goats, large rams,
some fatted pigs, and one domestic cow,
and cooked them for the feast.

Odysseus
was making haste to leave the countryside
for town. The swineherd spoke in lordly tones.

"Stranger, my master says that you can come
to town today, as you desire—though I
would rather leave you here to watch the farm.
But I am nervous that the master may
reproach me, and a master's curses fall
heavily on a slave. Now we must go.
The hour is late and it will soon get colder;
the sun is sinking low."

Odysseus
answered, "I understand. We can go now;
you lead the way. But if you have a stick,

give it to me to lean on, since I hear
the path is slippery."

With that, he slung
his bag across his shoulders by its string.
It was all tattered, full of holes. Eumaeus
gave him a serviceable stick. They left;
the dogs and herdsmen stayed to guard the farm.
The swineherd led his master into town
resembling a poor old beggar, leaning
upon a stick and dressed in dirty rags.
They walked along the stony path, and near
the town, they reached an ornate fountain, flowing
with clear streams, where the people came for water.
It had been built by Ithacus, Neritus,
and Polyctor. A circle of black poplars
grew round it, nurtured by the spring. Cool water
poured from the rocks above. There was an altar
built over it in honor of the Nymphs.
All passersby made offerings to them.
Melanthius the son of Dolius,
with two more herders, met them there. He was
driving the finest goats to feed the suitors.
On seeing them, he spoke abusively,
in brash, offensive language that enraged
Odysseus.

"One scoundrel leads another!
Makes sense: gods join like things with like. You foul
pig-man, where are you taking this old swine?
A scrounger, who will rub on many doors,
demanding scraps, not gifts for warriors.
If you let me have him to guard my farm,
and muck the pens and toss the kids their fodder,
he could drink whey and fatten his stick legs.

But he does not want work. He likes to traipse
around the town and beg for chow to stuff
his greedy belly. I predict, if he
reaches the palace of Odysseus,
a mass of hands will hurl stools at his head,
to pelt him through the house and bruise his ribs."

With that, he sauntered past him, and lunged out
to kick him on the hip bone. What a fool!
Odysseus was not pushed off the path;
he stood there fixed in place, and wondered whether
to rush at him, armed with his stick, and kill him,
or grab him by the ears and push him down
onto the ground. Instead, he braced himself
and kept his temper. When the swineherd saw
Melanthius insulting him, he prayed,
arms high.

"O Fountain Nymphs, O Zeus' daughters!
If ever King Odysseus brought bones
of lamb and goat in luscious fat for you, then now
fulfill my prayer! May spirits guide him home!
My master will put paid to all the bluster
of this rude man, who loafs round town and lets
the animals be ruined by bad herders."

Melanthius the goatherd sneered at him,
"Oh, very nice! This dog knows how to talk,
and it has learned some tricks. One day I will
take him by ship and row him far away
from Ithaca, and get a heap of treasure
by selling him. I wish Apollo would
shoot silver arrows at Telemachus
tomorrow in his house; or that the suitors

would kill him. I am sure Odysseus
is far away and never coming back."

With that, he left them—they were walking slowly,
and he rushed on ahead of them. He went
inside his master's house, and sat among
the suitors, with Eurymachus, his favorite.
The slaves brought out a piece of meat for him,
and a submissive house girl brought him bread.
The swineherd and Odysseus went in,
and stood, surrounded by the strumming sound
of the resounding lyre that Phemius
was tuning for his song. Odysseus
grabbed at the swineherd's hand and said,

"Eumaeus!
This is Odysseus' splendid palace.
It could be recognized among a thousand.
The rooms are all connected, and the courtyard
is fenced in by a wall with cornices,
and there are sturdy double doors. No man
could break through here. I notice many men
are feasting; I smell meat, and hear the lyre,
which gods have made companion to the feast."

Eumaeus answered, "Right! You are perceptive.
Now we must plan. Will you go inside first
to join the suitors, while I stay out here?
Or do you want to wait, and I will go?
But do not stay too long. If someone sees you,
you will be pelted, maybe beaten up."

Unflappable Odysseus said, "Yes,
I thought of that. You go, I will stay here.

I have been hit before. I know hard knocks.
I am resilient. I suffered war
and being lost at sea. So let this be.
There is no way to hide a hungry belly.
It is insistent, and the curse of hunger
is why we sail across relentless seas,
and plunder other people."

As they spoke,
Argos, the dog that lay there, raised his head
and ears. Odysseus had trained this dog
but with no benefit—he left too soon
to march on holy Troy. The master gone,
boys took the puppy out to hunt wild goats
and deer and hares. But now he lay neglected,
without an owner, in a pile of dung
from mules and cows—the slaves stored heaps of it
outside the door, until they fertilized
the large estate. So Argos lay there dirty,
covered with fleas. And when he realized
Odysseus was near, he wagged his tail,
and both his ears dropped back. He was too weak
to move towards his master. At a distance,
Odysseus had noticed, and he wiped
his tears away and hid them easily,
and said,

"Eumaeus, it is strange this dog
is lying in the dung; he looks quite handsome,
though it is hard to tell if he can run,
or if he is a pet, a table dog,
kept just for looks."

Eumaeus, you replied,
"This dog belonged to someone who has died

in foreign lands. If he were in good health,
as when Odysseus abandoned him
and went to Troy, you soon would see how quick
and brave he used to be. He went to hunt
in woodland, and he always caught his prey.
His nose was marvelous. But now he is
in bad condition, with his master gone,
long dead. The women fail to care for him.
Slaves do not want to do their proper work,
when masters are not watching them. Zeus halves
our value on the day that makes us slaves."

With that, the swineherd went inside the palace,
to join the noble suitors. Twenty years
had passed since Argos saw Odysseus,
and now he saw him for the final time—
then suddenly, black death took hold of him.

Telemachus first saw the swineherd coming.
He gave a nod to tell him to come over.
Glancing around, Eumaeus saw the stool
used by the boy who carved the suitors' meat.
He picked it up and set it down beside
Telemachus' table. There he sat;
the slave boy brought him meat and bread. And then
Odysseus approached and stepped inside,
looking like some poor homeless sad old man;
he hobbled on his stick, then slumped himself
down on the ash-wood threshold, leaning back
against the cypress doorpost, which a workman
had smoothed and straightened long ago. The boy
summoned the swineherd over, and picked up
a wheat loaf from the basket and as much
meat as his hands could hold, and gave it to him.
He said,

"Please take this food out to that stranger,
and tell him he should walk around the hall
and beg from all the suitors; shame is not
a friend to those in need."

The swineherd went
and told Odysseus, "Telemachus
gives you this food and says you ought to beg
from all these suitors; shame, he says, is not
fitting for those who have to live by handouts."

Odysseus prayed cautiously, "O Zeus,
bless this Telemachus, and may he have
all that his heart desires."

And with both hands
he took the food and set it at his feet,
on top of his old ragged bag, and ate,
and listened to the singer in the hall.
As he was finishing, the music stopped;
the suitors shouted, and Athena stood
beside Odysseus, and prompted him
to go among the suitors, begging scraps,
to find out which of them were bad or good—
although she had no thought of saving any
out of the massacre which was to come.
He went around and begged from left to right,
holding his hand out, like a practiced beggar.
They gave him food in pity, and they wondered
who this man was and whereabouts he came from.
They asked each other, and Melanthius,
the goatherd, said,

"You suitors of the queen,
listen to me about this stranger here.
I saw this man before; the swineherd brought him.
I know no more; I do not know his background."

Antinous began to scold the swineherd.
"Pig-man! You famous idiot! Why did you
bring this man here? Do we not have already
plenty of homeless people coming here
to spoil our feasts? Is it not bad enough
that they crowd round and eat your master's wealth?
You had to ask this other one as well?"

Eumaeus, you replied, "Antinous,
you are a lord, but what you say is trash.
Who would invite a stranger from abroad
unless he had the skills to help the people—
a prophet, or a doctor, or a builder,
or poet who can sing and bring delight?
No one would ask a beggar; they bring only
their hunger. Out of all the suitors, you
are meanest to the slaves, especially me.
But if the prudent queen and godlike prince
still live here in this house, I do not mind."

Telemachus said, "Shush. Antinous
does not deserve an answer. He is always
picking a fight, and goading on the others."

Then turning to Antinous, he said,
"You care for me so nicely, like a father!
You told me I should force the stranger out.
May no god make that happen! Go to him
and give him something; I can spare the food.

Go on, I tell you! You should pay no heed
to Mother or the other household slaves
belonging to my father. You were not
concerned about them anyway. You want
to gorge yourself, not share with other people."

Antinous replied, "You little show-off!
What nasty temper! What an awful comment!
If all the suitors gave the same as me,
this house could keep him checked for three whole months."

He had a footstool underneath the table,
for resting his soft feet on while he feasted;
he brandished it. The others all gave food
and filled the beggar's bag. Odysseus
had finished with his test; he could have walked
back to the threshold, no harm done. Instead,
he stood beside Antinous and said,

"Friend, give me something. You must be the best
of all the Greeks. You look like royalty,
so you should give more food than all the rest,
and I will make you known throughout the world.
I used to be a rich man, with a palace.
When needy beggars came from anywhere,
no matter who they were, I gave them food.
My slaves were numberless, my wealth was great;
I had the life men say is happiness.
But Zeus destroyed it all; he wanted to.
He prompted me to travel with some pirates
to Egypt; that long journey spelled my ruin.
I moored my galleys in the River Nile
and told my loyal men to stay and guard them,
and sent out scouts to all the lookout points.
But they were too impulsive, and they sacked

the beautiful Egyptian fields, and seized
women and children, and they killed the men.
The screaming reached the town; the people heard,
and rushed to come and help; at dawn the plain
was all filled up with foot soldiers and horses
and flashing bronze. Then Zeus, who loves the thunder,
caused panic in my men—disastrous panic.
Danger was all around us, and not one
stood firm. The sharp bronze swords killed many men,
and others were enslaved as laborers.
But they gave me to somebody they met,
a foreigner named Dmetor, king of Cyprus.
I came from there. Such is my tale of woe."

Antinous replied, "What god imposed
this pest to spoil our feast? Stay over there,
not near my table—or you can get lost!
Get killed in Egypt or enslaved in Cyprus!
You barefaced beggar! You come up to us,
and these men give you treats unthinkingly;
we have so much, and people do not mind
sharing another person's wealth."

Sharp-witted
Odysseus drew back from him and said,
"You handsome idiot! You would not give
a grain of salt from your own house. You sit
enjoying someone else's food, and yet
you will not give a crumb from this great banquet
to me."

Antinous was furious,
and scowling said, "That does it! You insult me?
You lost the chance to leave with dignity!"

He lifted up his stool and hurled it at
Odysseus' right shoulder, near his back.
It did not knock him over; like a rock
he stood there, shook his head, and silently
considered his revenge. Then he went back,
sat on the threshold and set down the bag,
all full of food, and told them, "Listen, suitors
of this world-famous queen; I have to speak.
When men are fighting for their own possessions,
for cows or sheep, there is no shame in wounds.
But now Antinous has wounded me
because I came here hungry; hunger brings
such suffering to humans. If there are
gods of the poor, or Furies to avenge us,
may he be struck by death, instead of marriage!

He answered, "Stranger, shut up, or be off!
If you keep talking, we young men will drag you
across the palace by your hands and feet
and have you flayed alive!"

But all the others
reproached Antinous insistently.
"You ought not to have hit a poor old beggar!
If he turns out to be a god from heaven
it will end badly! Gods disguise themselves
as foreigners and strangers to a town,
to see who violates their holy laws,
and who is good."

Antinous ignored
the suitors' words. The blow increased the pain
inside Telemachus' heart, but he
let fall no tears. He calmly shook his head
and thought about revenge.

Penelope
heard what had happened in the hall, and said
to all her slaves,

"I hope Apollo shoots
Antinous, just as he hit the beggar!"

And old Eurynome replied, "If only
our prayers were answered! None of them would live
to see the Dawn ride in upon her throne."

Penelope said, "Yes, dear, they are all
our enemies and mean to do us harm.
Antinous is the worst; he is like death.
Some poor old stranger wandered to this house
and asked the men for food, compelled by need.
The others helped him out and filled his bag;
Antinous hurled a footstool at his shoulder."

She had this conversation in her room
with her attendants, while Odysseus
was eating dinner. Then she called the swineherd.

"Eumaeus! Have the stranger come to me,
so I may welcome him, and ask if he
has heard or witnessed anything about
long-lost Odysseus. The stranger seems
as if he must have traveled far."

Eumaeus
replied, "Your Majesty, I wish these men
would quiet down! The tales the stranger tells
would charm your heart. For three days and three nights
I had him stay with me. He ran away

from off a ship, and came to my house first;
he started to describe his sufferings,
and had not finished. Like a singer, blessed
by gods with skill in storytelling—people
watch him and hope that he will sing forever—
so this man's tale enchanted me. He says
Odysseus and he are old guest-friends
through their forefathers. This man lived in Crete,
the home of Minos, and he traveled here
a rambling route, with dangers compassed round.
He says Odysseus is still alive
and near here, in the rich Thesprotian land,
and he is bringing home a pile of treasure."

Penelope said, "Call him over, let him
tell me in person, while the suitors have
their fun here in my house or at the doors;
their mood is festive. In their homes they have
untasted food and wine, which their house slaves
devour, while they are flocking to our house
each day to slaughter oxen, sheep, and goats,
to feast and drink our wine, with no restraint.
Our wealth is decimated. There is no man
here like Odysseus, who could defend
the house. But if Odysseus comes back
to his own native land, he and his son
will soon take vengeance for their violence."

Telemachus sneezed loudly and the noise
resounded through the hall. Penelope
laughed, and she told Eumaeus,

"Call the stranger!
My son just sneezed at what I said—you heard?
It is a sign of death for all the suitors;

no one can save them from their ruin now.
But listen: if I find this stranger speaking
the truth, give him nice clothes—a cloak and tunic."

At that, the swineherd went and stood beside
Odysseus. His words had wings.

"Now sir,
Penelope, Telemachus' mother,
has summoned you. She feels impelled to ask
about her husband, painful though it is.
If you tell her the truth—and she will know—
you will get clothes; you desperately need them.
And you can ask for food all through the town,
and fill your belly. Anyone who wants
can give you scraps."

Strong-willed Odysseus
answered, "Eumaeus, I will tell the truth,
the whole truth, to Penelope, and soon.
I know about Odysseus; we shared
in suffering. But I am very nervous
about the rowdy suitors. Their aggression
touches the iron sky. When I was walking
across the hall just now, quite harmlessly,
that man hurled something at me, and he hurt me.
Telemachus did nothing to protect me,
and nor did anybody else. So now,
tell her to stay right there until night falls,
however eager she may be. At dusk,
she can come nearer, sit beside the fire,
and ask about her husband's journey home.
I do have dirty clothes—you know it well,
since it was you I came to first for help."

The swineherd headed back; he crossed the threshold,
and sharp Penelope said,

"Are you not
bringing the traveler? Is something wrong?
Is he too scared or shy? A homeless man
can ill afford such shame."

Eumaeus answered,
"His words were common sense; he wants to stay
out of the suitors' way; they are aggressive.
He says you should stay here until sunset.
It is much better for you too, my queen,
to speak to him alone."

Penelope
replied, "The stranger is no fool at least.
There never were such bullies as these men,
and they intend us harm."

The swineherd went
back to the crowd of suitors, and approached
Telemachus, and tucked his head down close,
so no one else would hear. "My friend," he said,
"I have to go and watch the pigs, and all
your property, and mine. You should take care
of everything, but most of all, yourself.
Do not get hurt. So many mean you harm.
I pray that Zeus obliterates them all,
before they injure us!"

Telemachus
answered, "May it be so. First eat, then go;
come back at dawn with animals for meat.
The rest is up to me and up to gods."

So then Eumaeus sat down on the stool,
and ate and drank, then went back to his pigs,
leaving the palace full of banqueters.
It was already late, past afternoon;
music and dancing entertained the suitors.

BOOK 18

Two Beggars

Then came a man who begged throughout the town
of Ithaca, notorious for greed.
He ate and drank nonstop, so he was fat
but weak, with no capacity for fighting.
The name his mother gave him as a child
was Arnaeus, but all the young men called him
Irus, because he was their messenger.
Now this man tried to chase Odysseus
from his own home, and cursed him.

"Get away,
old man! Get out! Or else you will be dragged
out by the foot! Do you not see the suitors
winking to tell me I must throw you out?
This is embarrassing for me; I must
make you get up right now! Or we must fight!"

Scowling at him, Odysseus said, "Fool!
I did not do you wrong or speak against you.
I am not jealous of another beggar

receiving gifts, however much he gets.
This doorway can accommodate us both.
Do not hog all the wealth; it is not yours.
You seem to be a homeless man, like me.
Gods give all mortal blessings. Do not stir me
to fight or lose my temper. I am old
but I will crack your ribs and smash your face
to bloody pulp—then I will have a day
of peace tomorrow; you will not return
here to the palace of Odysseus."

Irus the vagabond was furious.
"This greedy pig yaks on like some old woman
scrubbing an oven! I will hurt him, punch him
two-fisted, and rip out his teeth, as farmers
pull out the tusks from pigs that damage crops.
Get ready! Let them watch. How could you be
so dumb, to pick a fight with someone younger?"

So on the threshold at the palace doors
their furious aggression reached its peak.
Antinous, that saintly lord, incited
the fight and with a chuckle told the suitors,

"My friends! We never had so fine a show
brought to this house before. The gods be thanked,
these two are getting ready for a brawl.
Quick, let us goad them on!"

They all jumped up,
laughing, and gathered round the ragged beggars.
Antinous addressed them.

"Listen, suitors!
Goat stomachs stuffed with fat and blood are roasting
over the fire for dinner. Let the beggar
who wins the fight choose one of these and take it;
and he can always eat with us in future,
and we will let no other beggar come
to share our company."

They all agreed.
The strategist Odysseus deceived them,
saying, "My friends, there is no way a man
as old as me, worn down by suffering,
can fight a younger man. My hunger forces
bad choices, tempting me to take the beating.
But swear a mighty oath that none of you
will step up to help Irus out and hit me
roughly with fists and make me lose to him."

All of them swore the oath as he had asked.
The holy prince Telemachus said,

"Guest,
if your brave spirit urges you to fight
against this challenger, you need not worry
about the others. Anyone who strikes you
will face a multitude. I am your host;
Eurymachus and this Antinous
are sensible and they agree with me."

They all consented, and Odysseus
took off his rags and tied them round his waist,
revealing massive thighs and mighty shoulders,
enormous chest and sturdy arms. Athena
stood near him and increased his strength, to suit

the shepherd of the people. All the suitors
were flabbergasted, and they said,

"This means
the end of Irus—brought upon himself!
What muscles underneath the old man's rags!"

Irus was deeply troubled and afraid;
his heart sank. But the house slaves made him gird
his tunic and get ready. He was shaking.
Antinous said,

"Haha, you big show-off!
You would be better dead than so afraid
of some old man worn down by suffering.
If this man beats you, proving he is stronger,
I will toss you on board a ship and send you
off to King Echetus in mainland Greece,
the lord of cruelty and pain. He will
cut off your nose and ears with pitiless bronze,
and then your genitals, and he will give them
raw to his dogs to eat."

These words increased
his shakiness. Escorted to the ring,
he stood. Both raised their fists. Odysseus,
who had endured so many insults, wondered
if he should hit him hard enough to kill him,
or give him just a tap to knock him down.
A light touch would be best, he thought, in case
the suitors cottoned on. They came to blows.
First Irus hit Odysseus' shoulder;
Odysseus punched Irus on his neck
below the ear, and broke his jaw. Red blood

gushed from his mouth, and with a moan he fell,
teeth chattering, legs flailing. Then the suitors
threw up their hands to cheer, and died of laughter.
Odysseus seized Irus by the foot,
dragging him through the gateway to the courtyard,
and propped him by the wall. He put a staff
into his hand, and said,

"Sit there and keep
the dogs and pigs away! You good-for-nothing!
You must not bully visitors and beggars,
or you will suffer even worse than this!"

Then picking up his ragged bag, he slung it
across his shoulders by the strap and sat
beside the door again. The suitors went
inside and raised their cups.

"May all the gods
and Zeus give you your heart's desire! That Irus
was sponging everywhere, the greedy pig.
You put a stop to him, and we will send him
to Echetus, the king of mass destruction."

Odysseus was thrilled to hear this omen.
Antinous set out the big goat's stomach,
stuffed full of blood and fat, in front of him.
Amphinomus provided two bread baskets,
and a gold cup of wine, and welcomed him.

"Sir, be our guest, and may your future luck
be good, though now you have so many troubles."

Odysseus replied, his wits about him,
"Amphinomus, you seem intelligent,
like Nisus of Dulichium, your father;
I heard about his wealth and excellence,
and that you are his son. You are well-spoken.
Take note of what I say. Of all the creatures
that live and breathe and creep on earth, we humans
are weakest. When the gods bestow on us
good fortune, and our legs are spry and limber,
we think that nothing can ever go wrong;
but when the gods bring misery and pain,
we have to bear our suffering with calm.
Our mood depends on what Zeus sends each day.
I once had what most people count as wealth,
great riches. I committed many crimes,
of violence, abuses of my power,
abetted by my brothers and my father.
No one should turn away from what is right;
a man should quietly accept whatever
the gods may give. I see how wickedly
the suitors are behaving—wasting wealth
and failing to respect the wife of one
who soon will come back to his family
and homeland. Very soon! May spirits guide you
home, so you do not meet him when he comes.
When he confronts the suitors in this hall
there will be blood."

He poured an offering
of sweet wine to the gods, and took a sip,
then passed the cup back to Amphinomus,
who took it, and then paced around the house,
troubled at heart, his head bowed low; he saw
the danger in his mind. But he was not

fated to live; Athena had condemned him
to be defeated by Telemachus
with his strong spear. Amphinomus sat down
on the same chair that he sat on before.

Athena, with her gray eyes glinting, gave
thoughtful Penelope a new idea:
to let the suitors see her, so desire
would open up inside them like a sail,
and so her son and husband would respect her.
Mysteriously, she laughed, and told her slave,

"Eurynome, I have a new desire:
to let the suitors see me, though I hate them.
I also want to give my son advice:
not to spend so much time with those proud men.
They talk impressively, but their intentions
are bad."

Eurynome replied, "My child,
your words make sense. But you should wash and oil
your skin, not go with blotches on your face
to have this conversation with your son.
You should not grieve forever, and your boy
is older now. You always begged the gods
to let you see him grown up, with a beard."

Penelope replied with circumspection,
"Eurynome, I know you care for me,
but do not tell me I should wash myself
and put on oil. The gods destroyed my beauty
that day my husband left in hollow ships.
Go call my slave girls, Hippodameia
and Autonoe—they must come with me

into the hall. I do not want to go
to meet the men alone. It would be shameful."
So the old woman went and called the girls.

Athena's eyes were bright with plans. She poured
sweet sleep onto Penelope, who lay
down on her couch; her joints relaxed; she slept.
Athena gave her gifts of godlike power,
to make the men astonished when they saw her.
She put ambrosial beauty on her face,
the kind that Aphrodite, wreathed in myrtle,
uses before she dances with the Graces.
She also made her shapelier and taller,
and made her skin more white than ivory.
The goddess left. The girls came in; their talking
woke up the queen. She felt her cheeks and said,

"Despite my bitter grief, a peaceful sleep
enveloped me. If only Artemis
would bring me gentle death right now to end
my misery. I waste my life in longing
for my beloved husband, who was good
at everything—the best of the Achaeans."

She went down from her sunny room upstairs.
The two slaves went with her. She reached the suitors,
and stood beside the central pillar, holding
her gauzy veil before her face. Her two
trustworthy slaves stood either side of her.
The suitors weakened at the knees; desire
bewitched them, and they longed to lie with her.
She spoke to her dear son, Telemachus.

"Telemachus, you are not thinking straight.
When you were still a child, you had good sense.
Now you are bigger; you have reached adulthood.
You are so tall and so good-looking now!
People can see you are a rich man's son;
even a foreigner would know at once.
And yet your judgment is askew. What happened,
that you allowed a guest to be insulted?
If strangers in our house are so abused,
what then? You will be shamed! Your reputation
will be destroyed!"

Telemachus replied
with calculated purpose. "Mother, I do not
blame you for being angry. In my heart
I do know right and wrong. I used to be
a child; I am not now. But I cannot
even afford to think my own heart's thoughts.
Those evil suitors keep distracting me,
and I have no one on my side. This fight
between the stranger and that beggar Irus
did not turn out as they had wished; the stranger
was much the stronger. Father Zeus! Apollo!
Athena! May the suitors in our house
be beaten and bow down their heads, some in
the house, and some outside. May each man's body
grow weak—like Irus, out there at the gate,
sitting with head slumped down, as if he were
intoxicated; he cannot stand up
nor go back home. His body is too frail."

And then Eurymachus spoke up and said,
"O Queen Penelope! Wise, prudent daughter
of great Icarius! If all the Greeks

could see you now, there would be far more suitors
feasting here in your house, from dawn to dusk,
because no other woman equals you
in beauty, stature, and well-balanced mind."

Penelope replied with caution. "No,
the deathless gods destroyed my looks that day
the Greeks embarked for Troy, and my own husband
Odysseus went with them. If he came
and started taking care of me again,
I would regain my good name and my beauty.
I am weighed down by grief. A spirit set
so many troubles on me. At the time
that he left Ithaca, my husband grabbed
my wrist, took my right hand, and said to me,
'Now wife, I do not think we armored Greeks
will all come home unharmed from Troy. They say
the Trojans are good warriors with arrows
and javelins, and they ride chariots
drawn by swift horses, which can quickly turn
the tide of war, in which so many die.
Some god may bring me home, or I may be
captured out there in Troy. I do not know.
You must remember this: my parents need
to be well cared for in our house, as much
as now or more so with me gone away.
When our son's beard has grown, you must get married
to any man you choose, and leave your house.'
Those were my husband's words. The time has come;
the night when I must marry is at hand.
Terrible! I am cursed! Zeus took away
my happiness. Another bitter thought
oppresses me: it is not right or proper
to court a decent woman in this way,

a rich man's wife, competing for her hand.
They ought to bring fat sheep and cows to feed
my family, and give fine gifts, not eat
what is not theirs, and offer nothing back."

Odysseus, who had endured so much,
was happy she was secretly procuring
presents, and charming them with pretty words,
while her mind moved elsewhere.

Antinous
said, "Wise Penelope, take all the presents
that any of the Greeks would like to bring.
Refusing gifts is not polite. But we
will not go back to our own farms or elsewhere,
until you choose the best of us to marry."

They all agreed and sent their men for gifts.
Antinous brought out a splendid robe,
patterned, and with twelve brooches of pure gold
pinned to the fabric. And Eurymachus
gave her a necklace, finely worked in gold
set in with amber beads that shone like sunlight.
Two slaves brought earrings from Eurydamas.
They sparkled beautifully, and triple clusters
like berries hung from each. Pisander's slave
brought her a lovely choker, finely made.
All of the suitors gave her different gifts.
The queen went upstairs to her room; her slaves
carried the splendid presents. Then the suitors
turned back to watch the dancing and enjoy
the captivating music. They stayed there
in pleasure, till black evening came. They set
three braziers to light the whole great hall,

stuffed with dry wood, well seasoned and fresh cut,
combined with kindling. The slave girls owned
by firm Odysseus took turns to light them.
The king himself had all his wits about him,
and said,

"Slave girls! Odysseus, your master,
has been long gone. Go back and sit beside
the queen and comfort her. Spin yarn or comb
the wool. I can provide these men with light.
If they decide to stay here till bright Dawn
rides on her lovely throne, I will not be
defeated. I am tough."

At that, the girls
began to giggle, peeking at each other.
Pretty Melantho, child of Dolius,
had been brought up by Queen Penelope,
who gave her toys and treated her just like
a daughter. But Melantho, unconcerned
about Penelope, was sleeping with
Eurymachus. She started to insult
Odysseus, and taunt him.

"Poor old stranger!
You are insane! You did not want to sleep
out in the smithy or the public shelter;
instead, you come here talking high and mighty
among this crowd of men. Are you not scared?
Wine may have dulled your senses, or perhaps
you always say such idiotic things.
Has your defeat of Irus made you crazy?
That beggar? Then watch out, a better man
may fight you soon, and punch your face so hard

you will be kicked out of this house all drenched
in blood."

Odysseus scowled back and said,
"You little dog! I will soon go and tell
Telemachus what you have said, so he
can slice you limb from limb!"

That made the women
tremble with fear; they thought he spoke the truth.
They scattered through the house. He took his stand
beside the braziers to keep them lit,
and looked at all the suitors. In his heart
he formed his plans, which soon would be fulfilled.

Athena wanted pain to sink down deep
inside Odysseus. She made the suitors
keep taunting him. Eurymachus was jeering
to make the others laugh.

"Now listen, suitors!
I have an intuition that this man
has come into Odysseus' house
through some god's will. His head is shining brightly
under the lanterns' light—perhaps because
he is completely bald!"

And then he turned
and asked Odysseus, the city-sacker,

"Stranger, if I was hiring, would you like
to labor on a distant farm for me?
You would be paid for sure, if you could plant
tall trees, and build stone walls, and I would give you

your meals all year and clothes, including footwear.
But you are only skilled at wickedness.
You have no wish to work. You like to beg,
traipsing around to stuff your greedy belly."

Crafty Odysseus said, "How I wish,
Eurymachus, that we could have a contest
in springtime in the meadow, when the days
are growing longer; I would have a scythe
of perfect curvature and so would you.
The grass would be abundant; we would test
our skill by working all day long, not eating
until late evening. Or if we could plow
using a pair of fine and well-fed oxen,
strong and both equal in their power to pull,
and if we had four acres of good soil,
then you would see if I know how to cut
a furrow straight. Or if Zeus suddenly
made war begin tomorrow, and I had
two spears, a shield, and a helmet all of bronze
close-fitted to my head, you would see me
amid the throng of fighters at the front—
and you would not hurl insults at my belly.
You act aggressive, and you think you are
a big strong man, because you spend your time
among this tiny group of lowborn louts.
But if Odysseus appeared, the doors—
which are quite wide—would start to seem too narrow,
as you were struggling to get away."

Scowling with rage, Eurymachus replied,
"You nasty hobo! I will make you pay
for showing off in front of all of us.
You should be scared! The wine has made you stupid,

or maybe you are always talking nonsense;
or you are all puffed up from having won
over the beggar Irus!"

Then he hurled
a footstool at Odysseus, who ducked
behind Amphinomus in fear; it hit
the right hand of the slave boy serving wine;
the wine jug fell and clattered on the ground.
The boy fell backwards on the dust and moaned.
The suitors' shouts resounded through the shadows:
"Too bad this foreign drifter did not die
before he came here causing all this bother!
These arguments with beggars are disrupting
our banquet; it is spoiling our nice evening.
This silly fuss is dominating things."

Telemachus spoke up with dignity.
"Most noble lords! This is insanity.
Perhaps you dined too well, or else some god
is stirring you. Now you have finished dinner,
go home and sleep, whenever you are ready.
I will not force you out."

They bit their lips,
surprised at the self-confidence he showed.
Amphinomus, the famous son of Nisus,
grandson of Lord Aretias, spoke out
to all of them.

"My friends! What he has said
was fair; no one need take offense. Do not
abuse the stranger, nor the slaves who work
in great Odysseus' house. The boy

should fill the cups with wine, so we can pour
libations, then go home. Telemachus
can take care of the stranger—after all,
the beggar came to his house."

They agreed.
And Moulius, the slave Amphinomus
had brought there from Dulichium, mixed wine
for all of them and shared the drinks around.
They poured libations to the gods and sipped
the cheering wine. When they had had enough,
each of them went back home, to his own bed.

BOOK 19

The Queen and the Beggar

Odysseus was left there in the hall,
and with Athena, he was hatching plans
for how to kill the suitors. Words flew fast:

"Telemachus, we have to get the weapons
and hide them. When the suitors see them gone
and question you, come up with good excuses.
You can explain, 'The soot had damaged them;
when King Odysseus marched off to Troy
their metal gleamed; now they are growing dull.
I put them safe away from all that smoke.
Some spirit also warned me if you drink
too much and argue, you could hurt each other,
dishonoring your banquet and your courtship.
Weapons themselves can tempt a man to fight.'"

Telemachus obeyed his father's word.
He summoned Eurycleia, and he told her,
"Shut up the women in their rooms, while I
carry my father's weapons to the storeroom.
They have got dirty since my father left

when I was just a little boy. I want
to keep them safe, protected from the smoke."

The loving nurse said, "Child, I wish you would
take charge of all the household management
and guard the wealth. Which girl should bring the torch?
You said the slaves were not allowed to walk
in front of you."

He said, "This stranger will.
A man who eats my bread must work for me,
even if he has come from far away."

She made no answer but locked up the doors
that led inside the hall. Odysseus
and his bright boy jumped up and got the helmets
and studded shields and pointed spears. Athena
stood by them with a golden lamp; she made
majestic light. Telemachus said,

"Father,
my eyes have noticed something very strange.
The palace walls, the handsome fir-wood rafters
and crossbeams and the pillars high above
are visible, as if a fire were lit.
Some god from heaven must be in the house."

But cautiously Odysseus replied,
"Hush, no more questions, discipline your thoughts.
This is the way of gods from Mount Olympus.
You need to go to bed. I will stay here,
to aggravate the slave girls and your mother,
and make her cry, and let her question me."

Telemachus went through the hall, lit up
by blazing torches, to his room. Sleep came,
and there he lay till Dawn. Odysseus
stayed in the hall, still plotting with Athena
how to destroy the suitors.

Then the queen,
her wits about her, came down from her room,
like Artemis or golden Aphrodite.
Slaves pulled her usual chair beside the fire;
it was inlaid with whorls of ivory
and silver, crafted by Icmalius,
who had attached a footstool, all in one.
A great big fleece was laid across the chair,
and pensively Penelope sat down.
The white-armed slave girls came and cleared away
the piles of bread, the tables, and the cups,
from which the arrogant suitors had been drinking.
They threw the embers from the braziers
onto the floor, and heaped fresh wood inside them
for light and warmth.

And then Melantho scolded
Odysseus again. "Hey! Stranger! Will you
keep causing trouble, roaming round our house
at night and spying on us women here?
Get out, you tramp! Be happy with your meal!
Or you will soon get pelted with a torch!
Be off!"

Odysseus began to scowl,
and made a calculated speech. "Insane!
You silly girl, why are you mad at me?
Because I am all dirty, dressed in rags,

and begging through the town? I have no choice.
That is how homeless people have to live.
I used to have a house, and I was rich,
respectable, and often gave to beggars;
I helped whoever came, no matter what.
I had a lot of slave girls too, and all
the things we count as wealth; the happy life.
Zeus ruined it. He must have wanted to.
Girl, may you never lose the rank you have
among the other slave girls—if your mistress
gets angry, or Odysseus arrives.
It might still happen. But if he is dead
and never coming back, his son is now
a man, praise be Apollo. He will notice
any misconduct from the women here.
He is a grown-up now."

Penelope
had listened warily, and now she spoke
to scold the slave. "You brazen, shameless dog!
I see you! You will wipe away your nerve,
your grand audacity, with your own life.
You knew quite well—I told you so myself—
that I might keep the stranger in the hall
to question him about my missing husband.
I am weighed down by grief."

And then she turned
to tell Eurynome, "Bring out a chair
and put a cushion on it, so this stranger
can sit and talk with me. I want to ask him
some questions."

So the woman brought a chair
of polished wood, and set a cushion on it.
Odysseus knew how to bide his time.
He sat, and circumspect Penelope
began the conversation.

"Stranger, first
I want to ask what people you have come from.
Who are your parents? Where is your home town?"

Cunning Odysseus said, "My good woman,
no mortal on the earth would speak against you;
your glory reaches up to the wide sky,
just like a virtuous and godlike king
who rules a mighty people with good laws;
he makes the black earth bear forth wheat and barley;
the trees are full of fruit; the sheep have lambs;
the sea brings fish and people thrive. This is
your house. You have the right to question me,
but do not ask about my family
or native land. The memory will fill
my heart with pain. I am a man of sorrow.
I should not sit in someone else's house
lamenting. It is rude to keep on grieving.
The slaves, or even you, might criticize
and say my tearfulness is caused by wine."

Penelope said cautiously, "Well, stranger,
the deathless gods destroyed my strength and beauty
the day the Greeks went marching off to Troy,
and my Odysseus went off with them.
If he came back and cared for me again,
I would regain my beauty and my status.
But now I suffer dreadfully; some god

has ruined me. The lords of all the islands,
Same, Dulichium, and Zacynthus,
and those who live in Ithaca, are courting
me—though I do not want them to!—and spoiling
my house. I cannot deal with suppliants,
strangers and homeless men who want a job.
I miss Odysseus; my heart is melting.
The suitors want to push me into marriage,
but I spin schemes. Some god first prompted me
to set my weaving in the hall and work
a long fine cloth. I said to all my suitors,
'Although Odysseus is dead, postpone
requests for marriage till I finish weaving
this sheet to shroud Laertes when he dies.
My work should not be wasted, or the people
in Argos will reproach me, if a man
who won such wealth should lie without a shroud.'
They acquiesced. By day I wove the web,
and in the night by torchlight, I unwove it.
I tricked them for three years; long hours went by
and days and months, but then, in the fourth year,
with help from my own fickle, doglike slave girls,
they came and caught me at it. Then they shouted
in protest, and they made me finish it.
I have no more ideas, and I cannot
fend off a marriage anymore. My parents
are pressing me to marry, and my son
knows that these men are wasting all his wealth
and he is sick of it. He has become
quite capable of caring for a house
that Zeus has glorified. And now, you must
reveal your ancestry. You were not born
from rocks or trees, as in a fairy tale."

The master of deception answered, "Wife
of great Odysseus, Laertes' son,
why will you not stop asking me about
my family? I will speak, if I must.
But you are making all my troubles worse.
It is the way of things, when someone is
away from home as long as I have been,
roaming through many cities, many dangers.
Still, I will tell you what you ask. My homeland
is Crete, a fertile island out at sea.
I cannot count how many people live there,
in ninety cities, and our languages
are mixed; there are Achaeans, native Cretans,
and long-haired Dorians and Pelasgians.
Knossos is there, a mighty city where
Minos, the intimate of Zeus, was king
for nine years, and my father was his son,
the brave Deucalion, whose other son
was Idomeneus, who sailed to Troy
with the two sons of Atreus. My name
is Aethon, and I am the younger brother.
In Crete, I saw Odysseus, and gave him
guest-gifts. A storm had driven him off course
at Malea, and carried him to Crete,
although he yearned for Troy. He narrowly
escaped the winds and found a refuge, mooring
his ships in Amnisus, beside the cave
of Eileithyia. He came up to town,
and asked to see my brother, who, he said,
was his good friend, a man he much admired.
But Idomeneus had sailed to Troy
ten days before. I asked him and his crew
inside and gave them all a lavish welcome;

our stores were ample, and I made the people
bring barley and red wine and bulls to butcher,
to satisfy their hearts. Those noble Greeks
stayed for twelve days; a mighty north wind trapped them;
so strong a person could not stand upright;
some spirit must have summoned it to curse them.
But on the thirteenth day, the wind died down;
they sailed away."

His lies were like the truth,
and as she listened, she began to weep.
Her face was melting, like the snow that Zephyr
scatters across the mountain peaks; then Eurus
thaws it, and as it melts, the rivers swell
and flow again. So were her lovely cheeks
dissolved with tears. She wept for her own husband,
who was right next to her. Odysseus
pitied his grieving wife inside his heart,
but kept his eyes quite still, without a flicker,
like horn or iron, and he hid his tears
with artifice. She cried a long, long time,
then spoke again.

"Now stranger, I would like
to set a test, to see if you did host
my husband and the men that followed him
in your own house, as you have said. Describe
his clothes, and what he looked like, and his men."

Odysseus the trickster said, "My lady,
that would be hard to say—his visit was
so long ago. It has been twenty years.
But I will tell the image in my mind.

Kingly Odysseus wore a purple cloak,
of double-folded wool, held fastened by
a golden brooch with double pins, that was
elaborately engraved. In its front paws
a dog held down a struggling dappled fawn.
All those who saw it marveled how the dog
could grip the fawn, and how the fawn could kick
its legs and try to get away, though both
were made of gold. I noticed his white tunic
was soft as dried-up onion peel, and shiny
as sunlight. It astonished many women.
But note, I do not know if he had brought
these clothes from home, or if a crew member
had given them to him on board the ship,
or some guest-friend. Odysseus had many
dear friends, since very few could match his worth.
And I myself gave him a sword of bronze,
a double-folded purple cloak, and tunic
edged with a fringe. I sent him off in glory
when he embarked. He had a herald with him,
I do remember, named Eurybates,
a man a little older than himself,
who had black skin, round shoulders, curly hair,
and was his favorite out of all his crew
because his mind matched his."

These words increased
her grief. She knew the signs that he had planted
as evidence, and sobbed; she wept profusely.
Pausing, she said, "I pitied you before,
but now you are a guest and honored friend.
I gave those clothes to him that you describe;
I took them from the storeroom, folded them,
and clasped that brooch for him. But I will never

welcome him home. A curse sailed on that ship
when he went off to see Evilium—
the town I will not name."

He answered shrewdly,
"Your Majesty, Odysseus' wife,
stop ruining your pretty skin with tears,
and grieving for your husband, brokenhearted.
I do not blame you; any woman would
mourn for a husband by whom she had children,
even if he were not the kind of man
they say your husband was—a godlike hero.
But stop your crying. Listen. I will tell you
a certainty. I will be frank with you.
I heard Odysseus is coming home.
He is alive and near here, in Thesprotia.
By hustling, he gained a heap of treasure
that he is bringing home. He lost his ship
at sea, and let his loyal men be killed
when he had left Thrinacia; Helius
and Zeus despised Odysseus, because
his men had killed the Cattle of the Sun.
So all those men were drowned beneath the waves,
but he himself was clinging to the rudder
and washed up in the land of the Phaeacians,
the cousins of the gods. They honored him
as if he were a god himself, and gave him
abundant gifts, and tried to send him home
safely. He would have been here long ago,
but he decided he should travel more
and gather greater wealth. No man on earth
knows better how to make a profit. Pheidon,
the king of the Thesprotians, told me this.
He poured libations and he swore to me

there was a ship already launched and crew
all set to take him home. But Pheidon said
good-bye to me first, as a ship of theirs
happened to be already on its way
to barley-rich Dulichium. He showed me
the treasure that Odysseus had gained—
enough to feed his children and grandchildren
for ten whole generations. Pheidon said
Odysseus had gone to Dodona,
to ask the rustling oak leaves whether Zeus
advised him, after all those years away,
to go home openly or in disguise.
I tell you, he is safe and near at hand.
He will not long be absent from his home
and those that love him. I swear this by Zeus,
the highest, greatest god, and by the hearth
where I am sheltering. This will come true
as I have said. This very lunar month,
between the waning and the waxing moon
Odysseus will come."

Penelope
said warily, "Well, stranger, I do hope
that you are right. If so, I would reward you
at once with such warm generosity
that everyone you met would see your luck.
In fact, it seems to me, Odysseus
will not come home. No one will see you off
with kind good-byes. There is no master here
to welcome visitors as he once did
and send them off with honor. Was there ever
a man like him? Now slaves, give him a wash
and make a bed with mattress, woolen blankets

and fresh clean sheets, to keep him warm till Dawn
assumes her golden throne. Then bathe and oil him;
seat him inside the hall, beside my son,
and let him eat. If any of these men
is so corrupt that he would harm our guest,
the worse for him! He will get nowhere here,
however much he rages. Stranger, how
could you have evidence that I excel
all other women in intelligence,
if you were kept in rags, your skin all sunburnt,
in my house? Human beings have short lives.
If we are cruel, everyone will curse us
during our life, and mock us when we die.
The names of those who act with nobleness
are brought by travelers across the world,
and many people speak about their goodness."

But devious Odysseus said, "Wife
of great Odysseus, I started hating
blankets and fine clean sheets the day I rowed
from cloudy, mountainous Crete. I will lie down
as I have spent so many sleepless nights,
on some rough pallet, waiting for bright Dawn.
I do not care for footbaths; do not let
any of these slave women in your house
come near my feet, unless there is an old one
whom I can trust, who has endured the same
heartbreak and sorrow as myself. If so,
I would not mind if she should touch my feet."

Penelope said thoughtfully, "Dear guest,
how well you speak! No visitor before
who came into my house from foreign lands

has ever been so scrupulous. I have
a sensible old woman, who brought up
my husband. She first took him in her arms
from his own mother as a newborn child.
She is quite weak, but she can wash your feet.
Get up now, Eurycleia, wash your master's
age-mate. By now, Odysseus himself
must have old wrinkled feet and hands like these.
We mortals grow old fast in times of trouble."

The old slave shed hot tears, and held her hands
across her face, and wailed,

"Oh, child! I am
so useless to you now! Zeus hated you
beyond all other men, although you are
so god-fearing! No human ever burned
so many thigh-bones to the Lord of Thunder,
or sacrificed so much to him. You prayed
that you would reach a comfortable old age
and raise your son to be respected. Now
you are the only one who cannot reach
your home. And when that poor Odysseus
stays at the palaces of foreign kings,
I think the women slaves are mocking him
as these bad girls are hounding you. You have
refused to let them wash you, to avoid
abuse. But wise Penelope has told me
to wash you, and reluctantly I will,
for her sake and for yours—you move my heart.
Now listen. Many strangers have come here
in trouble and distress. But I have never
seen any man whose body, voice, and feet
are so much like my master's."

He replied
shrewdly, "Old woman, everyone who sees
the two of us says we are much alike;
you were perceptive to observe the likeness."

Then the old woman took the shining cauldron
used for a footbath, and she filled it up
with water—lots of cold, a splash of hot.
Odysseus sat there beside the hearth,
and hurriedly turned round to face the darkness.
He had a premonition in his heart
that when she touched him, she would feel his scar
and all would be revealed. She kneeled beside him,
and washed her master. Suddenly, she felt
the scar. A white-tusked boar had wounded him
on Mount Parnassus long ago. He went there
with his maternal cousins and grandfather,
noble Autolycus, who was the best
of all mankind at telling lies and stealing.
Hermes gave him this talent to reward him
for burning many offerings to him.
Much earlier, Autolycus had gone
to Ithaca to see his daughter's baby,
and Eurycleia put the newborn child
on his grandfather's lap and said, "Now name
your grandson—this much-wanted baby boy."
He told the parents, "Name him this. I am
disliked by many, all across the world,
and I dislike them back. So name the child
'Odysseus.' And when he is a man,
let him come to his mother's people's house,
by Mount Parnassus. I will give him treasure
and send him home rejoicing." When he grew,
Odysseus came there to claim his gifts.
His cousins and Autolycus embraced him,

and greeted him with friendly words of welcome.
His grandma, Amphithea, wrapped her arms
around him like a vine and kissed his face
and shining eyes. Autolycus instructed
his sons to make the dinner. They obeyed
and brought a bull of five years old and flayed it,
and chopped it all in pieces, and then sliced
the meat with skill and portioned it on skewers
and roasted it with care, and shared it out,
and everybody got the same amount.
The whole day long they feasted, till the sun
went down and darkness fell. Then they lay down
and took the gift of sleep. When early Dawn,
the newborn child with rosy hands, appeared,
Autolycus went hunting with his dogs
and with his sons; Odysseus went too.
Up the steep wooded side of Mount Parnassus
they climbed and reached its windswept folds. The sun
rose from the calmly flowing depths of Ocean
to touch the fields, just as the hunters came
into a glen. The dogs had dashed in front,
looking for tracks. Autolycus' sons
came after, with Odysseus who kept
close to the dogs, and brandished his long spear.
A mighty boar lurked there; its lair was thick,
protected from the wind; the golden sun
could never strike at it with shining rays,
and rain could not get in; there was a pile
of fallen leaves inside. The boar had heard
the sound of feet—the men and dogs were near.
Out of his hiding place he leapt to face them,
his bristles standing up, his eyes like fire,
and stood right next to them. Odysseus

was first to rush at him, his long spear gripped
tight in his hand. He tried to strike; the boar
struck first, above his knee, and charging sideways
scooped a great hunk of flesh off with his tusk,
but did not reach the bone. Odysseus
wounded the boar's right shoulder, and the spear
pierced through. The creature howled and fell to earth.
His life flew out. Autolycus' sons
bustled around and skillfully bound up
the wound received by great Odysseus,
and stopped the black blood with a charm, and took him
back to their father's house, and nursed him well,
then gave him splendid gifts, and promptly sent him
back home to Ithaca, and he was glad.
His parents welcomed him and asked him questions,
wanting to know how he had got the wound.
He told them he was hunting with his cousins
on Mount Parnassus, and a boar attacked him;
the white tusk pierced his leg.

The old slave woman,
holding his leg and rubbing with flat palms,
came to that place, and recognized the scar.
She let his leg fall down into the basin.
It clattered, tilted over, and the water
spilled out across the floor. Both joy and grief
took hold of her. Her eyes were filled with tears;
her voice was choked. She touched his beard and said,

"You are Odysseus! My darling child!
My master! I did not know it was you
until I touched you all around your leg."

She glanced towards Penelope, to tell her
it was her husband. But Penelope
did not look back; she could not meet her eyes,
because Athena turned her mind aside.
Odysseus grabbed her throat with his right hand
and with the left, he pulled her close and whispered,

"Nanny! Why are you trying to destroy me?
You fed me at your breast! Now after all
my twenty years of pain, I have arrived
back to my home. You have found out; a god
has put the knowledge in your mind. Be silent;
no one must know, or else I promise you,
if some god helps me bring the suitors down,
I will not spare you when I kill the rest,
the other slave women, although you were
my nurse."

With calculation, Eurycleia
answered, "My child! What have you said! You know
my mind is firm, unshakable; I will
remain as strong as stone or iron. Let me
promise you this: if you defeat the suitors,
I will tell you which women in the palace
dishonor you, and which are free from guilt."

Odysseus already had a plan.
"Nanny, why do you mention them? No need.
I will myself make my own observations
of each of them. Be quiet now; entrust
the future to the gods."

The old nurse went
to fetch more washing water; all the rest

was spilt. She washed and oiled him, and then
he pulled his chair beside the fire again,
to warm himself, and covered up his scar
with rags. And carefully Penelope
spoke to him.

"Stranger, I have one small question
I want to ask you. It will soon be time
to lie down comfortably—at least for those
who can enjoy sweet sleep, no matter what.
But I have been afflicted by some god
with pain beyond all measure. In the day,
I concentrate on my work and my women's,
despite my constant grief. But when night comes,
and everybody goes to sleep, I lie
crying in bed and overwhelmed by pain;
worries and sorrows crowd into my heart.
As when the daughter of Pandareus,
the pale gray nightingale, sings beautifully
when spring has come, and sits among the leaves
that crowd the trees, and warbles up and down
a symphony of sound, in mourning for
her son by Zethus, darling Itylus,
whom she herself had killed in ignorance,
with bronze. Just so, my mind pulls two directions—
should I stay here beside my son, and keep
things all the same—my property, my slave girls,
and my great house—to show respect towards
my husband's bed and what the people say?
Or should I marry one of them—whichever
is best of all the suitors and can bring
most presents? When my son was immature,
and young, I could not leave my husband's house.
He would not let me. Now that he is big

and all grown-up, he urges me to go;
he is concerned that they are eating up
his property. Now how do you interpret
this dream of mine? I dreamed that twenty geese
came from the river to my house, and they
were eating grain and I was glad to see them.
Then a huge eagle with a pointed beak
swooped from the mountain, broke their necks, and killed them.
I wept and wailed, inside the dream; the women
gathered around me, and I cried because
the eagle killed my geese. Then he came back
and sitting on the jutting roof-beam, spoke
in human language, to restrain my grief.
'Penelope, great queen, cheer up. This is
no dream; it will come true. It is a vision.
The geese are suitors; I was once an eagle,
but now I am your husband. I have come
back home to put a cruel end to them.'
Then I woke up, looked round, and saw the geese
still eating grain beside the trough as they
had done before."

Odysseus, well-known
for his intelligence, said, "My dear woman,
there is no way to wrest another meaning
out of the dream; Odysseus himself
said how he will fulfill it: it means ruin
for all the suitors. No one can protect them
from death."

But shrewd Penelope said, "Stranger,
dreams are confusing, and not all come true.
There are two gates of dreams: one pair is made
of horn and one of ivory. The dreams

from ivory are full of trickery;
their stories turn out false. The ones that come
through polished horn come true. But my strange dream
did not come out that way, I think. I wish
it had, as does my son. The day of doom
is coming that will take me from the house
of my Odysseus. I will arrange
a contest with his axes. He would set them
all in a row, like ship's props. From a distance
he shot an arrow through all twelve of them.
I will assign this contest to the suitors.
Whoever strings his bow most readily,
and shoots through all twelve axes, will win me,
and I will follow him. I will be parted
from here, this lovely house, my marriage home,
so full of wealth and life, which I suppose
I will remember even in my dreams."

Scheming Odysseus said, "Honored wife
of great Odysseus, do not postpone
this contest. They will fumble with the bow
and will not finish stringing it or shooting
the arrow through, before Odysseus,
the mastermind, arrives."

She chose her words
with care: "If you would sit and entertain me,
guest, I would never wish to go to sleep.
But humans cannot stay awake forever;
immortal gods have set a proper time
for everything that mortals do on earth.
I will go up and lie down on my bed,
which is a bed of grief, all stained with tears
that I have cried since he went off to see

Evilium, the town I will not name.
I will lie there, and you lie in this house;
spread blankets on the floor, or have the slaves
make up a bed."

With that, she went upstairs,
accompanied by slave girls. In her room,
she cried for her dear husband, till sharp-sighted
Athena poured sweet sleep onto her eyes.

BOOK 20

The Last Banquet

Odysseus was lying at the entrance
on an untreated oxhide, over which
he heaped a pile of fleeces from the sheep
the suitors sacrificed. Eurynome
spread a thick blanket over him. He lay there
but did not sleep; his mind was plotting how
to kill the suitors. Then the girls who had
been sleeping with suitors slipped outside,
giggling and happy to be out together.
His heart was roused to rage; he wondered whether
to jump at them and slaughter every one,
or let them have one very final night
with those proud suitors—and his heart was barking,
just as a mother dog will stand astride
her little puppies, bristling to fight,
if she sees any man she does not know;
so his heart growled inside him; he was shocked
at their behavior. He slapped his chest
and told himself,

"Be strong, my heart. You were
hounded by worse the day the Cyclops ate
your strong companions. But you kept your nerve,
till cunning saved you from the cave; you thought
that you would die there."

So his heart held firm
and constant, but he writhed around, as when
a man rotates a sausage full of fat
and blood; the huge fire blazes, and he longs
to have the roasting finished. So he squirmed,
this way and that, and wondered how he could
attack the shameless suitors, being one
against a multitude. Athena came
from heaven and stood near him, at his head,
resembling a woman, and she said,

"Why are you wide awake, unlucky man?
This is your house, this is your wife inside,
and your own child, the son you hoped to have."

Clever Odysseus said, "Goddess, yes,
all that is true. But I am wondering how
I can attack those upstarts, who are always
clustered together, while I am alone.
My biggest fear is this: if you and Zeus
help me to kill them, then what? Where can I
run to escape my punishment? You tell me!"

With glinting eyes Athena said, "So stubborn!
Most men trust friends—even weaker, mortal friends,
whose judgment is far worse than mine. I am
a goddess, and throughout your many trials,
I have watched over you. If we were ambushed,

surrounded by not one but fifty gangs
of men who hoped to murder us—you would
escape, and even poach their sheep and cows.
Now go to sleep. To stay on guard awake
all night is tiring. Quite soon you will
distance yourself, Odysseus, from trouble."

With that, the goddess drenched his eyes with sleep,
then flew back to Olympus. Sleep took hold,
relaxed him, and released him from his worries.
Meanwhile, his faithful wife had woken up,
crying and sitting upright on her bed
against soft pillows. When her sobs subsided,
she prayed.

"O Artemis! Majestic goddess!
Daughter of Zeus! If only you would shoot
an arrow in my heart and kill me now,
or let a gust of wind take hold of me
and carry me across the misty clouds
and fling me where the waters of the Ocean
pour forth and back again, as when the breezes
took up the daughters of Pandareus,
after the gods destroyed their parents, leaving
the daughters orphaned. Aphrodite helped them,
and gave them honey, cheese, and mellow wine,
and Hera gave them beauty and good sense,
above all other women; Artemis
increased their height; Athena taught them how
to be most skillful in all handiwork.
Then Aphrodite went to Mount Olympus
to ask Zeus, Thunderlord, to grant the girls
good marriages—he knows all things, all fates,
both good and bad. But Harpies seized and forced them

to serve the cruel Furies. May the gods
annihilate me just like them! Or may
Artemis strike me dead, with my gaze fixed
upon Odysseus! Let me not make
a lesser husband glad. When someone weeps
all through the day quite overwhelmed by grief,
but sleeps at night, forgetting everything,
her pain is bearable. But I am cursed
with nightmares by some god. Last night, a man
was sleeping by me, just like him when he
marched off to war. My heart was cheered; it seemed
a vision, not a dream."

As she said this,
the golden Dawn arrived. Odysseus
heard his wife weeping, and became confused;
he thought that she was standing by his head,
and that she had already recognized him.
He took the cloak and fleece with which he slept,
and put them on a chair inside the palace,
and took the oxhide outside to the courtyard,
then raised his arms and prayed.

"O Father Zeus!
O gods! If you have brought me back on purpose
across dry land and sea to my own home,
after you made me suffer all that pain,
let someone inside speak in words of omen,
and Zeus, display another sign outside."

Zeus, Lord of Cunning, heard him, and he thundered
from bright Olympus, high above the clouds;
Odysseus was happy. Then a woman,

a wheat grinder, inside the house nearby,
spoke words of omen. Twelve slaves worked the mills
to grind the wheat and barley for the king.
The rest had finished and had gone to sleep.
The weakest one was still at work. She paused
her mill, and spoke—he heard it as an omen.

"Zeus, king of gods and humans! You made thunder
boom from a cloudless sky—a sign for someone.
Fulfill a poor slave's prayer: that this will be
the last day that the suitors dine in style
here in the old king's house. My knees are sore
from this exhausting work of grinding grain
for them. I pray this is their final meal!"

This sign and Zeus' thunder made her master
glad, and more certain he would get revenge
on those who did him wrong.

The other women
gathered and lit a fire in the hearth.
Godlike Telemachus got out of bed
and dressed, and slung his sword across his back.
He tied his sandals on his well-oiled feet,
and took his sharp and sturdy bronze-tipped spear.
Standing across the threshold, he called out
to Eurycleia.

"Nanny! Did you women
make sure our guest was honored, with a meal
and comfortable bed? Or did he lie there
neglected? This is typical of Mother!
She may be clever, but she acts on whims!

She treats unwanted guests with great respect,
and rudely sends the better ones away."

The nurse said tactfully, "Child, do not blame her,
not now. He drank some wine, and chose a chair.
He said he had already had his dinner—
she asked him. And at bedtime, she brought out
a cot, so that the girls could make his bed.
Poor destitute old man! He would not take
nice bedding. He slept outside on the porch,
on oxhide and a fleece; we spread a cloak
on top of him."

Telemachus marched off
out of the palace, with his sword in hand,
accompanied by two swift dogs, and went
down to the meeting place of the Achaeans.

Then noble Eurycleia, child of Ops,
called to the slaves.

"Now hurry! You girls sweep
the floors and sprinkle them. Spread purple cloths
across the chairs. You others, sponge the tables,
and wash the double-handled cups and bowls.
And you, go fetch the water from the spring.
Be quick! They will be coming soon; it is
a festival for all of them today."

They listened carefully and followed orders.
Twenty ran off to fetch the dark spring water;
the other well-trained slaves were working hard
around the house. The able-bodied men
came in and chopped the wood. They knew their work.

The women got back from the spring, and with them
the swineherd came with three fat pigs—his best.
He penned them in the yard to root around,
and kindly asked Odysseus,

"My friend,
are they now treating you with more respect,
or still abusing you, just as before?"

Odysseus, the cunning strategist,
replied, "Eumaeus, may the gods avenge
these upstarts for their wickedness and schemes!
The scoundrels have abused me in a house
which is not theirs! They show no shame!"

While they
were talking in this way, Melanthius
arrived with two more herders. They were driving
the very fattest she-goats from the flock—
a contribution to the suitors' banquet.
He tied the goats up on the portico,
and started picking on Odysseus.

"Stranger! Are you still here, still causing trouble,
with begging and annoying those inside?
I promise you a beating if you stay!
Your begging is not welcome! This is not
the only place in Greece where there is food."

Inscrutable Odysseus said nothing;
he bowed his head in silence, contemplating
his murderous plans.

The third and final herdsman,
Philoetius, an overseer, came
herding fat he-goats and an uncalved heifer,
brought by a ferryman to Ithaca—
the ferries also carry passengers
when anybody needs to get across.
Philoetius tied up his animals
outside, and asked the swineherd,

"Who is this
new guest who has arrived? Who are his people?
Where is his native land? His ancestry?
Poor man, he has a kingly look; his bearing
is like a lord's. When gods spin threads of pain,
even great kings are made to wander far
and suffer greatly."

Then he shook his hand
and greeted him. "Good morning, sir! You are
down on your luck; I hope things change for you.
No god is more destructive, Zeus, than you!
You are the father of humanity,
but you do not take pity on our pain.
My eyes are wet, my skin is damp with sweat,
as I think of Odysseus. If he
still lives and sees the sun, he must be lost,
and dressed in rags like these. Or if he has
already died, oh, Lord Odysseus!
I am so sorry! He entrusted me
with my first herd when I was just a boy,
in Cephallenia. His cattle now
are countless; they would not have multiplied
so well for someone else. But now these men

are telling me to drive the cows to them
for food. They do not care about the boy,
or tremble at the eyes of watchful gods.
My master has been gone a long time now.
They want to share his wealth among themselves,
and I keep turning over in my mind
that it would not be right to take the cows
and go to foreign lands, when master's son
is here. But it is worse to sit and suffer,
just taking care of other people's cattle.
I would have run away and gone to serve
another king; things are unbearable.
But I keep hoping my unlucky master
will come back from wherever he may be
and scatter all these suitors in his halls."

Crafty Odysseus replied, "I see
you are intelligent. So I will swear
a solemn oath to you. I vow by Zeus,
and hospitality, and by this hearth,
that while you are still here, Odysseus
will come back home, and if you want, you can
watch as the boys who swagger here are killed."

The cowherd answered, "Stranger, may Zeus make
your words come true—and you would see my strength,
and how prepared my hands would be to fight."
Eumaeus also prayed to all the gods
to bring his many-minded master home.

As they were talking in this way, the suitors
were planning how to kill Telemachus.
But then an eagle flew high on their left,

holding a wild dove. Amphinomus
said to them, "Friends, this plan of ours, this murder,
will fail. So let us think about our banquet."

They all agreed, and went inside the house
of godlike King Odysseus. They spread
cloths on the chairs and sofas, and they killed
large sheep, fat goats, big pigs, and one tame cow.
They cooked the innards and divided them,
and mixed the wine in bowls; the swineherd poured it
into the cups. Philoetius served bread
in baskets, and Melanthius passed round
the wine. They helped themselves to all the food.

Then thinking carefully, Telemachus
seated Odysseus inside the hall,
beside the stony threshold, and he brought
a table and a stool. He served him meat
and poured a gold cup full of wine, and said,

"Now you are sitting here and drinking wine
among them. I will stop them touching you
or mocking you. This is no public house!
Odysseus acquired it for me.
And you there, suitors! Please, no blows or insults.
We do not want to start an argument."

They bit their lips, surprised to hear the boy
speaking so boldly, and Antinous,
Eupeithes' son, declared,

"My lords, we must
accept the threats Telemachus has made,
annoying though they are. Zeus would not let us

kill him—or else by now we could have stopped
his speechifying in our banquet hall."

Telemachus ignored him, and meanwhile,
the house boys drove one hundred animals
through town for sacrifice. The Ithacans
assembled at Apollo's shady grove—
the lord of archery.

Inside the house,
the suitors cooked the meat kebabs, took out
the skewers, then divided up the portions—
a splendid feast. They served Odysseus
an equal portion with their own; his son,
Telemachus, had ordered them to do so.

But still Athena would not let the suitors
refrain from hurtful insults and abuse,
so even deeper bitterness would sink
into the heart of great Odysseus.
One lawless man from Same named Ctesippus,
encouraged by extraordinary wealth,
had come to court Odysseus' wife
because he had been absent for so long.
He shouted to the other reckless suitors,

"Listen! This stranger got an equal share,
as is appropriate. It would, of course,
be wrong to disrespect a guest who comes
to visit our Telemachus. Let me
give him a welcome gift, so he can give
gifts to the bath attendant or some other
house slave here in the palace."

Then he grabbed
an ox-foot from the basket, and he hurled it
towards Odysseus, who smoothly ducked,
bowing his head, and smiled in scornful rage.
The ox-foot struck the wall. Telemachus
scolded Ctesippus.

"You were very lucky
you failed to hit the stranger; he avoided
the blow himself. I would have thrust my sword
right through your belly, and your father would
have held your funeral, and not your wedding.
So from now on, you all should stay in check,
here in my house. I used to be a child,
but now I understand things, good and bad.
I have to watch and put up with all this:
the slaughtered sheep, the food, the wine. It is
hard for a single man to put a stop
to such a multitude. But please back down
from your hostility to me. Or if
you do still want to kill me with bronze swords,
go on; I want you to. It would be better
to die, than have to watch you suitors acting
so horribly—abusing strangers, dragging
the house girls through my home, molesting them."

They all fell silent. Agelaus spoke.

"My friends, his words are fair. Do not get angry
or argue back with him. Do not abuse
the stranger, or Odysseus' slaves.
Telemachus, I offer some advice
to you and to your mother, with respect.
I hope you can accept it. While you thought
your many-minded father would come home,

there was no harm in holding us at bay,
and waiting, in case he came back again.
Now it is obvious he will not come.
So boy, sit by your mother, and advise her
to choose the best, most generous of us
to marry; then you can enjoy the wealth
left by your father, eat and drink, and she
can go take care of someone else's house."

Telemachus inhaled, then answered, "Yes!
By Zeus and by my father's sufferings—
lost far from Ithaca, or maybe dead—
I will cause no delay, and I will tell her
to pick a husband, and I will provide
a lavish dowry. But I am reluctant
to force her if she does not want to go.
May no god make that happen!" So he spoke.

Athena turned the suitors' minds; they laughed
unstoppably. They cackled, and they lost
control of their own faces. Plates of meat
began to drip with blood. Their eyes were full
of tears, and they began to wail in grief.
The prophet Theoclymenus addressed them.

"What awful thing is happening to you?
Your faces, heads, and bodies are wrapped up
in night; your screams are blazing out like fire.
The ornate palace ceilings and the walls
are spattered with your blood. The porch is full
of ghosts, as is the courtyard—ghosts descending
into the dark of Erebus. The sun
has vanished from the sky, and gloomy mist
is all around."

At these words, they all laughed.
Eurymachus spoke up.

"This new arrival
has lost his mind! Quick, fellows, throw him out!
Make him go to the marketplace—he thinks
it is like night in here!"

The prophet answered,
"Eurymachus, I will not ask for guides.
I have good eyes and ears and feet; my mind
is working perfectly, and I am leaving.
I sense some evil coming for you all,
who sit here in Odysseus' house
tormenting and oppressing other people.
Not one of you will get away."

With that,
he left the palace and went down to meet
Piraeus, and was welcomed there.

The suitors,
with glances at each other, tried to tease
Telemachus by laughing at his guests.

"What awful luck you have with visitors!
Here is this dirty beggar, always wanting
more food and wine, who is unskilled in farmwork
or fighting—a mere burden on the earth!
That other one just stood there prophesying!
Now listen—I propose a better plan.
Pack up your strangers on a boat as slaves;
send them to Sicily, and make a profit!"

Telemachus ignored the suitors' words,
and watched his father quietly, still waiting
for when they should attack the shameless suitors.
The beautiful Penelope had wisely
set up her chair to face them, and she listened
to what each man was saying. They had killed
numerous animals, and made their banquet
with laughter. But no dinnertime could be
less welcome than the one the mighty man
and goddess would soon bring them, in revenge,
because they started it and wronged him first.

BOOK 21

An Archery Contest

With glinting eyes, Athena put a thought
into the mind of wise Penelope,
the daughter of Icarius: to place
the bow and iron axes in the hall
of great Odysseus, and set the contest
which would begin the slaughter. She went up
to her own room. Her muscular, firm hand
picked up the ivory handle of the key—
a hook of bronze. Then with her slaves she walked
down to the storeroom where the master kept
his treasure: gold and bronze and well-wrought iron.
The curving bow and deadly arrows lay there,
given by Iphitus, Eurytus' son,
the godlike man he happened to befriend
at wise Ortilochus' house, far off
in Lacedaemon, in Messenia.
Odysseus had gone to claim a debt—
some people of Messenia had come
in rowing boats and poached three hundred sheep

from Ithaca; they took their shepherds too.
Laertes and the other older men
had sent Odysseus to fetch them back
when he was still a boy. And Iphitus
had come there for his horses, twelve fine mares,
each suckling a sturdy mule. These horses
would later cause his death, when he had gone
to visit Heracles, who welcomed him,
but killed him, so that he could take the horses—
betraying hospitality, and heedless
about the watchful gods. Before all that,
when Iphitus first met Odysseus,
he gave this bow to him, inherited
from his own father. And Odysseus
gave Iphitus a sword and spear, to mark
their bond. But Iphitus was dead before
the friends could visit one another's houses.
So when Odysseus' black fleet sailed
to war, he did not take the bow, but stored it
in his own house, to use in Ithaca
in memory of his friend.

The queen had reached
the storeroom, and she stepped across the threshold
of polished oak; a skillful carpenter
had set it level, fixed the frame, and built
the dazzling double doors. She quickly loosed
the door-thong from its hook, pushed in the key
and with true aim, thrust back the fastenings.
The fine doors, as the key struck home, began
to bellow as a bull at pasture bellows.
At once, they flew apart. She stepped inside,
onto the pallet where the scented clothes

were stored in chests, and reached to lift the bow
down from its hook, still in its shining case.
She sat down on the floor to take it out,
resting it on her lap, and started sobbing
and wailing as she saw her husband's bow.
At last, she dried her eyes, and in her arms
picked up the curving bow and quiver, packed
with many deadly arrows, and she went
to meet her arrogant suitors. Slaves lugged out
a chest with their master's many axes
of bronze and iron, for the competition.
The queen came near the suitors, and she stopped
beside a pillar with a filmy veil
across her face. Two slave girls stood with her.
She said,

"Now listen, lords. You keep on coming
to this house every day, to eat and drink,
wasting the wealth of someone who has been
away too long. Your motives are no secret.
You want to marry me. I am the prize.
So I will set a contest. This great bow
belonged to godlike King Odysseus.
If anyone can grasp it in his hands
and string it easily, and shoot through all
twelve axes, I will marry him, and leave
this beautiful rich house, so full of life,
my lovely bridal home. I think I will
remember it forever, even in
my dreams."

She told Eumaeus he should set
the bow and pale-gray iron axes up
before the suitors, and in tears the swineherd

took them, and did as she had asked. The cowherd
wept also when he saw his master's bow.

Antinous began to scold and taunt them.
He said, "You idiots! You tactless peasants!
So thoughtless, so undisciplined! You fools,
your selfish crying is upsetting her!
Poor lady, she is sad enough already
at losing her beloved husband. Sit
and eat in silence, or go do your wailing
outside, and leave us suitors here to try
the deadly contest of the bow. I think
it will be difficult; not one of us
can match Odysseus. I saw him once
in childhood, and I still remember him."

He hoped he would be first to string the bow
and shoot through all the axes. But he would
be first to taste an arrow from the hands
of great Odysseus, whom he had mocked,
urging the others on to do the same.

Then Prince Telemachus addressed them all.
"Zeus must have made me stupid! My dear mother,
despite her usual common sense, has said
that she will marry someone else and leave
this house. But I am laughing, and my heart
feels foolish gladness. Well, come on, you suitors.
You want this prize—a woman unlike any
in holy Pylos, Argos or Mycenae,
or here in Ithaca or on the mainland.
No woman in Achaea is like her.
There is no need for me to praise my mother.
You know her worth. So do not make excuses,

do not put off the contest of the bow.
We want to watch. And I will try myself.
If I succeed in stringing it and shooting
all through, I will no longer mind if Mother
goes off with someone else, and leaves me here.
Success would prove me man enough to carry
my father's arms."

He stood up straight and tall,
tossed off his purple cloak, unstrapped his sword,
and dug a trench to set the axes up,
all in a line, and trod the earth down flat.
They were amazed to see him work so neatly,
though he had never seen it done before.
He stood astride the threshold and began
to try the bow. Three times he made it quiver,
straining to draw it back; three times he failed
to string the bow and shoot all through the axes.
He would have tried a fourth time; he was keen
to keep on pulling. But Odysseus
shook his head, stopping him. Telemachus
said,

"Ugh! It seems that I will always be
too weak and useless. Or perhaps I am
too young and inexperienced at fighting
in self-defense when someone starts a quarrel.
You all are stronger than I am. You try,
and we can end the contest."

With these words,
he set the bow down on the floor, propped up
against the polished, jointed double door,

and tucked the arrow up against the handle.
He sat back down where he had sat before.

Antinous called out, "Now, friends, get up,
from left to right, beginning with the man
next to the wine-slave!"

They agreed. The first
was Leodes, their holy man, who always
sat in the farthest corner, by the wine-bowl.
He was the only one who disapproved
of all their bullying. He grasped the bow
and stood astride the threshold, and he tried
to string it, but he failed. His hands were soft,
untrained by labor, and he grew worn out
trying to pull it back. He told the suitors,

"My friends, I cannot do it. Someone else
should have a turn. This bow will take away
courage, life-force, and energy from many
noble young men; but better we should die,
than live and lose the goal for which we gather
in this house every day. Each man still hopes
for marriage with Odysseus' wife,
Penelope. But if one tries and fails
to string the bow, let him go use his wealth
to court some other fine, well-dressed Greek lady.
And after that, Penelope will marry
whichever man can bring most gifts for her—
the man whom fate has chosen."

With these words,
he set the bow back down, and leaned it up

against the polished, jointed double door,
tucking the pointed arrow by the handle.
Antinous responded with a jeer.

"My goodness, Leodes! What scary words!
All your tough talk has made me really angry.
You cannot string the bow, so you are claiming
that it will take the life from proper men.
You surely were not born for archery.
The rest of us are actual warriors;
we will soon string this bow."

He told the goatherd,
"Melanthius, come on now, light a fire
and pull a chair beside it, with a fleece,
and bring out from the pantry a big hunk
of fat, so we young men can warm the bow,
grease it, and try it, and so end this contest."

Melanthius obeyed at once; he lit
a blazing fire, and pulled a chair beside it,
spreading a fleece on top, and brought the wheel
of fat. The young men warmed the bow, but still
they could not string it. They were far too weak.
Antinous and Eurymachus, the leaders,
strongest and most impressive of the suitors,
had still not had their turn.

Meanwhile the swineherd
and cowherd had both gone outside the house.
Odysseus himself came after them,
and when they were outside the gates, beyond
the courtyard, in a friendly voice he said,

"Cowherd and swineherd, I am hesitating
whether to speak out openly; my impulse
is to be frank. What if some god should guide
Odysseus, and suddenly, as if
from nowhere, he was here—how would you act?
Would you be with the suitors, or with him?
How are your hearts inclined?"

The cowherd said,
"O Father Zeus, please make this wish come true,
that he may come! May spirits guide him home!
Then you would see how well-prepared I am
to fight for him!" Eumaeus prayed in turn
that all the gods would bring Odysseus
back home. The man who thought of everything now knew
their minds, and said to them,

"I am here now.
I suffered terribly for twenty years,
and now I have come back to my own land.
I see that you two are the only slaves
who welcome my arrival. I have not
heard any others praying I would come
back to my home. I promise, if some god
brings down the noble suitors by my hands,
I will give each of you a wife and wealth,
and well-constructed houses, near my own.
You two will be Telemachus' brothers.
Now let me show you clearer proof, so you
can know me well and trust me. See my scar,
made by the boar's white tusk, when I had gone
to hunt on Mount Parnassus with my cousins."

So saying, he pulled back his rags and showed
the great big scar. They stared and studied it,
then both burst into tears. They threw their arms
around Odysseus, and kissed his face
and hugged him, overjoyed at seeing him.
Odysseus embraced them back and kissed them.
They would have wept till sunset, but he stopped them,
and said,

"Stop now; if someone steps outside
and sees you crying, they may tell the men.
Go in, not both at once but taking turns,
first me, then you, then you. And this will be
our sign: when all the noblemen refuse
to let me have the bow and set of arrows,
then you must bring them through the hall, Eumaeus,
and put them in my hands. Command the women
to shut up tight the entrance to the hall,
and go to their own quarters; if they hear
men screaming or loud noises, they must not
come out, but stay there quietly, and work.
And you, Philoetius, lock up the gates
leading out from the courtyard with the bolt
and put the rope on too. We must move fast."

With that, he went inside, and sat back down
on the same chair he sat on earlier.
Then the two slaves went in. Eurymachus
was handling the bow and warming it,
turning it back and forth beside the fire.
But even after that, he could not manage
to string it, and he groaned, and yelled in fury,

"This is disastrous! For all of us!
I do not even mind so much about
the marriage. There are lots of other women
on Ithaca, and in the other cities.
But that we should be proven so much weaker
than King Odysseus, that we should fail
to string his bow! Our deep humiliation
will be well-known for many years to come!"

Antinous said, "No, Eurymachus,
it will not be like that, as you well know.
No one should shoot a bow today; it is
a feast day for Apollo! We should sit
calmly and leave the axe heads standing there.
No one will come and take them. Let the boy
pour wine, so we can make drink offerings,
and leave the bow for now. At dawn, call back
Melanthius, to bring the finest goats,
so we can make our offerings to the god,
Apollo, lord of archery, then try
the bow again, and finish up the contest."

They all agreed with him. Attendants poured
water to wash their hands, and boys began
to mix the wine in bowls, and poured a serving
in every cup, so they could make libations
and drink. Odysseus, the lord of lies,
had carefully considered how to fool them.
He said,

"Now hear me, suitors of the Queen;
let me reveal the promptings of my heart.
Eurymachus and Lord Antinous,
I ask you specially, because you spoke

so well: now set the bow aside, and turn
towards the gods. At dawn, the god will choose
the victor and give him success. For now,
give me the polished bow, so I can try
my strength and find out if my hands still have
the suppleness and vigor of my youth,
or if it has been lost in all my years
of homelessness and poverty."

They bristled,
nervous in case he strung the polished bow.
Antinous said, "Foreigner! You fool!
Are you not grateful that we let you stay here
and eat with noblemen like us, and share
our feast, and hear us talk? No other beggars
can hear our conversation. This good wine
has made you drunk. It does have that effect
on those who gulp and fail to pace themselves.
Wine even turned the famous Centaur's head.
When Eurytion visited the Lapiths,
inside the house of brave Pirithous
the wine made him go crazy, and he did
terrible things. The warriors were outraged,
and dragged him from the house. Their ruthless swords
cut off his ears and cropped his nose right off.
He wandered, still insane and blown about
by gusts of madness. From that day, the Centaurs
and humans have been enemies. His drinking
was harmful to himself. If you should string
that bow, it would be worse for you. No man
will treat you kindly in our house. We will
send you by ship to Echetus, the king
of cruelty; you will find no escape.

Sit quietly, drink up, and do not quarrel
with younger men."

Astute Penelope
said, "No, Antinous, it is not right
to disrespect a guest Telemachus
has welcomed to this house. And do you think
that if this stranger's hands were strong enough
to string the bow, he would take me away
to marry him and live with him? Of course not!
He does not even dream of such a thing.
No need to spoil the feast by worrying
about such things; there is no need of that."

Eurymachus said, "Shrewd Penelope,
it is indeed unlikely that this man
would marry you. But we would feel ashamed
if some rude person said, 'Those men are weak!
They court a fighter's wife, but cannot string
his bow! Some random beggar has shown up
and strung it easily, and shot right through
all of the axes!' They will talk like that,
and we will be humiliated!"

Calmly,
Penelope replied, "Eurymachus,
people who waste the riches of a king
have lost their dignity. Why fuss at this?
The stranger is quite tall and muscular;
his father must be noble. Go on, give him
the bow, and let us watch. I tell you, if
he strings it by the blessing of Apollo,
I will give him a proper cloak and tunic,

fine clothes and sandals, and a two-edged sword
and dagger, sharp enough to ward away
both men and dogs, and I will help him go
wherever he desires to go."

With quick
intake of breath, Telemachus replied,
"No, Mother, no one has a better right
than I to give the bow to anyone
or to refuse it. No one on this island
or out towards the pasturelands of Elis,
and no man in this house can force my hand,
even if I should choose to give the bow
to him to take away. Go up and work
with loom and distaff; tell your girls the same.
The bow is work for men, especially me.
I am the one with power in this house."

She was amazed, and went back to her room,
taking to heart her son's assertive words.
Inside her bedroom with her girls, she wept
for her dear husband, her Odysseus,
until clear-eyed Athena let her sleep.

Meanwhile, the swineherd lifted up the bow.
The suitors made an uproar.

"Dirty pig-man!
Where are you taking it? Are you insane?
The dogs you raised yourself will eat you up
when you are out there with your pigs alone,
if we find favor with Apollo and
the other deathless gods."

He was afraid,
because there were so many people shouting
inside the hall, and set the bow he carried
down on the ground. Telemachus called out,
in forceful tones.

"No, Grandpa! Keep on going!
Keep carrying the bow! You will soon see
you have to choose which master to obey.
Though I am younger than you, I am stronger;
watch out, or I will chase you to the fields,
pelting your back with stones. I wish I had
an equal edge on all those who invaded
my home to court my mother and make mischief.
I would soon throw them out and make them pay!"

At that, the suitors all began to laugh;
their anger at Telemachus was gone.
Eumaeus went across the hall and gave
the bow to competent Odysseus.
And then he summoned Eurycleia, saying,

"Telemachus gave orders you must lock
the doors into the hall and tie them fast.
If any of you women hear a noise
of screaming men, stay up there in your quarters;
do not come out; keep quiet and keep working."

At that, she held her tongue and locked the doors
that led into the feast-hall. Philoetius
scurried outside to bolt the outer gates
that led into the courtyard. On the porch

lay a fresh-knotted cable made of byblos;
with that, he tied the gates, rushed in and sat
back down, and looked towards Odysseus.

The master was already handling
the bow and turning it this way and that,
to see if worms had eaten at the horn
while he was gone. The suitors told each other,

"He stares at it as if he were an expert
in bows. He acts the part! Perhaps he has
a bow like this at home or plans to make one.
See how this pitiful migrant fingers it!"
One confident young suitor said, "I hope
his future luck will match how well he does
in stringing it!"

So he had tricked them all.
After examining the mighty bow
carefully, inch by inch—as easily
as an experienced musician stretches
a sheep-gut string around a lyre's peg
and makes it fast—Odysseus, with ease,
strung the great bow. He held it in his right hand
and plucked the string, which sang like swallow-song,
a clear sweet note. The suitors, horrified,
grew pale, and Zeus made ominous thunder rumble.
Odysseus, who had so long been waiting,
was glad to hear the signal from the son
of double-dealing Cronus. He took up
an arrow, which was lying on the table.
The others were all packed up in the quiver,
soon to be used. He laid it on the bridge,
then pulled the notch-end and the string together,

still sitting in his chair. With careful aim,
he shot. The weighted tip of bronze flew through
each axe head and then out the other side.
He told his son,

"Telemachus, your guest
does you a credit. I hit all the targets
and with no effort strung the bow. I am
still strong, despite their jibes about my weakness.
Though it is daytime, it is time to feast;
and later, we can celebrate with music,
the joyful part of dinner."

With his eyebrows
he signaled, and his son strapped on his sword,
picked up his spear, and stood beside his chair,
next to his father, his bronze weapons flashing.

BOOK 22

Bloodshed

Odysseus ripped off his rags. Now naked,
he leapt upon the threshold with his bow
and quiverfull of arrows, which he tipped
out in a rush before his feet, and spoke.

"Playtime is over. I will shoot again,
towards another mark no man has hit.
Apollo, may I manage it!"

He aimed
his deadly arrow at Antinous.
The young man sat there, just about to lift
his golden goblet, swirling wine around,
ready to drink. He had no thought of death.
How could he? Who would think a single man,
among so many banqueters, would dare
to risk dark death, however strong he was?
Odysseus aimed at his throat, then shot.
The point pierced all the way through his soft neck.
He flopped down to the side and his cup slipped

out of his hand. A double pipe of blood
gushed from his nostrils. His foot twitched and knocked
the table down; food scattered on the ground.
The bread and roasted meat were soiled with blood.
Seeing him fall, the suitors, in an uproar,
with shouts that filled the hall, jumped up and rushed
to search around by all the thick stone walls
for shields or spears to grab—but there were none.
They angrily rebuked Odysseus.

"Stranger, you shot a man, and you will pay!
You will join no more games—you have to die!
For certain! You have killed the best young man
in all of Ithaca. Right here, the vultures
will eat your corpse." Those poor fools did not know
that he had killed Antinous on purpose,
nor that the snares of death were round them all.

Clever Odysseus scowled back and sneered,
"Dogs! So you thought I would not come back home
from Troy? And so you fleeced my house, and raped
my slave girls, and you flirted with my wife
while I am still alive! You did not fear
the gods who live in heaven, and you thought
no man would ever come to take revenge.
Now you are trapped inside the snares of death."

At that, pale fear seized all of them. They groped
to find a way to save their lives somehow.
Only Eurymachus found words to answer.

"If it is you, Odysseus, come back,
then we agree! Quite right, the Greeks have done
outrageous things to your estate and home.

But now the one responsible is dead—
Antinous! It was all his idea.
He did not even really want your wife,
but had another plan, which Zeus has foiled:
to lie in ambush for your son, and kill him,
then seize the throne and rule in Ithaca.
Now he is slain—quite rightly. Please, my lord,
have mercy on your people! We will pay
in public, yes, for all the food and drink.
We each will bring the price of twenty oxen,
and pay you all the gold and bronze you want.
Your anger is quite understandable."

Odysseus saw through him; with a glare
he told him, "Even if you give me all
your whole inheritance, and even more,
I will not keep my hands away from slaughter
until I pay you suitors back for all
your wickedness. You have two choices: fight,
or run away: just try to save your lives!
Not one of you will get away from death."

At that their knees grew weak, their hearts stopped still.
Eurymachus again addressed the suitors.
"My friends, this man will not hold back his hands.
Seizing the bow and arrows, he will shoot us
right from that polished threshold, till he kills
each one of us. Be quick, make plans for battle.
Draw out your swords, use tables as your shields
against the deadly arrows. All together,
rush at him, try to drive him off the threshold,
and out of doors, then run all through the town,
and quickly call for help. This man will soon
have shot his last!"

He drew his sharp bronze sword
and with a dreadful scream he leapt at him.
But that same instant, Lord Odysseus
let fly and hit his chest, beside the nipple,
and instantly the arrow pierced his liver.
The sword fell from his hand. He doubled up
and fell across the table, spilling food
and wine across the floor. He smashed his head
against the ground, and in his desperate pain
kicked up the chair, and darkness drenched his eyes.

Amphinomus attacked Odysseus.
He drew his sharp sword, hoping he could force him
to yield his place. Telemachus leapt in
and thrust his bronze spear through him from behind,
ramming it through his back and out his chest.
Face-first he crashed and thudded to the ground.
Telemachus dashed back—he left his spear
stuck in the body; he was terrified
that if he bent to pull it out, some Greek
would jump on him and stab him with a sword.
He ran and quickly reached his loyal father.
He stood beside him and his words flew out.

"Now Father, I will fetch a shield for you
and two spears and a helmet made of bronze,
and I will arm myself, and bring more arms
for our two herdsmen, since we all need weapons."

Odysseus, the master planner, answered,
"Run fast while I still have a stock of arrows,
before they force me from the doors—I am
fighting alone up here."

His son obeyed.
He hurried to the storeroom for the arms,
and took eight spears, four shields, and four bronze helmets
each fitted out with bushy horsehair plumes.
He hurried back to take them to his father,
and was the first to strap the armor on.
The two slaves also armed themselves, and stood
flanking their brilliant, resourceful leader.
As long as he had arrows, he kept shooting,
and one by one he picked the suitors off,
inside his own home. Then at last the king
ran out of arrows; he set down his bow
next to the sturdy doorpost, leaning up
against the palace walls, all shining white.
He slung the four-fold shield across his shoulders,
and put the well-made helmet on his head.
The crest of horsehair gave a fearsome nod.
He grasped a bronze-tipped spear in either hand.

There was a back gate in the castle walls,
providing access to the passageway,
with tightly fitted doors. Odysseus
ordered the noble swineherd to stand there
to guard it—there was only one way out.
Agelaus called out to all the suitors.

"Friends, one of us should slip out through that gate
and quickly tell the people, raise alarms.
That soon would put a stop to this man's shooting."

Melanthius the goatherd answered, "No!
My lord, that entryway is much too narrow,
and dangerously near the palace doors.
One man, if he was brave, could keep it guarded

against us all. So I will bring you armor
out of the storeroom, which I think is where
those two, our enemies, have hidden it."

Melanthius the goatherd climbed up past
the arrow-slits inside the castle walls,
into the chamber. There he took twelve shields,
twelve spears and twelve bronze helmets, each one crested
with horsehair. Then he hurried back downstairs
and handed all the weapons to the suitors.

Odysseus could see that they had arms;
their spears were brandished. His heart stopped, his legs
trembled—he was so shocked at their presumption.
At once his words flew out to tell his son,

"One of the women, or Melanthius,
is waging war against us, in my house!"

Wisely Telemachus owned up at once.
"Father, it was my fault, I am to blame.
I left the heavy storeroom door ajar.
Someone on their side must have kept good watch.
Go there, Eumaeus, shut the door, and see
if any of the women are against us,
or else, as I suspect, Melanthius."

Meanwhile, Melanthius was going back
to get more weapons from the room. The swineherd
saw him and told Odysseus,

"My Lord,
that little sneak, the man we all suspected,
is going to the stores! Odysseus,

you always have a plan for what to do:
so should I kill him, as I think is best,
or bring him here to you, so you can punish
his many crimes against you in your house?"

Odysseus already had a plan.
"Telemachus and I will keep the suitors
trapped in the hall—however much they rage.
You two, truss up his hands and feet behind him,
drag him inside the storeroom, string him up,
tying a knotted rope high on the column,
and hoist him to the rafters. Torture him
with hours of agony before he dies."

His word was their command; they hurried off,
and reached the weaponry. Melanthius
was unaware of them. As he was searching
for arms, they stopped on each side of the door
and waited. When he stepped across the threshold,
holding a lovely helmet in one hand,
and in the other hand, a rusty shield,
once carried by Laertes in his youth,
but now in storage, with its seams all loose.
The two men jumped on him and grabbed his hair
to drag him in and threw him on the floor,
shaking with fear. They bound his hands and feet
and yanked them painfully behind his back,
just as the lord of suffering had told them.
They tied him with a knotted rope and hoisted
his body up the column to the rafters.
Swineherd Eumaeus, you began to mock him:

"Keep watch the whole night through, Melanthius,
tucked up in this soft bed—it serves you right!
And wait there for the golden throne of Dawn

leaving the sea, that hour when you would lead
your goats to this house for the suitors' dinner."

There he was left, bound cruelly and stretched.
The herdsmen armed themselves and left the room,
shutting the door, and joined their cunning leader.
They stood there on the threshold, tense with purpose,
just four against so many men inside.
The child of Zeus, Athena, came to meet them;
her voice and looks resembled those of Mentor.
Odysseus was happy when he saw her,
and said, "Remember our old friendship, Mentor!
I have been good to you since we were boys.
So help me now!" He guessed it was Athena,
who rouses armies.

From the hall, the suitors
shouted their opposition. Agelaus
called, "Mentor, do not let Odysseus
sway you to help him and to fight against us.
I think this is how things will go. When we
have killed this father and his son, you will
die also, if you do as you intend,
and pay with your own life for all your plots.
Our bronze will strip your life away from you,
and we will seize whatever you may own
and mix it with the loot we get from here.
Your sons will not survive here in these halls,
nor will your wife and daughters still walk free
in Ithaca."

At that Athena's heart
became enraged, and angrily she scolded
Odysseus. "Where is your courage now?
You fought nine years on end against the Trojans,

for white-armed Helen, Zeus' favorite child.
You slaughtered many men when war was raging,
and formed the plan that made the city fall.
Now you are home at last, how can you flinch
from being brave and using proper force
against these suitors? Come now, stand by me
and watch how Mentor, son of Alcimus,
will treat your enemies as recompense
for all your service."

But she did not grant
decisive victory; she kept on testing
Odysseus' courage, and his son's.
She flew up like a swallow through the smoke
and nestled in the rafters of the roof.

Now Agelaus, Demoptolemus,
Eurynomus, Pisander, Amphimedon,
and Polybus were urging on the suitors.
Those were the most heroic of the group
who still survived and battled for their lives:
the others were defeated by the bow
and raining arrows. Agelaus told them,

"That Mentor's boasts were empty, friends! He left,
and they are all alone there at the entrance.
Now force this cruel man to stay his hands.
Do not hurl spears at him all in a mass,
but you six must shoot first and pray Lord Zeus
we strike Odysseus and win the fight.
Once he is down, the others will be nothing."

The six men threw their spears as he had said;
at once Athena made their efforts fail.
One pierced the doorpost of the palace hall,

another hit the closely fitted door,
another's spear of ash and heavy bronze
fell on the wall. The group of four avoided
all of the suitors' spears. Odysseus
had waited long enough.

"My friends," he said,
"they want to slaughter us and strip our arms!
Avenge my former wrongs, and save your lives!
Now shoot!"

They hurled their spears at once and hit.
Odysseus killed Demoptolemus;
Telemachus, Euryades; the swineherd
slaughtered Elatus, and the cowherd killed
Pisander. They all fell and bit the earth.
The other suitors huddled in a corner;
the four rushed up and from the corpses pulled
their spears. Again the suitors threw their weapons;
again Athena made them fail. One spear
struck at the doorpost, and another pierced
the door; another ash spear hit the wall.
Amphimedon's blow grazed Telemachus
right by the wrist: the bronze tore through his skin.
Ctesippus hurled his spear; it only scratched
the swineherd's shoulder, just above his shield,
flew past and fell down on the floor behind him.
The competent, sharp-eyed Odysseus
and his companions hurled their piercing spears
into the swarming throng. The city-sacker
skewered Eurydamas; Telemachus
slashed Amphimedon, and the swineherd struck
at Polybus; the cowherd sliced right through
Ctesippus' chest, and crowed,

"You fool! You loved
insulting us—now you have stopped your boasting.
The gods have got the last word; they have won.
This is a gift to pay you for that kick
you gave Odysseus when he walked through
his own house, as a homeless man in need."

Odysseus moved closer with his spear,
and pierced Agelaus; Telemachus
thrust at Leocritus, and drove his bronze
into his belly. He fell down headfirst,
face smashed against the floor.

Then from the roof
Athena lifted high her deadly aegis.
The frightened suitors bolted through the hall
like cattle, roused and driven by a gadfly
in springtime, when the days are getting longer.
As eagles with their crooked beaks and talons
swoop from the hills and pounce on smaller birds
that fly across the fields beneath the clouds;
the victims have no help and no way out,
as their attackers slaughter them, and men
watch and enjoy the violence. So these
four fighters sprang and struck, and drove the suitors
in all directions. Screaming filled the hall,
as skulls were cracked; the whole floor ran with blood.

Leodes darted up to supplicate
Odysseus; he touched his knees.

"Please, mercy!
I did no wrong, I swear, in word or deed
to any of the women in the house.
I tried to stop the suitors, tried to urge them

to keep their hands clean, but they would not listen.
Those fools deserved their fate. But I did nothing!
I am a priest—yet I must lie with them.
Will good behavior go unrewarded?"

The calculating hero scowled at him.
"If, as you claim, you sacrificed for them,
you must have often prayed here in my hall
that I would not regain the joys of home,
and that my wife would marry you instead,
and bear you children. You will not escape.
Suffer and die!"

Agelaus had dropped
his sword when he was killed. With his strong arm
Odysseus swung, slashed down and sliced right through
the priest's neck, and his head, still framing words,
rolled in the dust.

The poet Phemius,
who had been forced to sing to please the suitors,
was huddling by the back door with his lyre,
anxiously considering his choices:
to slip outside and crouch beneath the altar
of mighty Zeus, the god of home owners,
where his old masters burned so many thigh-bones;
or he could run towards Odysseus
and grasp him by the knees and beg for mercy.
He made his mind up: he would supplicate.
He set his hollow lyre on the ground
between the mixing bowl and silver chair,
and dashed to take Odysseus' knees,
beseeching him in quivering winged words.

"I beg you, Lord Odysseus! Have mercy!
Think! If you kill me now, you will be sorry!
I have the power to sing for gods and men.
I am self-taught—all kinds of song are planted
by gods inside my heart. I am prepared
to sing for you, as if before a god.
Wait, do not cut my throat! Just ask your son!
He will explain it was against my will
that I came here to sing to them after dinner.
They were too fierce and they outnumbered me.
I had no choice."

Then strong Telemachus
turned quickly to his father, saying, "Stop,
hold up your sword—this man is innocent.
And let us also save the house boy, Medon.
He always cared for me when I was young—
unless the herdsmen have already killed him,
or he already met you in your rage."

Medon was sensible: he had been hiding
under a chair, beneath a fresh cowhide,
in order to escape from being killed.
Hearing these words, he jumped up from the chair,
took off the cowhide and assumed the pose
of supplication near Telemachus,
and said,

"Friend, here I am! Please spare my life!
Your father is too strong, and furious
against the suitors, who skimmed off his wealth
and failed to honor you. Please, talk to him!"

Canny Odysseus smiled down and said,
"You need not worry, he has saved your life.

So live and spread the word that doing good
is far superior to wickedness.
Now leave the hall and go outside; sit down,
joining the famous singer in the courtyard,
so I can finish what I have to do
inside my house."

The two men went outside,
and crouched by Zeus' altar, on the lookout
for death at any moment all around.

Odysseus scanned all around his home
for any man who might be still alive,
who might be hiding to escape destruction.
He saw them fallen, all of them, so many,
lying in blood and dust, like fish hauled up
out of the dark-gray sea in fine-mesh nets;
tipped out upon the curving beach's sand,
they gasp for water from the salty sea.
The sun shines down and takes their life away.
So lay the suitors, heaped across each other.
Odysseus, still scheming, told his son,

"I need to say something to Eurycleia.
Hurry, Telemachus, and bring her here."

Telemachus was glad to please his father.
He pushed the door ajar and called, "Come, Nanny, quick!
You supervise the female palace slaves.
My father has to talk to you; come on!"

She had no words to answer him, but opened
the doors into the great and sturdy hall.
Telemachus went first and led the way.
Among the corpses of the slaughtered men

she saw Odysseus all smeared with blood.
After a lion eats a grazing ox,
its chest and jowls are thick with blood all over;
a dreadful sight. Just so, Odysseus
had blood all over him—from hands to feet.
Seeing the corpses, seeing all that blood,
so great a deed of violence, she began
to crow. Odysseus told her to stop
and spoke with fluent words.

"Old woman, no!
Be glad inside your heart, but do not shout.
It is not pious, gloating over men
who have been killed. Divine fate took them down,
and their own wicked deeds. They disrespected
all people that they met, both bad and good.
Through their own crimes they came to this bad end.
But tell me now about the household women.
Which ones dishonor me? And which are pure?"

The slave who loved her master answered, "Child,
I will tell you exactly how things stand.
In this house we have fifty female slaves
whom we have trained to work, to card the wool,
and taught to tolerate their life as slaves.
Twelve stepped away from honor: those twelve girls
ignore me, and Penelope our mistress.
She would not let Telemachus instruct them,
since he is young and only just grown-up.
Let me go upstairs to the women's rooms,
to tell your wife—some god has sent her sleep."

The master strategist Odysseus
said,

"Not yet; do not wake her. Call the women
who made those treasonous plots while I was gone."

The old nurse did so. Walking through the hall,
she called the girls. Meanwhile, Odysseus
summoned the herdsmen and Telemachus
and spoke winged words to them.

"Now we must start
to clear the corpses out. The girls must help.
Then clean my stately chairs and handsome tables
with sponges fine as honeycomb, and water.
When the whole house is set in proper order,
restore my halls to health: take out the girls
between the courtyard wall and the rotunda.
Hack at them with long swords, eradicate
all life from them. They will forget the things
the suitors made them do with them in secret,
through Aphrodite."

Sobbing desperately
the girls came, weeping, clutching at each other.
They carried out the bodies of the dead
and piled them up on top of one another,
under the roof outside. Odysseus
instructed them and forced them to continue.
And then they cleaned his lovely chairs and tables
with wet absorbent sponges, while the prince
and herdsmen with their shovels scraped away
the mess to make the sturdy floor all clean.
The girls picked up the trash and took it out.
The men created order in the house
and set it all to rights, then led the girls
outside and trapped them—they could not escape—
between the courtyard wall and the rotunda.

Showing initiative, Telemachus
insisted,

"I refuse to grant these girls
a clean death, since they poured down shame on me
and Mother, when they lay beside the suitors."

At that, he wound a piece of sailor's rope
round the rotunda and round the mighty pillar,
stretched up so high no foot could touch the ground.
As doves or thrushes spread their wings to fly
home to their nests, but someone sets a trap—
they crash into a net, a bitter bedtime;
just so the girls, their heads all in a row,
were strung up with the noose around their necks
to make their death an agony. They gasped,
feet twitching for a while, but not for long.

Then the men took Melanthius outside
and with curved bronze cut off his nose and ears
and ripped away his genitals, to feed
raw to the dogs. Still full of rage, they chopped
his hands and feet off. Then they washed their own,
and they went back inside.

Odysseus
told his beloved nurse, "Now bring me fire
and sulfur, as a cure for evil things,
and I will fumigate the house. And call
Penelope, her slaves, and all the slave girls
inside the house."

She answered with affection,
"Yes, dear, all this is good. But let me bring
a cloak and shirt for you. You should not stand here
your strong back covered only with those rags.
That would be wrong!"

Odysseus, the master
of every cunning scheme, replied, "No, first
I need a fire here, to smoke the hall."
His loving slave complied and brought the fire
and sulfur, and Odysseus made smoke,
and fumigated every room inside
the house and yard. Meanwhile, the old nurse ran
all through the palace summoning the women.
By torchlight they came out from their apartments,
to greet Odysseus with open arms.
They kissed his face and took him by the hands
in welcome. He was seized by sweet desire
to weep, and in his heart he knew them all.

BOOK 23

The Olive Tree Bed

Chuckling with glee, the old slave climbed upstairs
to tell the queen that her beloved husband
was home. Her weak old knees felt stronger now;
with buoyant steps she went and stood beside
her mistress, at her head, and said,

"Dear child,
wake up and see! At long last you have got
your wish come true! Odysseus has come!
He is right here inside this house! At last!
He slaughtered all the suitors who were wasting
his property and threatening his son!"

But cautiously Penelope replied,
"You poor old thing! The gods have made you crazy.
They have the power to turn the sanest person
mad, or make fools turn wise. You used to be
so sensible, but they have damaged you.
Why else would you be mocking me like this,
with silly stories, in my time of grief?

Why did you wake me from the sleep that sweetly
wrapped round my eyes? I have not slept so soundly
since my Odysseus marched off to see
that cursed town—Evilium. Go back!
If any other slave comes here to wake me
and tell me all this nonsense, I will send her
back down at once, and I will not be gentle.
Your old age will protect you from worse scolding."

But Eurycleia answered with affection,
"Dear child, I am not mocking you. I am
telling the truth: Odysseus is here!
He is the stranger that they all abused.
Telemachus has known for quite some time,
but sensibly he kept his father's plans
a secret, so Odysseus could take
revenge for all their violence and pride."

Penelope was overjoyed; she jumped
from bed and hugged the nurse, and started crying.
Her words flew fast.

"Dear Nanny! If this is
the truth, if he has come back to this house,
how could he have attacked those shameless suitors,
when he is just one man, and there were always
so many crowded in there?"

Eurycleia
answered, "I did not see or learn the details.
I heard the sound of screaming from the men
as they were killed. We huddled in our room
and kept the doors tight shut, until your son
called me—his father sent him. Then I saw

Odysseus surrounded by dead bodies.
They lay on top of one another, sprawled
across the solid floor. You would have been
thrilled if you saw him, like a lion, drenched
in blood and gore. Now they are all piled up
out by the courtyard gates, and he is burning
a mighty fire to fumigate the palace,
restoring all its loveliness. He sent me
to fetch you. Come with me, so both of you
can start to live in happiness. You have
endured such misery. Your wish came true!
He is alive! He has come home again,
and found you and your son, and he has taken
revenge on all the suitors who abused him."

Penelope said carefully, "Do not
start gloating. As you know, my son and I
would be delighted if he came. We all would.
However, what you say cannot be true.
Some god has killed the suitors out of anger
at their abuse of power and their pride.
They failed to show respect to visitors,
both good and bad. Their foolishness has killed them.
But my Odysseus has lost his home,
and far away from Greece, he lost his life."

The nurse replied, "Dear child! How can you say
your husband will not come, when he is here,
beside the hearth? Your heart has always been
mistrustful. But I have clear evidence!
When I was washing him, I felt the scar
made when the boar impaled him with its tusk.
I tried to tell you, but he grabbed my throat
and stopped me spoiling all his plans. Come with me.

I swear on my own life: if I am lying,
then kill me."

Wise Penelope said, "Nanny,
it must be hard for you to understand
the ways of gods, despite your cleverness.
But let us go to meet my son, so I
can see the suitors dead, and see the man
who killed them."

So she went downstairs. Her heart
could not decide if she should keep her distance
as she was questioning her own dear husband,
or go right up to him and kiss his face
and hold his hands in hers. She crossed the threshold
and sat across from him beside the wall,
in firelight. He sat beside the pillar,
and kept his eyes down, waiting to find out
whether the woman who once shared his bed
would speak to him. She sat in silence, stunned.
Sometimes when she was glancing at his face
it seemed like him; but then his dirty clothes
were unfamiliar. Telemachus
scolded her.

"Mother! Cruel, heartless Mother!
Why are you doing this, rejecting Father?
Why do you not go over, sit beside him,
and talk to him? No woman in the world
would be so obstinate! To keep your distance
from him when he has come back after twenty
long years of suffering! Your heart is always
harder than rock!"

But thoughtfully she answered,
"My child, I am confused. I cannot speak,
or meet his eyes. If this is really him,
if my Odysseus has come back home,
we have our ways to recognize each other,
through secret signs known only to us two."

Hardened Odysseus began to smile.
He told the boy,

"You must allow your mother
to test me out; she will soon know me better.
While I am dirty, dressed in rags, she will not
treat me with kindness or acknowledge me.
Meanwhile, we must make plans. If someone murders
even just one man, even one who had
few friends in his community, the killer
is forced to run away and leave his homeland
and family. But we have killed the mainstay
of Ithaca, the island's best young men.
So what do you suggest?"

Telemachus
said warily, "You have to work it out.
They say you have the finest mind in all
the world; no mortal man can rival you
in cleverness. Lead me, and I will be
behind you right away. And I will do
my best to be as brave as I can be."

Odysseus was quick to form a plan.
He told him, "Here is what I think is best.
The three of you should wash and change your clothes,
and make the slave girls go put on clean dresses.

Then let the godlike singer take the lyre
and play a clear and cheerful dancing tune,
so passersby or neighbors hearing it
will think it is a wedding. We must not
allow the news about the suitors' murder
to spread too far until we reach the woods
of our estate, and there we can decide
the best path forward offered us by Zeus."

They did as Lord Odysseus had said.
They washed and changed their tunics, and the slave girls
prepared themselves. The singer took the lyre,
and roused in them desire to hear sweet music,
and dance. The house resounded with the thump
of beating feet from all the dancing men
and girls in pretty sashes. Those outside
who heard the noises said to one another,

"So somebody is marrying the queen
who had so many suitors! Headstrong woman!
She must have lacked the strength to wait it out
and keep her husband's house safe till he came."
They spoke with no idea what really happened.

Eurynome the slave woman began
to wash strong-willed Odysseus. She rubbed him
with olive oil, and dressed him in a tunic
and handsome cloak. And then Athena poured
attractiveness from head to toe, and made him
taller and stronger, and his hair grew thick
and curly as a hyacinth. As when
a craftsman whom Athena or Hephaestus
has trained in metalwork, so he can make
beautiful artifacts, pours gold on silver—

so she poured beauty on his head and shoulders.
After his bath he looked like an immortal.
He sat down in the same chair opposite
his wife and said,

"Extraordinary woman!
The gods have given you the hardest heart.
No other wife would so reject a husband
who had been suffering for twenty years
and finally come home. Well, Nanny, make
a bed for me, so I can rest. This woman
must have an iron heart!"

Penelope
said shrewdly, "You extraordinary man!
I am not acting proud, or underplaying
this big event; yet I am not surprised
at how you look. You looked like this the day
your long oars sailed away from Ithaca.
Now, Eurycleia, make the bed for him
outside the room he built himself. Pull out
the bedstead, and spread quilts and blankets on it."
She spoke to test him, and Odysseus
was furious, and told his loyal wife,

"Woman! Your words have cut my heart! Who moved
my bed? It would be difficult for even
a master craftsman—though a god could do it
with ease. No man, however young and strong,
could pry it out. There is a trick to how
this bed was made. I made it, no one else.
Inside the court there grew an olive tree
with delicate long leaves, full-grown and green,
as sturdy as a pillar, and I built

the room around it. I packed stones together,
and fixed a roof and fitted doors. At last
I trimmed the olive tree and used my bronze
to cut the branches off from root to tip
and planed it down and skillfully transformed
the trunk into a bedpost. With a drill,
I bored right through it. This was my first bedpost,
and then I made the other three, inlaid
with gold and silver and with ivory.
I stretched ox-leather straps across, dyed purple.
Now I have told the secret trick, the token.
But woman, wife, I do not know if someone—
a man—has cut the olive trunk and moved
my bed, or if it is still safe."

At that,
her heart and body suddenly relaxed.
She recognized the tokens he had shown her.
She burst out crying and ran straight towards him
and threw her arms around him, kissed his face,
and said,

"Do not be angry at me now,
Odysseus! In every other way
you are a very understanding man.
The gods have made us suffer: they refused
to let us stay together and enjoy
our youth until we reached the edge of age
together. Please forgive me, do not keep
bearing a grudge because when I first saw you,
I would not welcome you immediately.
I felt a constant dread that some bad man
would fool me with his lies. There are so many
dishonest, clever men. That foreigner

would never have got Helen into bed,
if she had known the Greeks would march to war
and bring her home again. It was a goddess
who made her do it, putting in her heart
the passion that first caused my grief as well.
Now you have told the story of our bed,
the secret that no other mortal knows,
except yourself and me, and just one slave,
Actoris, whom my father gave to me
when I came here, who used to guard our room.
You made my stubborn heart believe in you."

This made him want to cry. He held his love,
his faithful wife, and wept. As welcome as
the land to swimmers, when Poseidon wrecks
their ship at sea and breaks it with great waves
and driving winds; a few escape the sea
and reach the shore, their skin all caked with brine.
Grateful to be alive, they crawl to land.
So glad she was to see her own dear husband,
and her white arms would not let go his neck.
They would have wept until the rosy Dawn
began to touch the sky, but shining-eyed
Athena intervened. She held night back,
restraining golden Dawn beside the Ocean,
and would not let her yoke her swift young colts,
Shining and Bright. Odysseus, mind whirling,
said,

"Wife, we have not come yet to the end
of all our troubles; there are more to come,
many hard labors which I must complete.
The spirit of Tiresias informed me,
that day I went inside the house of Hades
to ask about the journey home for me

and for my men. But come now, let us go
to bed together, wife; let us enjoy
the pleasure of sweet sleep."

Penelope,
who always thought ahead, said, "When you wish.
The bed is yours. The gods have brought you home,
back to your well-built house. But since a god
has made you speak about these future labors,
tell me what they involve. I will find out
eventually, and better to know now."

He answered warily, "You really are
extraordinary. Why would you make me tell you
something to cause you pain? It hurts me too,
but I will tell the truth, not hide it from you.
Tiresias foretold that I must travel
through many cities carrying an oar,
till I reach men who do not know the sea,
and do not eat their food with salt, or use
boats painted red around the prow, or oars,
which are the wings of ships. He said that I
will know I have arrived when I encounter
someone who calls the object on my back
a winnowing fan. Then I must fix my oar
firm in the earth, and make a sacrifice
to Lord Poseidon, of a ram and ox
and stud-boar, perfect animals, then come
back home and give a hecatomb to all
the deathless gods who live above the sky.
If I do this, I will not die at sea;
I will grow old in comfort and will meet
a gentle death, surrounded by my people,
who will be rich and happy."

Sensibly
Penelope said, "If the gods allow you
to reach old age in comfort, there is hope
that there will be an end to all our troubles."

They talked like this. Meanwhile, the slaves were working:
Eurynome and Eurycleia laid
soft blankets on the sturdy bed by torchlight.
The nurse went off to sleep; Eurynome
picked up the torch and led them to their bed,
then went to her room. Finally, at last,
with joy the husband and the wife arrived
back in the rites of their old marriage bed.

Meanwhile, the herdsmen and Telemachus
stopped dancing, made the women stop, and went
to bed inside the darkened house.

And when
the couple had enjoyed their lovemaking,
they shared another pleasure—telling stories.
She told him how she suffered as she watched
the crowd of suitors ruining the house,
killing so many herds of sheep and cattle
and drinking so much wine, because of her.
Odysseus told her how much he hurt
so many other people, and in turn
how much he had endured himself. She loved
to listen, and she did not fall asleep
until he told it all. First, how he slaughtered
the Cicones, then traveled to the fields
of Lotus-Eaters; what the Cyclops did,
and how he paid him back for ruthlessly
eating his men. Then how he reached Aeolus,

who welcomed him and helped him; but it was
not yet his fate to come back home; a storm
snatched him and bore him off across the sea,
howling frustration. Then, he said, he came
to Laestrygonia, whose people wrecked
his fleet and killed his men. And he described
the cleverness of Circe, and his journey
to Hades to consult Tiresias,
and how he saw all his dead friends, and saw
his mother, who had loved him as a baby;
then how he heard the Sirens' endless voices,
and reached the Wandering Rocks and terrible
Charybdis, and how he had been the first
to get away from Scylla. And he told her
of how his crew devoured the Sun God's cattle;
Zeus roared with smoke and thunder, lightning struck
the ship, and all his loyal men were killed.
But he survived, and drifted to Ogygia.
He told her how Calypso trapped him there,
inside her hollow cave, and wanted him
to be her husband; she took care of him
and promised she could set him free from death
and time forever. But she never swayed
his heart. He suffered terribly, for years,
and then he reached Phaeacia, where the people
looked up to him as if he were a god,
and sent him in a ship back home again
to his dear Ithaca, with gifts of bronze
and gold and piles of clothes. His story ended;
sweet sleep released his heart from all his cares.

Athena, bright-eyed goddess, stayed alert,
and when she thought Odysseus had finished
with taking pleasure in his wife and sleep,

she roused the newborn Dawn from Ocean's streams
to bring the golden light to those on earth.
Odysseus got up and told his wife,

"Wife, we have both endured our share of trouble:
you wept here as you longed for my return,
while Zeus and other gods were keeping me
away from home, although I longed to come.
But now we have returned to our own bed,
as we both longed to do. You must look after
my property inside the house. Meanwhile,
I have to go on raids, to steal replacements
for all the sheep those swaggering suitors killed,
and get the other Greeks to give me more,
until I fill my folds. But first I will
go to the orchard in the countryside
to see my grieving father. Then at dawn
the news will spread that I have killed the suitors.
Your orders, wife—though you are smart enough
to need no orders—are, go with your slaves
upstairs, sit quietly, and do not talk
to anyone."

He armed himself and called
the herdsmen and Telemachus, and told them
to put on armor too—breastplates of bronze.
Odysseus led all of them outside.
The light was bright across the earth. Athena
hid them with night and brought them out of town.

BOOK 24

Restless Spirits

Then Hermes called the spirits of the suitors
out of the house. He held the golden wand
with which he casts a spell to close men's eyes
or open those of sleepers when he wants.
He led the spirits and they followed, squeaking
like bats in secret crannies of a cave,
who cling together, and when one becomes
detached and falls down from the rock, the rest
flutter and squeak—just so the spirits squeaked,
and hurried after Hermes, lord of healing.
On open roads they crossed the Ocean stream,
went past the rock of Leucas and the gates
of Helius the Sun, and skittered through
the provinces of dreams, and soon arrived
in fields of asphodel, the home of shadows
who have been worn to weariness by life.

They found Achilles' ghost there, and Patroclus,
and Ajax, the most handsome of the Greeks
after unmatched Achilles. Agamemnon

had just arrived to join them, in deep grief
for his own death, and with him came the others
killed by Aegisthus and his bodyguards.
Achilles' ghost spoke first.

"O Agamemnon!
Men used to say that out of all the heroes,
Zeus, Lord of Lightning, favored you the most,
because you had command of a great army
in Troy where Greeks endured the pain of war.
But death, which no man living can avoid,
was destined to arrive at the wrong time.
If only you had died at Troy and won
the glory of your rank as a commander!
All of the Greeks and allies would have built
a tomb for you, and afterwards your son
would have received great honor. As it is,
it was your fate to die a dreadful death."

The ghost of Agamemnon answered him,
"Achilles, son of Peleus, you were
lucky to die at Troy, away from Argos.
The finest warriors of Greece and Troy
fought round your corpse and died. You lay a hero,
magnificent amid the whirling dust,
your days of driving chariots forgotten.
We fought all day, and would have fought forever,
but Zeus sent winds to stop us. Then we brought you
back to our ships, and laid you on a bier,
away from battle, and we bathed your skin
in heated water and anointed you
with oil. We wept for you and cut our hair.
Your mother heard the news, and with her nymphs
she came up from the waves. An eerie wailing
sounded across the sea. The men began

to tremble, and they would have rushed on board,
if wise old Nestor had not made them stop.
He always had the best advice for us,
and said, 'My lords, stay here. It is his mother,
coming with her immortal water nymphs
to find her own dead son.' At this, the Greeks
regained their courage. The old Sea King's daughters
gathered around you weeping, and they dressed you
in clothes of the immortals. All nine Muses
sang lamentations in their lovely voices.
No one could keep from crying at the sound,
so moving was their song. The gods and men
were mourning seventeen long nights and days
and then we gave you to the pyre, and killed
many fat sheep and cattle for your corpse.
You burned in clothes from gods; you were anointed
with oil and honey. Troops of warriors
on foot and horseback, fully armed, went marching
around your pyre, and made a mighty din.
At last Hephaestus' flame consumed your flesh.
When morning came, we gathered your white bones,
Achilles, and anointed them with oil
and unmixed wine. Your mother gave an urn
of gold with double handles, which she said
Hephaestus made and Dionysus gave her.
Your white bones lay inside it, Lord Achilles,
mixed with the bones of your dead friend Patroclus.
We laid the urn beside Antilochus,
the friend you most respected after him.
The army of Greek warriors assembled,
and with all reverence we heaped a mound
out on the headland by the Hellespont,
large enough to be visible to those
at sea, both now and in the years to come.
Your mother asked the gods for splendid prizes

and put them in the midst of an arena,
so the best athletes could compete for them.
You have seen many burials of heroes,
when young men tie their tunics to compete.
But you would have been startled at the riches
that silver-footed Thetis brought for you.
You were so dearly loved by all the gods.
You did not lose your name in death. Your fame
will live forever; everyone will know
Achilles. As for me, what good was it
that I wound up the war? When I came home
Aegisthus and my wicked, fiendish wife
murdered me. Zeus had planned it."

While they talked,
Hermes the guide came near them, with the suitors
killed by Odysseus. The two great lords,
astonished at the sight, rushed up to them,
and Agamemnon's spirit recognized
the son of his old friend, Melaneus,
with whom he stayed in Ithaca. He said,

"Amphimedon! What happened to you all?
Why have you all come down here to the land
of darkness? You are all so young and strong;
you must have been the best boys in your town.
Maybe Poseidon raised great waves and winds
to wreck your fleet? Or were you all attacked
by men on land while you were poaching cows
or flocks of sheep, or fighting for a city
and women? You must tell me! We are friends.
Do you remember when I visited
your home, when Menelaus and myself
were trying to persuade Odysseus
to join the fleet and sail with us to Troy?

It took a whole damned month to cross the sea;
we had to work so hard to sway that man,
who sacked the city."

Amphimedon's spirit
answered, "Great General, Agamemnon, yes,
I do remember everything you say.
And I will tell, in every gruesome detail,
the manner of our death. Odysseus
was gone for many years. We came to court
his wife, who had no wish to marry us,
but would not tell us no or make an end.
She planned black death for us, and tricked us, too.
She set a mighty loom up in the hall,
and wove a wide fine cloth, and said to us,
'Young suitors, now Odysseus is dead.
I know that you are eager for the wedding,
but wait till I am finished with this cloth,
so that my weaving will not go to waste.
It is a shroud for when Laertes dies,
so that the women in the town do not
blame me because a man who gained such wealth
was buried with no winding-sheet.' Her words
convinced us. So by day she wove the cloth,
and then at night by torchlight, she unwove it.
For three long years she fooled us; when the hours
and months had passed, the fourth year rolled around,
and then a girl who knew the truth told us;
and we found her unraveling her work.
We made her finish it. When she had washed
the marvelous huge sheet, she showed it to us,
bright as the sun or moon. And then some spirit
of ruin brought Odysseus from somewhere
to Ithaca; he went out to the fields,
to where the swineherd lived. His own dear son

sailed in his black ship back from sandy Pylos.
The two of them made plans to murder us.
They showed up at the palace—first the boy,
and then Odysseus propped on a stick
and dressed in dirty rags. He seemed to be
a poor old homeless man, who suddenly
appeared, led by the swineherd. None of us
could recognize him, even those of us
who were a little older than myself.
We hurled insulting words and missiles at him,
and for a while he patiently endured
abuse in his own home. But when the will
of Zeus awakened him, with his son's help,
he put the splendid weapons in the storeroom
and locked the door. Then came his cunning plan:
he told his wife to set for us the axes
and bow. The competition meant our doom,
the start of slaughter. None of us could string
the mighty bow—we all were far too weak.
But when it was his turn, we shouted out
that nobody should give the bow to him,
no matter what he said. Telemachus
alone insisted that he ought to have it.
At last Odysseus, with calm composure,
took it and strung it easily, and shot
all through the iron axes. Then he stood
astride the threshold with a fearsome scowl,
and started shooting fast. His arrow struck
Antinous, our leader. With sure aim
he shot his deadly arrows at more men;
those nearest to him fell. It was apparent
some god was helping them. Impelled by rage,
they rushed around the palace killing us
in turn. There was a dreadful noise of screaming
and broken skulls; the whole floor ran with blood.

So, Agamemnon, we were killed. Our bodies
still lie unburied in our killer's house.
Our families at home do not yet know.
They need to wash the black blood from our wounds
and weep for us and lay our bodies out.
This is the honor due the dead."

The ghost
of Agamemnon answered, "Lucky you,
cunning Odysseus: you got yourself
a wife of virtue—great Penelope.
How principled she was, that she remembered
her husband all those years! Her fame will live
forever, and the deathless gods will make
a poem to delight all those on earth
about intelligent Penelope.
Not like my wife—who murdered her own husband!
Her story will be hateful; she will bring
bad reputation to all other women,
even the good ones."

So they spoke together,
standing in Hades, hidden in the earth.

Meanwhile, Odysseus and his companions
had left the town and quickly reached the farm,
won by Laertes long ago—he fought
hard for it, and his house was there; the slaves,
who had to do his wishes, lived and slept
and ate their food in quarters that surrounded
the central house. One was from Sicily,
the old slave woman who took care of him
out in the countryside. Odysseus
spoke to his slaves and to his son.

"Go in,
choose the best pig and kill it for our dinner.
And I will test my father, to find out
if he will know me instantly on sight,
or not—I have been absent for so long."

At that he gave his weapons to the slaves.
They quickly went inside. Odysseus
walked to the fruitful orchard on his quest.
He did not find old Dolius, the steward,
nor any of his slaves or sons—he had
led them to gather rocks to build dry-walls.
Odysseus' father was alone,
inside the well-built orchard, digging earth
to make it level round a tree. He wore
a dirty ragged tunic, and his leggings
had leather patches to protect from scratches.
He wore thick gloves because of thorns, and had
a cap of goatskin. He was wallowing
in grief. The veteran, Odysseus,
seeing his father worn by age and burdened
by desperate, heartfelt sorrow, stopped beneath
a towering pear tree, weeping. Then he wondered
whether to kiss his father, twine around him,
and tell him that he had come home again,
and everything that happened on the way—
or question him. He thought it best to start
by testing him with teasing and abuse.
With this in mind, Odysseus approached him,
as he was digging round the plant, head down.
His famous son stood at his side and said,

"Old man, you know your trade and take good care
of this neat garden. Every plant and vine,

and tree—the figs, the pears, the olive trees—
and bed of herbs is nicely tended. But
I have to say something—please do not get
angry at me—you do not take good care
of your own self. You are unkempt, old man.
Your skin is rough and dirty and your clothes
are rags. Your master is neglecting you,
although you are not lazy. In your height
and face, you seem a leader, not a slave.
You look like someone who would bathe and eat
and sleep on fluffy pillows and fine sheets,
as is appropriate for older people.
But tell me this: whose slave are you? Whose garden
do you take care of? Also, have I come
to Ithaca, as somebody I met
was telling me just now? But he was not
a helpful man: when I was asking him
about a friend of mine, an old guest-friend,
whether he is alive or dead in Hades,
this fellow would not say, or even listen.
A while ago, in my own native land,
I had a guest to stay with me, who was
my dearest friend of all my visitors.
He said he was from Ithaca, and that
Laertes was his father. I had brought him
into my house, and welcomed him with warmth;
I can afford to be quite generous.
I gave him seven heaps of golden treasure,
a bowl made all of silver and inlaid
with flowers, twelve unfolded cloaks, and twelve
thick blankets, twelve fine mantles, and twelve tunics.
Also I gave him four well-trained slave women,
beautiful ones, whom he picked out himself."

His father answered through his tears, "Yes, stranger,
you have reached Ithaca. But cruel men
have taken over here. You will receive
nothing for all those gifts. If you had found him
still living in this land, he would have matched
your gifts and welcomed you with open arms
before he sent you home. Initial kindness
deserves due recompense. But tell me now,
how long is it since that unlucky man
visited you? Your guest was my own son!
Perhaps fish ate him out at sea, so far
from home and family; or birds and beasts
ate him on land. His mother did not lay
his body out and weep for him; nor I,
his father; nor Penelope his wife,
a wise and wealthy woman. She has not
closed her own husband's eyes or given him
a funeral. The dead deserve this honor.
But tell me now, who are you? From what city?
Who are your parents? Do you have a ship
docked somewhere, which conveyed you here with friends
and crew? Or did you sail as passenger
on someone else's ship, which now is gone?"

Lying Odysseus replied, "I will
tell you the truth completely. I am from
Alybas, and I have a palace there.
My name is Eperitus; I am son
of King Apheidas, son of Polypemon.
An evil spirit struck me and I came
from Sicily against my will. My ship
is docked away from town. It is five years
since poor, unfortunate Odysseus
came to my home. As he was setting out

we saw good omens—birds towards the right—
so we were hopeful we would meet again
as friends, and share more gifts."

At this, a cloud
of black grief wrapped itself around Laertes.
He poured two handfuls of the ashy dust
over his gray old head, and started sobbing.
Odysseus felt heart-wrenched to see his own
beloved father in this state; sharp pain
pierced through his nostrils. He rushed up to him
and threw his arms around him, kissing him,
and saying,

"Father! It is me! I have
been gone for twenty years, and now am home,
in my own father's country. Stop your tears.
I will explain, though we do not have long.
I killed the suitors in my house; I took
revenge for all the pain they caused."

Laertes
answered, "If you are really my own son
Odysseus come home, show me a sign;
let me be sure of it."

Odysseus
was quick to answer. "First, look here: the scar
made by the boar's white tusk when I had gone
to Mount Parnassus. You and Mother sent me,
to see my grandfather, Autolycus,
and get the gifts that he had promised me.
Next I will tell you all the trees that grow
in this fine orchard, which you gave to me.

When I was little, I would follow you
around the garden, asking all their names.
We walked beneath these trees; you named them all
and promised them to me. Ten apple trees,
and thirteen pear trees, forty figs, and fifty
grapevines which ripen one by one—their clusters
change as the weather presses from the sky,
sent down by Zeus."

At that, Laertes' heart
and legs gave way; he recognized the signs
Odysseus had given as clear proof.
He threw both arms around his ruthless son,
who caught him as he fainted. When his breath
and mind returned, he said,

"O Father Zeus,
you gods are truly rulers of Olympus,
if it is true the suitors have been punished
for all the monstrous things they did. But I
am terrified the Ithacans may soon
attack us here, and spread the news around
to all the towns of Cephallenia."

Scheming Odysseus said, "Do not fear.
Come to the farmhouse, where I sent my boy
to go with the two herdsmen, to prepare
dinner as fast as possible."

With this,
the son and father walked towards the house.
They found them serving generous plates of meat
and mixing wine. The slave from Sicily
washed brave Laertes, and she rubbed his skin

with olive oil, and wrapped a handsome cloak
around him. Then Athena, standing near,
made him grow taller and more muscular.
When he emerged, Odysseus was shocked
to see him looking like a god. His words
flew fast.

"Oh, Father! You look different!
A god has made you taller and more handsome."

Thoughtful Laertes said, "O Father Zeus,
Athena, and Apollo! If I were
as strong as when I took the sturdy fortress
of Nericus, out on the mainland shore,
when I was king of Cephallenia,
I would have stood beside you yesterday,
with weapons on my back, and fought with you
against the suitors who were in our house!
I would have brought so many of them down,
you would have been delighted!"

So they spoke.
The work of cooking dinner was complete,
and they sat down on chairs and stools, and reached
to take the food. The old slave Dolius
approached them with his sons, who had been working.
Their mother, the Sicilian old woman,
had gone to call them. She took care of them,
and also the old man, made weak by age.
They saw Odysseus and stared, then stopped,
astonished. But he spoke to reassure them.

"Old man, sit down and eat. The rest of you,
put your surprise entirely out of mind.

We have been waiting ages; we are eager
to have our dinner here."

But Dolius
ran straight to him with arms outstretched, and took
Odysseus' wrist and kissed his hand,
and let his words fly out.

"My friend! You have
come home! We are so very glad to see you!
We never thought this day would come! The gods
have brought you here! A heartfelt welcome to you!
I pray the gods will bless you!—Does your wife
know you have come back home? Or should I send
a message?"

But Odysseus said coolly,
"Old man, she knows already. Do not bother."

So Dolius sat back down on his chair.
His sons were also clustering around
their famous owner, Lord Odysseus,
to welcome him and hold him in their arms.
Then they sat down in turn beside their father.
They had their meal together in the farmhouse.

Meanwhile, swift Rumor spread the news all through
the city, of the suitors' dreadful murder.
When people heard, they rushed from all directions
towards the palace of Odysseus,
with shouts and lamentations. Then they brought
the bodies from the house and buried them.
The ones from distant towns were sent back home
by ship. The mourners gathered in the square,

heartbroken. When the people were assembled,
Eupeithes first stood up and spoke to them.
This man was inconsolable with grief
for his dead son Antinous, the boy
Odysseus killed first. His father wept,
tears falling as he spoke.

"This scheming man,
my friends, has done us all most monstrous wrongs.
First, he took many good men off to sail
with him, and lost the ships, and killed the men!
Now he has come and murdered all the best
of Cephallenia. Come on, before
he sneaks away to Pylos or to Elis,
we have to act! We will be shamed forever
unless we take revenge on him for killing
our sons and brothers. I would have no wish
to live; I would prefer to die and join
the boys already dead. We have to stop them
escaping overseas! Come on, right now!"

He spoke in tears, and pity seized them all.
But Medon and the bard had woken up;
they came outside and stood among the crowd.
They all were terrified, and Medon said,

"Now listen, Ithacans. Odysseus
could not have done such things without the help
of gods. I saw a god myself, disguised
as Mentor, sometimes standing at his side,
giving him will to fight, and sometimes rushing
all through the hall to make the suitors scatter.
They fell like flies."

Pale terror seized them all.
Then Halitherses, an old warrior,
the only one to know both past and future,
stood up; he wished them well. He said to them,

"Now hear me, Ithacans. My friends, it was
because of your own cowardice this happened.
You did not listen to me, or to Mentor,
when we were telling you to stop your sons
from acting stupidly. They did great wrong,
through their impulsiveness; they skimmed the wealth
of an important man, and disrespected
his wife, believing he would never come.
But listen now. We must not go and fight,
or we will bring more ruin on our heads."

At that, some stayed there, huddling together,
but more than half jumped up with shouts. They thought
Eupeithes had the right idea. They rushed
to arms, and strapped their gleaming armor on,
and gathered in a mass before the town.
Eupeithes was their leader—to his cost.
He thought he would avenge his murdered son.
In fact, he would not come back home; it was
his fate to die out there.

And then Athena
spoke to the son of Cronus.

"Father Zeus,
highest of powers! Tell what hidden thoughts
lie in you. Will you now make yet more war
and bitter strife, or join the sides in friendship?"

The Gatherer of Clouds replied, "My child,
why ask me this? The plan was your idea,
to have Odysseus come take revenge.
Do as you wish. But here is my advice.
He has already punished all the suitors,
so let them swear an oath that he will be
the king forever, and let us make sure
the murder of their brothers and their sons
will be forgotten. Let them all be friends,
just as before, and let them live in peace
and in prosperity."

Athena was
already eager; at these words she swooped
down from Olympus.

Meanwhile, they had finished
dinner, and battle-scarred Odysseus
said, "Somebody must go and see if they
are coming near." A son of Dolius
obeyed and went. As he stepped out, he stood
across the threshold, and he saw them all
near to the house. At once his words took wings.
He told Odysseus,

"Those men are near!
We have to arm, and fast!"

They quickly armed.
Odysseus, his son and their two slaves
made four, and Dolius had his six sons.
Laertes and old Dolius were also
needed as fighters, though they had gray hair.
When all of them were dressed in gleaming bronze,

they opened up the gates and went outside;
Odysseus was leading them. Athena
came near, disguised as Mentor. When he saw her,
weathered Odysseus was glad and turned
towards Telemachus and said,

"Dear son,
soon you will have experience of fighting
in battle, the true test of worth. You must
not shame your father's family; for years
we have been known across the world for courage
and manliness."

Telemachus inhaled,
then said, "Just watch me, Father, if you want
to see my spirit. I will bring no shame
onto your family. You should not speak
of shame."

Laertes, thrilled, cried out, "Dear gods!
A happy day for me! My son and grandson
are warring with each other for achievement!"

With glinting eyes, Athena stood beside him
and said, "You are my favorite, Laertes.
Pray to the bright-eyed goddess and her father,
then lift and hurl your spear."

As she said this,
Athena breathed great energy inside him.
Laertes quickly raised and hurled the spear,
and struck Eupeithes through his bronze-cheeked helmet,
which did not stop the weapon; it pierced through.
Then with a thud he fell; his armor clanged

around him on the ground. Odysseus
charged the front line, his radiant son beside him;
they hacked with swords and curving spears. They would
have killed them all and made sure none of them
could go back home—but then Athena spoke.
Her voice held back the fighters.

"Ithacans!
Stop this destructive war; shed no more blood,
and go your separate ways, at once!"

Her voice
struck them with pale green fear and made them drop
their weapons. They were desperate to save
their lives, and they turned back towards the city.
Unwavering Odysseus let out
a dreadful roar, then crouched and swooped upon them,
just like an eagle flying from above.
But Zeus sent down a thunderbolt, which fell
in front of his own daughter, great Athena.
She looked at him with steely eyes and said,

"Odysseus, you are adaptable;
you always find solutions. Stop this war,
or Zeus will be enraged at you."

He was
glad to obey her. Then Athena made
the warring sides swear solemn oaths of peace
for future times—still in her guise as Mentor.

NOTES

BOOK 1 SUMMARY

The poet invokes the Muse. The gods hold a council: Athena appeals to Zeus about Odysseus, who is trapped far from home, on the island of the nymph Calypso. Zeus promises to send Hermes, the messenger god, to make Calypso help Odysseus go home. Athena goes to Ithaca in the guise of Mentes and inspires Telemachus, assuring him that his father is alive. Then she flies away, like a bird. The singer, Phemius, begins to sing about Troy; Penelope is made upset by the topic, and tries to stop him. Telemachus, to her surprise, intervenes, scolds her, and makes her go upstairs. Telemachus announces that he will be calling a meeting the next day. Antinous and Eurymachus speak to him nastily and try to find out who Athena was.

1.29–30 *Aegisthus, who was killed / by Agamemnon's famous son Orestes*: Agamemnon was killed on his return home by the usurper Aegisthus, with the help of Agamemnon's adulterous wife, Clytemnestra. Orestes, Agamemnon and Clytmenestra's son, came back and killed his mother and Aegisthus.

1.63 *why do you dismiss Odysseus?*: The word in the original for Zeus' hostile treatment of Odysseus, *odussomai* ("to hate" or in this version, "to dismiss") is reminiscent of the name "Odysseus." See also the notes to 19.274–75 and 19.408.

1.105 *the Taphian leader*: The Taphians were an island people from the Ionian Sea.

1.145 *observing proper order*: There may be an implication that the suitors seat themselves according to some kind of rank, with the more important ones in the group getting a more honorable position.

BOOK 2 SUMMARY

Telemachus calls an assembly and speaks to the elite men of Ithaca about the trouble caused him by the suitors. Antinous, a leading suitor, explains Penelope's trick with the loom. Zeus sends two eagles that attack the faces of the men in the crowd, and an Ithacan named Halitherses explains that this is a prophecy that Odysseus is on his way home. Mentor speaks up for Telemachus; the suitors (Eurymachus and Leocritus) resist the warnings. Telemachus asks for a ship to travel in search of news about his father. He prays for Athena's help; disguised as Mentor, she appears to him and promises to help him and equip a ship for him. At dinner, the suitors tease Telemachus. He slips out secretly, gets provisions with the help of Eurycleia, and goes down to the shore, where Athena, disguised as Mentor, has prepared the ship, borrowed from Noëmon, and assembled a crew. They pack up and set sail.

2.53 *choose who should be her husband*: Here, Telemachus makes it sound as if it is Icarius who will choose a new husband for Penelope, although later, in response to Antinous, he suggests that it is up to Penelope herself (2.131). The ambiguity is part of a larger tension in the poem about how much agency Penelope has.

2.71 *Friends, leave me be*: Telemachus switches from addressing the suitors to addressing the general population of Ithaca.

2.73–74 *Or did Odysseus, my warlike father, / deliberately do harm to our own side?*: Irony: Telemachus assumes that it is obvious that Odysseus was always a helper to the Greek side.

2.154 *their talons ripped each face and neck*: The original may mean "at each other's faces and necks" or, more likely, "ripping at their own faces and necks" (as if in a gesture of mourning, perhaps for the sorrows of the house of Telemachus—although it is hard to see how a flying bird could actually do this). The interpretation given here is linguistically difficult, but was proposed in late antiquity, and makes better sense of the sign, since the birds are presumably meant to be parallel to Telemachus and Odysseus, who will attack the suitors.

2.155 *to the right they flew, across the town*: Signs on the right side were supposed to be lucky, so this is a good omen.

2.160 *excelled at prophecy and knew the birds*: Prophets observed bird flight in order to predict the future.

2.190–91 *he will be hurt, and never get to act / on any of these prophecies of yours*: This line about Telemachus' being unable to act on the prophet's words is believed to be spurious by many editors.

2.317–19 *I will try to bring down doom / on your heads here at home or when I go / to Pylos*: These lines were thought to be spurious by an ancient editor (Aristarchus), presumably because they suggest that Telemachus is not sure whether he will go to Pylos or not, and hence, not sure whether he will destroy the suitors directly, or from afar.

2.320–21 *I do not own / a ship or have a crew—because of you!*: Telemachus has seen through Antinous' false promise that the Greeks will provide a ship, and he is suggesting that, if he had not been deprived of his inheritance by the suitors, he would already have the means for his journey without having to rely on others.

2.386–87 *the son of Phronius, / Noëmon*: Both names suggest wisdom or mindfulness, and the name Phronius occurs only here.

BOOK 3 SUMMARY

Telemachus reaches Pylos, home of old King Nestor, where he receives a warm welcome. Nestor tells how the Greeks destroyed Troy, and then were cursed by Athena. The brothers Agamemnon and Menelaus quarreled, the troops split up, and the fleet was scattered on their homeward journey. Nestor himself reached home safely; Agamemnon was killed by Aegisthus, who had seduced his wife; Menelaus was swept off to Egypt by a storm. Nestor warns Telemachus to remember the story of Aegisthus, and be wary. He advises him to go visit Menelaus, and then go back home. Nestor insists that Telemachus must stay the night, and sends him off in the morning with gifts, a carriage to get to Sparta, and his son Pisistratus as a companion.

3.1 *Leaving the Ocean's streams*: The Ocean was imagined as a vast river running round the landmass of the world.

3.2 *the sky of bronze*: The word used in the original, *polychalkos*, translates literally as "of much bronze," which could mean that the gods in heaven are well supplied with bronze implements, or that the sky is solid and firm, like bronze, or that it is bright and shiny.

3.68 *Gerenian Nestor*: Gerenia is a town where Nestor took refuge when Heracles was attacking Pylos; Nestor was the sole survivor of his generation.

3.91 *Amphitrite's waves*: Amphitrite, the wife of Poseidon, is a sea goddess, used here as a metonym for the sea itself.

3.133 *some of us had neither sense nor morals*: Ajax raped the Trojan priestess Cassandra (daughter of Priam) in a temple to Athena; Nestor alludes to this violation but never spells it out. The pollution to her temple is what caused the unappeasable rage of Athena and Zeus.

3.137–38 *they called the people / at sunset, not observing proper norms*: The suggestion is that the Greeks will inevitably be tired and drunk if called to a meeting at the wrong time, after dinner.

3.170–73 *Should we travel north . . . or under Chios, passing blustery Mimas?*: The latter is the longer but safer route, with less open sea.

3.178 *nightfall in Geraestus*: Geraestus was the southernmost part of Euboea.

3.189 *Achilles' son led home the Myrmidons*: The Myrmidons are a Thessalian tribe and Achilles' men in *The Iliad.* Neoptolemus (also known as Pyrrhus) was Achilles' son; he led the tribe after his father's death.

3.190 *Philoctetes came back home with glory*: Philoctetes was a hero with a wounded foot that never healed; his bow was essential in the final destruction of Troy.

3.191–92 *Idomeneus led back his crew / to Crete*: Idomeneus is a Cretan king; he will appear later in Odysseus' false tales of traveling in Crete.

3.217–18 *he will come home and take revenge, alone, / or with an army of the Greeks*: "He" must be Odysseus, although it is striking that Nestor meanders away from the topic of Telemachus' revenge, to that of Odysseus, and back again—perhaps a mark of his senility, or perhaps he is veering around the possibility that Telemachus is being too passive.

3.268 *Fate forced the queen to yield*: The original is ambiguous about whether Fate subdued Clytemnestra (the most likely option) or Aegisthus or the poet. The original is also vague about how exactly Clytemnestra made the switch from resistance to "mutual desire."

3.292–95 *steep rock rises sheer above the sea / near Gortyn . . . west to Phaestus*: Phaestus and Gortyn were cities in Crete, a place that is prominent in the poem (and which Odysseus chooses for his fictional birthplace in Books 13–14 and 19). The apparent precision of these details may not reveal actual knowledge of the place, since archaeologists have tried in vain to fit the text to the material record.

3.326 *My sons can guide you all the way to Sparta*: Nestor lavishly suggests that multiple sons will accompany Telemachus; however, as it turns out, only one of Nestor's sons, Pisistratus, goes with the Ithacan.

3.369–70 *Give him a carriage, / drawn by your strongest and most nimble horses*: The word translated here as "carriage," *diphros*, is literally a "two-person carriage," a type of vehicle on which two people could ride on a standing board drawn by two horses. There are many different words for horse-drawn carriages in Homer, and I have tried not to overuse the word "chariot," which usually connotes a vehicle used for war or racing; the *diphros* was used sometimes for warfare and other times, as here, for travel.

3.371–72 *Athena flew away, transformed / into an ossifrage*: An ossifrage is a type of vulture, also known as a lammergeier.

3.406–7 *polished stones / that stood outside his palace, bright with oil*: The stones that mark Nestor's judgment seat have been anointed, a mark of their sanctity.

3.445 *sprinkle barley-groats and ritual water:* Before sacrifice, one washed hands and sprinkled barley grains at the victim and the altar—to ensure that the sacrifice was legitimate. It was then traditional to cut a few hairs from the victim's head, as Nestor does, to make the animal no longer inviolate before it dies.

3.452 *began to chant*: The verb for chanting, *oluluzo,* suggests a ritual loud cry, usually performed by women on occasions of prayer, thanksgiving, triumph, or, more rarely, lamentation.

3.452–54 *The men / hoisted the body, and Pisistratus / sliced through her throat*: The animal had to be held up, facing the gods, while its neck was slit; the blood would then be collected in the designated bowl.

3.456–57 *covered them / with double fat and placed raw flesh upon them*: The thighbones were presented to the god, covered with a double layer of fat, and then with little pieces of the rest of the raw carcass on top.

BOOK 4 SUMMARY

Telemachus and Pisistratus find Menelaus and Helen in their rich home at Sparta, in the midst of a lavish celebration of the marriages of Menelaus' two children. They are welcomed warmly; Menelaus tells the story of his long journey back from Troy, expressing grief for those who died and were lost—especially, his brother Agamemnon and his dear friend Odysseus. Telemachus starts crying. Helen appears and identifies Telemachus; Pisistratus explains the reason for their visit. Everyone weeps about the absence of Odysseus, but Pisistratus intervenes and Helen pours a magical drug into the wine to remove all capacity for grief. She describes how Odysseus at Troy disguised himself and snuck through the city on a spy mission; Menelaus tells how determined he was inside the Wooden Horse. They all go to sleep. In the morning, Menelaus tells the story of how, on his way back from Troy, he stopped and accrued wealth in Egypt, and then met and temporarily captured Proteus, the old sea god, who gave him some news of his fellow warriors, such as the murdered Agamemnon. Menelaus offers Telemachus fine gifts to take home. Meanwhile, on Ithaca, the suitors discover about the boy's trip and plot to kill Telemachus on his return journey. Penelope also finds out and is full of grief. The suitors set up the ambush. Athena sends a dream phantom to comfort Penelope.

4.187–88 *irreplaceable Antilochus, / killed by the noble son of shining Dawn*: Antilochus was a son of Nestor (so brother to Pisistratus), killed at Troy by Memnon, son of the Dawn Goddess.

4.232 *They are the Healer's people*: The Healer, Paieon, is the doctor to the gods. He was later identified with Apollo.

4.276 *Godlike Deiphobus was following you*: There was a legend that Helen married Deiphobus, another son of Priam, after the death of Paris. Some scholars (now and in antiquity) believe that this line was a later interpolation, put in as a reference to this legend. But others argue that the line does not imply that Helen was married to Deiphobus; it simply explains why Helen's behavior is dangerous: a Trojan witnesses it and therefore the whole Wooden Horse plan is threatened.

4.402–3 *the daughters / of lovely Lady Brine*: The obscure word *halosudne*, translated here as "Lady Brine," suggests something like "daughter of the salty sea" or "female saltwater person"; it is elsewhere an epithet of Thetis, mother of Achilles, but here seems to imply a different sea goddess.

4.499 *Ajax was drowned*: The Ajax referred to here is Locrian Ajax, also known as Lesser Ajax—not the hero known for his shield and skill in defensive warfare. He had raped Cassandra, the prophet daughter of Priam, in the temple of Athena. Outraged, Athena asked Poseidon to take revenge.

4.516–17 *where all farms / are finished*: This suggests that there are lands beyond the limits of agriculture and, hence, beyond civilized culture.

BOOK 5 SUMMARY

Zeus and Athena again discuss the fate of Odysseus; Zeus sends Athena to protect Telemachus, and Hermes to rescue Odysseus from Calypso. Hermes tells Calypso to let Odysseus go; reluctantly, she agrees. Odysseus constructs a raft and almost reaches Phaeacia, when Poseidon spots him and sends a storm to wreck the raft. Odysseus is helped by Ino, the White Goddess. He clings to a plank from the broken raft, and then swims towards shore. With the aid of Athena, he finds a good place to rest, in a gentle river's mouth. He crawls out of the water, hides in some bushes, and goes to sleep.

5.75 *the deathless god who once killed Argos*: One of the standard epithets for Hermes, *argeiphontes*, may suggest "killer of Argos" (a giant with a hundred eyes who was employed by Hera to guard Io, one of her husband Zeus' girlfriends. Hermes was employed by Zeus to kill the spy). However, it has also been interpreted to mean "shining" or associated with the god's masterly ability to appear and disappear at will.

5.108 *they wronged Athena*: At the time of the sack of Troy, the Lesser Ajax's rape of Cassandra in the temple of Athena caused the goddess to be enraged against the Greeks (whom she originally favored). Athena's anger is one of the reasons that the Greek army had such a difficult time getting home.

5.256–57 *He heaped the boat with brush . . . to keep the water out*: The construction of Odysseus' boat has been much discussed by scholars. The poet seems to be limited by the fact that most epic descriptions of boatbuilding deal with the construction of large ships (like the *Argo*), not one-man rafts. Ancient ships were generally built starting with the innards, the keel, the stem, and the sternpost, with ribs added on after—a reverse of the modern practice. The brush is apparently heaped in the bottom of the boat to protect the cargo from the bilgewater. It is unclear how wicker could do anything to keep out leaks.

5.274 *the only star that has no share of Ocean*: The idea is that the Plow (the Big Dipper) is the only constellation that stays above the horizon all year round. This is not true in astronomical fact; other constellations also remain visible year round.

5.289 *the rope of pain that binds him*: *Peirar,* the word translated here as "rope," can have literal meanings ("binding" or "rope") and metaphorical ones ("end," "completion," "boundary").

5.311 *Peleus' son*: The reference is to Achilles.

5.340 *create an odyssey of pain for you?*: The original uses a verb that puns on our hero's name: *odysat',* which means "he hated" or "he was angry at."

5.422 *famous Amphitrite*: See the note to 3.91.

5.435 *A mighty wave rolled over him again*: The verb in the original—rendered here as "rolled over," but more literally "covered"—is *kalypsen*, an important term in this book since it is cognate with Calypso's name.

5.477–78 *two bushes grown together, / of olive and thorn*: The species of the first bush may be wild olive, fig, or evergreen thorn. The olive wood is, as ever, significant in that it is Athena's tree: the goddess is still watching over her hero.

5.491–92 *So was Odysseus concealed in leaves. / Athena poured down sleep to shut his eyes*: The Greek words translated here as "covered" (*kalypsato*) and "shut" (*amphikalypsas*) are again cognate with Calypso's name.

BOOK 6 SUMMARY

Athena appears in a dream to the Phaeacian princess Nausicaa and tells her to go to the washing pools and do laundry, in preparation for her putative future marriage. Nausicaa sets out on this trip with a packed lunch, a wagon full of dirty laundry, and some helpful slave girls. After laundry and lunch, the girls are playing ball and start screaming when the ball is lost. Odysseus pops up from his hiding place and appeals for help to Nausicaa. She gives him a set of clothes, and provides instructions about how to get into town and to her parents' palace, keeping behind her so as to evade the criticism or suspicion of the people. Odysseus waits in Athena's sanctuary outside the town and prays for the help of the goddess.

6.293 *his orchard and estate*: The "estate," *temenos*, is land set apart for a king or a temple precinct.

BOOK 7 SUMMARY

Nausicaa gets home. Odysseus walks to town; Athena hides him in magic mist, and then, as a little girl, guides him to the palace. He supplicates Arete, the queen. Alcinous, the king, welcomes him warmly and gives him food and wine. Arete notices that Odysseus is wearing clothes that she made herself. Odysseus explains that Nausicaa gave them to him. Odysseus is offered a comfortable bed out on the porch, where he goes to sleep for the night.

7.53 *First greet the queen*: The prominence of Queen Arete in this account is puzzling, especially since when Odysseus reaches the palace, the queen makes no response to his appeal.

7.54 *Arete is her name*: The name suggests "Prayed For" or "Wanted."

7.81 *Erechtheus' palace*: Erechtheus was a legendary king of Athens.

7.108 *oil was dripping from the woven fabric*: The oil may be from the fabric itself if it is wool, or perhaps the women are applying olive oil to the material to make the weaving easier.

7.198 *the heavy ones, the Spinners*: The Spinners (*Klothes*) are imagined in Greek mythology as three old female figures who construct the thread of human destiny—associated here with Fate (*Aisa*), the "share" allotted to humans in life.

7.323–24 *they carried fair-haired Rhadamanthus / to visit Tityus, the son of Gaia*: Rhadamanthus is the mythical son of Zeus and Europa, closely associated with Crete; Tityus is a Titan, one of the generation before the Olympian gods; and Gaia is the original Earth Goddess. The story of Rhadamanthus' visit to Tityus is entirely unknown beyond this passage.

BOOK 8 SUMMARY

At the Phaeacian council place, Alcinous invites the lords of Phaecia to his palace for a feast to welcome the stranger. He orders men to equip a ship, to help the visitor on his way. Everyone assembles and eats; after the meal, Demodocus the blind poet sings about a quarrel of Odysseus and Achilles. Odysseus starts crying.

Alcinous, noticing, suggests that everybody go outside and play sports. There are competitions in sprinting, wrestling, discus, and boxing. Then Laodamas, Alcinous' youngest son, invites Odysseus to participate; another son, Euryalus, taunts Odysseus that he is no athlete. Odysseus hurls a discus far beyond the others and is congratulated by Athena in disguise. Demodocus sings a second, longer song, about the adulterous affair of Aphrodite and Ares; Odysseus is pleased. The Phaeacians give Odysseus lavish gifts, bathe him, and feed him. He asks Demodocus to sing the song of the Wooden Horse; when the poet complies, Odysseus weeps desperately. Alcinous notices and asks Odysseus to explain who he is.

8.52–53 *tying / each to its leather thole-strap*: Tholes are pins set in the side of a boat to keep the oar in place.

8.81–83 *Apollo had foretold . . . through the plans of Zeus*: Apparently the Delphic oracle (Pytho) told Agamemnon that Troy would be destroyed when the "best of the Achaeans" were quarreling.

8.108–14 *Many young athletes stood there . . . Naubolus' son*: These names are all invented to suggest the Phaeacians' skill in seafaring: Acroneüs = "Topship," Ocyalus = "Sharpsea," Elatreus = "Driver," Nauteus = "Shipman," Thoön = "Quick," Anchialus = "Seaside," Eretmeus = "Oarsman," Anabesineus = "Embarker," Ponteus = "Deep-Sea," Prymneus = "Sternman," Proreus = "Prowman," Amphialus = "Sea-Girt," Polynaus = "Many-Shipped," Tecton = "Shipwright," Naubolus = "Ship-Launcher," and Euryalus = "Wide-Sea."

8.124–25 *the length / of a field plowed by mules*: The length-across area of land that could be plowed in a day was a standard unit of measurement. The distance imagined here is probably about two hundred feet (an unlikely margin for a race).

8.518 *to find Deiphobus' house*: After Paris was killed, Helen was appropriated by Deiphobus, another Trojan prince; Odysseus killed him and mangled his corpse, and Menelaus reclaimed his wife.

BOOK 9 SUMMARY

Odysseus begins to tell his story. He tells how, after sacking Troy, he and his fleet were blown off course. They reached the land of the Cicones, where they sacked the city, killed the men, and enslaved the women as concubines. Odysseus' party remained on the shore, drinking; the Cicones retaliated, and some of Odysseus' men were killed. Another storm struck the fleet, and the ships reached the land of the Lotus-Eaters, who tempted some of the men to eat the lotus fruit and forget all thoughts of home. Odysseus ordered the whole crew back on board. They reached the island of the Cyclopes, where they found a cave inhabited by a large, solitary shepherd, named Polyphemus. Odysseus left most of his crew with the ships, taking twelve men and a sack of special wine with him to visit the native inhabitant. Finding him absent, they broke into the cave; the men tried to persuade Odysseus to steal Polyphemus' cheese and animals and then make a quick escape. Odysseus insisted on staying. When the Cyclops came home, Odysseus demanded a gift; Polyphemus refused and ate two of the men; he then went to sleep. The door-stone of the cave was too heavy for the men to move, so they were trapped inside. Next morning, Polyphemus ate two more men, and then set out for pasture with his flock. Odysseus prepared a sharp olive wood stake to blind Polyphemus. When the Cyclops returned, he ate two more men; Odysseus then offered him some wine. He drank too much. Odysseus claimed his name is "Noman." When the Cyclops passed out, Odysseus and his men shoved the stake into his eye. Polyphemus called for help, but no one came, because he said that "No man" has hurt him. Next morning, the blinded Cyclops opened the door-stone, counting the sheep and goats as he let them out to pasture. Odysseus and his men escaped by clinging to the animals' bellies. As they sailed away, Odysseus shouted back to taunt Polyphemus and revealed his true name. Polyphemus hurled a huge rock that almost destroyed the ship and called on his father Poseidon to curse Odysseus.

9.27–28 *my Ithaca is set apart, most distant, / facing the dark*: The suggestion is that Ithaca is farthest west, facing the setting sun ("the darkness"), whereas the other islands are more east. It is impossible to reconcile this claim with actual geography.

9.41 *the Cicones in Ismarus.*: The Cicones, a Thracian people, were allies of Troy. But the passage does not suggest that Odysseus' piracy is motivated by any particular military objective.

9.125 *red-cheeked ships*: Ships were decorated with red at the prow.

9.298 *unmixed milk*: The word for "unmixed" is generally used for wine undiluted with water. The text is making a sort of joke since milk is the equivalent of wine for this mostly teetotal character.

9.302 *feeling for his liver*: Odysseus imagines having to move by feel, since the cave is entirely dark.

9.349 *a holy offering*: The term used here is usually applied to drink offerings given to the gods.

9.414 *the "no man" maneuver*: There is a pun here in the Greek: *metis* means "nobody" but also "cunning." "Maneuver" is designed to hint at the wordplay.

BOOK 10 SUMMARY

The fleet reached the floating island of Aeolus, guardian of the winds, who gave Odysseus a bag containing multiple winds as a gift to help him on his way. The fleet almost reached Ithaca, but Odysseus fell asleep at the rudder. The men, jealous that Odysseus was acquiring all the treasure on the trip and sharing none of it, opened the bag of winds, and the ship was blasted back to Aeolus' palace, from which they are then sent harshly away. They reached the land of Laestrygonia, and all the men except Odysseus moored inside the harbor. The inhabitants turned out to be cannibal giants, who skewered all those in the harbor and ate them. The lone remaining ship sailed to the land of Circe, who turned half of Odysseus' men into pigs. With the help of Hermes, Odysseus managed to persuade Circe to turn them back into human form. They all stayed with Circe for a year, recuperating. Then Odysseus asked Circe to help them on their way, but she told him they must first visit the house of Hades and consult the dead spirit of the prophet Tiresias, who would advise him about his journey. Before they left, the youngest crew member, Elpenor, fell from the attic in Circe's house and died.

10.82 *Lamos*: Lamos is apparently the founder of this mythical place.

10.83–84 *A herdsman there . . . another herdsman going out*: The idea is that in this strange country, herdsmen work around the clock, a day shift and a night shift.

10.87 *the paths of day and night are close together*: This odd phrase presumably means that the nights are almost nonexistent here, as in areas near the Arctic Circle during the summer. Attempts to plot Laestrygonia on a real map have not been convincing; this is a fictional place, melding several elements of actual geography.

10.178–79 *and took / their cloaks down from their faces*: People in Homer cover their faces in grief; the men in this small band of survivors have been grieving at the loss of the other eleven ships and their crew members.

10.236 *Pramnian wine*: Apparently, a particular type of wine rather than from a particular location; it is described as black and harsh by the medical writer Galen. The same wine is used for the potion made in Nestor's cup in *Iliad* Book 11.

10.304 *this plant Moly*: Moly is probably an imaginary plant, although the legend may be connected to the ancient idea that garlic (which also has a white flower and dark root) can be used against bad spirits and vampires.

10.518 *a cubit wide and long*: A cubit is a unit of measure roughly equivalent to a human forearm.

10.520 *honey-mix*: A mixture of honey with some other substance, perhaps milk.

BOOK 11 SUMMARY

They reached the dark land of the Cimmerians, and Odysseus performed a sacrifice, praying to reach his homeland. He dug a ditch and filled it with blood; the spirits of the dead appeared. First was Elpenor, who asked for proper burial. Next came the spirit of Anticleia, Odysseus' mother; but Odysseus spoke first to the prophet Tiresias, who foretold many dangers ahead. Odysseus spoke to his mother, wept for her death, and tried to embrace her, but she slipped away. Then came a parade of famous mythical women, all associated with even more famous male heroes and gods. Odysseus pauses his story, but Alcinous begs him to continue. He tells of meeting the ghost of Agamemnon, who told him how he was murdered, and the ghost of Achilles, who regretted trading his life for honor. The ghost of Ajax refused to speak to Odysseus. After glimpsing other male heroes, seeing the torments of the dead, and speaking to Heracles, Odysseus returned to his ship.

11.85 *Autolycus' daughter Anticleia*: The name of Odysseus' maternal grandfather, Autolycus, suggests "Wolf Man."

11.172–73 *Or did the archer Artemis destroy you / with gentle arrows?*: Artemis, goddess of hunting and childbirth, was particularly associated with the deaths of women.

11.297–98 *Iphicles set him free as his reward / for prophecy*: The story goes that the prophet Melampus, after an unsuccessful attempt to drive off Iphicles' cattle and win his daughter's hand, prophesied that Iphicles, who had been impotent, would be able to have more children. In reward for the good prophecy, Iphicles set Melampus free. For a different version of the story, see the note to 15.227–28.

11.304–5 *They live and die alternately, and they / are honored like the gods*: Castor and Polydeuces (also known as Pollux), the twins associated with the constellation Gemini, were given by Zeus the privilege of being alive on every other day, taking turns. According to many versions of the myth, Zeus was actually their father, having seduced Leda in the guise of a swan (so that the twins are brothers of Helen and Clytemnestra).

11.322–23 *Then I saw Phaedra, Procris . . . dangerous Minos*: Phaedra was the elder daughter of Minos, the legendary king of Crete; she married Theseus of Athens and fell in love with his son, her stepson, with disastrous results. Procris was the daughter of Erechtheus, another king of Athens; she was killed unintentionally by her husband, Cephalus.

11.326–27 *Artemis killed her on the isle of Día, / when Dionysus spoke against her*: Ariadne, another daughter of King Minos of Crete, helped Theseus through the Cretan labyrinth to kill her half brother, the Minotaur, and was taken off with Theseus on his ship. In later versions of the legend, Theseus abandoned her, and she was then whisked away by Dionysus. This Homeric version implies that she somehow offended Dionysus—it is unclear how, and this story is otherwise unknown.

11.329 *accepting golden bribes, she killed her husband*: Eriphyle accepted the bribe of a gold necklace to persuade her husband, Amphiaraus, king of Argos, to go on a doomed raid against Thebes.

11.522 *since Priam bribed his mother*: After the death of Achilles, Priam bribed Eurypylus' mother to persuade her son to fight for the Trojans.

11.544–46 *I won / Achilles' armor, when the case was judged / beside the ships*: Achilles' mother, the Sea Goddess Thetis, gave him armor crafted by the god Hephaestus. After Achilles' death, the Greeks held a meeting beside their ships to judge which other hero should get the divine armor. Ajax hoped to win, but the judgment went in Odysseus' favor, and Ajax killed himself. According to some versions of the myth, Ajax was first driven mad by Athena (a story used in Sophocles' *Ajax*).

11.573 *I saw great Orion*: Mythical hunter, who was turned into the constellation Orion.

11.577 *Tityus, the son of Gaia*: See note for 7.723–24.

11.600–602 *I saw a phantom of great Heracles. / The man himself is . . . with fine-ankled Hebe*: Heracles, a son of Zeus, was supposed to have been rewarded after all his Labors with a place among the Olympian gods. The confusing suggestion that his phantom is with the dead, while his real self is with the gods, may be a reflection of various views about whether or not Heracles really was apotheosized.

BOOK 12 SUMMARY

Back on Circe's island, they held a funeral for Elpenor. Circe gave Odysseus advice about his route. They sailed past the Sirens; Odysseus, tied to the mast, was the only one who heard their song. They reached the six-headed Scylla and the whirlpool Charybdis; Scylla devoured six men. They were marooned on the island of Helius, the Sun God, and the men were half starved; while Odysseus napped, they killed the forbidden cattle and ate them. When they left, Zeus wrecked the ship and all the men drowned. Odysseus, the sole survivor, was swept back; he clung to a fig tree above the whirlpool Charybdis, then jumped into the water, clutched a broken ship's timber, and managed to row out of the way of Scylla. After ten days of drifting, he reached the island of Calypso; and so the story of the wanderings comes full circle.

12.65–66 *Zeus must send another to restore / the number of the flock*: There may be an obscure reference here to the legend of a lost Pleiad. The Pleiades were seven sisters who were hunted by Orion and turned first into doves and then into stars.

12.70–71 *Only the famous Argo sailed through there / returning from the visit with Aeetes*: The Greek hero Jason sailed in the *Argo* to get the Golden Fleece from King Aeetes of Colchis. The journey of Jason and the Argonauts was supposed to have taken place a generation before the wanderings of Odysseus. Jason was the favorite of the goddess Hera.

12.125 *Cratais*: The name means "mighty force."

12.133 *Phaethousa and Lampetia*: The names literally mean "shining."

12.251–52 *long rod and line set round with oxhorn / to trick the little fishes with his bait*: The technology implied by the reference to oxhorn is unclear, but probably a tube of hollow oxhorn was used to protect the line above the hook (perhaps to stop fish biting through the line when they took the bait).

12.357 *on the ship there was no barley*: Barley is a component of a ritual sacrifice.

BOOK 13 SUMMARY

The Phaeacians give Odysseus a rich array of gifts and put him on a magical self-steering ship, equipped with talented rowers, to go back to Ithaca; he falls asleep on the journey and they lay him, still asleep, on the shore of his homeland, beside the cave of the Nymphs. When the ship approaches Phaeacia, Poseidon wrecks it, turns it to stone, and threatens to cover the country with a mountain. Odysseus wakes up and, because Athena has disguised the island, does not recognize Ithaca. She approaches, in the guise of a young man, reveals that they are in Ithaca, and questions Odysseus. He pretends to come from Crete. She praises his caution and capacity for deceit, expresses her love for him, and reveals the truth. They hide the treasure in the cave, and form plans about how to kill the suitors. Athena disguises Odysseus as an old beggar, and then goes to fetch Telemachus from Sparta.

13.144 *an elder so high-ranking*: There are different traditions about whether Zeus or Poseidon was the elder brother. The text here might suggest that Poseidon is the older, or only that he is one of the older generation of Olympian gods (in contrast to relative newcomers like Aphrodite and Dionysus).

13.150–54 *But now . . . I want / to smash it in the sea . . . to prevent them / from ever guiding travelers again*: It is unclear whether Poseidon is threatening to wipe out the whole Phaeacian people, by crushing them, or simply intends to block their way out to the open sea, by surrounding the city and its harbor with a mountain. It is also unclear what actually happens to the Phaeacians.

BOOK 14 SUMMARY

In his disguise, Odysseus visits Eumaeus, the swineherd. The guard dogs set on the visitor, but Eumaeus rescues him and welcomes him into his humble abode. Eumaeus expresses his loyalty to his master and grief for his supposed death; Odysseus predicts the return of Odysseus. He tells a convoluted false story about his history, saying he came from Crete, stayed in Egypt, was tricked by a Phoenician, shipwrecked, landed in Thesprotia (where he heard about Odysseus), was again tricked and enslaved, landed on Ithaca with the slave ship, and eventually escaped from the traffickers, ending up in Eumaeus' hut. Eumaeus responds that he does not believe Odysseus is en route; he explains his skepticism of tricksters. They eat, then Odysseus tells a story about Odysseus tricking one of his men into giving him a cloak. Eumaeus gives him a cloak as a reward for a good story. They go to sleep—Odysseus in the hut, and Eumaeus out with the pigs.

14.182 *Arcesius' line*: Arcesius was the father of Laertes; he may have been more prominent in earlier versions of the myth.

14.328–30 *Odysseus . . . had gone off / to Dodona, to ask the holy oak / what Zeus intended*: Dodona in Epirus was the seat of the most ancient oracle of Zeus. A holy oak there was supposed to deliver the god's voice, perhaps through rustling leaves.

14.337 *Thesprotians*: A Greek tribe with a friendly relationship to the Ithacans.

14.378 *Aetolian*: Aetolians were a Greek tribe living on the north coast of the Gulf of Corinth, a mountainous region; they were reputed to be a wild or primitive people.

14.453 *Taphians*: See note to 1.105.

BOOK 15 SUMMARY

Athena urges Telemachus to set out for home. Menelaus and Helen send Telemachus and Pisistratus off with ample gifts. Telemachus explains to his companion that he will not accompany him back to his father Nestor's house; instead, Telemachus sets off for Ithaca by ship. While boarding, he meets Theoclymenus, who is in exile for murder and is exceptionally skilled at prophecy. Meanwhile, in the swineherd's cottage, Eumaeus urges Odysseus to stay with him rather than go into town to beg. He shares news of Odysseus' parents and tells the story of how he himself, born into a king's family, was enslaved as a little child, bought by Laertes, and raised by Anticleia alongside Odysseus' own sister. Telemachus approaches Ithaca and receives a promising sign. He sends Theoclymenus to stay with Piraeus, who had sailed home with him.

15.227–28 *Melampus, who once lived in Pylos, land / of sheep*: The story told here elliptically is that Melampus, a famous prophet who was the great-grandfather of Theoclymenus, lived in Pylos, and his brother fell in love with the daughter of Neleus, Pero. Neleus demanded the herds of Phylacus as the bride-price; Melampus tried to steal them for his brother, but he was imprisoned by Phylacus. He noticed that worms were eating the wooden beams of his prison, and foretold their fall. Phylacus, impressed at his prophetic talent, released him; he brought the herds to Neleus, won Pero for his brother, and moved to Argos. For another version of the story, see the note to 11.297–98.

15.248–49 *he was killed at Thebes, / because his wife took bribes*: The mythical Theban War was initiated by the two sons of Oedipus, Polyneices and Eteocles, over control of the city. Eriphyle, wife of Amphiaraus, was bribed with a gold necklace by Polyneices to persuade Amphiaraeus to join his army, although he was doomed to die if he did so.

15.299 *Needle Islands*: It is unclear which islands are meant, and the epithet translated as "Needle" is mysterious—it could suggest "sharp" or "swift," an odd term for islands.

15.405–6 *Syria, where the sun turns round, above / Ortygia*: The concept is that the sun, like a competitor in a Greek race, turns round on its course when it reaches the farthest point—presumably towards the west. The place-names here do not seem to correspond to any real geography.

BOOK 16 SUMMARY

Telemachus arrives at Eumaeus' hut and is greeted warmly by the swineherd, who introduces him to the "stranger." Telemachus sends Eumaeus to take news of his arrival to Penelope. Athena transforms Odysseus, so he looks young and strong again; he tells the startled Telemachus who he really is. After weeping together, they start making plans for how to kill the suitors. Odysseus tells Telemachus he must hide almost all the weapons, so that the suitors will be unarmed, and must keep his father's identity secret, even from Laertes and Penelope. Telemachus explains how many suitors there are and proposes a slight modification of Odysseus' plan. Meanwhile, news reaches the palace that Telemachus has come back safe. The suitors are angry at the foiling of their plan to murder him, but continue to scheme. Amphinomus speaks against killing the boy. Penelope speaks out against the suitors, then goes upstairs. Eumaeus returns to his cottage, telling Telemachus and Odysseus that the suitors have returned from their failed attempt at ambush. They eat and sleep.

BOOK 17 SUMMARY

Telemachus heads out, telling Eumaeus that the stranger will have to go begging his way. When the boy reaches home, Eurycleia greets him warmly, as does a tearful Penelope. Piraeus brings Theoclymenus to the palace; Telemachus invites him in as a guest. Penelope questions Telemachus about his trip. Theoclymenus intervenes to report the promising sign. Eumaeus and Odysseus set out towards the town center. At the fountain they meet the goatherd Melanthius, who insults them and kicks Odysseus. Eumaeus prays for revenge. Melanthius returns to the palace and eats. Argos, the old dog left behind by Odysseus as a puppy twenty years earlier, recognizes his master and then dies. Odysseus enters his own home as a beggar. Telemachus gives him food and tells him to beg from all the suitors. They each give him scraps, except Antinous, who hurls a footstool at him. Odysseus curses him, and the others reproach Antinous. Telemachus sneezes. Penelope invites the supposed beggar to talk to her, promising him new clothes if he tells her the truth about any news he has of Odysseus. Odysseus puts off the conversation.

BOOK 18 SUMMARY

Odysseus, still in his guise as a beggar, encounters a real beggar, Irus, at the palace, who taunts him. Challenged by the suitors, they fight, and Odysseus wins; the suitors reward him with a meal. Odysseus tells Amphinomus, a kind suitor, a false autobiographical story of which the moral is that the suitors will be punished when Odysseus comes back: "there will be blood." Amphinomus almost heeds the warning, but Athena makes him stay in the palace to die. Penelope is inspired by Athena to show herself in her full beauty to the suitors; she comes downstairs and reproaches Telemachus for his treatment of the beggar, and declares that she must soon marry one of the suitors. Odysseus is glad and the suitors give her gifts. The slave woman Melantho taunts Odysseus, who responds aggressively. Eurymachus taunts him and hurls a footstool at him. The suitors have a final drink, then go off to their homes.

18.7 *Irus, because he was their messenger*: An allusion to Iris, the messenger and rainbow goddess. The name also seems to be related to the word *hieros*, meaning "holy" or "strong."

18.74 *the end of Irus—brought upon himself!*: Literally, he will be "not-Irus," with an allusion to the name's link with the word for "strong."

18.117 *Odysseus was thrilled to hear this omen*: This omen—an utterance that has resonance for the future undetected by the speaker—is presumably the suitors' wish for Odysseus to get his heart's desire. They do not know that his desire is to kill them.

18.164 *so her son and husband would respect her*: This passage has been much discussed since antiquity. It can be read as hinting that Penelope has secretly recognized Odysseus already, or as reflecting an earlier version of the story, in which her recognition might have happened earlier. Alternatively, and perhaps more likely, it is Athena, not Penelope herself, who wants to make Odysseus and Telemachus honor Penelope more. Whichever view one takes, the ambiguity is important in itself: we are reminded that we do not fully understand what is happening in Penelope's head. Similarly, her mysterious laugh is open to multiple interpretations—suggesting her confidence in her own powers, or her discomfort at her own impulses.

BOOK 19 SUMMARY

Athena makes a magic light shine in the hall. Odysseus sends Telemachus to bed and lurks downstairs. Melantho is rude to him; Penelope scolds her. Penelope tells Odysseus about her weaving trick, which held the suitors at bay for a while. Odysseus tells her a false autobiographical story, claiming to come from Crete and to know Odysseus. She weeps. Odysseus promises that Odysseus will be home within the month. Penelope offers him a nice bed with clean sheets; he refuses, saying he is used to sleeping rough, but he is willing to let an old slave women wash his feet. Eurycleia, the old nurse, washes Odysseus, finds the scar on his leg from an old hunting wound, and recognizes him. He got the scar on a trip to his grandfather Autolycus, who named him as a baby. Odysseus makes Eurycleia keep the secret of his identity. Penelope tells Odysseus of her suffering and also of her dream about the geese killed by an eagle. Odysseus is glad. Penelope explains her plan tomorrow to set up the contest of the bow and the axes; the winner will gain her hand.

19.26 *This stranger will*: Eurycleia's question implies an assumption that carrying the light is the job of a woman, a female slave; there is a momentary surprise that the answer is a man.

19.108 *My good woman*: With heavy dramatic irony, Odysseus addresses Penelope with a word that means both "woman" and "wife"—both here and throughout the book. The word can be understood by Penelope as simply a form of address (like "Madam"), but the text allows us to read it in the other sense as well.

19.179–80 *Minos . . . was king / for nine years*: The original could also mean "nine-year-old Minos." There are various theories about what the line means. Some have theorized, speculatively, that the Cretan kingship may have been held for nine years, after which the king was killed and a new one took his place.

19.183–84 *My name / is Aethon*: The name "Aethon" can suggest either "shining" or "brown." It may suggest foxy tricks, since the word is applied to the reddish color of the fox in Pindar (*Olympian* 11.19).

19.190–91 *Amnisus, beside the cave / of Eileithyia*: Amnisus is the port of Knossos in Crete. Eileithyia is a goddess associated with childbirth.

19.206–8 *the snow that Zephyr / scatters across the mountain peaks; then Eurus / thaws it*: Zephyr is the West Wind, Eurus the East. The West Wind is imagined to bring the snow that is melted by the East Wind of springtime.

19.258–59 *Evilium— / the town I will not name*: Penelope coins a compound word suggesting "Bad Troy" (*Kakoïlion*; Troy = Ilium).

19.274–75 *Helius / and Zeus despised Odysseus*: The verb here, *odussomai*, is the same one associated with the name Odysseus elsewhere in the poem (1.63). It means "to be angry at [somebody]" or "to hate," and it is a cognate with a noun for "pain" (*odune*). See also the note to 19.408.

19.356–57 *wash your master's / age-mate*: The original also has a temporary ambiguity (suggested here by enjambment), where the reader or listener may wonder if Penelope has already recognized her husband and may be about to say, "Your master's . . . feet."

19.408 *I dislike them back*: Autolycus uses the same verb *odussomai* as in 19.274, which sounds like the name "Odysseus" and can mean either "I am angry at" or "I am the cause of anger (in others)." See also the note to 1.63.

19.520 *the daughter of Pandareus*: This is the earliest instance of the myth of the nightingale, most influentially retold by Ovid. In this version, Aedon, daughter of Pandareus, king of Crete, married Zethus, king of Thebes, and tried to kill one of the children of her sister-in-law, Niobe, in a fit of jealousy. By mistake, she killed her own son, Itylus (called Itys in other versions of the myth). She was turned into a nightingale, whose song is supposed to be a constant lament for the dead boy.

BOOK 20 SUMMARY

Odysseus lies at the entrance of the palace and is aware of slave women slipping out to meet the suitors. He is enraged, but Athena calms him, promising to protect him and his interests. Penelope weeps and prays. Odysseus hears his wife weeping as he wakes up. He prays and hears a slave praying for an end to the suitors' banquets. Telemachus wakes and worries that his mother has failed to treat his father properly; Eurycleia reassures him. Under her supervision, the slaves prepare the house for a special feast day. Melanthius the goatherd appears and insults Odysseus. Another herdsman, Philoetius, arrives and speaks politely to Odysseus. Philoetius and Eumaeus both swear their loyalty to their master. The suitors reconsider the plan to kill Telemachus, following the advice of Amphinomus. Telemachus helps Odysseus to food and warns the suitors not to abuse him. One of them, Ctesippus, hurls an ox-foot at Odysseus. Telemachus speaks out against their behavior. Athena makes the suitors laugh unstoppably; after the prophet Theoclymenus foretells their death, he leaves the house. The suitors tease Telemachus, who does not react; he and Odysseus wait for their moment.

20.19–20 *You were / hounded by worse*: The original conveys that Odysseus' heart has suffered "something more doglike" before. The Greek word for "doglike" usually suggests shame or shamelessness.

20.53 *distance yourself, Odysseus, from trouble*: The word used in the original for "distance yourself" (more literally, "rise up out of") sounds somewhat like the name Odysseus.

20.65–66 *where the waters of the Ocean / pour forth and back again*: See note to 3.1.

20.66–67 *the breezes / took up the daughters of Pandareus*: According to later sources, Pandareus stole a golden dog made by Hephaestus from a temple of Zeus; the gods punished him, his wife, and his daughters. The story told in Book 19, that a daughter of Pandareus killed her son by accident and was turned into a nightingale, has been seen by some scholars as contradicting this passage. But the passage does not say that all the daughters were swept away by the winds. There are no other sources for this story.

20.211 *Cephallenia:* Cephallenia is apparently the name of Ithaca and all the other towns under the dominion of the Ithacan king. It is not, in this text, identical with the modern Ionian island of Cephalonia.

20.243 *an eagle flew high on their left*: The left side is unlucky.

20.275 *one hundred animals*: A hecatomb—a ritual sacrifice of one hundred animals—may be understood as the sacrifice of a large number, not necessarily literally one hundred. But some scholars have traced a connection between the hundred animals and the roughly one hundred suitors (108 is the usual count), who are also soon to be killed. There was an ancient festival to Apollo, the Hecatombia, which may be referred to here; the festival may have been associated, like the return of Odysseus, with the new moon.

BOOK 21 SUMMARY

Penelope takes the storeroom key and fetches Odysseus' bow; her slaves bring the axes. Telemachus tries the bow first and fails to string it; Odysseus makes him stop trying. Leodes, the suitors' prophet, tries and fails. Antinous sneers, and asks Melanthius to light a fire and bring some fat, to grease the bow. Even so, they fail to string the bow; only Antinous and Eurymachus have still not tried it when they stop. Meanwhile, Odysseus reveals himself to Eumaeus and Philoetius. Eurymachus fails to string the bow. Antinous uses the excuse of the feast day to Apollo (god of archery) to put off the contest. Odysseus suggests that, while waiting for the real contest the next day, they should let him try the bow. Antinous and Eurymachus speak against allowing it; Penelope speaks up for the beggar; Telemachus scolds her and sends her upstairs. Eumaeus gives Odysseus the bow. Eurycleia locks up the women in their quarters; Philoetius secures the gate of the house. Odysseus effortlessly strings the bow and shoots through all the axes.

21.16 *in Lacedaemon, in Messenia*: Lacedaemon, also known as Laconica, is the region around Sparta; Messenia is an area within that region.

21.46 *with true aim, thrust back the fastenings*: The door seems to be fastened with a leather thong attached to a bolt, which is tied to a hook on the outside when not in use; the key is used to open the door from the outside. The key is presumably a kind of large bronze hook, not serrated in a specific pattern like a modern key.

21.73–74 *shoot through all / twelve axes*: The mechanics of the axe competition are unclear, but it seems most likely that these are axe heads, without handles, and with round, drilled holes in the end through which the wooden handle could be inserted. The axe heads are lined up, with the holes all aligned straight. The goal of the contest is to shoot an arrow through all of the holes. Scholars debate whether the contest takes place inside the feast hall or in the courtyard outside. It seems most likely that it is inside, with the axes resting on a pile of earth, and perhaps also on some kind of platform, to reduce the danger of spectators being shot.

21.121 *trod the earth down flat*: If the contest is taking place in the feast hall—which has a finished floor, not dirt—the earth seems to be brought in and heaped up to provide a base for the axes.

21.144 *Leodes, their holy man*: The holy man is literally a man who performs sacrifices. However, the job description is somewhat fluid, and he also serves as a prophet or diviner.

21.153–55 *This bow will take away / courage, life-force, and energy from many / noble young men:* Leodes speaks in prophetic language, perhaps unconsciously. His words could suggest only that the attempt to string the bow will discourage those who fail in the attempt; but they can also mean that the bow will kill many men.

21.296 *Wine even turned the famous Centaur's head*: The passage refers to the famous drunken brawl between the Lapiths, a Thessalian tribe, and the Centaurs, a wild mountain-dwelling people, later imagined as half-human and half-horse.

21.352–53 *The bow is work for men, especially me. / I am the one with power in this house*: These two lines echo the words of Hector to Andromache in Book 6 of *The Iliad*: "War is a job for men, especially me."

21.392 *byblos*: A fiber from the papyrus plant, imported to Greece from Egypt and known for its strength.

21.403–5 *"I hope / his future luck will match how well he does / in stringing it!"*: Dramatic irony: the suitor assumes he will fail in the bow stringing and hopes his life will continue badly thereafter.

21.417 *double-dealing Cronus*: Cronus, leader of the Titans (divine descendants of Sky and Earth), was persuaded by his mother, Earth, to castrate his father, Sky, which he did with a sickle. Sky threatened revenge, but Cronus killed him, and ruled the world with his sister/wife Rhea. They became the parents of most of the Olympian gods. Cronus swallowed his children when they were born, but Zeus, the sixth child, organized a war against his father, which he won, and he became king in turn.

BOOK 22 SUMMARY

As Antinous lifts his wine-cup, Odysseus shoots him through the neck. He reveals his identity to the suitors and shoots Eurymachus through the nipple. Armed with their personal swords as well as chairs and tables, the suitors try to defend themselves. Telemachus kills Amphinomus, then goes to fetch more weapons from the storeroom. The suitors hope to slip out the back; Melanthius sneaks to the storeroom and gets weapons for them. Odysseus instructs the herdsmen to intercept him and torture him by trussing him up and hanging him from the storeroom roof. In the guise of Mentes, Athena joins Odysseus; many are slaughtered. Phemius and Medon are spared. Soon all the men are dead. Odysseus tells Telemachus to hack to death the girls who slept with the suitors; instead, he hangs them, and the herdsmen mutiliate and slaughter Melanthius. The surviving slave women are brought out to greet their master.

22.74 *use tables as your shields*: In the usual Greek arrangement, there were light side tables by each diner, rather than a single larger dining table; the suitors are to pick up their tables for self-defense.

22.126–27 *There was a back gate in the castle walls, / providing access to the passageway*: The exact architectural layout of Odysseus' palace is difficult to work out from the text. This passage, which has been viewed by some scholars as a later addition to clear up a possible problem with the plot, explains that there is only one exit apart from the main doors of the palace, and it is impossible for the suitors to escape by that route to raise the alarm.

22.222 *Your sons will not survive here in these halls*: It is unclear in the original whether Agelaus is threatening to kill Mentor's sons or only banish them.

22.228 *Zeus' favorite child*: The original epithet, *eupatereios*, is an unusual one, suggesting "well fathered."

22.230 *the plan that made the city fall*: The trick of the Wooden Horse.

22.423 *tolerate their life as slaves*: There is an important interpretative question in this line. Some scholars think that the original *doulosune* ("slavery") here suggests sexual slavery, and that the line (the Greek reads *doulosunes apechesthai*) should be interpreted to mean "to hold off against (sexual) enslavement"—that is, to resist the kind of advances made by the suitors.

22.432 *who made those treasonous plots while I was gone*: The Greek verb *mechanoonto* ("plotted"—with implications of cunning strategy reminiscent of Odysseus himself) suggests that these girls were deliberately hoping to work against their master—a suggestion that goes well beyond Odysseus' evidence. I use "treasonous" for a word that can suggest lack of shame as well as other kinds of dangerous or inappropriate behavior (*aeikea*): it can suggest sexual "shamelessness," but is not limited to that connotation.

BOOK 23 SUMMARY

Eurycleia tells Penelope that the old beggar is really Odysseus, and that he has killed all the suitors. She is reluctant to believe her slave. Telemachus scolds her. Odysseus tells him they will recognize each other in time, through secret signs; meanwhile, they must make noise as if of a wedding party, to delay the moment when the people of Ithaca realize what has been done to the suitors. Penelope, testing Odysseus, tells Eurycleia to pull the bed frame out of the room and make up the bed for the guest. Odysseus is horrified and tells the story of how he built the bed himself, using a still-living tree that grows in the middle of the palace. Penelope acknowledges him as her husband. They weep. Odysseus tells her about his next journey, to the land of people who do not know the sea. They go to bed together. He tells her an edited version of his adventures. In the morning, Odysseus sends her upstairs while he prepares to fight off the Ithacans.

23.21 *Evilium*: The same pun as at 19.258–59.

23.160 *Athena or Hephaestus*: Gods associated with skill in handicrafts and technology.

23.221 *That foreigner*: The foreigner is Paris, who came from Troy in the Near East, to Sparta in Greece. The connection between Helen's situation and that of Penelope herself is not spelled out, and some readers, in antiquity as well as more recently, have argued that the passage is an interpolation. But there are no linguistic grounds for excluding the lines, and they can make perfectly good sense if the reader is prepared to do some interpretative work. Penelope is using Helen as an example of two distinct facts about her situation: first, that trusting strangers can be disastrous (so Penelope is not wrong to mistrust this particular stranger), and second, that people in general, and perhaps women in particular, may not be fully in control of their actions, and may not be able to see the consequences of choices that they are forced to make (so, she may hint, Penelope too might not have been to blame if she had ended up marrying a suitor).

23.230 *Actoris*: Actoris is mentioned only here, and it is possible that she has died, to be replaced by Eurynome—which would explain why Penelope is sure that Actoris has not told the stranger the secret.

23.318–19 *wrecked / his fleet and killed his men*: There is a line here in some of the texts, missing from most, which reads, "All of them. And Odysseus alone escaped in his black ship." This is likely to be a later addition, since the reference to the speaker himself by name seems implausibly clumsy.

BOOK 24 SUMMARY

Hermes leads the spirits of the dead suitors down to Hades. Achilles and Agamemnon are conversing; Agamemnon tells Achilles about Achilles' funeral. Agamemnon greets the dead suitors; Amphimedon, a suitor, tells how they died. Agamemnon expresses jealousy of Odysseus for having a loyal wife, unlike his own, who killed him. Odysseus goes to the countryside and meets his old father, Laertes, in his orchard. He pretends to think Laertes is a slave and makes up a fake story about his own identity, claiming to be a guest-friend of Odysseus. Laertes is overwhelmed by grief. Odysseus at last reveals his identity, proving it with a childhood memory of being taught about all the trees in the orchard. When they return to the hut, Odysseus reveals himself to the slaves. Meanwhile, news of the suitors' murder has got out. The people gather in outrage outside the palace, and Eupeithes, the bereaved father of Antinous, speaks out against Odysseus. Old Halitherses tries to restrain the crowd, reminding them that the suitors behaved badly and fighting is risky. But over half still want to fight. Athena and Zeus agree that Odysseus should be appointed as king in Ithaca and there should be peace. Odysseus, his son, his father, and his slaves all arm; Athena, disguised as Mentor, joins them. They begin killing. Eupeithes dies first, and all the rebel Ithacans would have been slaughtered, but Athena intervenes and stops the bloodshed, even though Odysseus himself is eager to keep killing.

24.42 *your days of driving chariots forgotten*: Achilles is usually known as "swift-footed," a quick sprinter on foot rather than on a horse or chariot. The most famous episode in which he uses a chariot is near the end of *The Iliad*, when he drags the body of his slaughtered enemy Hector round the walls of Troy—a gesture of brutality that is forgotten in Achilles' own splendid death scene.

24.97 *wound up the war?*: The metaphor, present in the original, is of winding a skein of yarn.

24.113–14 *fighting for a city / and women?*: The idea is that a group like the suitors, all strong young men, are the type to be chosen for a naval expedition, hunting party, or similar expedition. Agamemnon is trying to think of situations in which a group of young men might all be killed together.

24.120 *we had to work so hard to sway that man*: According to legend, Odysseus tried to get out of going to the Trojan War by feigning madness. The usual story is that he was demonstrating his insanity by plowing his field using a donkey and an ox yoked together (animals with different strides who would not plow well together). Palamedes, a Greek who had come on the embassy with Agamemnon and Menelaus, put the newborn Telemachus in front of the plow, and Odysseus veered away from his son—thus demonstrating his sanity.

24.147–48 *she showed it to us, / bright as the sun or moon*: This passage seems to reflect a different version of the story, in which Odysseus arrives on Ithaca at the exact moment that Penelope is forced to finish the weaving, and to alternative versions in which Odysseus and Penelope colluded together to kill the suitors.

24.208–9 *he fought / hard for it, and his house was there*: It is unclear whether Laertes won his land by wresting it from its natural, untilled state to cultivation, or by taking it from the original inhabitants—either is possible.

24.236–37 *he wondered / whether to kiss his father, twine around him*: The Greek verb translated here as "twine around" means literally, "to grow around," as if the embracer is a vine growing around the tree of the embraced.

24.274 *I gave him seven heaps of golden treasure*: Literally, seven "talents." It is unclear exactly what measurement the Homeric "talent" is, and perhaps it is not very exact. The term is used only of gold in Homer. The later Attic talent, used for measurement of silver, was about fifty-seven pounds.

24.304–7 *I am from / Alybas. . . . My name is Eperitus . . . Apheidas, son of Polypemon*: Alybas is probably a made-up place, perhaps coined by analogy with *alaomai*, "to wander"; ancient scholars thought it was in southern Italy. The made-up name Eperitus suggests "picked" or "chosen." The fictional father's name, Apheidas, suggests "Generous," and the grandfather, Polypemon, "Rich" or "Much Suffering."

24.321 *pierced through his nostrils*: The oddly specific physiological detail has been taken as metaphorical by some commentators, but it seems best to take it as entirely literal: the sudden welling up of tears puts pressure on the sinuses.

24.357 *Cephallenia*: See the note to 20.211.

24.385–86 *The old slave Dolius / approached them with his sons*: Dolius is also the father of Melantho and Melanthius, who were slaughtered by Odysseus, unbeknownst to him. The poem never shows us his reaction when he finds out what his master has done to his other children.

24.389 *also the old man, made weak by age*: Presumably the old man is Dolius, even though the same slave also cares for old Laertes.

GLOSSARY

PRONUNCIATION KEY

a as in *cat*	*er* as in *bird*	*or* as in *bore*
ah as in *father*	*eu* as in *lurk*	*ow* as in *now*
ai as in *light*	*g* as in *good*	*oy* as in *toy*
aw as in *raw*	*i* as in *sit*	*s* as in *mess*
ay as in *day*	*j* as in *joke*	*ts* as in *ants*
dew as in *dew*	*k* as in *kite*	*u* as in *us*
e as in *pet*	*o* as in *pot*	*ur* as in *sir*
ee as in *street*	*oh* as in *no*	*you* as in *you*
ehr as in *air*	*oo* as in *boot*	*zh* as in *vision*

´ marks a stressed syllable.

Each entry ends with a reference to the book and line number of the name's first appearance in the poem.

Acastus (*a-kas´-tus*): king of Dulichium. 14.340.

Achaean (*a-kee´-an*): the collective name for inhabitants of Achaea, as mainland Greece was called. 1.272.

Acheron (*a´-ker-on*): a mythical river in the land of the dead; also a real river in Thesprotia. 10.516.

Achilles (*a-kil´-eez*): important Greek warrior, central character in *The Iliad.* Son of Peleus and the Sea Goddess Thetis. Leader of a band of fighters known as the Myrmidons. 3.106.

Acroneüs (*ak-ro´-nee-us*): Phaeacian nobleman; the name suggests "Top-ship." 8.108.

Actoris (*ak´-to-ris*): slave woman owned by Penelope. 23.230.

Adraste (*ad-ra´-stee*): slave girl of Helen. 4.122.

Aeaea (*ee-ee´-a*): the mythical island of Circe. 10.135.

Aeetes (*ee-ee´-teez*): brother of Circe. 10.138.

Aegae (*ee´-jee*): a city in northern Peloponnese, sacred to Poseidon. 5.381.

Aegisthus (*ee-jis´-thus*): son of Thyestes; onetime ruler of Mycenae. Aegisthus killed his uncle Atreus to restore his father to the throne, exiling Menelaus and Agamemnon to Sparta. Menelaus later drove Atreus and Aegisthus out of Sparta, and put his brother Agamemnon on the throne. When Agamemnon and Menelaus were gone to Troy, Aegisthus seduced Agamemnon's wife Clytemnestra and took the throne of Mycenae back. When Agamemnon returned, Aegisthus and Clytemnestra killed him, but Agamemnon's son Orestes eventually returned from exile and killed Aegisthus and Clytemnestra, his own mother. 1.29.

Aegyptius (*ee-jipt´-ee-us*): nobleman of Ithaca; father of Eurynomus. 2.15.

Aeolus (*ee-oh´-lus*): the guardian of the winds, sometimes said to be the son of Poseidon (although this is not mentioned in *The Odyssey*). The Aeolus mentioned at 11.236 as the father of Cretheus may be a different character. 10.1.

Aeson (*ee´-son*): son of Tyro and Cretheus, and father of Jason. 11.260.

Aethon (*ee´-thon*): an assumed name used by Odysseus in disguise; suggests "Burning," "Blazing," or "Reddish Brown." 19.184.

Agamemnon (*ag´-a-mem´-non*): king of Mycenae and brother of Menelaus. The leader of the Greek forces against Troy, he was killed by his wife's lover, Aegisthus, on his return home from the war. 1.30.

Agelaus (*a-je-lay´-us*): one of Penelope's suitors; he speaks up for Telemachus and later tries to spread the word to the Ithacans about the massacre, but is killed by Odysseus. 20.322.

Ajax (*ay´-jax*): (1) Greek (Achaean) warrior in the Trojan War, son of Telamon, known for his sturdy shield and physical strength; in myth, he hoped to win the armor of Achilles after that hero's death. When the armor was instead won by Odysseus, Ajax killed himself. Odysseus meets the spirit of the dead Ajax in Book 11, and he refuses to speak to him. 3.109. (2) Greek warrior, son of Oileus, known as Locrian or Lesser Ajax. 4.499.

Alcandre (*al-kand´-ree*): wife of Polybus; queen of Egyptian Thebes. 4.125.

Alcimus (*al´-sim-us*): father of Mentor. 22.234.

Alcinous (*al-sin´-oh-wus*): king of the Phaeacians. 6.11.

Alcippe (*al-sip´-ee*): slave woman owned by Helen. 4.123.

Alcmaeon (*alk-mai´-on*): son of Amphiarus. 15.250.

Alcmene (*alk-mee´-nee*): mother of Heracles. 2.120.

Alector (*al-ek´-tor*): a Spartan man whose daughter marries Menelaus' son, Megapenthes. 4.11.

Aloeus (*al-oh´-us*): husband of Iphimedeia, mentioned in the parade of heroines. 11.306.

Alpheus (*al´-fee-us*): god associated with a river of the same name, in the western Peloponnese. 3.490.

Amnisus (*am-nee´-sus*): a port city of Knossos in northern Crete. 19.190.

Amphialus (*am-fee´-al-us*): Phaeacian nobleman whose name means "Sea-Girt." 8.112.

Amphiaraus (*am-fai´-a-rus*): king of Argos, one of the seven warriors who fought against Thebes—all were killed. 15.245.

Amphilochus (*am-fi´-lo-kus*): son of Amphiaraus. 15.250.

Amphimedon (*am-fi´-me-don*): one of Penelope's suitors; killed by Telemachus. He is a guest-friend of Agamemnon, and after death, his spirit explains to the spirit of Agamemnon what happened to the suitors. 22.242.

Amphinomus (*am-fin´-o-mus*): one of Penelope's suitors, said to be intelligent and liked by Penelope. He is kind to Odysseus in his guise as beggar. Odysseus warns him to leave the palace before the slaughter, but Athena prompts him to stay. He is killed by Telemachus. 16.350.

Amphion (*am-fee´-yon*): (1) son of Zeus and Antiope; co-founder of Thebes. 11.263. (2) king of Orchomenos. 11.283.

Amphithea (*amf-i-thee´-ya*): wife of Autolycus; grandmother of Odysseus. 19.416.

Amphitrite (*amf-i-tree´-tee*): sea goddess. 3.91.

Amphitryon (*amf-i´-tree-yon*): husband of Alcmene. 11.268.

Amythaeon (*am-ee´-thee-yon*): son of Tyro and Cretheus; mentioned in the parade of heroines. 11.260.

Anabesineus (*an-a-be-si´-nee-yus*): 8.111.

Anchialus (*an-kai´-a-lus*): (1) father of Mentes. 1.180. (2) young Phaeacian nobleman; his name suggests "Seaside." 8.110.

Andraimon (*an-drai´-mohn*): father of Thoas. 14.500.

Anticleia (*an-ti-klay´-a*): daughter of Autolycus; wife of Laertes; mother of Odysseus. 11.85.

Anticlus (*an´-ti-klus*): Greek warrior, one of those hiding inside the Trojan Horse. Helen imitated the voice of his wife, Laodameia, to persuade him to come out; Odysseus clamped his hands over his mouth to stop him from talking. According to some versions, not *The Odyssey*, Odysseus killed him by strangling him. 4.286.

Antilochus (*an-ti´-lo-kus*): (1) dead son of Nestor. 3.112; (2) son of Amphiaraeus. 11.469.

Antinous (*an-ti´-no-us*): a leading suitor whose father, Eupeithes, was protected by Odysseus and whom Odysseus held on his lap when he was a little boy. Antinous jeers at Telemachus and is an instigator in the plan to kill the prince. He is cruel to Eumaeus and to Odysseus in his guise as a beggar, hurling a stool at him. Antinous instigates the fight between Odysseus and the real beggar, Irus. He is the first suitor killed by Odysseus, with an arrow through the neck. In Book 24, Antinous' father speaks in grief of his murdered boy, and calls for revenge. 1.383.

Antiope (*an-ti´-oh-pee*): mother of Amphion and Zethus by Zeus; mentioned in the parade of heroines. 11.262.

Antiphates (*an-ti´-fa-teez*): (1) king of the Laestrygonians. 10.108. (2) son of Melampus and the father of Oïcles. 15.244.

Antiphus (*an´-ti-fus*): (1) son of Aegyptius, who goes as a crew member with Odysseus and is killed by the Cyclops. 2.17. (2) Ithacan elder. 17.68.

Apeire (*a´-pay-ree*): mythical home of Eurymedusa, the slave of Nausicaa; location unknown. 7.9.

Apheidas (*a-fay´-das*): fictional father of Odysseus. 24.307.

Aphrodite (*a-fro-dai´-tee*): goddess associated with sexual desire, and the daughter of Zeus. Born from the sea with no other mother, she is traditionally accompanied by the Graces (lowlier female divinities representing three aspects of attractiveness). She is married to Hephaestus, the metal-working god, but has a long-standing affair with Ares. 4.15.

Apollo (*a-pol´-oh*): son of Zeus and Leto, and a god associated with the sun and with music, poetry, and archery; he typically carries a bow and a lyre. He is also referred to by the epithet Phoebus. It is a festival day to Apollo at the end of *The Odyssey*, when Odysseus uses his bow to kill the suitors. 3.279.

Arcesius (*ar-kes´-ee-us*): son of Zeus (or, according to other sources, son of a she-bear and a human named Cephalus). Father of Laertes and grandfather of Odysseus. Zeus doomed Arcesius to have a single line, of only sons. 14.182.

Ares (*air´-eez*): the god of war; son of Zeus and Hera. He has an affair with Aphrodite. 8.115.

Arete (*a-ree´-tee*): queen of Phaeacia. When Odysseus visits Phaeacia, he is first told that the queen is the most important person in the court, although later, Alcinous, the king, seems to be more powerful. 7.54.

Arethusa (*a-re-thoo´-sa*): a spring in Ithaca. 13.409.

Aretias (*a-ree´-tee-as*): grandfather of Amphinomus. 18.414.

Aretus (*a-ree´-tus*): son of Nestor. 3.413.

Argives (*ar´-gaivs*): inhabitants of Argos, in the Peloponnese; used as a general name for Greeks. 2.173.

Argo (*ar´-go*): mythical ship, imagined in Greek legend to be the first large-scale ship in the world, used by Jason and the Argonauts to travel in search of the Golden Fleece. 12.70.

Argos (*ar´-gos*): (1) a city in the northeast Peloponnese and the area surrounding it, or, more vaguely, mainland Greece. 1.211. (2) giant with a hundred eyes. 5.75. (3) old dog owned by Odysseus. 17.291.

Ariadne (*ar-ee-ad´-nee*): daughter of Minos. She helped the Greek hero Theseus kill the Minotaur (her bull-headed brother), and went away with him, only to be abandoned on an island; the god Dionysus then took her as a bride. In the *Odyssey* version, she was denounced by Dionysus and killed by Artemis, for reasons that are not explained. 11.323.

Arnaeus (*ar-nai´-us*): the real name of the beggar Irus (q.v.). 18.6.

Artaky (*ar´-ta-kee*): a spring on the island of the Laestrygonians. 10.107.

Artemis (*ar´-te-mis*): virgin goddess associated with hunting, wild places, the moon, childbirth, and diseases of women. Daughter of Zeus and Leto, and twin sister of Apollo. 4.121.

Arybas (*a´-ri-bas*): nobleman in Sidon and the father of Eumaeus' nurse. 15.426.

Asphalion (*as-fa´-lee-on*): a slave of Menelaus. 4.216.

Asteris (*as´-ter-is*): island near Ithaca. 4.846.

Athena (*ath-ee´-na*): the goddess associated with technical and strategic skill, warfare, weaving, and other kinds of expertise. Her plant is the olive tree; she is associated with birds of prey and has particularly quick sight. She is the daughter of Zeus by Metis (a Titan representing cleverness): Zeus, afraid of a prophecy that said Metis' son would overthrow him, turned her into a fly and swallowed her, but Athena, who was already conceived in Metis, grew inside Zeus' head and sprang out, already fully armed. She is also referred to by the epithet Pallas. 1.44.

Athens (*ath´-ens*): a city in Attica, a region of mainland Greece. 3.306.

Atlas (*at´-las*): the Titan who holds up the sky. 1.52.

Atreus (*ay´-tree-us*): father of Agamemnon and Menelaus; king of Mycenae. Along with his brother Thyestes, he was exiled for killing their half brother; later, suspecting Thyestes of having an affair with his wife, Atreus killed Thyestes' children and made him eat them. This myth is not mentioned in Homer. 3.136.

Autolycus (*aw-to´-li-kus*): father of Anticleia and maternal grandfather of Odysseus. His name means "The Wolf Himself" or "Real Wolf." He gives Odysseus his name. 11.85.

Autonoe (*aw-to´-noh-ee*): slave of Penelope. 18.184.

Boreas (*bor´-ee-as*): the North Wind. 5.296.

Cadmus (*kad´-mus*): the founder of Thebes; hence "Cadmeans" (*kad´-mee-ans*) = Thebans. 5.334.

Calypso (*kal-ip´-so*): a goddess (or nymph) who lives on the island of Ogygia and hopes to keep Odysseus there as her husband. Daughter of Atlas, the Titan who holds up the world. 1.14.

Cassandra (*kas-ahn´-dra*): one of the daughters of Priam, king of Troy; she was raped by Apollo and rewarded with the gift of true prophecy—but with the inability to make anybody believe her words. She was taken as a slave concubine by Agamemnon, brought back to his home in Greece, and then murdered by Agamemnon's wife, Clytemnestra, and her lover, Aegisthus. 11.422.

Castor (*kas´-tor*): (1) son of Zeus and Leda, and the brother of Helen, Clytemnestra, and Polydeuces. 11.301. (2) son of Hylax ("Castor Hylacides") and fictional father of Odysseus. 14.200.

Cauconians (*kaw-koh´-nee-yanz*): a tribe of southwest Pylos. 3.367.

Cetians (*see´-tee-yanz*): a people led by Eurypylus. 11.521.

Chalcis (*kal´-sis*): a town in western Greece, not the Chalcis in Euboea. 15.294.

Charybdis (*ka-rib´-dis*): a monstrous goddess in the form of a giant whirlpool. 12.104.

Chios (*kee´-os*): an Aegean island. 3.172.

Chloris (*klor´-is*): wife of Neleus and mother of Nestor. 11.282.

Chromios (*krom´-ee-os*): son of Neleus and Chloris. 11.287.

Cicones (*si´-koh-neez*): Trojan allies in Thrace, north of Troy. 9.41.

Cimmerians (*sim-air´-ee-anz*): a people living near the land of the dead. 11.13.

Circe (*sur´-see*): daughter of Helius, the Sun God, and a sea nymph (Perse); she lives on the island of Aeaea and has magical powers, especially the ability to change humans into animals. 8.448.

Clitus (*klee´-tus*): human son of Mantius, taken by the goddess Dawn. 15.251.

Clymene (*kli´-men-ee*): the name of several mythical characters, including an Amazon, a Titan, and a sea-nymph; it is not clear which is meant. 11.328.

Clytemnestra (*klai-tem-nes´-tra*): twin sister of Helen; daughter of Zeus and Leda; wife of Agamemnon. 3.263.

Clytius (*kli´-tee-us*): father of Piraeus. 16.328.

Clytoneus (*kli-toh´-nee-us*): son of Alcinous and Arete, and the brother of Nausicaa. 8.119.

Cocytus (*ko´-see-tus*): a river in the land of the dead, literally meaning "lamentation." 10.514.

Corax (*kor´-ax*): a rock in Ithaca; since the name means "raven," presumably it is a black rock. 13.408.

Cratais (*kra´-tais*): a sea monster; mother of Scylla. The name suggests "Force." 12.125.

Creon (*kree´-on*): king of Thebes, and the father of Megara. 11.270.

Cretheus (*kree´-thee-us*): husband of Tyro. 11.236.

Cronus (*kro´-nus*): a titan-god; son of Uranus and father of Zeus. Cronus castrated Uranus with a sickle and overthrew him. Cronus had many children by his wife, Rhea, and ate them all, because they were destined to overthrow him. But Rhea hid Zeus, who grew up, freed his siblings from his father's belly, and killed him and the other titans—beginning the reign of the Olympian gods. 1.386.

Crouni (*kroo´-nee*): a place-name meaning "streams"; location unknown. 15.294.

Ctesippus (*ktee-si´-pus*): one of Penelope's suitors; killed by Philoetius. 20.288.

Ctesius (*ktee´-see-us*): father of Eumaeus, and the king of the two provinces of Syria. 15.413.

Ctimene (*kti´-men-ee*): younger sister of Odysseus. 15.363.

Cyclopes (*sai´-klo-peez*): a race of one-eyed giants. Their name suggests "round-eyed" or "round-faced. 1.71.

Cydonians (*si-doh´-nee-ans*): a people from northwest Crete. 3.291.

Cyprus (*sai´-prus*): a large island in the eastern Mediterranean. 4.82.

Cythera (*si´-the-ra*): an island south of Cape Malea, at the southeastern tip of the Peloponnese. 9.82.

Deiphobus (*day-if´-o-bus*): son of Priam; killed by Odysseus and Menelaus during the sack of Troy. According to some traditions, he married Helen after the death of Paris. 4.276.

Delos (*dee´-los*): one of the Cycladic islands in the Aegean; sacred to Apollo, it is the birthplace of Apollo and Artemis. 6.162.

Demeter (*de-mee´-ter*): the goddess of agriculture and the harvest; daughter of Cronus and Rhea, and mother of Persephone. 5.125.

Demodocus (*de-mod´-o-kus*): the court bard of the Phaeacians. 8.44.

Demoptolemus (*day-mop-tol´-e-mus*): one of Penelope's suitors, killed by Odysseus. 22.241.

Deucalion (*dew-kayl´-ee-on*): king of Crete; son of Minos; father of Idomeneus and Aethon, whose identity Odysseus assumes. 19.181.

Día (*dee´-a*): an island in the Aegean Sea, off the northern coast of Crete. 11.326.

Diocles (*dai´-o-kleez*): king of Pherae; son of Ortilochus and grandson of Alpheus. 3.488.

Diomedes (*dai-o-mee´-deez*): son of Tydeus, king of Argos; he fought on the side of the Greeks in the Trojan War. 3.167.

Dionysus (*dai-o-nai´-sus*): the god of wine; son of Zeus and Semele. 11.327.

Dmetor (*dmee´-tor*): king of Cyprus to whom Odysseus, in diguise, claims to have been enslaved. 17.444.

Dolius (*do´-lee-us*): an Ithacan herdsman, and the father of Melantho and Melanthius. 4.734.

Dorians (*dor´-ee-ans*): one of the major ethnic and linguistic subgroups into which the archaic Greeks classified themselves. Dorians are included in the list of tribes that inhabit Crete. 19.177.

Dulichium (*doo-lik´-ee-um*): one of the islands under Odysseus' rule, mentioned together with Same, Zacynthus, and Ithaca; its precise location has been debated since antiquity. 1.246.

Dymas (*doo´-mas*): Phaeacian sailor; father of Nausicaa's unnamed friend. 6.23.

Echeneus (*ek-ee´-nee-us*): Phaeacian elder. 7.155.

Echephron (*ek´-e-fron*): one of Nestor's sons. 3.412.

Echetus (*ek´-e-tus*): king in mainland Greece, infamous for his cruelty. 18.84.

Eidothea (*ay-do´-thee-a*): a sea-nymph; she helps Menelaus and his men escape from Egypt by explaining how to capture her father, Proteus. 4.363.

Eileithyia (*ay-lay-thwee´-a*): the goddess associated with childbirth. 19.191.

Elatreus (*e-lat´-ree-us*): Phaeacian nobleman who excels at discus throwing. His name means "Driver." 8.109.

Elatus (*e´-lat-us*): one of Penelope's suitors; killed by Eumaeus. 22.268.

Elis (*el´-is*): an area in the northwestern Peloponnese. 4.636.

Elpenor (*el-pee´-nor*): crewmate of Odysseus who dies after he falls drunkenly from an upper room in Circe's house. His is the first shade Odysseus encounters in Hades. He asks Odysseus and his men to return to Aeaea to bury him, which they do at the beginning of Book 12. 11.50.

Elysium (*e-lis´-ee-um*): a paradise inhabited after death by the most famous Greek warriors. 4.562.

Enipeus (*e-nip-ee´-us*): a river and a river god with whom Tyro fell in love. Ancient scholars placed the river in Thessaly or Elis. 11.237.

Epeians (*e-pee´-ans*): a group of people that rules Elis, in the northwestern Peloponnese. 13.276.

Epeius (*e-pee´-us*): son of Panopeus, who built the Trojan Horse with Athena's help. 8.494.

Eperitus (*e-pe-ree´-tus*): fictional name of Odysseus, suggesting "Picked" or "Chosen." 24.306.

Ephialtes (*ef-ee-alt´-eez*): giant; son of Iphimedeia and Poseidon. With his brother, Otus, he waged war with the Olympians and was killed by Apollo. 11.309.

Ephyra (*e-fai´-ra*): a city in Thesprotia, on the western mainland of Greece. 1.260.

Epicaste (*e-pi-kast´-ee*): mother of Oedipus; wife of Laius, king of Thebes. In other versions of the myth, she is known as Jocasta. 11.272.

Erebus (*e´-reb-us*): a dark underworld location. 10.530.

Erechtheus (*e-rek´-thee-us*): legendary king of Athens. 7.81.

Eretmeus (*e-ret´-mee-us*): Phoenician athlete; the name suggests "Oarsman." 8.110.

Eriphyle (*e-rif-eel´-ee*): wife of Amphiaraus; one of the shades of heroines Odysseus encounters in the underworld. 11.328.

Erymanthus (*e-ree-man´-thus*): a mountain range on the border between Achaea and Elis, in the northwestern Peloponnese. 6.103.

Eteoneus (*e-tee-o´-nee-us*): Menelaus' guard in Sparta. 4.22.

Ethiopia (*ee-thee-o´-pee-ya*): the most distant place imaginable, located "between the sunset and the dawn"; a mythical place, not identical with the modern country. Poseidon's visit to Ethiopia provides the opportunity for the gods to discuss Odysseus' return home. 1.22.

Euanthes (*you-anth´-eez*): father of Maron. 9.199.

Euboea (*you-bee´-a*): a large island east of mainland Greece. Nestor lands there on his way back from Troy. 3.175.

Euenor (*you-ee´-nor*): father of Leocritus. 2.241.

Eumaeus (*you-may´-us*): loyal slave of Odysseus; he takes care of his pigs and helps Odysseus kill his wife's suitors. 14.54.

Eumelus (*you´-mel-us*): husband of Penelope's sister, Iphthime. 4.798.

Eupeithes (*you-pay´-theez*): father of Antinous; the name suggests "Persuasive." 20.269.

Eurus (*yor´-us*): the East Wind. 5.295.

Euryades (*yur-ai-ad´-eez*): one of Penelope's suitors; killed by Telemachus. 22.267.

Euryalus (*yur-ai´-a-lus*): Phaeacian; son of Naubolus. He is second only to Laodamas in beauty and strength, and he excels at wrestling. His name suggests "Wide-Sea." 8.114.

Eurybates (*yur-i´-ba-teez*): squire of Odysseus. 19.245.

Eurycleia (*yur-i-klay´-a*): old slave woman who took care of Telemachus as a baby; she now protects Odysseus' domestic stores. 1.427.

Eurydamas (*yur-i´-da-mas*): one of Penelope's suitors; killed by Odysseus. 18.297.

Eurydice (*yur-i´-di-see*): queen of Pylos, and wife of Nestor. 3.452.

Eurylochus (*yur-i´-lo-kus*): a self-assertive member of Odysseus' crew. 10.205.

Eurymachus (*yur-i´-ma-kus*): one the most prominent and vocal of Penelope's suitors. 1.400.

Eurymedon (*yur-i´-me-don*): king of the Giants, whom he killed, and great-grandfather of Alcinous. 7.56.

Eurymedusa (*yur-i-me-doo´-sa*): old slave who attends to Nausicaa. 7.7.

Eurymus (*yur´-i-mus*): father of Telemus, who prophesied to Polyphemus that he would lose his sight at Odysseus' hands. 9.509.

Eurynome (*yur-i´-no-mee*): servant of Penelope. 17.495.

Eurynomus (*yur-i´-no-mus*): one of Penelope's suitors; son of Aegyptius. 2.21.

Eurypylus (*yur-i´-pi-lus*): son of Telephus, leader of the Cretans; he was killed by Neoptolemus during the Trojan War. 11.518.

Eurytion (*yur-i´-tee-on*): a centaur who, at the wedding of Pirithous, king of the Lapiths, got drunk and tried to abduct the bride; in the ensuing brawl, many on both sides (centaurs and Lapiths) were slaughtered. 21.297.

Eurytus (*yur´-i-tus*): king of Ochalia, and father of Iphitus; killed by Apollo when he proposed an archery contest with the god. 8.224.

Gaia (*gai´-a*): the earth; mother of Tityus. 7.324.

Geraestus (*ger-ais´-tus*): a promontory on the coast of Euboea, where Nestor puts in for a night on his way back from Troy. 3.178.

Gerenian (*ger-ee´-nee-an*): an epithet for Nestor, referring to Gerenia, the town in Messenia where Nestor took refuge when Heracles was attacking Pylos. 3.68.

Giants: a race of beings that waged war with the Olympians. They were ruled over, and eventually killed, by Eurymedon. 7.57.

Gorgon (*gor´-gon*): a legendary monster whose gaze could turn onlookers to stone. 11.635.

Gortyn (*gor´-tin*): a city in south central Crete. 3.293.

Graces: daughters of Zeus and Eurynome; attendants of Aphrodite. 6.19.

Greeks: Greek-speaking inhabitants of the southern Balkan penninsula, as well as of parts of southern Italy, Crete, the Aegean islands, and the coast of Asia Minor. The original text usually calls them "Achaeans." 1.11.

Gyrae (*gee´-rai*): a (perhaps mythical) rocky outcropping in the Aegean Sea, onto which Poseidon drove the Lesser Ajax to shipwreck. 4.501.

Hades (*hay´-deez*): the land of the dead, and the god who rules there (a brother of Zeus, another son of Cronus and Rhea). 3.409.

Halitherses (*hal-i-ther´-seez*): old Ithacan; son of Mastor. He is noted for his skill in prophecy and augury, and he interprets the omen of the two eagles. 2.158.

Halius (*ha´-lee-us*): Phaeacian; son of Alcinous. 8.119.

Hebe (*hee´-bee*): daughter of Zeus and Hera, and the cup bearer for the Olympian gods. Goddess of youth, her name means "Youth." 11.602.

Helen: daughter of Zeus and Leda, and wife of Menelaus; mother of Hermione, and sister of Castor, Pollux, and Clytemnestra. Her abduction by Paris prompted the Trojan War. 4.13.

Helius (*hee´-lee-us*): the Olympian god associated with the sun. Often referred to just as the Sun God (q.v.), and distinct from Apollo. 12.4.

Hephaestus (*he-fais´-tus*): the god of fire and metallurgy; a master craftsman, he is the son of Hera and husband of Aphrodite. 4.616.

Hera (*hee´-ra*): goddess associated with the hearth and marriage; she is the daughter of Cronus and Rhea, and the sister and wife of Zeus. 4.512.

Heracles (*he´-ra-kleez*): deified mortal hero; son of Zeus and Alcmene, he was persecuted by Hera. 8.224.

Hermes (*her´-meez*): the messenger of the gods; son of Zeus and Maia. 1.39.

Hermione (*her-mai´-o-nee*): daughter of Helen and Menelaus. 4.14.

Hippodamia (*hip-o-da´-mee-ya*): slave girl of Penelope. 18.183.

Hyperesia (*hai-per-ee´-see-a*): a town in Achaea, in the northern Peloponnese; home of Polypheides. 15.257.

Hyperia (*hai-pehr´-ee-a*): the former home of the Phaeacians, near the land of the Cyclopes. 6.4.

Hyperion (*hai-pehr´-ee-on*): father of Helius. 12.262.

Iasion (*ya´-see-on*): son of Zeus and Electra; loved by Demeter. 5.127.

Icarius (*i-kar´-ee-us*): father of Penelope and brother of Tyndareus. 2.52.

Icmalius (*ik-may´-lee-us*): Ithacan craftsman; he made Penelope's footstool. 19.55.

Idomeneus (*i-dom-i-nay´-us*): Cretan king who fought on the side of the Greeks in the Trojan War. 3.191.

Ilus (*ail´-us*): king of Ephyra. 1.263.

Ino (*ai´-no*): daughter of Cadmus; a sea goddess also called the White Goddess. 5.333.

Iolcus (*yol´-kus*): a city in Thessaly; the home of Nestor's uncle Pelias, who sent Jason in quest of the Golden Fleece. 11.257.

Iphicles (*if´-ik-lees*): king of Phylace. 11.292.

Iphimedeia (*if-i-me-day´-a*): wife of Aloeus; mother, by Poseidon, of Otus and Ephialtes. 11.306.

Iphitus (*if´-i-tus*): son of Eurytus; he gives Odysseus his father's bow. 21.13.

Iphthime (*if-thee´-mee*): daughter of Icarius; sister of Penelope; wife of Eumelus. 4.797.

Irus (*ai´-rus*): Ithacan beggar; also known as Arnaeus (q.v.). 18.7.

Ismarus (*is´-mar-us*): a city in Thrace; home of the Cicones. 9.41.

Ithaca (*ith´-a-ka*): an Ionian island in western Greece; home to the Ithacans, including Odysseus. 1.18.

Ithacus (*ith´-a-kus*): one of the builders of an ornate fountain in Ithaca. 17.206.

Itylus (*i´-til-us*): son of Zethus, the king of Thebes, and Aedon. He was accidentally killed by his mother. 19.525.

Jardan, River (*jar´-dan*): a river in Crete. 3.290.

Jason: Thessalian hero; he led the Argonauts in their quest for the Golden Fleece. 12.73.

Knossos (*kuh-nos´-os*): a city in Crete where King Minos ruled. 19.178.

Laerces (*lay-ur´-seez*): Pylian goldsmith. 3.424.

Laertes (*lay-air´-teez*): father of Odysseus; son of Arcesius. 1.188.

Laestrygonia (*lai-stri-go´-nee-a*): a mythical place visited by Odysseus, inhabited by a race of giant cannibals, the Laestrygonians. 10.81.

Lamos (*lai´-mos*): apparently, the founder of Laestrygonia. 10.82.

Lampetia (*lam-pet´-ee-a*): daughter of Helius and Neaira; one of the caretakers of Helius' cattle on Thrinacia. Her name means "Shining." 12.133.

Laodamas (*lay-o´-da-mas*): Phaeacian prince, son of Alcinous and Arete. 7.170.

Leda (*lee´-da*): wife of Tyndareus; mother by Zeus of Castor and Polydeuces. 11.300.

Lemnos (*lem´-nos*): an island in the northeast Aegean; inhabited by the Sintians. 8.283.

Leocritus (*lee-ok´-ri-tus*): one of Penelope's suitors, and son of Euenor. He is killed by Telemachus. 2.241.

Leodes (*lee-oh´-deez*): the prophet of the suitors. 21.144.

Lesbos (*les´-bos*): a large island in the northeastern Aegean Sea, off the coast of Asia Minor. 3.169.

Leto (*lee´-to*): goddess; mother by Zeus of Apollo and Artemis. 6.106.

Libya (*lib´-ee-ya*): a land on the northern coast of Africa; vaguely imagined and not necessarily co-extensive with the modern country. 4.84.

Maera (*mai´-ra*): one of the heroines whose shades Odysseus encounters in the underworld. 11.328.

Malea (*ma´-lee-a*): a cape at the southeastern tip of the Peloponnese, famous for its treacherous sailing conditions. 3.286.

Mantius (*man´-tee-yus*): son of Melampus; father of Clitus and Polypheides; grandfather of Theoclymenus. 15.243.

Marathon (*ma´-ra-thon*): a town northeast of Athens, near the northeast coast of Attica. 7.80.

Maron (*mah´-ron*): priest of Apollo; son of Euanthes. He gave Odysseus the wine that Odysseus uses to intoxicate Polyphemus. 9.199.

Mastor (*mas´-tor*): father of Halitherses. 2.158.

ORPHAN HOLD
DO NOT SHIP

H1–000000000396

ISBN 9780393356250

Odyssey

CLIENT	Alternate Sourcing
STATION	TPP Receiving Station 03
HELD	2026–10–08 12:19

SHELF

If its order arrives, scan this label at a receiving station.

Medon (*mee´-don*): slave boy in Ithaca; spared by Odysseus. 4.676.

Megapenthes (*me-ga-pen´-theez*): son of Menelaus by a slave woman. 4.12.

Megara (*me´-ga-ra*): daughter of Creon and wife of Heracles; one of the shades of heroines Odysseus encounters in the underworld. 11.270.

Melampus (*me-lam´-pus*): prophet; great-grandfather of Theoclymenus. 11.293.

Melaneus (*me-lan-ai´-us*): father of the suitor Amphimedon. 24.104.

Melanthius (*me-lanth´-ee-yus*): goatherd for the suitors; brother of Melantho. He is killed by Odysseus. 17.212.

Melantho (*me-lanth´-oh*): sister of Melanthius and slave of Penelope. She has a sexual relationship with Eurymachus and is hanged by Telemachus, along with eleven others. 18.320.

Memnon (*mem´-non*): son of the Dawn Goddess; killed Antilochus at Troy. 11.520.

Menelaus (*me-ne-lay´-us*): king of Sparta; husband of Helen; brother of Agamemnon. 1.285.

Mentes (*men´-teez*): leader of the Taphians; a guest-friend of Odysseus whose identity is assumed by Athena. 1.105.

Mentor (*men´-tor*): son of Alcimus; a trusted friend of Odysseus whose identity is often assumed by Athena. 2.225.

Mesaulius (*mes-ow´-lee-yus*): slave of Eumaeus. 14.450.

Messenia (*mes-ee´-nee-ya*): a region of the southwest Peloponnese. 21.16

Mimas (*mai´-mas*): a promontory on the coast of Asia Minor, opposite Chios. 3.173.

Minos (*mai´-nos*): son of Zeus; legendary king of Crete; judge of the dead in the underworld. 11.323.

Minyans (*min´-yans*): inhabitants of Orchomenus. 11.283.

Moulius (*moo´-lee-yus*): slave brought by Amphinomus from Dulichium. 18.423.

Muse: one of nine daughters of Zeus and Mnemosyne who preside over various arts. 1.2.

Mycenae (*mai-see´-nee*): a palatial city in the northeastern Peloponnese, and home of Agamemnon. 3.304.

Mycene (*mai-seen´*): legendary heroine. 2.120.

Myrmidons (*mur´-mi-dons*): a Thessalian tribe and Achilles' men in *The Iliad*. Neoptolemus, Achilles' son, led the tribe after his father's death. 3.189.

Naubolus (*now´-bo-lus*): father of Euryalus. His name suggests "Ship-Launcher." 8.114.

Nausicaa (*now´-sik-ah*): Phaeacian princess; daughter of Alcinous and Arete. 6.16.

Nausithous (*now-sith´-o-wus*): king of the Phaeacians before his son, Alcinous, succeeded him. He resettled the Phaeacians in Scheria due to harrassment from their neighbors, the Cyclopes. 6.7.

Nauteus (*now´-tee-yus*): Phaeacian who competes in the athletic contests during Odysseus' stay in Scheria. His name suggests "Shipman." 8.109.

Neaira (*nee-ai´-ra*): mother, by Helius, of Phaethousa and Lampetia. 12.134.

Neion, Mount (*nay´-on*): a mountain in Ithaca; alternative name for Mount Neriton. 3.81.

Neleus (*nee´-lee-yus*): father of Nestor, and his predecessor as king of Pylos. 3.79.

Neoptolemus (*nee-op-tol´-e-mus*): son of Achilles; leader of the Myrmidons at Troy after his father's death. 11.508.

Nereids (*nee´-ree-ids*): nymphs of the sea. 13.104.

Neriton, Mount (*ne´-rit-on*): a mountain in Ithaca. Also referred to as Mount Neion. 9.24.

Neritus (*ne´-ri-tus*): one of the builders of an ornate fountain in Ithaca. 17.206.

Nestor (*nes´-tor*): king of Pylos; son of Neleus; father of Antilochus and Pisistrarus. 1.284.

Nisus (*nai´-sus*): son of Aretias, and father of Penelope's suitor Amphinomus, from Dulichium. 16.396.

Noëmon (*noh-wee´-mon*): son of Phronius. He lends a ship to Telemachus. 2.387.

Notus (*noh´-tus*): the South Wind. 5.296.

Ocean: the vast river running around the landmass of the world; also a personage. 3.1.

Ocyalus (*o-kee´-yal-us*): Phaeacian who competes in the athletic contests during Odysseus' stay in Scheria. His name suggests "Sharpsea." 8.109.

Odysseus (*o-dis´-ee-yus*): king of Ithaca; son of Laertes and Anticleia; grandson of Arcesius and Autolycus; father of Telemachus. 1.21.

Oedipus (*eed´-i-pus*): king of Thebes who killed his father, Laius, and married his mother, Epicaste (known as Jocasta in other versions). 11.272.

Ogygia (*o-ji´-ja*): the mythical island home of Calypso, where Odysseus washes up and stays for seven years. 1.85.

Oïcles (*oh´-i-kles*): son of Antiphates and father of the famous Argive warrior-prophet Amphiaraus. 15.245.

Olympus (*o-lim´-pus*): a mountain in northeastern Thessaly. The tallest peak in Greece, it is home to the Olympian gods. 1.27.

Ops (*ops*): father of Eurycleia. 1.428.

Orchomenus (*or-ko´-me-nus*): a city in Boeotia, home to the Minyans. 11.284.

Orestes (*o-res´-tees*): son of Agamemnon and Clytemnestra. Orestes went into exile after the murder of Agamemnon by Clytemnestra and Aegisthus, but eventually returned to Mycenae and killed them. 1.30.

Orion (*o-rai´-yon*): mythical hunter, turned into a constellation after his death. 5.122.

Orsilochus (*or-sil´-o-kus*): son of Idomoneus, the leader of Cretan forces at Troy. 13.261.

Ortilochus (*or-til´-o-kus*): son of Alpheus and father of Diocles. 3.489.

Ortygia (*or-ti´-ja*): a small Sicilian island separated from the mainland by a very narrow channel, although the mention of Ortygia here does not seem to correspond to any real geographical place. 15.406.

Ossa (*o´-sa*): a mountain in the region of Thessaly, just south of Mount Olympus. 11.315.

Otus (*oh´-tus*): son of Iphimedeia and Poseidon. 11.309.

Pallas (*pal´-las*): an epithet used of Athena, of unknown origin and meaning. 1.125.

Pandareus (*pan-dar´-ee-yus*): king of Crete and father of Aedon, the wife of Theban founder Zethus. 19.520.

Panopeus (*pan-oh´-pee-yus*): a Greek town near the border of Boeotia. 11.579.

Paphos (*pay´-fos*): a city in southwest Cyprus; as the supposed site of Aphrodite's birth, it was an important center of worship of the goddess. 8.362.

Parnassus, Mount (*par-nas´-us*): a mountain in central Greece where a boar wounded Odysseus during his childhood. 19.395.

Patroclus (*pat-ro´-klus*): Achilles' companion; killed by Hector. 3.110.

Pelasgians (*pe-las´-jee-ans*): a people who were either pre-Greeks or the ancestors of the Greeks, inhabitating regions of Greece, including Crete, Thessaly, and Epirus, and parts of northwestern Asia Minor. 19.177.

Peleus (*pee´-lee-us*): son of Aeacus; father of Achilles; husband of the Sea Goddess Thetis. 5.311.

Pelias (*pee´-lee-as*): king of Iolcus and son of Tyro and Poseidon; murdered by his daughters at the persuasion of Medea. 11.254.

Pelion (*pee´-lee-on*): a mountain in Thessaly. 11.315.

Penelope (*pe-ne´-loh-pee*): daughter of the Arcadian king Icarius; wife of Odysseus, with whom she has a son, Telemachus. 1.222.

Periboea (*pe-ri-boy´-ya*): daughter of Eurymedon; mother, by Poseidon, of Nausithous; grandmother of the Phaeacian king Alcinous. 7.60.

Periclymenus (*pe-ri-kli´-me-nus*): son of Neleus and Chloris. 11.287.

Perimedes (*pe-ri-mee´-dees*): one of Odysseus' men. 11.23.

Pero (*pe´-ro*): daughter of Neleus and Chloris; wooed by Melampus and his brother Bias. 11.288.

Perse (*pur´-see*): daughter of Ocean; mother, by the Sun God, of Circe and Aeetes. 10.140.

Persephone (*pur-se´-fo-nee*): goddess; daughter of Zeus and Demeter; and, after he abducted her, wife of Hades. According to mythological tradition, Persephone spends part of the year with her husband Hades in the underworld, and part of the year in the world above with her mother. 10.492.

Perseus (*pur´-see-yus*): a son of Nestor. 3.413.

Phaea (*fai´-ya*): a port on the coast of Elis. 15.297.

Phaeacians (*fai-yay´-shuns*): the inhabitants of the island of Scheria. 5.36.

Phaedimus (*fai´-di-mus*): king of Sidon. 4.617.

Phaedra (*fai´-dra*): elder daughter of Minos, the king of Crete; wife of Theseus. 11.322.

Phaestus (*fai´-stus*): a city in south central Crete. 3.295.

Phaethousa (*fai-thoo´-sa*): daughter of the Sun God Helius and Neaira; together with her sister, attendant of her father's cattle. Her name means "Shining." 12.133.

Pharos (*fehr´-os*): an island off the coast of Egypt. 4.355.

Pheidon (*fay´-don*): king of the Thesprotians. 14.316.

Phemius (*fee´-mee-yus*): bard in the household of Odysseus on Ithaca, 1.154.

Pherae (*fehr´-ai*): a city in the Peloponnese, between Pylos and Sparta. 3.488.

Pheres (*fehr´-eez*): son of Tyro and Cretheus. 11.260.

Philoctetes (*fi-lok-tee´-teez*): Thessalian hero and companion of Heracles. On the way to fight at Troy, Philoctetes was bitten by a snake. The wound festered and stank, so Philoctetes' companions abandoned him on the island of Lemnos. It was later prophesied that Troy could be captured only with Philoctetes' bow, so Odysseus was sent to Lemnos to retrieve him. Philoctetes returned to Troy and was healed. 3.190.

Philoetius (*fi-loy´-tee-us*): enslaved herdsman loyal to Odysseus. 20.186.

Philomeleides (*fi-lo-mee´-lee-dees*): mythical king of Lesbos who challenged all vistors to wrestle him; most failed, but Odysseus won. In 17.135, he is known as Philomedes. 4.343.

Phoebus (*fee´-bus*): an epithet for Apollo meaning "Bright." 3.279.

Phoenicia (*fu-nee´-sha*): the region of modern-day Lebanon, Israel, Jordan, and Syria that was dominated by the loosely organized seafaring civilization known as the Phoenicians. 4.83.

Phorcys (*for´-kis*): an ancient sea god who presides over a harbor on the island of Ithaca. 1.72.

Phronius (*fro´-nee-yus*): father of Noëmon. 2.386.

Phrontis (*fron´-tis*): the pilot of Menelaus' ship; killed at Sounion by Apollo. 3.280.

Phthia (*fthee´-ya*): the kingdom of Peleus and Achilles, located in central Greece. 11.497.

Phylace (*fee´-la-see*): a city in the Greek region of Thessaly. 11.292.

Phylacus (*fi´-la-kus*): the founder of Phylace; father of Pero. 15.232.

Phylo (*fai´-loh*): slave of Helen. 4.124.

Pieria (*pai-e´-ree-ya*): a region in northern Greece. 5.50.

Piraeus (*pai-ray´-yus*): one of Telemachus' companions. 15.541.

Pirithous (*pe-ri´-tho-wus*): a mythical hero, king of the Lapiths and son of Zeus. According to tradition, Pirithous—together with his friend and companion, the hero Theseus—attempted to kidnap Helen when she was a child; the pair also attempted to kidnap Persephone from the underworld. On the occasion of Pirithous' wedding to Hippodameia, the Centaurs, the mythological half-horse, half-human race, attempt to kidnap the Lapith women, precipitating a major battle between the Centaurs and Lapiths. 11.631.

Pisander (*pai-san´-dur*): one of Penelope's suitors. 18.299.

Pisenor (*pai-see´-nor*): Telemachus' herald. 2.36.

Pisistratus (*pai-sis´-tra-tus*): youngest son of Nestor and companion of Telemachus. 3.37.

Pleiades (*play´-a-deez*): the seven daughters of Atlas; they were chased by Orion and turned into a constellation. 5.271.

Polites (*po-lai´-teez*): one of Odysseus' men. 10.223.

Polybus (*po´-li-bus*): (1) father of Eurymachus, one of Penelope's principal suitors. 2.177. (2) king of Thebes. 4.126. (3) a Phaeacian artisan. 8.373. (4) one of Penelope's suitors. 22.243.

Polycaste (*po-li-kas´-tee*): Nestor's eldest daughter. 3.465.

Polyctor (*po-lik´-tor*): one of the builders of an ornate fountain in Ithaca. 17.207.

Polydamna (*po-li-dam´-na*): wife of Thon. 4.229.

Polydeuces (*po-li-dew´-seez*): one of the two twin sons of Leda and Zeus, and thus a brother of Helen and Clytemnestra. With his twin, Castor, famed for abilities as horsemen and called the Dioscuri. On their deaths, they were given immortality to share, spending alternate days in the underworld or the world above. 11.301.

Polynaus (*po-li-nay´-us*): a Phaeacian; son of Tecton and father of Amphialaus. His name suggests "Many-Shipped." 8.113.

Polypemon (*po-li-pee´-mon*): fictional grandfather of Odysseus; the name suggests "Rich" or "Much Suffering." 24.307.

Polypheides (*po-li-fai´-deez*): a prophet, son of Mantius. 15.253.

Polyphemus (*po-li-fee´-mus*): son of Poseidon and the nymph Thoösa. One of the Cyclopes (so he is a Cyclops), he lives in a cave with his sheep and goats. Odysseus' mistreatment of Polyphemus is a major component in Poseidon's rage against Odysseus. 1.70.

Ponteus (*pon´-tee-yus*): a Phaeacian. His name suggests "Deep-Sea." 8.111.

Pontonous (*pon-to´-no-wus*): slave of Alcinous. 7.179.

Poseidon (*po-sai´-dun*): a god; son of Cronus and brother of Zeus. After drawing lots with his brothers Zeus and Hades, Poseidon gained the sphere of the sea and earthquakes. He is often associated with horses. Much of the adversity that Odysseus faces is the result of Poseidon's anger at Odysseus, caused by the Greek violation of Trojan temples in the sack of Troy (in, for example, the rape of Cassandra in the temple of Athena), and Odysseus' actions in tricking and blinding Poseidon's son, Polyphemus. 1.20.

Priam (*prai´-yam*): son of Laomedon and the last king of Troy. With his wife, Hecuba, and many slave women, he had fifty sons and between twelve and fifty daughters. In *The Iliad*, after Achilles killed his son, Hector, and deliberately abused the dead body, Priam went by night to the Greek camp to ask his enemy to return the body for proper burial. During the sack of Troy, Priam was murdered by Achilles' son Neoptolemus on the altar of Zeus. 3.108.

Procris (*pro´-kris*): daughter of Erechteus and wife of Cephalus. 11.322.

Proreus (*pror´-ee-yus*): 8.112.

Proteus (*proh´-tee-yus*): a sea god who shape-shifts and makes prophecies. Menelaus captured Proteus in Egypt, and Proteus gave Menelaus news of his companions, including his brother Agamemnon. 4.349.

Prymneus (*prim´-nee-yus*): a Phaeacian. His name suggests "Sternman." 8.111.

Psara (*psa´-ra*): an island in the Aegean Sea. 3.172.

Psyria (*psee´-ree´-ya*): 3.171.

Pylos (*pai´-los*): the city and kingdom of Nestor; located in Messenia on the Peloponnese. The inhabitants are Pylians. 1.94.

Pyriphlegethon (*pi-ri-fle´-ge-thon*): a tributary of the Styx in the underworld. Its name means "Stream of Fire." 10.514.

Pytho (*pai´-tho*): another name for Delphi, as well as the oracle of Apollo based there. The name alludes to the earth dragon (the Python) that originally lived in Delphi, and which was killed by Apollo (who is therefore also known as Pythian Apollo). 8.80.

Rhadamanthus (*ra-da-manth´-us*): son of Zeus and Europa; a Cretan king. 4.563.

Rhexenor (*rex-een´-or*): son of Nausithous and brother of the Phaeacian king Alcinous. 7.64.

Salmoneus (*sal-mohn´-ee-yus*): father of Tyro. 11.235.

Same (*say´-mee*): an island in the eastern Aegean near Ithaca, also known in Homer as Samos. Note that this is not the same as the modern island of Samos. 1.246.

Scheria (*ske´-ree-ya*): the land of the mythological people, the Phaeacians, which does not seem to correspond to a real geographical place, although scholars have proposed many possible locations. 5.35.

Scylla (*ski´-la*): a sea goddess who lives in a cave near Charybdis. The daughter of Cratais and Phorcys, she has six heads, each with the voice of a hungry dog. 12.85.

Scyros (*skai´-ros*): an island in the Aegean Sea, and the home of Achilles' son Neoptolemus. 11.509.

Sidon (*sai´-don*): a major Phoenician city, on the eastern coast of the Mediterannean; now in modern Lebanon. 4.84.

Sintians (*sint´-ee-yans*): a mythical people who inhabited areas of Thrace and the island of Lemnos. 8.294.

Sirens: mythical female creatures whose seductive singing causes sailors to forget their homes and waste away until they die. 12.38.

Sisyphus (*si´-see-fus*): son of Aeolus, the mythical progenitor of the Aeolians, and father of Glaucus. A consummate trickster who seduced his brother's wife and killed travelers and guests, Sisyphus was condemned to punishment in the underworld: he had to roll a rock up a mountain, but every time, just before he reached the top, the rock rolled back down. 11.593.

Solyma, Mount (*sol´-im-a*): a mountain in Lycia, in eastern Greece. Poseidon pauses here on his return from Ethiopia. 5.282.

Sounion (*soo´-nee-yon*): a cape located at the southernmost end of Attica; the site of an important temple dedicated to Poseidon. 3.278.

Sparta: a Doric city in the region of Lacedaemon in the Peloponnese, ruled by Menelaus. 1.94.

Stratius (*stray´-tee-yus*): a son of Nestor. 3.412.

Styx (*stix*): the river that forms the boundary of the underworld. 5.185.

Sun God: a Titan descended from Hyperion, the Olympian god associated with the sun. Also called Helius (q.v.), and distinct from Apollo. 1.8.

Syria (*si´-ree-ya*): a seemingly fictional geographical place that does not correspond to the modern state in the Middle East. 15.405.

Tantalus (*tan´-ta-lus*): king of an Anatolian city called Sipylus and, like Sisyphus, a mythological criminal. Tantalus' crime varies according to mythological tradition: according to some, he was granted a wish by Zeus and asked to live like a god, while according to others he stole nectar and ambrosia from the gods. Tantalus' punishment in the underworld is to stand in water that retreats whenever he tries to drink it, and to have fruit hovering above him that pulls back when he reaches for it. 11.584.

Taphos (*tay´-fos*): an island in the Ionian Sea; its inhabitants, the Taphians, are often described as pirates. 16.429.

Taygetus (*tai´-ge-tus*): a mountain range in the southern Peloponnese. 6.102.

Tecton (*tek´-ton*): a Phaeacian. His name means "Shipwright." 8.113.

Telamon (*te´-la-mon*): son of Aeacus and brother of Peleus. He is the father of Ajax and Teucer, the Trojan War heroes. 11.553.

Telemachus (*te-le´-ma-kus*): the only son of Odysseus and Penelope. Telemachus goes in search of his father in Books 1–4 (often called the "Telemachy"). On his return to Ithaca, Telemachus assists his father in the massacre of the suitors. 1.113.

Telemus (*te´-le-mus*): son of Eurymus; he lived among the Cyclopes as a soothsayer. 9.508.

Telephus (*te´-le-fus*): the son of Heracles and Auge; he fought in the Trojan War on the side of the Troy and was killed by Neoptolemus. 11.519.

Telepylus (*te-le-pai´-lus*): a town in Laestrygonia; the name suggests "Far Gate." 10.82.

Temese (*te´-me-see*): a city in Bruttium, the Greek colony in the "toe" region of Italy (modern-day Calabria). 1.185.

Tenedos (*te´-ne-dos*): an island in the northeast Aegean Sea. 3.159.

Thebes (*theebs*) (1) a city in Upper Egypt. 4.126. (2) a city in the Greek region of Boeotia. 11.264.

Theoclymenus (*thee-yo-cli´-men-us*): a seer from Argos, whom Telemachus brings back to Ithaca. 15.259.

Theseus (*thee´-see-yus*): son of Poseidon and Aethra, a mythological hero associated with Athens. With the help of Ariadne, daughter of Minos, Theseus killed the Minotaur, the son of Minos, a man-bull hybrid enclosed in the king's labyrinth on Crete. Theseus and Ariadne fled, but Theseus abandoned her before he returned to Athens. 11.324.

Thesprotia (*thes-proh´-sha*): a region of Epirus in Greece. Its inhabitants are Thesprotians. 14.316.

Thetis (*the´-tis*): a sea goddess; daughter of Nereus and the sea goddess Doris; mother, with Peleus, of Achilles. According to most versions of the legend, she was engaged to Peleus against her will and attempted in vain to escape him by shape-shifting into various forms. 11.546.

Thoas (*thoh´-was*): Greek warrior in Odysseus' fictional story to Eumaeus. 14.500.

Thon (*thohn*): Egyptian nobleman and husband of Polydamna. 4.229.

Thoön (*tho´-ohn*): Phoenician athlete; the name suggests "Quick." 8.110.

Thoösa (*tho-woh´-sa*): mother, by Poseidon, of Polyphemus. 1.72.

Thrace (*thrays*): a region of northeastern Greece. 8.361.

Thrasymedes (*thra-si´-mee-deez*): a son of Nestor. 3.39.

Thrinacia (*thri-nay´-sha*): a mythical island where Helius the Sun God kept his cattle, attended by his daughters. 11.107.

Thyestes (*thai-yes´-teez*): son of Pelops; brother of Atreus; and father of Aegisthus. In exile with Atreus after their joint murder of their half brother, Thyestes seduced Atreus' wife and attempted to seize the throne of Mycenae from Atreus, but was banished. According to some versions of the legend, Atreus served Thyestes a meal of his own children, with the exception of Aegisthus, who lived to take revenge on Atreus' son Agamemnon. 4.517.

Tiresias (*tai-ree´-see-yas*): famous blind Theban seer. 10.493.

Tithonus (*ti-thoh´-nus*): a son of Laomedon and the brother of Priam. He was abducted by Dawn to be her lover. According to legend, Dawn requested immortality for Tithonus but not eternal youth, so he aged and wasted away until only his voice was heard, chirping like a grasshopper. In some versions of the myth he was transformed into a cicada or grasshopper. 5.1.

Tityus (*ti´-tee-yus*): son of Zeus and Elara. To hide Elara's pregnancy, Zeus concealed her under the earth, which then birthed out the giant Tityus. He was shot dead by Artemis and Apollo, and punished in the underworld by having two vultures eat away at his innards. 7.324.

Tyndareus (*tin-da´-ree-yus*): king of Sparta and husband of Leda. According to variations in traditions, either he or Zeus was the father of Helen, Castor, and Polydeuces; he is also the father, with Leda, of Clytemnestra. 11.299.

Tyro (*tai´-roh*): daughter of Salmoneus and wife of Cretheus. 2.120.

Zacynthus (*za-kin´-thus*): an island in the Ionian Sea. 1.246.

Zephyr (*ze´-feer*): the West Wind. 2.421.

Zethus (*zee´-thus*): son of Zeus and Antiope. Together with his brother Amphion, the founder of the city of Thebes in Greece. Zethus married Aedon, who mistakenly murdered their son. 11.263.

Zeus (*zoos*): most powerful of the pantheon of Greek gods, associated with masculine power, kingship, fatherhood, and hospitality. The husband of Hera, he is often linked with eagles. As the god of the sky, he controls lightning and thunderbolts. 1.9.

ACKNOWLEDGMENTS

First thanks go to Pete Simon at Norton, whose wonderful idea it was that I should translate the *Odyssey*. Pete is an amazing editor who combed through my first drafts of every book with an unfailingly keen ear for clarity, English idiom, and poetic impact, and inspired me to keep at it. This book would not exist without him.

In the process of planning and creating this translation, I have shared pieces of my work in progress, as well as thoughts about the process, with engaged and helpful audiences at several institutions. I will not be able to thank by name all those who asked questions and made useful comments on those occasions, but I would like to extend a general and heartfelt thank you to those who invited me, listened to me, and engaged with me, at the Barnard Center for Translation Studies; classics graduate students at City University of New York; undergraduates and faculty at Swarthmore College (especially Rosaria Munson and Grace Ledbetter); various people at Columbia University (especially Julie Crawford, Jenny Davidson, and Molly Murray), and the Department of Languages and Cultures at the University of Delaware. I was lucky to be able to participate in a Penn Alumni Travel cruise round Sicily and the coast of Italy toward the end of this project; I am grateful to Emilie de la Rosa for inviting me, and to all my fellow passengers for discussing Homer with me while we sailed past the land of the Cyclops.

In my home institution, the Penn Humanities Forum provided two years of partial course relief and the stimulating company of two very different but equally impressive groups of scholars in the humanities; the *Odyssey* was part of the Year of Violence and then, equally suitably, the Year of Sex. I am grateful to all those who participated in those groups and helped expand my mind, with particular gratitude to Jennifer Conway, Jim English, David Stern, and Zeb Tortorici. Thanks also to the members of the Penn Undergraduate Humanities Forum on Translation, and to Andrea Goulet for inviting me to speak with them; to the lively students of the Penn Philomathean Society; and to all the students in Peter Struck's *Iliad* class, as well as Peter himself. Warm thanks to all those who attended my Library Tea presentation at Van Pelt here at Penn, and especially to Rebecca Stuhr, our classical studies librarian, who has been an engaged and thoughtful interlocutor for this project. Thank you also to all the graduate students who took my seminar on Greek poetry in translation.

I presented pieces of this project at two different Penn Classical Studies Colloquia, and am grateful to the audience members who asked useful questions on both occasions. I have benefited enormously from the company of my colleagues at Penn, especially those in the Classical Studies Department. I owe particular thanks to Bridget Murnaghan, magnificent Homerist and fellow translator, who generously read and commented on the majority of this volume, and who has taught me an enormous amount about the values and narrative strategies of the *Odyssey*. Thank you to all those faculty, graduate students, and post-bac students who regularly showed up, in the middle of their own busy weeks, to listen to me reading books-in-progress at "Homer Reading Group," and offer comments, questions, and suggestions for improvement. Particular thanks to my colleague Cynthia Damon, for wonderfully incisive questions about characterization, tone, and narrative perspective. Thank you to all the graduate students who participated in this context, including but not limited to: Lucy Ayers, Amelia Bensch-Schaus, Wes Hanson, Amy Lewis, Daniel Mackey, Isabella Reinhardt, and Jeffrey Ulrich. Thank you also to all the occasional visitors to the group, including Rita Copeland, Seth Schein, and Mira Seo.

In the final stages of this large project, I was greatly helped by a team of classicist readers whose eagle eyes saved me from innumerable infelicities. Thank you most especially to Alice Hu and Bill Beck, both extraordinarily quick, acute, and diligent readers of Homer and of me, who commented on the entire poem and introduction and helped me compile the glossary. Thank you to Jacob Feeley and Brian Rose for help with the maps, as well as the fine cartographer who drew them, Adrian Kitzinger. Deep thanks for alert, prompt, thoughtful reading and commenting on individual books and the introduction go to Addie Atkins, Ginna Closs, Tom Elliott, Matthew Farmer, Julie Nishimura-Jensen, Hannah Rich, Ralph Rosen, Lydia Spielberg, Alison Traweek, Caroline Whitbeck, and Kate Wilson.

I have been lucky to have the help of Joanne Dubil, the ever-reliable administrator in my alternate home, the Program in Comparative Literature and Literary Theory, for providing a warm and secure environment in which to work. I am also grateful to my mother, Katherine Duncan-Jones, who read many early sections of the poem, and to my sister, Bee Wilson, for essential emotional support.

I would like to thank those who have tried to educate me over the years, especially Jasper Griffin, with whom I first read Homer in Greek, and the late-lamented Oliver Lyne and David Quint, both of whom, in different ways, taught me to look for the stories and voices of losers in epic. Looking further back, I would like to thank the women who taught me Greek at Oxford High School for Girls, including Deborah Bennett, Eda Forbes, and Caroline Mayr-Harting. I would also like to thank the teachers at St. Barnabas Primary School, Oxford (especially Mr. Penfold, aka The Cyclops), for inspiring my eight-year-old self with a lifelong interest in the *Odyssey*.

Thanks to Trent Duffy for his excellent copyediting services, without which the line numbering and capitalization would have been hopelessly inconsistent. All remaining errors are, of course, my fault. Thank you also to Gerra Goff at Norton, who has helped keep everything on schedule.

Thank you to Holly Danesi, for the tattoo of Athena's owl that has helped me through the project.

Thank you to each of my three daughters, for letting me work sometimes, and for sharing my love of stories, pretend-play, magic, goddesses, adventures, and home. Thank you also to all the wonderful staff of St. Mary's Nursery School/Afterschool Program, without whom I could not have finished this book.

Finally, I am grateful to and for David Foreman. Thank you.

On the occasion of this new edition, I would like to offer my deepest thanks to the vast number of helpful and attentive readers who have drawn my attention to various typos, Britishisms, and infelicities of phrasing, of meter and rhythm, or of interpretation. I have made a number of small corrections in response to these generous readers, which have included a tweak to the type of bag carried by Odysseus as a beggar (now a "satchel," not a "tote bag"—although I had thought the latter would be more suitable for carrying snacks), and couple of crucial changes to the description of Odysseus' curly-haired herald (whom I should not, as the work of Dr. Jackie Murray has shown me, have described as a "valet"—a choice that imported entirely anachronistic presumptions about race into the poem). I am also truly grateful to the editorial assistants at W. W. Norton, Zeba Arora and Kadiatou Keita, who kept track of many very fiddly details with impressive competence and grace. Thank you all.

EU Authorised Representative:
Easy Access System Europe
Mustamäe tee 50, 10621 Tallinn, Estonia

www.ingramcontent.com/pod-product-compliance
Ingram Content Group UK Ltd.
Pitfield, Milton Keynes, MK11 3LW, UK
UKHW041918090926
475376UK00004B/4

9780393356250